THE
100 BEST
STOCKS
TO BUY IN
2017

THE 100 BEST STOCKS TO BUY IN 2017

PETER SANDER
AND
SCOTT BOBO

Avon, Massachusetts

Published by
Adams Media, a division of F+W Media, Inc.
57 Littlefield Street, Avon, MA 02322. U.S.A.
www.adamsmedia.com

ISBN 10: 1-4405-9602-6
ISBN 13: 978-1-4405-9602-5
eISBN 10: 1-4405-9603-4
eISBN 13: 978-1-4405-9603-2

Printed in the United States of America.

10   9   8   7   6   5   4   3   2   1

Cover design by Sylvia McArdle.

This book is available at quantity discounts for bulk purchases.
For information, please call 1-800-289-0963.

Contents

PART I

THE ART AND SCIENCE OF INVESTING IN STOCKS

By Peter Sander

The Art and Science of Investing in Stocks

As the saying goes, a tie score "is like kissing your kid sister."

We know that feeling. Not because we have kid sisters, nor because we've kissed any family members against our will lately.

It's because our *100 Best Stocks 2016*, the oh-so-carefully crafted list put together to guide you through thick and thin and make you a winner for our 2016 measurement year, in fact finished in a virtual dead heat with our main benchmark, the S&P 500 Index.

In fact, we were 0.3 percent—*three-tenths of 1 percent*—ahead of the benchmark, so technically we get to count it as another win. Our seventh in a row, seven out of seven since your author team of Scott and Peter took over this franchise in 2010. Not bad, and we like to win . . . but is three-tenths of 1 percent, two-tenths of that simply based on dividends, a real win? Is a year where Public Storage and Campbell Soup were the two biggest winners a showcase for our skills and talents?

We wonder. But we'll take it.

These days, when ties occur in most big league sports, they go into overtime to settle the score. We couldn't come up with a practical way to do that, so no "sudden death" for us. Any other way to feel better about this year's tie?

Back in the "old days" when sports teams tied, and even when they lost a close one, they looked for *consolation*. "We lost, but our pitching held them close and our defense was brilliant" is something you'll hear to this day. We looked—and found—some pretty interesting consolations.

First, we probably *should* have lost. Those of you who have followed our stock picking over the years know that we play defense with a little offense; that is, we look to beat the markets when they're up, but even more importantly we want to do better, i.e., lose less, when they're down. Growth and income, yes, but with a measure of safety.

You also know that we pick excellent businesses in good industries and tend to stay with those businesses even in times of turbulence and volatility. We trust their strength. We trust their management teams to guide them successfully through the rough waters of "down" business cycles. We don't typically jump ship unless there's ample evidence that the core business itself has changed.

Additionally, you know that we favor relatively simple companies that produce something tangible that can be branded and differentiated among competitors; that can be exported overseas as a way to bring income back to the U.S. and as a way to expand the business. We like companies with a strong overseas presence.

We like U.S. manufacturers. We like companies engaged in the business of agriculture, for food will always be in demand; and in fact the growth in population and standard of living leads to a projected 70 percent growth in agricultural demand by the year 2050 in an environment where available agricultural land has almost all already been put to use.

And we like companies that slant toward meaningful innovation in areas like alternative energy. Companies that can innovate—products, processes, or customer interfaces—are sowing the seeds for better business fundamentals in the future. Better innovation and marketplace intangibles today lead to better business results down the road.

Trouble is, these major investment "themes" didn't work very well this year.

The persistently strong dollar trashed exports again. Throughout the book we had to repeat that tired refrain over and over: "Company A reported a 4 percent increase in revenues, which would have been 8 percent in constant currency."

The energy bust, and the adjacent commodity bust, trashed our materials, energy, and agriculture plays. We think we are just emerging from one of the sharpest down cycles in history in energy, where prices dropped 50 percent in one year and 40 percent the next. We didn't have that many energy stocks (only six of the 100) but the collateral damage in the rest of the commodity industry and with manufacturers geared to supplying things (like steel pipe or industrial gases) to the energy industry added weight to our "losers" list.

You would have thought manufacturers would have prospered in an environment of low energy and commodity input costs. Yes, so far as it goes—but the downward drive of emerging market slowdowns (China in particular) and the strong dollar trashed that concept too.

Yes, we should have lost. We should have lost in a year of headwinds for manufacturers, commodity, and agricultural firms. We also took hits in the retail sector as the Millennial-driven shift to online commerce seems to be picking up steam.

Instead, our defensive stocks pulled us through. Public Storage, Campbell Soup, McCormick, Kimberly-Clark, Sysco, AT&T—hats off to you guys—and welcome back to the 2017 *100 Best Stocks* list for another go.

Yet the "we should have lost" consolation is good only so far as it goes. Not very positive, and certainly not very inspiring for you readers new to the

100 Best Stocks series. But then, as we dug deeper into what really happened this year, we found a second consolation that, in our book, carries greater significance. Which is another way of saying, it makes us feel better.

Despite our virtual tie with the S&P 500, *we beat most other sectors of the market*, as defined by the Lipper Mutual Fund Index Benchmarks. As you'll soon see in Table 0.1, we beat everything from Global Large Cap Growth to Global Multicap Value to Science and Technology to Financial Services.

We beat 36 out of 40 groups, and lost out only to Precious Metals Equity, Utility, Telecommunications, and Intermediate Municipal Debt. And the latter three—only by a tiny margin. Oh well. We'll take it.

Pretty darned good to beat all those groups. In fact, 29 out of the 40 groups *lost* ground for the measurement year (April 1, 2015–April 1, 2016) so we feel pretty special just to be in positive territory.

Okay, enough grasping at straws. We won despite carrying more losers than usual. We beat most of the market if you look beyond the S&P. We had 85 of our stocks *raise* dividends through the year.

We did well, despite the virtual tie. We did well in a particularly wacky and challenging market year.

And we think we're positioned pretty well for the coming year—come rain or shine in the markets.

* * *

Enough about last year, last year's performance, and the important "consolations" that helped make the year feel like a winner despite the dim top line.

You bought this book because you wanted to hear more about this coming year, 2017, and beyond. So on to that frontier we will now go.

With the "dim" performance and so many disruptions in previously "staid" industries like energy and agriculture, you might have expected wholesale changes in this year's list.

That didn't happen. We made nine changes—nine new companies for the 2017 *100 Best Stocks* list.

That doesn't mean we didn't carefully consider making *more* changes. You'll see many instances through the 100 narratives for this year where we hung on to a company, like Schlumberger or Deere or Macy's or ConocoPhillips or Union Pacific—not because of its recent performance (which was pretty dismal) but rather out of a combination of patience and perseverance and a justified focus on the future.

Patience because by habit we pick solid companies with solid management and track records; a business cycle downturn is nothing new and certainly nothing a seasoned company can't handle. It is nothing a seasoned investor can't handle either—if we always bought high and sold low into the business cycle, where would we be, anyway? "Sell when there's something better to buy" is our perhaps overused but continuously prescient operating mantra when it comes to such decisions.

Perseverance because we know that the "best" companies such as the ones we pick are dedicated to the proposition of "sharpening their saws" when the going gets rough. They take decisive actions to improve operating efficiency, making them ever stronger and more profitable when their business does eventually come back. They continue to "cut fat" but better yet to invest in everything from physical plant in the case of railroads to online presence in the case of retailers. They fine-tune processes, invest in brand building and customer interfaces—all toward becoming better "machines" when the business turns around.

We continue to tip our caps to the advance of the Millennial generation—those born after 1982 and raised with a digital silver spoon— who now outnumber the rest of the population and are starting to make their weight felt in the marketplace. We recognize the Millennial tastes and attitudes—which bring a new emphasis on experiences, work-life balance, customization and personalization, and healthy living among other things. We recognize that Millennials don't put so much weight on "standards" of the past—everything from handwritten letters to buying IBM—and we're once again adjusting our stock list accordingly.

Goodbye, IBM and Wal-Mart. Hello, Amazon and WhiteWave Foods. Yes, this year we finally ditched IBM after years of not being able to make the right business adjustments—but we think, also, for a loss of critical brand cachet with the new generation. And, yes, we've finally added Amazon to the list. No dividend, lots of debt, sky-high price-to-earnings ratio there may be, but we noted that e-commerce has now reached 10 percent of U.S. retail— and we see signs everywhere that Millennials are not going to stores in droves.

So we jumped the fence to put an Internet stock on the list. One which, by the way, has developed an immense and immensely profitable cloud "side business" to help pay the bills and profit further from the inevitable Millennial shift.

We think Millennials are also driving an irreversible shift toward healthy and organic foods, thus our WhiteWave pick; a shift toward acquiring experiences rather than things, thus our Carnival Corporation (cruise lines) pick; and our shift from the staid old ponies of Ralph Lauren's stable to the practical outdoorsy chic of Columbia Sportswear.

You get the idea. Our list isn't necessarily for Millennials; it's for everyone. But as we continue to base our prospects for financial excellence on prospects for marketplace excellence (another underlying *100 Best* theme), it's impossible—as well as imprudent—not to embrace this marketplace shift.

So, there you have it. Patience, perseverance, and Millennials. Three of our most important investing themes for the coming year.

* * *

Once again, as we wind down this opening statement we'll share a few other miscellaneous topics on our minds related to this edition and how we connect with you as readers and investors.

First of all, we continue to enjoy your feedback. I (Peter) first offered my e-mail address three years ago (ginsander@hotmail.com) as an experiment, and it's worked quite well. We've fielded many fine questions that, frankly, we enjoyed answering. Not only do we appreciate the dialogs, but we learn from them too. The number of—and quality of—the questions and feedback continues to increase. Keep them coming.

We continue to be measurement minded. We still enjoy the praise given by "Buffetfan" on Amazon for the *100 Best Stocks* 2015 edition:

"Another plus is that they have the courage of their conviction and review the performance of their previous year's stock picks; something not seen too often in other books of this type."

We agree, and appreciate the comment. It's not hard to find investment suggestions, but it's much harder to find advice—or advisors, for that matter—who regularly measure and report their successes and failures. Not only is it good form (especially for us engineer types) to measure the quality of what we're providing, it also helps us understand how well our approach is working. As author Katherine Neville put it in her exquisite novel *The Eight*, "What can be measured can be understood; what can be understood can be altered."

As usual, we continue to produce this book not only to give you our annual selections (fish) but also provide a model for *how* we make our selections (teach you to fish). This Part I narrative has elements of both—and we apologize once again for parts of it that might seem repetitive, year after year—for those of you faithful enough to buy each year's edition. (For those of you who would like still more insight on how to fish, I'll point you to two of my other works: *The 25 Habits of Highly Successful Investors*, from this publisher, and *All about Low Volatility Investing*, from McGraw-Hill.) Anyway, for us, investing is a thought process, which we hope you acquire over time—not just through our investment tenets and philosophies shared in the narrative, but also by watching us *do* it (the *100 Best* list) and ultimately through your own experience.

Speaking of thought processes, last year we noticed ourselves making a couple of quick "acid test" checks when sifting through the universe of thousands of potential companies for the *100 Best* list. Once again we think that we can recognize a good company—at least one into which to drill down further—by assessing two characteristics:

1.   Are dividends meaningful and rising?
2.   Is the company buying back shares?

If a company is doing both, it suggests that other business attributes are going well—the company has sufficient capital, management thinks things are improving (else why would they commit capital to dividends and share buybacks?)—and finally, they are shareholder oriented. If the company has sufficient capital, things are getting better, and management cares about shareholders, what more do we need to know? (Lots, actually, but it's a good place to get started.) It's like meeting someone new and exciting at a party or online—first impressions are important and things may just click, but you need to find out more. Chalk it up as another *100 Best* investing theme.

Finally, some of our best "media" appearances and contacts with the public have come from meeting and presenting the *100 Best Stocks* at investment clubs. We've found investment clubs to be great forums to exchange ideas, insights, and experiences. We also enjoy evaluating investment club portfolios and comparing them to our *100 Best* list. Once again, if anyone out there wants to engage us for an investment club meeting, we can work out "consideration" (often just a free lunch; we know you've bought at least one book and we also know we aren't Registered Investment Advisors) and the means, perhaps teleconference or some such. Anyhow, the door is open; contact me (Peter) at the aforementioned e-mail.

As always, enjoy *The 100 Best Stocks to Buy in 2017*; invest long and prosper, and we hope to see you in the winner's circle again after a more decisive victory than in the 2016 year gone by.

Beating the Averages—Most of Them, Anyhow

Three years ago, we created a "temporary" analysis and table comparing the performance of the *100 Best Stocks* list against major sector benchmarks as measured by Lipper, a division of Thomson Reuters and a major supplier of quality financial information and analytics especially for the mutual fund sector. Our "temporary" analysis has once again proven quite interesting for our 2016 picks. In a year where we beat our main benchmark by the oh-so-narrow margin of 0.3 percent, it turns out that we beat other major market benchmarks quite handily. The following "temporary" Table 0.1 shows what we're talking about.

For 2016 Table 0.1 shows that while we once again "lost out" to four benchmarks—and three of them only by a small margin—our *100 Best* list is intended to be a pretty "steady-Eddie" bunch. That's borne out in the fact that we were only beaten by Precious Metals Equity, Utility, Telecommunications, and Intermediate Municipal Debt. So—that means we're a pretty good defensive list too, as it turns out. At least, we think we are. What the table does not show—but is interesting—is how well we've done in general over the past four years against these benchmarks. While the "winners" rotated every year, we've come in consistently in a Number Four or Number Five position each year for four years. Not the winner, but a steady-Eddie placement toward the top of the pack in both up and "sideways" markets. Perhaps we haven't really had a good "down market" test, but we'd be pretty curious to see how that would come out. (No, we're *not* rooting for a down market!) Anyway, if you prefer tortoises to hares, we may just have the right collection of stocks for you.

▼ Table 0.1: Performance Compared to Major Benchmarks

100 BEST STOCKS 2016 COMPARED TO LIPPER MUTUAL FUND INDEX BENCHMARKS

ONE-YEAR PERFORMANCE, APRIL 1, 2015–APRIL 1, 2016

Fund Benchmark	1-year return
Precious Metals Equity	12.5%
Utility	3.8%
Telecommunications	3.6%
Intermediate Municipal Debt	3.0%
100 BEST STOCKS TO BUY 2016	2.65%

Fund Benchmark	1-year return
Real Estate	2.5%
General U.S. Treasury	2.4%
S&P 500 with Dividends Reinvested	2.35%
General U.S. Government	1.2%
Short/Intermediate U.S. Government	0.7%
Short U.S. Government	0.4%
Inflation Protected Bond	0.1%
International Small/Mid Cap Growth	-0.4%
General Bond	-0.4%
Science and Technology	-1.1%
Multisector Income	-1.7%
International Small/Mid Cap Value	-2.2%
Global Large Cap Growth	-2.3%
International Small/Mid Cap Core	-2.7%
Global Large Cap Core	-3.8%
High Yield Bond	-4.0%
Japan Region	-4.6%
Financial Services	-4.8%
Global Large Cap Value	-4.9%
Global Multicap Core	-5.0%
Global Multicap Value	-5.3%
Global Multicap Growth	-5.4%
European Region	-5.8%
International Multicap Growth	-5.9%
International Large Cap Growth	-7.1%
International Multicap Core	-7.8%
Pacific Region	-7.8%
International Large Cap Value	-9.3%
International Multicap Value	-9.5%
Pacific Ex-Japan	-9.5%
International Large Cap Core	-9.8%
Latin American	-10.7%
Emerging Markets	-11.6%

Fund Benchmark	1-year return
China Region	-14.1%
Health/Biotech	-16.8%
Natural Resources	-23.2%

Source: Lipper/Thomson Reuters, *Barron's Weekly*

A Seven-Year Stretch Run

A couple of years ago we realized that it had been five years since we took over the publication of *The 100 Best Stocks to Buy* series from John Slatter, the previous author. That, and a couple of poignant reader queries got us to ask ourselves: "So how well did we do?" How well did we achieve the goals of applying solid, value-based, marketplace-based investing techniques and philosophies to picking great companies, the *100 Best* of them for you to invest in? More simply stated, would you have been better off to not buy our book, not take the time to pursue individual stock investing, and throw it over the wall to a low-cost S&P 500 index fund?

Always being sensitive to this sort of question, we checked this out, and found the results encouraging. If you had invested an initial $100,000 and reinvested in each of our lists from 2010 through 2014, you would have ended up with $303,461 on your $100,000 investment, compared to $243,899 if you had invested in an S&P 500 index fund with reinvested dividends. We thought the additional $59,562 in total return was quite worthwhile for having to shell out $16.99 (or less) to buy our book each year.

Like our other "oh-point temporary" table, we got rather fond of the message delivered by this one too, so we decided to repeat this table again for the 2015 list, and now, for the 2016 list as well. Seven years in all. Now it won't surprise you that, with last year's 2.65 percent gain, 0.3 percent ahead of the S&P 500, we didn't pull very far ahead in 2016. But a little bit here compounded on top of a *lot* over there makes for a pretty good story: Our $100,000 invested seven years ago would have produced $77,393 more than an equivalent investment in the S&P as of the end of our 2016 measurement year. Cumulatively, on percentage terms, our picks are almost 25 percent ahead of the S&P.

Not bad, especially for an investment of $16.99 per year for the book. And the win streak continues.

▼ Table 0.2: Performance Compared to Major Benchmarks

SIX-YEAR PERFORMANCE COMPARISON: 100 BEST STOCKS VERSUS S&P 500

ANNUAL PERFORMANCE OF EACH 100 BEST LIST AND COMPOUNDED CUMULATIVE PERFORMANCE

		2010	2011	2012	2013	2014	2015	2016
100 Best Stocks	Gain, percent	62.5%	20.0%	5.5%	19.2%	23.8%	15.0%	2.65%
	Compounded	62.5%	94.9%	105.6%	145.1%	203.5%	249.0%	258.2%
	$100,000 invested in 2010	$162,500	$194,919	$205,639	$245,122	$303,461	$348,980	$358,228
S&P 500	Gain, percent	44.6%	13.1%	5.4%	15.6%	22.4%	12.5%	2.35%
	Compounded	44.6%	63.5%	72.4%	99.3%	143.9%	174.4%	180.8%
	$100,000 invested in 2010	$144,600	$163,543	$172,374	$199,264	$243,899	$274,387	$280,835
Net advantage, $100K invested, 100 Best Stocks		$17,900	$31,376	$33,265	$45,858	$59,562	$74,593	$77,393

For 12-month periods beginning April 1 of previous year, dividends included after 2011

Individual Investor: This Book Is for You

If you bought this book, you're probably an astute and experienced individual investor who invests in individual stocks in individual companies. Are you alone? Heck no. You have more company than ever. In fact, shoved along a bit by the hits most people took in the Great Recession, more and more investors are putting themselves in the driver's seat. Why? It's simple, and easily explained by the old adage: "Nobody cares about your money more than you do."

The trend toward self-directed investing was highlighted in an April 2013 *Wall Street Journal* article entitled "A New Era for Do-It-Yourself Investing." We realize this article might be a bit dated for a 2017 book but don't think the figures or the main message have changed that much—for one thing, we've seen no update to this article nor to its figures.

In the study central to the article, the researchers asked mostly middle-tier investors whether they were relying more or relying less on advisors since the 2008–09 financial crisis. Some 50 percent of respondents said "less"; only 21 percent said "more." (The rest said "no change.") They cited a trend toward "investors wanting to be more involved" and toward brokerages offering do-it-yourself services with only occasional help from professional advisors when requested.

Does this mean that everyone is picking their own stocks? No, not necessarily, and not entirely. They may still be using any of among the 14,000 mutual funds or roughly 1,600 exchange-traded fund (ETF) "products" (or hedge funds, if they're wealthy enough) that do the driving for them. But more and more investors are making informed choices themselves; fewer are leaving the choice of those products—or individual stocks, for that matter—to someone else. What's really emerging is more of a hybrid model, where investors are making their own decisions, but sprinkling in some help in the form of professional advice, or professional management given by mutual fund managers, and automatic diversification as given by index funds, ETFs, and other kinds of instruments. Individually picked investments—with some help along the way. (We don't accept the newfangled "robo-advisors" as this sort of professional help, by the way.)

Where does *The 100 Best Stocks to Buy* fit in? Every edition of *The 100 Best Stocks* is intended as a core tool for the individual investor, especially those investors inclined to buy individual stocks. Most of you probably aren't inclined to buy individual stocks for your entire portfolio—nor should you be unless you have the time and it's your thing to do. Sure, it makes sense to round out your portfolio with funds and ETFs, or perhaps it makes sense to round out your ETF and fund portfolio with a few individual stocks of your choosing.

And, as far as individual stock investing goes, we know that *100 Best Stocks* is hardly the only tool available. The Internet has made this book one of hundreds of choices for acquiring investing information. With the speed of cyberspace, our book will hardly be the most current source. In fact, we know, despite recent changes to the publishing schedule, that we're still at least six months out-of-date. If you check our research, you'll be able to come up with two to three calendar quarters of more current financial information, news releases, and so forth.

So does the delay built into the publishing cycle make our book a poor source? Not at all. It works because the companies we choose don't change much and because they avoid the temptation to manage short-term, quarter-to-quarter performance. We chose these companies *because* they have sustainable performance, so who cares if the latest details or news releases are included? In *The 100 Best Stocks to Buy in 2017*, as with all previous editions, we focus on the *story*—the story of each company—not just the latest facts and figures.

To that same point, *100 Best Stocks* goes well beyond just being a stock screen or a study of stocks to invest in. Analysis forms the base of *100 Best Stocks*, but it isn't the rigid, strictly numbers-based selection and analysis so often found in published "best stocks" lists. Sure, we look at earnings, cash flow, balance sheet strength, and so forth, but we'll also look far beyond those things. We'll look at the intangible and often subtle factors that make truly great businesses—that is, companies—great. That is, once again, the *story.*

Great companies have good business fundamentals, but what makes them really great is the presence of intangibles and subtleties—the brands, the marketplace successes, the management style, the competitive advantages—that will *keep* them great or make them greater in the future. In our view, *good intangibles today lead to better business fundamentals down the road.*

100 Best Stocks is not a simple numbers-based stock screen like many found on the Internet and elsewhere today. It is a selection and analysis of really good businesses you would want to buy and own, not just for past results, but for future outcomes. Does "future" mean "forever"? No, not anymore. While the *100 Best Stocks* list correlates well with the notion of "blue-chip" stocks, the harsh reality is that "blue chip" no longer means "forever."

We feel that the 100 companies listed and analyzed in the pages that follow are the best companies to own for 2017, and generally, beyond. That said, the word "own" has become a more active concept these days. Gone are the days of "own forever," like the halcyon days when Peter's parents, Jerry and Betty Sander, bought their 35 shares of General Motors, lovingly placed the stock certificate in their safe-deposit box, and henceforth bought nothing but GM cars. Today, there is no forever; the economy, technology, and consumer tastes simply change too fast, and the businesses that participate in the economy by necessity change with it. Ownership is a more active concept than it was even 10 or 20 years ago.

So going forward, we offer the *100 Best* companies to own now and for 2017, those that have the best chances of not only surviving but evolving with—or even ahead of—the economy based on their current market position and approach to doing business. We think these are the best companies to (1) stay with or perhaps stay slightly ahead of business change, (2) provide short- and long-term returns in the form of cash and modest appreciation, and (3) do so with a measure of safety or at least reduced volatility so that you can burn your energy doing other things besides staring at stock quotes day and night.

Bottom line: Our intent is simple and straightforward. We provide a list and a set of facts and stories. You take the information as it's presented, do your own assessment, reach your own conclusions, and take your own actions. Anything more, anything less, won't work. You're in charge. And we suspect that you like it that way.

What's New for 2017

For those of you who've stayed with us over the years, this edition will take the same approach as before. For those of you reading for the first time, here are some guidelines and ideas we follow.

First and once again: no changes to the author team of Scott and Peter (we'll introduce ourselves in a minute). Once again, no significant changes to the structure or format of our presentation. Continuing is our emphasis on sustainable value, strong market position and other intangibles, and sustainable and growing cash returns to investors, in the form of dividends and share buybacks as well as share appreciation. We continue to take interest in the persistency of dividend increases above and beyond the yield itself, and we continue to stay focused on total shareholder returns. For the most part, we are playing the hand that got us here.

However, although we say every year that our investing style and presentation has remained essentially the same, the style of the best artists, writers, or even software programmers evolves over time; as with any blend of science and art, investing most certainly included, the approach evolves; the style acquires a little of this and a little of that and loses a little of something else as time goes on. Experience matters and is taken into account. Changes in the world investing context and environment factor in. And heck—we're getting older and perhaps a bit wiser. Maybe we see things a little differently than we did seven years ago . . . and certainly 35 years ago. All of these factors influence the mix; here are a few directions we've taken recently (or have continued with emphasis) with this edition:

- *Low-volatility bias.* We continue to think it's important to get good returns but also to sleep at night. *Steady* growth, *steady* returns, *steady* dividend increases—that's what we prefer. While we present "beta" as a measure of market correlation, we look deeper into the actual patterns and history of earnings, dividends, cash flow, and yes, share price. If it's a wild ride (or if there *are* no earnings, cash flows, etc.), we don't get on; we prefer to watch instead. You'll never find the likes of Twitter on our list. We know—as the markets continue to rise through the years, the chances for corrective "volatility" increase—there isn't a whole lot we can do about that except to stick to our knitting. That said, we've reached outside our normal "core" type of holding for the second year in a row to pick up a few more aggressive companies that seem at the forefront of change. Indeed, we now have four companies—CarMax, Itron, Amazon, and WhiteWave—that don't pay dividends, a 100 percent increase over last year's two. We are still mostly about the steady-Eddie traditional blue-chip core, but we think a few more aggressive plays are in order as (1) change is everywhere and (2) a lot of our "core" has gotten pretty expensive.

- *Still playing defense.* We took a more defensive stance for 2014 and almost wound up with some explainin' to do as the markets forged ahead. We did that again in 2015 and don't think we missed much of what the markets had to offer as a consequence. And for 2016 defense remained a prominent theme—and we managed a small gain while many sectors lost.

Our lists continue to be constructed to provide enough growth opportunity to beat the market but also to beat the market in a *down* market, that is, to be down only 5 percent if the market dropped 10 percent. We continue to take that position. Once again, a number of our *100 Best Stocks* seem fully valued at this juncture. We were nervous about riding them any further. We evaluate all of our picks carefully using our "sell if there's something better to buy" philosophy and try to visualize how they would do "on a sloppy track." And we continue to avoid "momentum" plays as they have a tendency to beat a "mo" path downward at the slightest sign of change.

- *Focus on millennials.* The January 2015 *New York Times* headline summed it up perfectly: "Millennials Set to Outnumber Baby Boomers." There are about 75 million of each, with Millennials counted as being born between 1982 and 1997, and more importantly, with a digital silver spoon in their mouths. Hmmm, we thought. Have we embraced this adequately in our stock picks, given that we like companies with at least steady, and preferably improving, brand strength and loyal customer bases? Millennials are typically typecast as digitally fluent, preferring unstructured environments, having a taste for customizable products, healthy foods, immediate gratification—all with short attention spans and relatively less loyalty to companies and brands than their non-digital ancestors. We had to ask ourselves—Do they drink Coke? Buy IBM? Eat Big Macs? Wash their clothes with Tide? Go to movie theaters?—and a thousand other questions. Are we seeing—or about to see—a major shift in consumer preferences as Millennials gradually take charge of the commercial world? Do our long-standing brands like Coke and Corn Flakes have cachet with these groups like they once did with us older folks?

  We've seen considerable recent evidence in the retail world that the "Millennial" megatrend is large and here to stay. Online shopping is no longer just a novelty—it has captured 10.4 percent of the U.S. retail market. Shopping malls and mall stores in particular have seen sales and traffic declines. We took Wal-Mart and Tiffany off of the 2017 list and probably would have taken Macy's off if it weren't for its head start on its e-commerce strategy and attractive valuation. We're still worried about Macy's and about every one of our stocks that has a consumer-facing element that might be disrupted by the Internet and the overarching demographic and market shift.

- *Another investment product.* In 2014 we tiptoed into the "investment product" space adding a real estate investment trust (REIT) rather unimaginatively called "Health Care REIT, Inc." (now Welltower). Our goal was to gain the diversification, yield, and defensiveness of a managed portfolio, in this case a portfolio of senior housing and health facilities. Although that investment didn't work out so well for 2014, we doubled down on the approach in 2015 with Public Storage (PSA), another good business built on a foundation of self-storage facilities. Both worked *very* well in 2015. For 2016, we added a new and smaller "mid-cap" REIT—Empire State Realty Trust—that just happens to own the most revered office building in the world—the Empire State Building (how's *that* for a brand?). Now, for 2017, we've liked this "formula" enough that we're going to the well again—this time to add logistics real estate trust Prologis. Once again, a good business (logistics and especially e-commerce logistics solutions) built on top of a real estate portfolio. We will continue to consider investment products—REITs, other types of investment trusts, funds, ETFs, and others from time to time, but we won't add them unless we (1) understand them, (2) have a specific rationale, and (3) feel that they provide a "*100 Best*" opportunity to deploy your hard-earned cash.

Other than that, for 2017 and beyond we continue on a value-driven track, looking for the very best businesses to invest in with an emphasis on "sell if there's something better to buy." We didn't respond too much to short-term concerns that affected everyone, like the rising dollar or falling agricultural prices. We thought about bringing some of our "eggs" home and out of foreign baskets to mitigate dollar impacts and reduce foreign event risk somewhat, but figured the dollar thing would stabilize or reverse itself just about the time we made the changes, and we consider the headline risk an omnipresent ongoing factor that would nearly equally harm "domestic" investments—we're in a global economy, after all. Finally, while we did take a close look at the energy and commodity sectors and make a few changes, once again this year for the most part we dismissed the recent market disruption as a cycle like many others we've waited through patiently in the past. In our view, the best businesses will survive, even thrive, in the deepest cycles. Our "good" companies will implement efficiency measures, lose competitors, and emerge ever stronger in our view. The trick is to make sure the cycle is really a cycle, rather than a sign of structural business change

About Your Authors

If you're a regular reader of the *100 Best Stocks* series you've probably seen the following before. It's about us, and not much has changed about us, so feel free to skip this section if it's altogether too familiar—or if it doesn't matter much to begin with.

Peter Sander

Peter is an independent professional researcher, writer, and journalist specializing in personal finance, investing, and location reference, as well as other general business topics. He has written 46 books on these topics, as well as numerous financial columns, and performed independent, privately contracted research and studies. He came from a background in the corporate world, having experienced a 21-year career with a major West Coast technology firm.

He is, most emphatically, an individual investor, and has been since the age of 12 (okay, so Warren Buffett started when he was 11), when his curiosity at the family breakfast table got the better of him. He started reading the stock pages with his parents. He had an opportunity during a "project week" in the seventh grade to read and learn about the stock market. He read Louis Engel's *How to Buy Stocks*, then the pre-eminent—and one of the only—consumer-friendly books about investing available at the time. He picked stocks, and made graphs of their performance by hand with colored pens on graph paper. He put his hard-earned savings into buying five shares of each of three different companies. He watched those stocks like a hawk and salted away the meager dividends to reinvest. He's been investing ever since. (Incidentally, Warren Buffett bought Cities Service preferred shares, Peter bought Burlington Northern preferred shares following much the same principles, and how ironic that Mr. Buffett came to own all of Burlington Northern. Perhaps Peter will come to own a big oil company some day.)

Yes, Peter has an MBA from Indiana University in Bloomington, but it isn't an MBA in finance. He also took the coursework and certification exam to become a certified financial planner (CFP). By design and choice, he has never held a job in the financial profession. His goal has always been to share his knowledge and experience in an educational way, a way helpful for the individual as an investor and a personal financier to make his or her own decisions.

He has never earned a living giving direct investment advice or managing money for others, nor does he intend to.

A few years ago, it dawned on Peter that he has really made his living finding value, and helping or teaching others to find value. Not just in stocks, but other things in business and in life. What does he mean by value? Simply, the current and potential *worth* of something as compared to its price or cost. As it turns out, he's made a career out of assessing the value of people (for marketers), places (as places to live), and companies (for investors).

Scott Bobo

Peter and Scott have been friends and colleagues since, roughly, tenth grade (a long time!). Scott has been part of the team for seven years now and has been huge not only in identifying the *100 Best Stocks*, but also analyzing them and explaining their pros and cons crisply and in plain English so that you can make the best use of the list. Having Scott on the team allows you to get the combined wisdom and observations of two people, not just one, in an arena where one plus one almost always equals something greater than two.

Scott has been an investor since age 14, when he made the switch from analyzing baseball box scores to looking at the numbers and charts in the business section. In his 20-plus years in engineering and technology management, he's learned that a unique product value proposition is important to the success of any company. He has also learned (the hard way) that proper financial fundamentals are critical. From a development manager's perspective, comprehending a new product's risk/reward proposition is one of the keys to a company's success. From an investor's perspective, it's also one of the keys to successful value investing in a dynamic, innovation-driven market.

Scott adds a strong analytical touch. But he is most at home as an applications engineer, explaining how a company's products work and how they apply to a customer's needs. Consequently, and in addition to analytical legwork, Scott really adds an extraordinary and very real-world sense of how a company's products "fit" in the marketplace. Determining whether a company's products are relevant, best-in-class, and have a competitive advantage over others is an oft-overlooked core skill for a value investor. Scott brings this skill to the table in a big way.

How do these diverse experiences of Peter and Scott translate into picking stocks? Just like customers or places to live, we want companies that produce the greatest return, the highest value, *per dollar invested*. And *for the amount of risk taken*. The companies we will identify as among the *100 Best* have, in our assessment, the greatest and most persistent long-term *value*, and if you can buy these companies at a *reasonable price* (a factor that we largely leave out of this analysis because this is a book and prices can change considerably), then these investments deliver the best prospects while keeping the downsides manageable.

Later we'll come back to describe some of the attributes of value that we look for.

A "Low-Volatility" Investing Book

You've heard about—and just read about—the new trend toward low-volatility investing. This term means investing to minimize risk and volatility—to be able to sleep at night and count on your otherwise unpredictable retirement—and achieve decent investing returns all the same. That's the subject of Peter's book *All About Low Volatility Investing* (McGraw-Hill, 2014), and some of the "DNA" from that book has leaked into this one. But that's not what this subsection is about.

What we're getting at here is the low-volatility nature of the sequential editions of this book. We try to keep them useful and relatively simple year after year. The analysis is the same, and for the most part the presentations are the same. Each year we make a few adjustments, pruning away a few stocks and adding a few others. We do that adhering to our core principles without having any particular number of changes in mind.

When we first took over this series from John Slatter for the 2010 edition, we made 26 changes, not a revolution but perhaps a strong evolution of the philosophy toward core value principles, strong competitive advantages and intangibles, and healthy cash returns. After that first year we went back to more of a fine-tuning mode, changing 14 stocks for the 2011 list, 12 for 2012, and back to 14 for 2013. In 2014 we held the line in a measure of defense and the simple inability to find "better horses," and changed only eight stocks. For 2015 and with the heady gains in the markets (almost 24 percent) we felt that a few more of our horses might be ready to fade and brought in 13 fresh ones for that year's ride. The pattern continued mostly unchanged in 2016 when we changed ten stocks.

With all the turmoil in the oil patch, commodity, and export businesses this year, it might surprise you that for the 2017 *100 Best Stocks* list, we replaced nine stocks. You can see our patience with business cycles and our "sell when there's something better to buy" principle hard at work here.

The overall methodology used for analysis and selection of the *100 Best Stocks* remains largely unchanged. We continue to focus on fundamentals that really count, like cash flow; profit margins and balance sheet strength; and those intangibles such as brand, market share, channel and supply-chain excellence, and management quality that really determine success *going forward*. We continue to place more focus on dividends and more generally, investor returns. More and more, especially in today's volatile markets, we feel that investors should get paid something to commit their precious capital to a company; it's a sign of good faith to investors and provides at least some return while waiting for a larger return in the future—or if things go south later on. This year, as mentioned previously, 96 of this year's *100 Best* pay at least some dividends—down from 98 over the past several years. The two "legacy" culprits that don't pay are CarMax and Itron; the two "new" nonpayers are Amazon and organic food producer WhiteWave Foods. These stocks are included because of other prospects; we can turn our heads the other way on the dividend for a while but would expect some dividends eventually as the business models mature.

In a "hallmark" factor, differentiating our approach, we continue to prefer companies with a track record for regular dividend *increases*. A few years ago we started tracking, for each company, the number of dividend increases or *raises* (yes, you can think of them as comparable to a raise in your own wage or salary) in the past ten years. We are proud to report that of the 98 *100 Best* stocks paying dividends in 2016, fully *85* of them *raised* their dividend from 2015 to 2016 (yes, that's down from 93 in 2015— mostly due to uncertainties facing energy and commodity stocks). Of the 85, *44* of them have raised their dividends in each of the past ten years, and 18 more have raised them each of the past eight or nine years (most of these took a year or two off during the Great Recession), adding up to 62 or almost two-thirds of our stocks able and willing to give you annual raises. Pretty good stuff, in our view.

As in all editions, we review the performance of our 2016 picks in some detail, and continue with our "stars" lists identifying the best stocks in six different categories:

1. Yield Stars (stocks with solid dividend yields—Table 6)
2. Dividend Aggressors (companies with strong and persistent records and policies toward dividend *growth*—Table 6.1)
3. Safety Stars (solid performers in any market—Table 7)
4. Growth Stars (companies positioned for above-average growth— Table 8)
5. Prosperity Stars (formerly Recovery Stars—companies poised to do particularly well in a strong economy—Table 9)
6. Moat Stars (companies with significant sustainable competitive advantage—Table 10)

So, if you're an investor partial to any of these factors, such as safety, these lists are for you.

2015–2016: A Dead Heat and a Wild Ride

Now we diagnose what happened in the year gone by and try to turn that into a prognosis for the coming year. Always a challenge in any year—and this one in particular.

It was a weird year that ended up pretty much where it started—the benchmark S&P 500 index, excluding dividends, advanced a mere 0.25 percent ahead of where it started, not including dividends during our measurement year April 1, 2015 to April 1, 2016—far short of the 10.5 percent advance in 2015 and 22.4 percent rise in 2014. Pretty dull, right? Not too much to diagnose, right?

Wrong. It was a wild ride, starting with a spring and early summer advance to new highs in 2015, a brief dip in August and September, a strong and sharp recovery, a larger "bear market" swoon in January–February 2016, followed by yet another strong, sharp recovery.

It wasn't a year for the faint of heart. And it certainly wasn't a year that lent itself to predicting what was going to happen *this coming* year—2017.

For the year, we noted five factors that drove the markets:

- *Accommodative Fed policy—for now.* With interest rates hovering near zero for the better part of eight years, many began to wonder just when the Fed would end that cycle and start to nudge rates upward. The "for" argument, of course, centered on keeping inflation in check, sending a signal that, yes, the economy is doing better, and keeping some powder dry for the next downturn. The "against" argument hung its hat on avoiding the same sort of debacle that occurred in 1937 as the nascent recovery then slammed against a wall of the Fed's making, and avoiding the strengthening of the dollar (higher interest rates attract overseas capital and thus drive up the value of the dollar) which would be hard on an already export-starved domestic production sector. As 2017 unfolds the Fed appears to be taking a very measured and transparent approach; some interest rate increases are likely but we don't expect anything large enough to be disruptive. Still, any time a rate rise is even hinted—or when any key economic indicator goes the wrong way—the markets have reacted in a frightened, oversensitized manner.

- *Economic turmoil overseas, especially in emerging markets.* Both high- and low-growth overseas markets have become very difficult to figure. China, which accounts for such a large portion of world demand and supply for goods, has seen its growth rates drop from the high to mid-single digits—which has caused a lot of disruption to trade and especially commodity markets. Other economies, some wrecked by the oil bust, have retrenched considerably, while Europe, which had seemed to be emerging from a funk, seems to have ducked back into another one. Commodity-producing countries like Canada, Australia, and many developing countries, have taken big hits as world commodity demand has fallen below world supplies. While we think a lot of this is cyclical, some may be permanent as (1) we think world demand for physical goods has waned a bit (downsizing boomers, lack of space for "stuff" for the world's new emerging market professionals), and (2) new supplies recently turned on during the commodities boom have proven difficult to turn off.

- *Commodity supply/demand out of whack.* One of the biggest and most dynamic factors affecting the U.S. economy and U.S. stocks in 2015–2016 is the strong cyclical swing first in energy and then pretty much across the board through the commodity sector. Oft-cited slowing China and emerging market demand was clearly a factor, but most of the cause appears to be large market oversupplies due to ramped up production—which strong emerging market and China growth stimulated years ago. In the energy sector, the additional supply boost given by the new "fracking" technology also helped throw that market out of whack. In almost all of these markets—oil, gas, copper, iron ore, fertilizer ingredients—supply has exceeded demand for a few years, but as production capacity declines slowly and demand picks up slowly, we expect these markets to be approaching a better balance in 2017. This will help the U.S. markets across the board—not just the commodity producers themselves but all the financial, equipment-producing, logistical, and other companies that support them. It also helps exports as strapped foreign commodity-producing countries balance their economies, too. Balanced commodity markets should prove quite beneficial for *100 Best* stocks and stock markets in general.

- *U.S. manufacturing growth on hold.* Although it is still slowing, in part due to commodity and emerging market cycles just noted, we still see a steady, if not ground-shaking, reshoring of manufacturing to American soil. Companies finally got the memo that it isn't just about labor costs—long, inflexible supply chains and the inability to control quality negate the savings, sometimes in a big way. Chinese labor costs are going up, and improved availability and declining costs of U.S. energy resources, especially natural gas, are helping even more. True, some supply chains, especially for electronics products, simply aren't deep enough to support U.S. manufacturing. The strong dollar has slowed reshoring a bit recently, but as dollar gains moderate or reverse, we would expect the trend to continue. Many of our companies, like W.W. Grainger and Illinois Tool Works, benefit from reshoring.

• *Persistence of share buybacks.* Companies have accumulated huge hoards of cash, as they have learned how to manage expenses and leverage their infrastructure to produce more for less. Although a big chunk of that cash is parked overseas for tax reasons, companies continue to actively buy back shares, producing rather silent but persistent returns to existing shareholders. S&P's Howard Silverblatt estimates that S&P 500 companies bought back an estimated $561 billion in 2015, mostly on par with the $553 billion bought back in 2014 (the record is $589 billion repurchased in 2007). More than half the companies on our *100 Best Stocks* list could be classified as "buyback aggressors," retiring 10–20 percent and as much as 50 percent of outstanding float since 2004. This, of course, serves to increase returns, both to the shareholders who sell and to those who remain to enjoy a higher rate of return on the remaining shares. We did see a moderation of that trend as the year went on, as the energy industry and others responded to new uncertainties, and—possibly due to high share prices—a few of our companies reduced buybacks in favor of cash dividends paid outright to shareholders.

Report Card: Recapping Our 2016 Picks

Once again, we weren't too excited with this year's 2.65 percent gain (2.3 percent of which was dividends), nor were we too excited about our "margin of victory" over the S&P 500's 2.35 percent—the "margin" being almost all in dividend yield (2.3 percent versus 2.1 percent). We got a little more excited, however, when we realized that we had beaten 36 out of the 40 Lipper sector indexes (as shown in Table 0.1). So—last year didn't make us (or you) rich, but we (you) were made less poor than a lot of other folks! At this juncture, we'll once again do a short refresher on how we evaluate our gains. There are many ways to evaluate the performance of a group of stocks over time. Some are simplistic, such as simply averaging the percent gain in each share price. But such a method may not weight a portfolio very realistically, for it assumes you buy the same number of shares of W.W. Grainger at $240 as you would Daktronics at $8. We feel it's better to take the approach of an investor with $100,000 to invest—who invested $1,000 in each of the *100 Best Stocks* across the board, regardless of share price. Sure, you end up with some weird quantities of shares in your portfolio, but the portfolio, and thus the performance metrics, isn't weighted in favor of more expensive stocks.

The Bottom Line

If you had invested $100,000 in our *100 Best Stocks 2016* list on April 1, 2015—$1,000 in each of the 100 stocks—you would have ended up with $100,334 on April 1, 2016, not including dividends paid during that period. That's a paltry 0.33 percent gain (yes, that's less than 1 percent!). Including dividends of some $2,318, you would have ended up with $102,652. The S&P, as measured by the buyable SPDR S&P 500 ETF Trust ("SPY"), was ahead just 2.35 percent, including dividends ($102,351) during that period. We were ahead of the S&P by some $301 for the year on a $100,000 investment—almost all of that on dividends. Although it's a win and a win's a win, we needed a flash photo at the finish line to assure our trip to the winner's circle.

Winners and Losers

The full list of the *100 Best Stocks 2016* and how they did through the comparison period can be found in Appendix A. At this point, we'll give a short overview of what really worked and what didn't within the list. First, the winners:

▼ Table 1: Performance Analysis: *100 Best Stocks 2016*

TOP WINNERS, 1-YEAR GAIN/LOSS, APRIL 1, 2015–APRIL 1, 2016

Company	Symbol	Price 4/1/2015	Price 4/1/2016	% change	Dollar gain per $1,000 invested
Public Storage	PSA	$197.14	$275.52	39.8%	$430.56
Campbell Soup	CPB	$46.55	$65.16	40.0%	$426.64
WD-40 Company*	WDFC	$79.95	$110.69	38.4%	$404.25
Cincinnati Financial*	CINF	$48.54	$65.96	35.9%	$397.20
McCormick	MKC	$77.11	$100.53	30.4%	$324.86
General Electric	GE	$24.81	$31.93	28.7%	$324.06
Kimberly-Clark	KMB	$107.11	$136.20	27.2%	$302.03
Sysco	SYY	$37.73	$47.08	24.8%	$280.15
Pall Corporation	PLL	$100.39	$127.20	26.7%	$278.61

* = New for 2016

Company	Symbol	Price 4/1/2015	Price 4/1/2016	% change	Dollar gain per $1,000 invested
Nike	NKE	$48.92	$61.59	25.9%	$271.26
Starbucks	SBUX	$48.97	$61.02	24.6%	$260.77
AT&T	T	$32.65	$39.05	19.6%	$253.91
Schnitzer Steel	SCHN	$15.86	$18.94	19.4%	$241.49
Aqua America	WTR	$26.35	$31.93	21.2%	$238.33
Fair Isaac	FICO	$88.72	$108.80	22.6%	$227.23
Ross Stores	ROST	$48.97	$58.64	19.7%	$210.74
Visa	V	$65.41	$77.59	18.6%	$194.16
Stryker Corporation	SYK	$92.25	$108.52	17.6%	$192.09
Fresh Del Monte*	FDP	$36.47	$42.96	17.8%	$191.66
Coca-Cola	KO	$40.55	$46.83	15.5%	$187.92

* = New for 2016

This year, our "winning percentage" of 57 winners out of 100 picks was *way* off from 79 for the 2015 list and 89 for 2014. Of course we're not proud about this low percentage but it isn't too surprising given our statistical dead heat for the year.

Our biggest winners—Public Storage and Campbell Soup—came as quite a surprise. We figured those stocks to be "steady Eddies," but outright winners? Not in our dreams. It shows what kind of a mixed year we had, and the success of these more defensive stocks shows how much commodity exposure and dollar exposure really hurt most of our list.

Many of our other top winners came from the same "defensive" part of our list—McCormick, Kimberly-Clark, Sysco, Aqua America (another dreamy surprise for the Top 20 list), AT&T, and Coca-Cola. We had our usual takeover for the year (Pall Corporation). More predictably, a few of our more aggressive growth picks (Nike, Starbucks, Visa, Fair Isaac, Schnitzer Steel, Ross, Stryker, and Fresh Del Monte) made the Top 20—a refreshing confirmation that our more aggressive growth picks actually do grow.

One pleasant surprise comes in the appearance of three of our "new" picks (out of ten total) on this list—WD-40, Cincinnati Financial, and Fresh Del Monte. Those of you continuing on from last year may remember that five out of the *bottom* 20 were new picks on the 2015 *100 Best* list—not a good place to be. As for our "sell when there's something better to buy" mantra, this year is far more confirming than last.

Now, for the losers:

▼ Table 2: Performance Analysis: *100 Best Stocks 2016*

TOP LOSERS, 1-YEAR GAIN/LOSS, APRIL 1, 2015–APRIL 1, 2016

Company	Symbol	Price 4/1/2015	Price 4/1/2016	% change	Dollar gain/loss per $1,000 invested
St. Jude Medical	STJ	$65.40	$55.19	-15.6%	$(138.07)
Tiffany	TIF	$88.01	$73.77	-16.2%	$(143.62)
ResMed	RMD	$71.78	$58.99	-17.8%	$(161.74)
Norfolk Southern	NSC	$102.95	$82.97	-19.4%	$(171.15)
State Street Corp	STT	$73.53	$58.95	-19.8%	$(174.35)
Steelcase	SCS	$18.94	$14.93	-21.2%	$(187.43)
Monsanto	MON	$112.54	$87.87	-21.9%	$(200.91)
Johnson Controls	JCI	$50.44	$39.15	-22.4%	$(201.23)
Archer Daniels Midland	ADM	$47.54	$36.47	-23.3%	$(208.88)
Daktronics	DAKT	$10.81	$8.03	-25.7%	$(220.17)
Perrigo	PRGO	$165.55	$126.73	-23.4%	$(231.35)
Ralph Lauren	RL	$131.50	$97.26	-26.0%	$(245.17)
CarMax	KMX	$69.01	$51.75	-25.0%	$(250.11)
Union Pacific	UNP	$108.31	$78.92	-27.1%	$(251.04)
McKesson	MCK	$226.20	$157.41	-30.4%	$(299.34)
Seagate Technology	STX	$52.03	$33.69	-35.2%	$(309.05)
Macy's	M	$64.91	$42.96	-33.8%	$(315.98)
ConocoPhillips	COP	$62.26	$39.78	-36.1%	$(321.55)
Harman International	HAR	$133.63	$86.75	-35.1%	$(340.49)
Mosaic	MOS	$46.06	$26.84	-41.7%	$(393.40)

* = New for 2016

Once again, our Top Losers list was populated by companies susceptible to the commodity and oil down cycle, including Mosaic, ConocoPhillips, and coal and oil transporters Union Pacific and Norfolk Southern. The related agriculture bust also dinged Mosaic, Archer Daniels, and Monsanto. But this year more than some others, we had a lot of flameouts on the more aggressive growth side (maybe fitting as we had more success with aggressive stocks too)—Harman, Macy's, McKesson, Seagate, Perrigo, CarMax, Daktronics, Ralph Lauren, Steelcase, and ResMed. In the case of Harman, Seagate, Johnson Controls, and Ralph Lauren, we deemed the change structural enough to remove them from the list (more to follow). The others? We decided to get back up on these horses again; we don't think the likes of McKesson, Perrigo, and others are ready to put out to pasture just yet.

As engineering types we always attempt to learn from our mistakes. We're not sure what we learned here. One of our valued mantras (besides "sell when there's something better to buy") is to not overreact to down cycles—but maybe we waited too long to respond to changes at Ralph Lauren and Seagate, which have been "racked" by Millennial and mall shifts, and high-tech commodity competition respectively—we might have seen those coming a bit sooner. File this one away under "Experience."

Which brings us to . . .

Value—Now More Than Ever

Those of you who take in our book every year have seen this before, but we remain steadfast in the principles of value investing.

For intelligent investors, chasing the latest fad doesn't work; buying something and locking it away forever doesn't work anymore, either. Investors must make intelligent choices based on true value and follow those choices through time and change. It all points to taking a value-oriented approach to investing and to staying modestly active with your investments.

The next obvious task is to define what we mean by a "value" approach. Essentially, it is to think of buying shares in a company as buying the company itself; it is about putting yourself in an entrepreneurial frame of mind, not just an investment frame of mind. Would you want to own that business? Why or why not?

Fundamentally, whether or not you want to own the business depends on two factors: first, the *returns* you expect to receive on your investment in the near- and long-term future, and second, the *risk* you'll take in generating those returns. Fortunately, the third factor the prospective entrepreneur must consider—"Do I have the time to run this business?"—is less of an issue for the investor.

You are looking for tangible value—tangible worth—for your precious, scarce, and hard-earned investment capital. That return can come in the form of immediate cash returns (dividends), longer-term cash returns (dividends and especially growing dividends), or as growth in the value of assets longer term. If you realize your return in the form of owning a share of a larger company eventually, that's still a legitimate return. Cash flow received later in the form of a higher share price or a takeover is still cash return; it is just less certain because of the forces of change that may take place in the interim. It is also theoretically worth less because of the nature of discounting—a dollar received tomorrow is worth more than a dollar received 20 years in the future.

The point: Many investment experts distinguish between "value" and "growth" investing; in fact, mutual funds are often classified as being one or the other. We dismiss this separation; growth can be an essential component of a firm's value. That growth can come either in the form of asset values or cash returns—i.e., growing dividends.

Value also implies safety. The safety comes in three forms. First is the fundamental quality and soundness of the firm's financial fundamentals— that is, income, cash flow, and the balance sheet. Value companies have plenty of reserves, a large enough *margin of safety*, to weather downturns and unforeseen events in the marketplace. Second, they have strong enough intangibles (brands, market position, supply-chain strength, etc.) to *maintain* their position in that marketplace and generate future returns. When we say this year, as we do *every* year, that our list should fare better in a *down* market than the S&P 500 as a whole, it's these safety factors, and particularly the intangibles, that support our premise.

Third, if you're really practicing value-investing principles, you buy these companies at reduced prices, when the markets are down, when the company is out of favor. You're looking for situations where the price is less than what you perceive to be the value, although calculating the value that precisely is elusive. When you "buy cheap" you provide another margin of safety; that margin makes it less likely that the stock will drop further. It gives you room for error if you turn out to be wrong about a choice. Again, it's much like buying a business of your own—you want to pay as little as possible in case things don't turn out as you'd expect. In today's markets, admittedly it's hard to buy cheap, but many of the nine new adds for 2017 for the moment at least, appear to have value relative to the market and the other choices we could have made, although are hardly in bargain territory. Sell when there's something better to buy.

Stay Active

What do we mean by "stay active"? Staying active means that you should remain abreast of your investment and, like any business you own, keep an eye on its performance. Periodically review the business and the stock as you would your own finances to see if it is making money and generally doing what you think it should be doing. You should keep an eye on company-related news, financials, earnings reports, and so forth—it's all part of being an individual investor and owner of companies.

Beyond that, time permitting, you should listen in on investor conference calls (usually at earnings announcements) to see what management has to say about the business. In addition, you should watch your business in the marketplace. See how many people are going to your local Starbucks and whether they are enjoying the experience, and look for other signs of excellence. See how many are milling around the Ralph Lauren department at Macy's—unfortunately not so many these days. We're not talking about constantly monitoring the stock price. Instead, we're suggesting an oversight of the business as though it were one you happen to own that, while professionally managed, requires an occasional glance to make sure everything is still acting according to your best interests. We also recommend a periodic review—at least annually—of whether your investments are still your best investments. Evaluate each investment against its alternatives. If you still perceive it to be the best value out there, keep it. If not, consider a swap for something new. Sell if there's something better to buy.

The *100 Best Stocks* for 2017: A Few Comments

As we head into 2017 we expect the economy to still be growing, albeit slowly, in a generally favorable interest rate and tax environment. We expect—a little stronger than hope for—a few more tailwinds for our *100 Best Stocks* list—a modest (emphasis on modest) recovery in energy and commodity prices as supply and demand gradually balance; a moderation or possibly a small pullback in the dollar, which will help exporters; and better news in the farm sector.

These external environmental factors should help our list achieve—and achieve better than the S&P 500 at large because we tilt toward manufacturers, exporters, agriculture, and the infrastructure that supports them.

But there's another factor in play, one that seems to be a recurring theme as we read company material and one that should provide a tailwind to most if not all of our *100 Best* list. Recent weakness in key markets, manufacturing, and export has motivated most quality U.S. companies to clean up their act and operate more efficiently. They've not only "cut the fat" but have taken a more realistic view of how and where to deploy capital—the energy industry is a good example—to produce the best returns, rather than trying to do everything. Companies are learning to "rightsize," to spin off non-congruent businesses, and to invest and invest wisely—a fact that has dragged a bit on many providers of business infrastructure like information technology products. We think both businesses and public sector spenders are reaching the end of that efficiency cycle and will start spending again, much to the aid of *100 Best* entries like Oracle, GE, Itron, and Valmont.

Beyond that, as demand picks up for most of our companies—as it will as exports, commodities, and agriculture strengthen if nothing else—companies will be more efficient and be able to reap more income from the sales surge. Revenues will rise faster than expenses, and shareholders of well-run companies will benefit.

Another "background" factor we see helping our *100 Best* list over the next few years is the continued semi-subconscious adjustment in our economy away from low value–add industries toward a back-to-basics, make-things-that-people-need mentality; with capital allocated to things like research labs and factories, not housing and real estate. We see manufacturing, scientific, food and agriculture, and infrastructure plays coming out ahead of financial stocks, real estate developers and builders, and service industries. It's just a hunch.

Still of concern is the rapid and still-uncontrolled rise in healthcare costs. Recent data showed that almost half the jobs created since the trough of the Great Recession are in healthcare-related fields. Healthcare businesses should prosper, but healthcare also acts like a tax for the rest of us—unless we start exporting healthcare in a meaningful way (many of the companies we choose in the sector do export healthcare in the form of pharmaceutical products or healthcare technologies). The Affordable Care Act made some important structural changes and expanded the reach of covered health-care but basically kicked the can down the road so far as healthcare costs are concerned. We continue to think this could start to be a real drag on the economy in 2017 and especially beyond—unless something, like competitive Medicare pharmaceutical bidding, is done about it.

While lower energy prices have kept inflation in check (which should also attenuate interest rate hikes), we still see more inflation at a personal level than we'd like and wonder sometimes just what numbers the Fed and Bureau of Labor Statistics are really looking at. Anyone who has bought meat, airline tickets, hotel accommodations—not to mention health insurance—knows what I'm talking about. We wonder where we would be without cheap energy, and as suggested earlier, we do think energy prices will gradually rise to something close to their previous equilibrium, as supply adjusts and demand continues its steady, if moderate, rise.

We also fret about the growing income gap; clearly the rich are getting richer at the expense of everyone else; that the second-largest category of job increases was in food service, retail, and hospitality suggests that the benefits of economic recovery aren't as helpful to some as others; good-paying jobs still exit our shores. While we applaud current downsizing trends in consumer spending, and see a very slight shift from physical goods to experiences and services, we feel that the economy in general as well as our *100 Best* list would be greatly helped out by an increase in capital spending—which isn't likely to come on fast if consumers aren't spending. A weaker dollar could supplant domestic spending through exports—but that weaker dollar would require forestalling interest rate increases, which would create excessive money supply. As usual, it's complicated.

All of this takes us to the usual place: We stick to companies with great business models, which have brand, marketplace, and financial strength sufficient to master the crosscurrents of change and the emergence of megatrends. We do factor in such megatrends as the cloud, the demise of paper in the workplace, the "always-on" nature of personal connectivity (and the prospect of marketers taking advantage of it), and availability of healthcare for everyone—and now the emergence of the Millennial generation. We've wanted to see a megatrend toward more energy wisdom; that one's been put on hold by cheap energy and new domestic energy supplies although we're still betting on it for the longer term. We continue to see a "national" economy, where large national brands gradually usurp local favorites, providing extra lift for big brands and big names like Coke and Smucker and Starbucks. (We do, however, especially with Millennials in mind, watch for localization trends in key industries like food processing; the beer industry, where local microbrews have gained significant share, provides an example.) For 2017, as always, we look for companies with good business models, which produce high-value-add things that people (or companies) need, do it efficiently, and generate a lot of cash. Good businesses. Not just companies that make a lot of money, but good businesses with a sustainable future. We think our "core" list is still pretty good regardless of what the market does; this year the nine changes we've made take in some of the themes we've mentioned previously; occasionally we switched horses where we felt it made sense. Sell when there's something better to buy. As is our custom, we'll start with the companies removed from the 2016 list:

▼ **Table 3: Companies Removed from 2016 List**

Company	Symbol	Category	Sector
Harman International	HAR	Aggressive Growth	Consumer Discretionary
Hillenbrand Inc.	HI	Aggressive Growth	Industrials
IBM	IBM	Conservative Growth	Information Technology
Johnson Controls	JCI	Conservative Growth	Industrials
Pall Corporation	PLL	Conservative Growth	Industrials
Ralph Lauren	RL	Aggressive Growth	Consumer Discretionary
Seagate Technology	STX	Aggressive Growth	Information Technology
Tiffany	TIF	Aggressive Growth	Retail
Wal-Mart	WMT	Conservative Growth	Retail

This year's "cut" list starts with Pall Corporation, acquired midyear by a private equity firm. Then come Harman and Seagate, two tech favorites. Harman had a bad year during a good "car" year; we think the industry is anticipating automotive electronic solutions from the likes of Apple and Google, which could push Harman out into the street. Seagate's once-promising solid-state drive products became commodities rather too quickly, with not enough new and profitable products down the pipe. Hillenbrand, our "new pick" from last year, has too much invested in machinery that serves the energy and mining industries, and layers that on top of a declining (but not dead yet) traditional funeral industry. Didn't come to life during the year as we had hoped.

Johnson Controls had a lackluster year and annoyed us by threatening to "invert" its headquarters to Ireland to avoid taxes just a few years down the road from Federal government bailouts of GM and Chrysler which probably saved their bacon—we prefer companies with a stronger sense of corporate responsibility. And Tiffany—well, seems too dependent on selling expensive tchotchkes to foreign tourists at its Fifth Avenue store; this is not a business model we have much faith in. We haven't liked their recent designs so much either (but hey, we don't buy a whole lot of jewelry!).

Once again our fine-tooth comb was directed at companies that would feel increased pain in an atmosphere where Millennials have become demographically dominant. The research is abundant—summing it up, among other things Millennials like customization and personalization, are health conscious, change preferences rapidly (brought on in part by rapid-fire social media; less loyal is another way to put it), like edgy new things, embrace and use information technology for everything, and tend not to do things the way Mom and Dad always did them. We looked through our list at companies that would have trouble dealing with this shift. Would Millennials buy IBM and embrace its heritage and brand? We decided not and cut IBM amidst its perpetually less-than-fruitful restructuring exercise. Would Millennials fawn over Ralph Lauren ponies on shirts and jackets? Not so much—not as much as *we* did at their age. And what about the Millennial transformation of shopping to a regular online experience we noted earlier? This will happen slowly, but stands to hurt the sizeable Wal-Mart the firstest and mostest—though we worry about other retailers like Macy's and Target that retain their positions on our list for now. Once again, we're likely not done making changes to the *100 Best* list to embrace this demographic shift—stay tuned next year.

Sell when there's something better to buy. So we did that in nine cases, and here they are:

▼ Table 4: New Companies for 2017

Company	Symbol	Category	Sector
AbbVie	ABBV	Aggressive Growth	Healthcare
Amazon	AMZN	Aggressive Growth	Retail
Carnival Corporation	CCL	Aggressive Growth	Consumer Discretionary
C.H. Robinson	CHRW	Aggressive Growth	Transportation
Columbia Sportswear	COLM	Aggressive Growth	Consumer Staples
Ormat Technologies	ORA	Aggressive Growth	Energy
Prologis	PLD	Growth and Income	Real Estate
Qualcomm	QCOM	Aggressive Growth	Technology
WhiteWave Foods	WWAV	Aggressive Growth	Consumer Staples

And now for the fun part—introducing our new "draft choices" for the 2017 season! We "sell when there's something better to buy" and tend to try to keep the mix of sectors relatively constant for diversification's sake and so as not to overload in any sector or industry. Aside from that, our only real theme for this year's new picks was a tilt—not surprisingly based on what we've said so far—toward the ever-growing Millennial demographic. So here goes:

AbbVie is the research pharma spinoff from the old Abbott Laboratories, a former *100 Best* pick we cast off to await the establishment of the new derivative companies. AbbVie appeals to us in its branding and extension of its core products to capture new markets; we like their portfolio and how they manage it for long-term success, and shareholder returns are attractive.

To varying degrees, Amazon, Columbia, Prologis, Qualcomm, and WhiteWave Foods all owe their inclusion on the list to the Millennial influence. E-commerce is here to stay, and Amazon as we all know plays hard in this space and has one of the world's most effective cloud-hosting businesses under its wing as well. E-commerce demands high-performance logistics and supply-chain solutions, and that's where our latest REIT, Prologis, plays with at least part of its business. Columbia Sportswear has become a branded favorite for outdoors enthusiasts and business-casual wearers alike and replaces Ralph Lauren for staid-chic couture (in our view, anyway). Qualcomm is a perennial innovator in the mobile phone space; we like their long-term visions and strategies for how to use mobile technologies for things like healthcare management as well as their generous shareholder returns today. WhiteWave is a very well-positioned but aggressive pure play in the organic food space, another Millennial favorite. (We like the idea too that WhiteWave, Columbia, and a few others not only appeal to the Millennials but to some of the more hip elements of the older generations too—who among other things have plenty of disposable income.)

So enough about Millennials. We mentioned "supply chain" in introducing Prologis; we think supply chains are becoming more high performance, more integrated, and more outsourced—trends that favor both C.H. Robinson and Prologis. This trend works well since many companies are looking at supply chains as one of the last frontiers to achieve meaningful efficiency gains and market expansions most large companies (and a lot of smaller ones) seek.

Carnival Corporation is a particularly well-run travel provider that follows a latent trend for people to buy experiences instead of expensive goods. We think the all-inclusive vacation is gaining traction among younger travelers—especially with greater varieties of ways to customize experiences to your tastes and travel budget. Okay, we're convinced—score another one for the Millennial transition.

Finally—there's Ormat. We continually look for companies that put promising new technologies to work, and we like companies that do things well in the alternative energy space. Ormat does both, as market leader of a narrow but growing niche of geothermal energy. They produce power as a utility from geothermal sources and make thermal recovery equipment for others, including the capture of waste heat from industrial processes. Always keen to separate good businesses from good ideas, we think Ormat has made the transition from the latter to the former.

As usual, we like to sum up the changes by sector after we do our picks. The sector balance is indicative at a high level of the nature of the changes we make each year. We don't like to change the sector balance too much unless there's a strong and compelling reason.

Table 5 (following) sums up this year's nine changes by sector. Reductions were a little more concentrated than in years past, with three in Industrials and two each in Retail, Consumer Discretionary, and Information Technology. Increases came pretty much across the board. The heaviest weightings remain Consumer Staples, Healthcare, and Industrials.

▼ Table 5: Sector Analysis and 2017 Change by Sector

NUMBER OF COMPANIES:

Sector	On 2016 list	Added for 2017	Cut from 2016	On 2017 list
Business Services	2			2
Consumer Discretionary	5	1	-2	4
Consumer Staples	13	2		15
Consumer Durables	1			1
Energy	6	1		7
Entertainment	1			1
Financials	5			5
Healthcare	14	1		15
Heavy Construction	0			0
Industrials	16		-3	13
Information Technology	8	1	-2	7
Materials	6			6
Real Estate	2	1		3
Restaurants	1			1
Retail	9	1	-2	8
Telecommunications Services	3			3
Transportation	5	1		6
Utilities	3			3

Yield Signs

We continue to like dividend-paying stocks. We like stocks that pay meaningful dividends, and especially stocks that have a tendency to have their dividends raised over time.

With dividend-paying stocks, especially those inclined toward dividend increases, you get an attractive yield from the day you buy the stock, but you'll also get handsome raises over time. As we reported earlier, 85 of the 98 dividend-paying stocks on the 2016 *100 Best* list raised their dividends in 2015, and 44 of those have raised their dividends in each of the past ten years. We like this. We like it a lot. A company that raises its dividend 10 percent will roughly double the payout in just seven years. (Calculation? Rule of 72—divide the percent increase into 72 and you'll get the number of years it takes to double: 72/10 equals 7.2 years.) You could end up with twice the income in addition to any gains or growth in the price of the stock.

DIVIDEND-PAYING, DIVIDEND-RAISING STOCKS—NOW AND FOREVER

The Rule of 72 and dividend-paying stocks lessons should be taken to heart by prudent investors, particularly those who fret about the effects of rising interest rates on their income-oriented investments (and who follow such fret in the financial media). When interest rates rise, bond prices fall, as the implied yield must adjust somehow; that is, a bond that generates a fixed income stream is worth relatively less in a higher interest–rate environment. Often, as we've seen, dividend-paying stocks take a tumble along with their bond brethren anytime even the rumor of rising interest rates is unsheathed. But the rising dividend provides the difference, and we feel that most of the investing world, particularly those attempting to build a comfortable retirement stream, should take note.

If you invest in a bond over a ten-year period, that bond will pay back its original principal at the end of the ten years, plus the interest as prescribed initially when the bond is sold. Nothing more, nothing less—so long as you wait ten years assuming no default—and you might not get your original principal if you decide to sell the bond sooner in a rising interest–rate environment (note that the interest payments don't go up—only that the bond value goes down).

If you invest in a dividend-paying stock with a persistent dividend raise policy and track records, as some two-thirds of the *100 Best* list represents, you enjoy the benefits of—and the protection of—the rising dividend. If your company raises its dividend 10 percent each year, the dividend will double in 7.2 years, and if it's paying 3 percent today, that implies 6 percent in 7.2 years—or a *doubling in the stock price* if the same yield is maintained (which is affected by a lot of factors besides the yield). If your company raises its dividend only 5 percent each year, it doubles in 14.4 years, but is still up roughly 70 percent in the ten-year period just described. That's still a handsome payout as well as giving solid potential for stock appreciation.

This favorable scenario simply does not exist for bonds. Bonds may be a bit more safe, as the interest payments are less likely to be cut (a cut is a default) and will be paid before dividends. But when we put a stock on the *100 Best* list, we feel that not only is the dividend itself fairly secure, but so is the potential for increase. We should also add that dividends receive favorable tax treatment for those of you holding investments outside of retirement accounts.

We continue to feel that investing in dividend-paying, dividend-growing stocks is the best way to save for a financially secure future.

Last year we came to the realization that we use two simple and key indicators to suggest a good stock for further analysis: (1) strong and growing yield, and (2) the persistence of share buybacks. Like that pretty face at a party, those two features suggest that we should learn the rest of the story. We continue to focus on those healthy companies willing to not only share a portion of their profits but also to give you, the investor, a periodic raise to recognize the value of your commitment of precious investment capital. In that spirit, in our presentation format we show the number of dividend increases in the past ten years in the header right after Current Yield. We know of no other financial publication that does this.

We also present the Dividend Aggressors list in our Stars lists, which you'll see shortly. Dividend aggressors are companies with substantial payouts that are also growing those payouts at a persistent and substantial rate. They have indicated through both words and performance that they continue to do so and have the resources to do it. So it isn't enough to raise the dividend each year by just a penny; it must be substantial. It also isn't enough to raise the dividend each year but still only be yielding 0.5 percent. There are lists of "dividend achievers" floating around on the Internet, and there are even a few funds constructed around a dividend achievers index. Our Aggressors are—well—a bit more aggressive.

The climate for dividend growth continues to be favorable albeit a bit diminished from past years. Estimates call for dividend growth somewhere in the 7 percent range over the next five years as energy and certain other companies regain their footing; raises had been in the 9–10 percent range for the prior two years. On the plus side, companies are still swimming in cash ($1.3 trillion for the "500" in early 2016). Rather than commit to expensive wages or business investments that might not pan out, they are simply returning cash to previously starved shareholders. This may be further helped along by lower energy and commodity input prices as they become baked into company performance.

Dancing with the Stars

We continue developing and sharing our "star" categories—groups of stocks essentially the "best of the best" in categories we chose to highlight—yield stars, dividend aggressors, safety and stability stars, growth stars, prosperity stars, and moat stars. We provide these stars lists because we know that every investor has his or her own preferences, and thus there are no "best" stocks within our "best" list, that is, there is no number one, two, and so on within the list.

Table 6 shows the top 20 stocks on our *100 Best* list by percentage yield as of mid-2016.

▼ Table 6: Top 20 Dividend-Paying Stocks

Company	Symbol	Projected 2016 dividend	Yield %	Dividend raises, past 10 years
Total S.A.	TOT	$2.73	5.6%	7
Daktronics	DAKT	$0.40	5.0%	7
Welltower	HCN	$3.44	5.0%	10
AT&T	T	$1.92	4.9%	10
Schnitzer Steel	SCHN	$0.75	4.7%	3
CenterPoint Energy	CNP	$1.03	4.6%	10
Macy's	M	$1.51	4.6%	8
ConocoPhillips	COP	$1.98	4.5%	9
Verizon	VZ	$2.26	4.5%	9
Valero	VLO	$2.40	4.4%	9
Chevron	CVX	$4.28	4.2%	10
Otter Tail Corporation	OTTR	$1.25	4.2%	4
Qualcomm*	QCOM	$2.12	3.8%	10
AbbVie*	ABBV	$2.28	3.6%	2
Prologis*	PLD	$1.68	3.5%	4
General Electric	GE	$0.92	3.4%	8
Procter & Gamble	PG	$2.68	3.3%	10
Target Corporation	TGT	$2.24	3.3%	10
Coca-Cola	KO	$1.40	3.2%	10
Paychex	PAYX	$1.68	3.1%	8

Table 6.1 shows our list of Dividend Aggressors for 2017:

▼ **Table 6.1: Companies with Strong Dividend Track Records**

Company	Symbol	Estimated 2016 dividend	Yield %	Dividend raises, past 10 years
3M Company	MMM	$4.44	2.6%	10
AT&T	T	$1.92	4.9%	10
CenterPoint Energy	CNP	$1.03	4.6%	10
Chevron	CVX	$4.28	4.2%	10
Cincinnati Financial	CINF	$1.92	2.8%	10
Coca-Cola	KO	$1.40	3.2%	10
Deere	DE	$2.40	3.0%	10
General Electric	GE	$0.92	3.4%	8
General Mills	GIS	$1.84	2.9%	10
Kimberly-Clark	KMB	$3.68	2.9%	10
Macy's	M	$1.51	4.6%	8
NextEra Energy	NEE	$3.48	2.9%	10
Paychex	PAYX	$1.68	3.1%	8
Public Storage	PSA	$7.20	2.8%	8
Qualcomm*	QCOM	$2.12	3.8%	10
Target Corporation	TGT	$2.24	3.3%	10
United Parcel Service	UPS	$3.12	3.0%	10
Valero	VLO	$2.40	4.4%	9
Verizon	VZ	$2.26	4.5%	9
Welltower	HCN	$3.44	5.0%	10

REMEMBER, THERE ARE NO GUARANTEES

While dividends and especially high yields are attractive, investors must remember that corporations are under no contractual or legal obligation to pay them! Interest payments on time deposits and bonds are much more clearly defined, and failure to pay can represent default. With dividends, there is no such safety net. Companies can—and do—reduce or eliminate dividends in bad times, as most strikingly observed with BP in the wake of the Deepwater Horizon Gulf spill disaster in 2010 and most bank stocks after the 2008 dive. More recently, energy price declines have hurt many U.S. oil producers, particularly more indebted ones engaged in the more expensive "fracking" process—and many of these players have cut or omitted dividends recently—ConocoPhillips on our *100 Best* list is a current example. Dividend investors should therefore keep an eye out for changes in a company's business prospects and shouldn't put too many eggs in a single high-yielding basket. On the flip side, as investors become more conscious of returns, and as corporate management teams become more aware of such investor consciousness, we've seen a lot of companies loudly trumpet their recent dividend increases to their investors and the investing public. It's a nice sound that we hope to continue to hear.

Safety Stars

Safety stars are companies we think will hold up well in volatile and negative stock markets as well as recessionary economies. They have stable products and customer bases, and long traditions of being able to manage well in downturns. We made no changes from last year's list. Several others, including the likes of Colgate-Palmolive, Coca-Cola, and Procter & Gamble from the remainder of the *100 Best* list would probably qualify.

▼ Table 7: Top 10 Stocks for Safety and Stability

Company	Symbol
Aqua America	WTR
Becton, Dickinson	BDX
Bemis	BMS
Campbell Soup	CPB
Clorox Company	CLX
General Mills	GIS
Johnson & Johnson	JNJ
Kimberly-Clark	KMB
McCormick	MKC
Sysco	SYY

Growth Stars

Looking at the other side of the coin, we picked ten stocks we feel are especially well positioned to grow, even in a negative economy and especially in a positive one. We made a couple of changes mostly to replace companies that not only weren't growing but were cut from our *100 Best* list altogether (Harman, Seagate) and replaced them with Amazon and WhiteWave Foods, two bellwether growth stocks in today's markets.

▼ **Table 8: Growth Stars: Top 10 Stocks for Growth**

Company	Symbol
Amazon	AMZN
Apple	AAPL
CarMax	KMX
Corning	GLW
Nike	NKE
Novo Nordisk	NVO
ResMed	RMD
Starbucks	SBUX
Visa	V
WhiteWave Foods	WWAV

Three years ago we shifted into post–Great Recession gear, replacing our "recovery stars" list with a "prosperity stars" selection. For this year we removed Tiffany (not so prosperous and a little too dependent on foreign tourist and Wall Street prosperity) and replaced it with logistics real estate provider Prologis, which should do well in a healthy economy.

▼ **Table 9: Prosperity Stars: Top 10 Stocks for a Growing Economy**

Company	Symbol
CarMax	KMX
DuPont	DD
General Electric	GE
Grainger, W.W.	GWW
Illinois Tool Works	ITW
Prologis	PLD

Company	Symbol
Schnitzer Steel	SCHN
Southwest Airlines	LUV
Steelcase	SCS
Whirlpool	WHR

Moat Stars

Finally, we get back to one of the basic tenets of value investing—the ability of a company to build a sustainable and unassailable competitive advantage. Value investing aficionados call such an advantage a "moat," for it represents a barrier to entry for competitors that will likely preserve that advantage for some time. The moat can come in the form of technology, the use of technology, a brand, enduring customer relationships, channel relationships, size or scale, or simply a really big head start into a business that makes it hard or even impossible for competitors to catch up. The appraisal of a moat is hardly an exact science; here we give our top ten picks based on the size and strength (width?) of the moat. For 2017 we cut Pall (acquisition) and Tiffany and Ralph Lauren, whose moats apparently served them poorly (a good moat doesn't fix declining demand or help a bad business). We added Amazon (lots of e-commerce competitors but nobody will ever catch up), Public Storage (also easy to mimic but hard to catch up), and Stryker, who dominates the growing market in orthopedic devices. Again, these are subjective picks, and good moats exist throughout our *100 Best* list.

▼ Table 10: Moat Stars: Top 10 Stocks for Sustainable Competitive Advantage

Company	Symbol
Amazon	AMZN
Apple	AAPL
Coca-Cola	KO
McCormick	MKC
Monsanto	MON
Public Storage	PSA
Starbucks	SBUX
Stryker Corporation	SYK
Visa	V
WD-40 Company	WDFC

What Makes a Best Stock Best?

We have proclaimed that we could identify a good *100 Best* candidate on two simple features: increasing dividend and declining share counts. But these, of course, aren't the whole story: Where do we go from there? What comes next? What is it that defines excellence—*sustainable* excellence—among companies? That's been a topic of considerable debate for years, and with all the study that's gone into it, nobody has hit upon a single formula for deciphering undeniable excellence in a company. That may seem amazing at first, but when you think about it, it isn't.

That's largely because "excellence" isn't as scientific as most of us would like or expect it to be. Much like finding your "match" and life partner, it defies data and mathematical formulation. Take the square of net profits, multiply by the cosine of the debt-to-equity ratio, add the square root of the revenue-per-employee count, and what do you get? Some nice numbers, but not a clear picture of how things work together or how a company will sell its products to customers and prosper going forward. And you certainly wouldn't want to select your ideal "match" this way.

Fundamentals such as profitability, productivity, and asset efficiency tell us how well a company has done and, by proxy, how well it is managed and how well it has done in the marketplace. Fundamentals are about what the company has already achieved and where it stands right now, and if a company's current fundamentals are a mess (or your potential partner is in bankruptcy court)—stop right now; there isn't much point in going any further.

In most cases, what really separates the great from the good are the intangibles: the "soft" factors of market position, market acceptance, customer "love" of a company's products, its management, its aura. These features create competitive advantage, or "distinctive competence," as an economist would put it, that cannot be valued. Furthermore, and most importantly, they are more about what a company is set up to achieve in the future. When you think about it, it's the intangibles that provide the spark for most of our personal matches, too.

To paraphrase Buffett at his best: Give me $100 billion, and I could start a company; but I could never create another Coca-Cola.

What does that mean? It means that Coca-Cola has already established a worldwide brand cachet; the distribution channels, customer knowledge, and product development expertise cannot be duplicated at any cost. When companies have competitive advantages that cannot be duplicated at any cost, they have an enduring grip on their markets. They can charge more for their products. They have a moat that insulates them from competition, or makes it much more expensive for competitors to participate. They're perceived by loyal customers as having top-line products worth paying more for.

A company with exceptional intangibles can control price and, in many cases, can control its costs.

Strategic Fundamentals

Let's examine a list of strategic fundamentals that define, or keep score of, a company's success. This list can be used as a checklist, although it's hard to find a company that shows excellence in all of these areas.

Are Gross and Operating Profit Margins Growing?

We like profitable companies; who doesn't? But what really counts is the size of the margin and especially the growth. If a company has a gross margin (sales minus costs of goods sold) exceeding that of its competitors, that shows that it's doing something right, probably with its customers and/or with its costs. But competitive analysis is elusive; there is no dependable source of "industry" gross margins, and comparing competitors can be difficult because no two companies are exactly alike; it's easy to mix apples and oranges.

We like to see what direction gross margin is moving in—up or down. A growing gross margin also signals that the company is doing something right and is gaining strength in its markets and/or its supply chain. That isn't perfect, either; as the economy moved from boom to bust, many excellent companies reported declines in gross and especially operating margins (sales minus cost of goods sold minus operating expenses) as they laid off workers and used less capacity. Still, in a steady-state environment, it makes sense to favor companies with growing margins. In a declining market, companies that can *protect* their margins will come out ahead.

Does a Company Produce More Capital Than It Consumes?

Make no mistake about it—we like cash. Pure and simple, we also like it when a company produces more cash than it consumes.

At the end of the day, cash generation is the simplest measure of whether a company is being successful, especially over the long term. Sure, if a company buys an airplane or opens a factory or a bunch of stores in a given quarter, it will be cash-flow negative. But that should be a temporary thing; over the long haul, it should produce, not consume, cash. Companies that continually have to borrow or sell shares to raise enough cash to stay in business are on the wrong track.

So how do you determine this? You'll have to become familiar with the Statement of Cash Flows or equivalent in a company's financial reports. "Cash flow from operations" is usually positive and represents cash booked from sales less cost of goods sold, with adjustments for noncash items like depreciation and for increases or decreases in working capital. In simple terms, is the cash going into the cash register from the daily operations of the business? Or from other sources?

"Cash used for investing purposes" or similar is a bit of a misnomer and represents net cash used to "invest" in the business—usually for capital expenditures, but also for short-term noncash investments like securities and a few other smaller items usually beyond scope. This figure is typically negative unless the company sells some part of its infrastructure. Over the long haul, cash generated from operations should well exceed cash used to invest in the business.

Companies in expansion mode may not show this surplus, and that's where "cash from financing activities" comes in. That's the cash generated from issuing debt or selling securities—or paying off debt or repurchasing shares, if things are going well—and dividends are included here as well. Again, a successful company will produce more cash—capital—from the business than it consumes, just as a successful household does the same, or else it goes into debt. Smart investors track this surplus over time.

Are Expenses under Control?

Just like your household, company expenses should be under control, and anything else, especially without explanation, is a yellow flag.

The best way to test this is to check whether the "Selling, General, and Administrative" expenses (SG&A) are rising, and more to the point, rising faster than sales. If so, that's a yellow, not necessarily a red, flag, but if it continues, it suggests that something is out of control, and it will catch up with the company sooner or later. In a downturn, companies that are able to reduce their expenses to match revenue declines scored more points, too.

Is Working Capital under Control?

Working capital is a hard concept to grasp—even for small entrepreneurs who live with its ups and downs on a daily basis. Insufficient working capital is one of the biggest causes of death for small businesses, and working capital and especially changes in working capital can signal success or trouble.

Using a simple analogy, working capital is the circulatory lifeblood of the business. Money comes in and money goes out, and working capital is what circulates in the veins in between. In its purest sense, it is cash, receivables, and inventory, less short-term debts. It's what you own less what you owe aside from fixed assets like plant, stores, and equipment.

If receivables are increasing, that sounds like a good thing—more people owe you more money. But if receivables are rising and sales aren't, that suggests that people aren't paying their bills, or worse, the business has to finance more to achieve the same level of sales. Similarly, a rise in inventory without a rise in sales means that it costs the business more money—more working capital—to do the same amount of business. That costs twice, because unless the firm is lucky, more inventory means more obsolescence and potentially more deep-discount sales or more write-offs down the road.

So a sharp investor will check to see that major working capital items— receivables and inventory—aren't growing faster than sales; indeed, a company that generates more sales with a decrease in working capital is becoming more productive.

Is Debt in Line with Business Growth?

Like many other "fundamentals" items, you can tear your hair out looking at debt figures and trying to decide whether they're in line with asset levels, equity levels, and industry norms. A simpler test is to check and see whether long-term debt is increasing or decreasing, and in particular, whether it is increasing faster than business growth. Gold stars go to companies with little to no debt, and to companies able to grow without issuing mountains of long-term debt. It's also worth checking to make sure the company isn't simply issuing debt to buy back shares—a little of this is okay, but some companies take on expensive debt just to increase per-share earnings (and management bonuses). This isn't a good strategy; in fact, it isn't a strategy at all.

Is Return on Equity Steady or Growing?

Return on equity (ROE) is another of those hard-to-grasp concepts, and another subjective measure when valuing assets and earnings. But at the end of the day, it's what all investors really seek: a return on their capital investments.

Like many other figures pulled from income statements and balance sheets, an ROE number, without any context, is hard to interpret. Does a 26.7 percent ROE mean, in itself, that a company is excellent? The figure sounds healthy, to be sure—it's a heck of a lot better than investing your money in a CD or T-bill. But because earnings and asset values are subjective, it may not represent true success. In fact, a company can increase ROE simply by borrowing money (yes!) and investing it into the business, even if it isn't invested as productively as other previous funds were invested. The math is complicated; we won't go into it here.

So the true test of ROE success is to check whether it is steady or increasing. Increasing—that makes sense. Why *steady*? Because if a company makes profits in a previous period and reinvests them in the business, that amount of money becomes part of equity (retained earnings). If the company reinvests productively, it will produce more returns, and ROE will at least keep up. If the company can't reinvest those earnings productively, ROE will drop—and perhaps it should be paying the earnings to you as dividends instead of investing them unproductively in the business. So if ROE is steady, the company still has good investments to make, and management is probably doing the right thing.

We should note that many investment analysts today prefer "Return on Invested Capital" (ROIC) as a metric over ROE. ROIC is return, or profit, divided by total equity *plus* debt. This gets you past the distortions that adding debt to the balance sheet might cause. Since the traditional balance sheet equation holds that "Assets = Liabilities + Capital," you can simply use total assets as the denominator—essentially the measure is "return on assets." Some analysts prefer to go farther by removing the cash balance from the asset denominator, to reflect the assets deployed and in use to generate returns and to get around the distortions of large reserve capital infusions often found at startup companies.

Does the Company Pay a Dividend?

Different people feel differently about dividends, and as described previously, we place great emphasis on dividend-paying stocks and especially those that *grow* their dividends. After all, save for the eventual sale of the company to someone else, a dividend is the only true cash that an investor will realize from buying a stock in a corporation, other than by selling the stock. At least in theory, investors should receive some compensation for their investments once in a while.

Yet, many companies don't pay dividends or don't pay dividends that compete very effectively with fixed-income yields. Why do investors put up with this? Because, in theory anyway, a company in a good business should be able to reinvest profits more effectively than the investor can (or else why would the investor have bought the company in the first place?). Investors trust that reinvested profits will eventually bring the growth in company value that will be reflected in the share price, or eventual takeover, or an eventual payment of a dividend or, better yet, growth in that dividend.

That's the theory, anyway, but there are still lots of companies that get away with paying no dividend at all. Can we tolerate this? Yes, if a company is really doing a great job with their retained profits, like Apple before they started paying dividends three years ago, or CarMax, or, now, Amazon and WhiteWave Foods. But we favor companies that offer at least something to their investors in the short term, some return on their hard-earned and faithfully committed capital. If nothing else, it keeps management teams honest and shows that management understands that shareholder interests are up there somewhere on the list of priorities. And getting an ever-*increasing* dividend—and owning a stock that has most likely appreciated because the dividend has increased—is like having your cake and eating it, too: a true favorite among investors, as noted in our previous sidebar (Dividend-Paying, Dividend-Raising Stocks—Now and Forever).

Strategic Intangibles

When you look at any company, perhaps the bottom-line question follows the Buffett wisdom: If you had $100 billion in cool cash to spend (and we'll assume the genius intellect to spend it *well*), could you re-create that company?

If the answer is yes, it may still be a great company, but it may not be great enough to fend off competition and keep its customers forever. If the answer is no, the company truly has something unique to offer in the marketplace, difficult to duplicate at any cost. That distinctive competence, that sustainable competitive edge—whatever it is, a brand, a trade secret, a lock on distribution or supply channels—may be worth more than all the factories and high-rise office buildings and cash in the bank a company could ever have.

What we're talking about are the intangibles, the "soft" factors that make companies unique and that add up to more than the sum of their parts, the factors that ultimately drive future revenues. Intangibles not only define excellence, they define the future, while fundamentals mainly define the past. Seven key intangibles follow, although you'll think of more, and some industries may have some unique ones of their own, like intellectual property in the technology sector.

Does the Company Have a Moat?

A business moat performs much the same role as its medieval castle equivalent—it protects the business from competition. Whatever factors create the moat, ultimately those are the factors that prevent you, with your $100 billion, from taking their business. Moats are usually a combination of brand, product technology, design, marketing and distribution channels, and customer loyalty all working together to protect a company. A moat doesn't just protect the existence of a company, it helps it command higher prices and earn higher profits.

Whether a company has a narrow moat, a wide moat, or none at all is a subjective assessment for you to make. However, you can get some help at Morningstar (www.morningstar.com), whose stock ratings include an assessment of the moat.

Coca-Cola has a moat because of the sheer impossibility of surpassing its brand and brand recognition worldwide. CarMax has a moat because it is farther along in putting retail-style dealerships on the ground and applying management information technologies to its business than anyone else; it would take years for a competitor to catch up. Amazon has a moat because of its immediately recognized brand, its size, and its technology leadership in delivering an industry-leading e-commerce experience. WD-40 has a moat because it's virtually the only game in town and the only recognized brand for its relatively simple product. The Moat Stars list presented earlier identifies the top ten stocks with a solid and sustainable competitive advantage.

DOES THE COMPANY HAVE AN EXCELLENT BRAND?

It's hard to say enough about brand, especially in today's fast-moving, highly packaged, highly national and international marketplace. A strong brand means consistency and a promise to consumers, and consumers sold on a brand will prefer it over any other, almost regardless of price. People still buy Tide; Starbucks is still synonymous with high quality and ambience. Good brands command higher prices and foster loyalty, identity, and even customer "love."

Ask yourself if a company has a sought-after brand, a brand customers would pay extra to buy or align with, a brand that would be difficult to duplicate at any cost. Would customers rather fight than switch? Think about Starbucks, Coca-Cola, Allstate, Smucker's, Scotts, Southwest, or Nike, or the brands within a house, like Minute Maid (Coke), Tide (P&G), KitchenAid (Whirlpool), Horizon Organics (WhiteWave Foods), or Varathane, DAP, or Rust-Oleum (RPM International).

IS THE COMPANY A MARKET LEADER?

Market leadership usually—but not always—goes hand in hand with brand. The trick is to decide whether a company really leads in its industry. Often—but not always—that's a factor of size. The market leader usually has the highest market share, and the important point is that it calls the shots with regard to price, technology, marketing message, and so forth—other companies must play catch-up and often discount their prices to keep up. Apple is a market leader in digital music, Monsanto in systematized agriculture, Nike in sports apparel, and Starbucks in beverages—and so forth.

Excellent companies tend to be market leaders, and market leaders tend to be excellent companies. However, this relationship doesn't always hold true—sometimes the nimble but smaller competitor is the excellent company and *headed for* market leadership. Examples like CarMax, Perrigo, Valero, Columbia Sportswear, and Southwest Airlines can be found on our list.

Does the Company Have Channel Excellence?

"Channels" in business parlance means a chain of players to sell and distribute a company's products. It might be stores, it might be other industrial companies, it might be direct to the consumer. If a company is considered a top supplier in a particular channel, or a company has especially good relations with its channel, that's a plus.

Excellent companies develop solid channel relationships and become the preferred supplier in those channels. Companies such as Patterson, Deere, Fair Isaac, McCormick, Nike, Novo Nordisk, Procter & Gamble, Scotts Miracle-Gro, Sysco, WD-40, and Whirlpool all have excellent relationships with the channels through which they sell their product.

Does the Company Have Supply-Chain Excellence?

Like distribution channels, excellent companies develop excellent and low-cost supply channels. They are seldom caught off guard by supply shortages and tend to get favorable and stable prices for whatever they buy. This is often not an easy assessment unless you know something about a particular industry. Fresh Del Monte, Nike, Target, or Procter & Gamble again, are examples of companies that have done a good job managing their supply chains.

Does the Company Have Excellent Management?

It's not hard to grasp what happens if a company *doesn't* have good management: Performance fails and few inside or outside the company respect the company. It's not easy for an investor to determine if a management team does a good job or acts in shareholder interests. Clues can include candor and honesty and the ability of company management to speak in accessible, easily understood terms about the company and company performance (it's worth listening to conference calls as a resource). A management team that admits errors and eschews other forms of arrogance and entitlement (i.e., luxury perks, office suites, aircraft) is probably tilting its interests toward shareholders, as is the management team that can cough up some return to shareholders once in a while in the form of a dividend.

This may be the most subjective and elusive assessment of all, as few investors work with these folks on a daily basis. Still, over time, you can garner a strong hunch about whether a management team is effective and on your side. We're reluctant to keep mentioning WD-40 in this section, but a trip through their website and especially their "values" page (www .wd40company.com/about/values/) will give you (as it gave us) comfort with their management style. Of course, be careful: It can be difficult to separate the "business B.S." from the true indicators of excellence; it becomes largely a matter of gut feel and personal assessment of what they say—again, we're back to what it takes to make that relationship "match."

ARE THERE SIGNS OF INNOVATION EXCELLENCE?

This question seems pretty obvious, but it's not just about the products that a company sells. True, if the company is leading the industry in innovation, that's usually a good thing, for "first to market" definitely offers business advantages.

The less obvious part of this question is whether the company makes the best *use* of technology to make operations and customer interfaces as efficient and effective as possible. Southwest Airlines may have missed our list in the past because of the difficulty of achieving excellence in an industry where players can't control prices or costs. While airlines have enjoyed better times, we still don't like them in general—but Southwest continues to make our list today, not only because of brand and management excellence, but also innovation excellence. Why? Simply because, after all of these years, amazingly, it still has the best, simplest, easiest-to-use flight booking and check-in in the industry. Sometimes such innovations mean a lot more than bringing new, fancy products and bells and whistles to the market. You can also look to Amazon, Apple, CarMax, CenterPoint Energy, C.H. Robinson, Daktronics, FedEx, Itron, Novo Nordisk, ResMed, Steelcase, UPS, and Visa on our list for more obvious examples of companies that have deployed technology and innovative customer interfaces to achieve sustainable competitive advantage.

Choosing the *100 Best*

With all of this in mind, just how was this year's *100 Best Stocks* list actually chosen?

The answer is more subtle than you might think. If we could give you a precise formula, you wouldn't need this book. You'd be able to do it yourself. In fact, every investor would be able to do it on his or her own. Our book would simply be the result of yet another stock screener, and every investor would invest in the same stocks. Is that a feasible or practical solution? Hardly. Everyone would scramble to buy the same 100 best stocks. The prices would be sky high, and the price of other stocks would melt to nothing.

SIGNS OF VALUE

Following are a few signs of value to look for in any company. This is not an exhaustive list by any means, but it's a good place to start:

» Rising dividends

» Declining share count

» Gaining market share

» Can control price

» Loyal customers

» Growing margins

» Producing, not consuming, capital (free cash flow)

» Steady or increasing ROE

» Management forthcoming, honest, understandable

SIGNS OF UNVALUE

. . . and signs of trouble, or "unvalue":

» Declining margins

» No brand or who-cares brand

» Commodity producer, must compete on price

» Losing market dominance or market share

» Can't control costs

» Must acquire other companies to grow

» Management in hiding, off message, making excuses, difficult to understand, or in the news for all the wrong reasons

Fortunately or unfortunately, however you want to look at it, it isn't that simple. There are so many fundamentals, so many intangibles, and so many unknown and unknowable weighting factors to combine the fundamentals and intangibles that—well—it just wouldn't work. No screener could recreate the subtle judgment that gets applied to the cold, hard facts. It's that judgment, the interpretation of the facts and intangibles, that makes it worth spending money on a book like this.

While we didn't apply a specific formula or screener to the universe of stocks, we did take a few measurable factors into account to narrow the list from thousands to a few hundred issues. Those factors came from several sources, but at this point we must tip our cap to Value Line and the research and database work they do as part of the Value Line Investment Survey. If you aren't familiar with Value Line, it's worth a look for any savvy individual investor, either online at www.valueline.com or, in many cases, at your local library. It is an excellent resource.

When to Buy? Consider When to Sell

We've said it over and over: Sell when there's something better to buy.

Selling is hard. So is removing something from our *100 Best* list (unless it became part of a takeover transaction). If it's hard to figure out when to buy a stock, it's even harder to figure out when to sell. People tend to get married to their investment decisions, feeling somehow that if it isn't right, maybe time will help and things will get better. It's human nature.

Or they're just too arrogant to admit that they made a mistake. That's also human nature.

There are lots of reasons why people hold on to investments for too long a time.

Here's the fundamental truth: Buying and selling should be much the same process. Let's look at it from the point of view of selling. When should you sell? Simply, as we've said repeatedly, when there's *something else better to buy*. Something else better for future returns, something else better for safety, something else better for timeliness or fit with today's go-forward worldview; a *megatrend* as we've referred to it. That something else can be another stock, a futures contract, or a house, or any kind of investment. It can also be cash—sell that stock when . . . when what? When cash is a better investment. Or when you need the money, which is another way of saying that cash is a better investment—at least it's safer for the time being.

Similarly, if you think of a buy decision as a best possible deployment of capital because there's no better way to invest your money, you'll also come out ahead. It really isn't that hard, especially if you've done your homework. And it's also made easier if you avoid rash overcommitments; that is, you avoid buying all at once in case you've made a mistake or in case better prices come later down the road.

ETFs: Different Route, Same Destination (Almost)

The 100 Best Stocks to Buy series continues to be about—well—the 100 best *individual companies* in which you can buy shares to build into your investment portfolio. The objective is to use these selections as a starting point to build a customized portfolio of your very own, a portfolio that earns decent, better-than-market, long-term returns from excellent companies while—because they're excellent companies—taking less risk than you would with most investments. Because you're doing it yourself, you save money on fees and expenses and come away with the pride of ownership of doing it yourself.

That said, not everyone has the time or inclination to do this. Not everyone wants to sail through the treacherous channels of company financial information and the foggy mysteries of intangibles and marketplace performance to figure out which companies are really best to own and to keep a finger on the pulse to make sure they stay that way. You may want to own individual stocks. But just as buying a kit makes many aspects of building a new outdoor deck easier, so does buying a stock "kit": a product or package of stocks to do what you might otherwise have to struggle through on your own. If you could get such a kit product cheap enough and aligned to your needs, then why wouldn't you? It will save time, and you'll be firing up the barbecue and enjoying those outdoor parties with your friends a lot sooner. Or, perhaps at the risk of more tiring analogies, buying individual stocks is like ordering à la carte from a menu. You're not sure if what you're getting works together, so why not do a *prix fixe* to let the chef do some of the driving? Okay, enough . . .

Such is the impulse to find investment products—packages, *prix fixe* menus—that mimic the performance of the *100 Best* stocks. Honestly, we would *still* love it if some fund company would come to us and "buy" our index to build a fund you could buy, but that hasn't happened yet (but we as optimists never give up hope!). So in that spirit—and because we've written a lot about the merits of individual stock versus fund investing before—we'd like to offer this special section about using exchange-traded funds (ETFs) as a path to own portfolios crafted with many of the *100 Best Stocks* principles in mind.

The ETF Universe

We're talking about ETFs here, not traditional mutual funds. Although total traditional mutual fund assets still outweigh ETF-held assets by a factor of eight to one, traditional mutual funds are more expensive and haven't performed as well as ETFs—or the market benchmarks—over time. So we will limit this discussion to ETFs, but if you're working with a professional advisor or are limited to traditional funds through your 401(k) or some other investment platform, the discussion can apply to traditional funds, too.

ETFs are packaged single securities trading on stock exchanges (rather than directly through a mutual fund company), which create a basket of securities that track the composition of specially designed indexes. With most ETFs (excluding "actively managed" ETFs) there are no fund managers making individual stock purchase or sale decisions. The fund follows the index.

These indexes started out as broad, bland, and obvious—the first ETF, the SPDR S&P 500 ETF Trust, has tracked the S&P 500 index since 1993. Since that inception, hundreds of new indexes have been created to track everything from broad baskets of stocks to the price of certain commodities in Australian dollars. Three years ago we made an attempt to identify the indexes—and the funds built around them—that mimic *100 Best Stocks* principles.

As of early 2016, there are about 1,600 exchange-traded products, of which about 1,400 are ETFs and 200 are so-called "exchange-traded notes," or ETNs, which are actually fixed-income securities adjusted in value to track an index without actually owning the components of the index. Growth in the ETF space has slowed as recently some funds have closed due to the lack of interest; the total number has stayed relatively constant over the past three years. Total assets were about $2 trillion, or 13 percent of the total "fund" market at the end of 2015. There are generalized and specialized ETFs covering stocks, bonds, fixed-income investments, commodities, real estate, currencies, and the so-called "leveraged and inverse" funds designed to achieve specialized investing objectives. Within each of those groups, the segments available could fill a chapter in and of themselves with divisions by market cap, style (growth versus value), industry, sector, strategy, country, and region—just to name a few.

ETF Advantages

There are numerous advantages of ETFs over traditional funds—reasons why they are "where the puck is going" in packaged investments:

- *Easy to research.* ETFs are relatively easy to understand and easy to screen using commonly found screening tools at online brokers.
- *Transparency.* It's easy to learn what individual stocks an ETF owns and what comprises the underlying index, both through the online portals and through the index providers' websites. (Want to know what's in the Focus Morningstar Health Care Index? Just put the index name into a search engine, and you'll find out.)
- *Low fees, low cost.* Fees typically range from 0.1 percent for the most generic index funds to 0.2–0.8 percent for more specialized funds—about half of the typical figures found in traditional mutual funds. One fund provider—Vanguard—has traditionally been the lowest cost provider in this regard.
- *Easy to buy and sell.* It's like buying and selling an ordinary stock.
- *Easy to match your objectives and style.* New funds are showing up every day, and many match a quality, low-volatility, value-oriented style we're aligned with.

Dining with the 100 Best: A Special ETF Menu

Our *100 Best Stocks* list doesn't really follow any investment style. It isn't just growth or value. It isn't just large cap, it isn't just high yield, nor is it just tied to certain industries or sectors of the economy. It is a blend of excellent companies in the right businesses, doing well in those businesses, with a potential for strong, steady, and growing investor returns. There is no index or any other screenable classification to select those companies. If there were, there'd be little reason to publish this book.

So as we search for ETFs that run with the same tailwinds as our *100 Best* list, we start with the name of the fund and the index that the fund follows. "Dividend Achievers" or "Buyback Achievers" tells us we're looking on the right part of the menu. Then we dig in and look at the actual portfolio composition (again, most investing portals and brokerage sites let you do this—we use Fidelity [www.fidelity.com]). If we see lots of *100 Best* stocks on the list, it confirms that we're on the right track.

Three years ago we selected eight ETFs that we thought most closely followed our *100 Best* style and principles, and could be used to build or supplement parts of your portfolio. For the second year in a row, we reviewed the list of available funds and found no others that fit better than what we had. We share the list in the following table, and in the typical spirit of our presentations, we show the performance of these eight funds during our measurement period.

The results for 2016 were—in a word—surprising!

As Table 11 shows, almost every *100 Best*-style ETF beat the *100 Best 2016* list (as well as the S&P 500) handily. By several percentage points to almost five times the performance including dividends.

What gives? We're not 100 percent sure, but there seem to be at least a few factors at work. During the past year in particular, the low-volatility investing style has really caught on with baby boomers trying to eke out a bit more savings for retirement without exposure to too much risk. The low-volatility investing style is intended to achieve slightly above-market returns with less risk or volatility (again see my book *All About Low Volatility Investing*). It fits right in with what the boomers are trying to achieve.

So they loaded up on low-volatility ETFs, including most of the entries on the list. Billions of dollars flowed in, and those dollars had to be invested, by definition, in the stocks "indexed" in the fund. Such true low-volatility stocks, like Campbell Soup, went up with these new investments, and the valuation of the ETFs went up as a result.

So why didn't the *100 Best 2016* list track this rise? Because, while we have *many* low-volatility stocks, we are not 100 percent invested in this style. We have energy, resource, and industrial stocks that, while we think they're pretty safe, aren't on these indexes. So we enjoyed some of the gains—as with Campbell Soup—but had other picks that these funds managed to avoid.

So is it time now to buy these ETFs? Frankly, it's a bit risky—the fund values, as well as the underlying stock values, are pretty high. Required rebalancings of ETF portfolios—to realign the values of individual holdings to the index—may result in selloffs in many or most of these stocks. This will potentially hurt *100 Best* also, but will hurt the funds more as they are "all in" on these higher-priced "safe" stocks. We should note that even with this cloud over the low-volatility funds and stocks, they are still pretty safe bets compared to the alternatives. So is the *100 Best 2017* list—for that matter!

Selecting ETFs is an art in itself and was covered in a now-dated but still relevant earlier book we did in this series called *The 100 Best ETFs You Can Buy 2012*. Unfortunately that book didn't find a large enough market to be updated each year, but it is still useful in its original form and is still available. There are many other ETF resources, again at your online broker

▼ Table 11: *100 Best Stocks*—ETF "Imitators"

ETFS WITH STRONG "100 BEST" COMPOSITION AND STRATEGIES, PERFORMANCE 2015–2016

ETF	Symbol	Sponsor	Total assets	Expense ratio (%)	Price 4.1.2015	Price 4.1.2016	% gain share value	2015–6 dividend	Yield %	Total return	What attracted us:
Spdr S&P Dividend ETF	SDY	State Street	$13.6B	0.35%	$73.48	$80.69	9.8%	$4.56	6.2%	16.0%	Diverse portfolio, "Dividend Aristocrats" index
First Trust Morningstar Dividend Leaders Index Fund	FDL	First Trust	$1.42B	0.45%	$23.20	$25.70	10.8%	$0.83	3.6%	14.4%	Lots of *100 Best Stocks*
iShares Dow Jones Select Dividend Index Fund	DVY	Blackrock	$14.6B	0.39%	$75.70	$82.04	8.4%	$2.62	3.5%	11.8%	Growth plus income, lots of *100 Best Stocks*
iShares MSCI USA Minimum Volatility Index Fund	USMV	Blackrock	$12.4B	0.15%	$40.17	$43.77	9.0%	$0.87	2.2%	11.1%	Low-volatility focus, lots of *100 Best Stocks*, low cost
Powershares S&P 500 High Quality Portfolio	SPHQ	Invesco	$899.1M	0.29%	$22.80	$24.70	8.3%	$0.46	2.0%	10.4%	Growth and stability of dividends, lots of *100 Best Stocks*
Market Vectors Wide Moat ETF	MOAT	Van Eck	$705.1M	0.49%	$30.48	$32.34	6.1%	$0.62	2.0%	8.1%	Compelling strategy, new fund, low cost
Powershares S&P 500 Low Volatility Portfolio	SPLV	Invesco	$6.8B	0.25%	$37.08	$39.04	5.3%	$0.86	2.3%	7.6%	Low-volatility focus, lots of *100 Best Stocks*, low cost
100 Best Stocks 2016 Portfolio										2.65%	
Powershares Buyback Achievers Portfolio	PKW	Invesco	$1.64B	0.63%	$48.18	$45.66	-5.2%	$0.59	1.2%	-4.0%	Compelling strategy, strong long-term results

or through a specialized ETF portal called ETFdb (www.etfdb.com). This portal and its classification page (www.etfdb.com/type) can be helpful in finding individual ETFs that suit your taste.

We'll leave the ETF discussion here for this year; the good news continues to be that you can invest in ETFs and still follow the *100 Best* style.

Now the moment of truth—we invite you to accompany us in the unveiling of *The 100 Best Stocks to Buy in 2017*. Drum roll, please.

Part II

THE 100 BEST STOCKS TO BUY

The 100 Best Stocks to Buy

Index of Stocks by Company Name (*New for 2017)

Company	Symbol	Category	Sector
3M Company	MMM	Conservative Growth	Industrials
—A—			
*AbbVie	ABBV	Aggressive Growth	Healthcare
Aetna	AET	Conservative Growth	Healthcare
Allstate	ALL	Conservative Growth	Financials
*Amazon	AMZN	Aggressive Growth	Retail
Apple	AAPL	Aggressive Growth	Consumer Discretionary
Aqua America	WTR	Growth and Income	Utilities
Archer Daniels Midland	ADM	Conservative Growth	Consumer Staples
AT&T	T	Growth and Income	Telecommunications Services
—B—			
Becton, Dickinson	BDX	Conservative Growth	Healthcare
Bemis	BMS	Conservative Growth	Consumer Staples
—C—			
Campbell Soup	CPB	Conservative Growth	Consumer Staples
CarMax	KMX	Aggressive Growth	Retail
*Carnival Corporation	CCL	Aggressive Growth	Consumer Discretionary
CenterPoint Energy	CNP	Growth and Income	Utilities
Chevron	CVX	Growth and Income	Energy
Cincinnati Financial	CINF	Growth and Income	Financials
Clorox Company	CLX	Conservative Growth	Consumer Staples
Coca-Cola	KO	Conservative Growth	Consumer Staples
Colgate-Palmolive	CL	Conservative Growth	Consumer Staples
*Columbia Sportswear	COLM	Aggressive Growth	Consumer Staples
Comcast	CMCSA	Aggressive Growth	Telecommunications Services
ConocoPhillips	COP	Growth and Income	Energy
Corning	GLW	Aggressive Growth	Information Technology
Costco Wholesale	COST	Aggressive Growth	Retail
CVS Health	CVS	Conservative Growth	Retail
—D—			
Daktronics	DAKT	Aggressive Growth	Information Technology
Deere	DE	Aggressive Growth	Industrials
DuPont	DD	Growth and Income	Materials

Index of Stocks by Company Name (continued)

Company	Symbol	Category	Sector
—E—			
Eastman Chemical	EMN	Conservative Growth	Materials
Empire State Realty Trust	ESRT	Growth and Income	Real Estate
—F—			
Fair Isaac	FICO	Aggressive Growth	Business Services
FedEx	FDX	Aggressive Growth	Transportation
Fresh Del Monte	FDP	Conservative Growth	Consumer Staples
—G—			
General Electric	GE	Growth and Income	Industrials
General Mills	GIS	Growth and Income	Consumer Staples
Grainger, W.W.	GWW	Conservative Growth	Industrials
—H—			
Honeywell	HON	Aggressive Growth	Industrials
—I—			
Illinois Tool Works	ITW	Conservative Growth	Industrials
International Flavors & Fragrances	IFF	Aggressive Growth	Consumer Staples
Itron	ITRI	Aggressive Growth	Information Technology
—J—			
Johnson & Johnson	JNJ	Growth and Income	Healthcare
—K—			
Kimberly-Clark	KMB	Growth and Income	Consumer Staples
Kroger	KR	Conservative Growth	Retail
—M—			
Macy's	M	Aggressive Growth	Retail
McCormick	MKC	Conservative Growth	Consumer Staples
McKesson	MCK	Conservative Growth	Healthcare
Medtronic	MDT	Aggressive Growth	Healthcare
Microchip Technology	MCHP	Aggressive Growth	Technology
Monsanto	MON	Aggressive Growth	Industrials
Mosaic	MOS	Aggressive Growth	Materials

Index of Stocks by Company Name (continued)

Company	Symbol	Category	Sector
—N—			
NextEra Energy	NEE	Growth and Income	Utilities
Nike	NKE	Aggressive Growth	Consumer Discretionary
Norfolk Southern	NSC	Conservative Growth	Transportation
Novo Nordisk	NVO	Aggressive Growth	Healthcare
—O—			
Oracle	ORCL	Aggressive Growth	Information Technology
*Ormat Technologies	ORA	Aggressive Growth	Energy
Otter Tail Corporation	OTTR	Growth and Income	Energy
—P—			
Patterson	PDCO	Aggressive Growth	Healthcare
Paychex	PAYX	Aggressive Growth	Information Technology
Perrigo	PRGO	Aggressive Growth	Healthcare
Praxair	PX	Conservative Growth	Materials
Procter & Gamble	PG	Conservative Growth	Consumer Staples
*Prologis	PLD	Growth and Income	Real Estate
Public Storage	PSA	Growth and Income	Real Estate
—Q—			
*Qualcomm	QCOM	Aggressive Growth	Technology
Quest Diagnostics	DGX	Aggressive Growth	Healthcare
—R—			
ResMed	RMD	Aggressive Growth	Healthcare
*C.H. Robinson	CHRW	Aggressive Growth	Transportation
Ross Stores	ROST	Aggressive Growth	Retail
RPM International	RPM	Aggressive Growth	Basic Materials
—S—			
Schlumberger	SLB	Aggressive Growth	Energy
Schnitzer Steel	SCHN	Aggressive Growth	Industrials
Scotts Miracle-Gro	SMG	Growth and Income	Materials
J.M. Smucker	SJM	Growth and Income	Consumer Staples
Southwest Airlines	LUV	Aggressive Growth	Transportation
St. Jude Medical	STJ	Aggressive Growth	Healthcare
Starbucks	SBUX	Aggressive Growth	Restaurant
State Street Corp	STT	Conservative Growth	Financials
Steelcase	SCS	Aggressive Growth	Industrials
Stryker Corporation	SYK	Aggressive Growth	Healthcare
Sysco	SYY	Conservative Growth	Consumer Staples

Index of Stocks by Company Name (continued)

CONSERVATIVE GROWTH

3M Company

Ticker symbol: MMM (NYSE) ❑ S&P rating: AA– ❑ Value Line financial strength rating: A++ ❑ Current yield: 2.6% ❑ Dividend raises, last 10 years: 10

Company Profile

The 3M Company, originally known as the Minnesota Mining and Manufacturing Co., is a $30 billion diversified manufacturing technology company with leading positions in industrial, consumer and office, healthcare, safety, electronics, telecommunications, and other markets. The company has operations in 30 U.S. states and in more than 70 countries and serves customers in nearly 200 countries; 63 percent of the company's sales are international. 3M also operates 36 laboratories worldwide and spends about 5.8 percent of revenues on R&D. Due to the breadth of their product line and the global reach of their distribution, the company has long been viewed as a bellwether for the overall health of the world economy.

3M's operations are divided into five business segments (approximate revenue percentages in parentheses):

- The Industrial business (34 percent of 2015 sales) serves a variety of vertical markets, including automotive, automotive aftermarket, electronics, paper and packaging, appliance, food and beverage, and construction. Products include industrial tapes, a wide variety of abrasives, adhesives, specialty materials, filtration products, closures, advanced ceramics, automotive insulation, filler and paint system components, and products for the separation of fluids and gases.
- The Safety and Graphics business (18 percent) serves a broad range of markets that increase the safety, security, and productivity of workers, facilities, and systems. Major product offerings include personal protection, like respirators and filtering systems, safety and security products such as reflectorized fabrics and tapes, energy control products, traffic control products including sheeting for highway signs, building cleaning and protection products, track and trace solutions, and roofing granules for asphalt shingles.
- The Healthcare business (18 percent) serves markets that include medical clinics and hospitals, pharmaceuticals, dental and orthodontic practitioners, and health information systems. Products and services include medical and surgical supplies, skin health and infection prevention

products, drug-delivery systems, dental and orthodontic products, health information systems, and antimicrobial solutions. The Healthcare business is the most profitable, with operating margins of 31.8 percent versus margins in the low 20s for the other four businesses.

- The Electronics and Energy segment (17 percent) serves the electrical, electronics, communications, and renewable energy industries, including electric utilities. Products include electronic and interconnect solutions, microinterconnect systems, high-performance fluids and abrasives for semiconductor and disk drive manufacture, high-temperature and display tapes, telecommunications products, electrical products, and optical film materials that support LCD displays and touch screens for monitors, tablets, mobile phones, and other products.

- The Consumer segment (14 percent) serves markets that include retail, home improvement, building maintenance, office, and other markets. Products in this segment include office supply products such as the familiar Scotch tapes, Post-it notes, Scotch-Brite cleaning abrasives, stationery products, construction and home improvement products, home-care products, protective material products, and consumer healthcare products. This segment grew considerably with the 2012 acquisition of the Avery Dennison office products line.

Near-term strategies include streamlining the organization structure, combining 40 businesses into 26, a more general cost containment effort, and a greater emphasis on leveraging and promoting the brand across all businesses. The company has also adjusted its portfolio with five small acquisitions and five divestitures in 2015 (we were sorry to see the Library Systems business go). It appears that continued small acquisitions and an emphasis on fast-track R&D will also be themes going forward.

Financial Highlights, Fiscal Year 2015

The usual crosscurrent of upsides including innovations, small acquisitions, and focus on higher-margined businesses swirled with the downsides of currency, emerging market headwinds, and a manufacturing slowdown in FY2015; revenues dropped for the first time in recent memory by 5 percent to just over $30 billion. Earnings dropped 2.5 percent but on a per-share basis actually advanced just over 1 percent. The outlook for FY2016 and beyond is more rosy with moderate organic revenue growth in the 1–3 percent range depending on currency effects and 2–6 percent in total and across most businesses for FY2017 and beyond. Earnings growth should come in at the 3–4 percent range for FY2016 and expand to 5–7 percent thereafter, and per-share earnings gains are targeted in the 8–11 percent range (see following note on buybacks). 3M took more big strides in cash returns to shareholders, with a 20 percent dividend raise and a 3 percent share buyback (21 million shares) in 2015. We expect more of the same: healthy dividend raises and share buybacks over the next few years.

Reasons to Buy

3M is a classic exercise in brand excellence, marketplace and niche strength, and steady performance (although FY2015 was a slight exception). The company makes and distributes many repeat-sale products essential to manufacturing and day-to-day operations of other companies and organizations and seemingly essential to most of us, e.g., Post-it notes and Scotch tape. The company appears to do better than the markets during strong periods and also holds value better than most during downturns. There is a persistent focus on innovation here, both in its products and in its internal operations and marketing—and it's more the slow, steady variety than a flash in the pan. Cash flows are strong and growing, and continue to be shared liberally with shareholders.

Reasons for Caution

3M is, and always will be, vulnerable to economic cycles, and 2015 was a pretty strong case in point. Notwithstanding a short but steep and temporary share price drop, suggesting there might be more risk here than in the past, in general the business holds up pretty well in down cycles. We also worry that 3M could go on a larger acquisition rampage to boost growth, but so far have been comfortable with the types of acquisitions the company has made. We still think there's value here.

SECTOR: **Industrials** ◻ BETA COEFFICIENT: **1.10** ◻ 10-YEAR COMPOUND EARNINGS PER-SHARE GROWTH: **7.0%** ◻ 10-YEAR COMPOUND DIVIDENDS PER-SHARE GROWTH: **8.5%**

		2008	2009	2010	2011	2012	2013	2014	2015
Revenues (mil)		25,269	23,123	26,662	29,611	29,904	30,871	31,821	30,274
Net income (mil)		3,460	3,193	4,169	4,283	4,445	4,659	4,956	4,833
Earnings per share		4.89	4.52	5.75	5.96	6.32	6.72	7.49	7.58
Dividends per share		2.00	2.04	2.10	2.20	2.36	2.54	3.42	4.10
Cash flow per share		6.65	6.15	7.43	7.85	8.35	9.09	10.02	10.29
Price:	high	84.8	84.3	91.5	98.2	95.5	140.4	168.2	170.5
	low	50.0	40.9	68.0	68.6	82.0	94.0	123.6	124.0

Website: www.3m.com

AGGRESSIVE GROWTH

NEW FOR 2017

AbbVie Inc.

Ticker symbol: ABBV (NYSE) ❑ S&P rating: A- ❑ Value Line financial strength rating: A ❑ Current yield: 3.7% ❑ Dividend raises, past 10 years: 2

Company Profile

Spun off from the former combined Abbott Laboratories in 2013, today's AbbVie is a leading research-based biopharmaceutical company specializing in developing and marketing treatments and therapies for a range of complex diseases. The former Abbott Laboratories was a favorite and perennial *100 Best Stock* but we weren't too clear on the strategy or the outcome of the split (the other half of the split is still called Abbott Laboratories [we wish they hadn't done that; it's confusing]) and specializes mainly in making and distributing a line of medical supplies. We had liked the combined business model where the supplies business anchors, steadies, and funds the more volatile and often more profitable research pharma business, but the company split, citing focus on specific business models for specific markets. Anyway, we've come to like what is happening at AbbVie, both product-wise and financially, and so we go with the name for the 2017 *100 Best* list.

AbbVie's products help treat conditions, such as chronic autoimmune diseases, in rheumatology, gastroenterology and dermatology; oncology, including blood cancers; virology, including the hepatitis C virus (HCV) and human immunodeficiency virus (HIV); neurological disorders, such as Parkinson's disease; metabolic diseases, including thyroid disease and complications associated with cystic fibrosis; as well as other serious health conditions. AbbVie also has a pipeline of new medicines, including over 50 compounds or indications (20 in late-stage development), such as immunology, virology/liver disease, oncology, neurological diseases, and women's health. Its product portfolio includes Humira, Imbruvica, HCV products, additional virology products, metabolics/hormones products, endocrinology products, and other products.

Accounting for 61 percent of FY2015 sales, Humira is by far the largest product—really, it's a franchise. An immunological agent initially developed to treat rheumatoid arthritis, the company (and the FDA) have found it quite useful for treating other immunological diseases such as psoriasis, psoriatic arthritis, and a number of other diseases in the rheumatology, gastroenterology, and dermatology space. The patent for the "composition of matter" expires at the end of 2016—and normally with 61 percent of sales this would be a huge red flag—but the company has an extensive "patent estate" of several dozen patents for the product covering other uses, formulations, manufacturing processes, and other patents extending well into the next decade. By 2020 the company expects Humira to account for about 50 percent of sales and a large share of profits.

Other major emerging drug platforms include Imbruvica, a hematology (blood oncology) and HCV drug acquired through the 2015 acquisition of Pharmacyclics which is projected to reach 13 percent of sales by 2020, Viekira for hepatitis C (8 percent by 2020) and the just-approved Duopa for Parkinson's disease (3 percent by 2020). As exemplified by the Humira platform, the company continually looks for ways to extend existing and modified formulations into additional disease categories with new delivery and dosage models added in where feasible (Duopa uses an implant to provide more steady levels of dopamine for advanced Parkinson's patients, for example).

More recently, the company has announced an agreement with German drug maker Boehringer Ingelheim for a line of monoclonal antibodies, again for immunology, and also announced the larger $5.8 billion acquisition of oncology drug maker Stemcentrx in early 2016 to strengthen its oncology offerings. The company markets its products in 170 countries; about 40 percent of sales are overseas.

Financial Highlights, Fiscal Year 2015

Making the most of its existing and new platforms, the company has been on a roll of late and has emerged in three short years to produce some of the best results among its research pharma peers. In part driven by acquisitions, FY2015 revenues advanced 15 percent, while operating margins advanced a full 6 percent to a very healthy 45.5 percent, guiding profits to a 31 percent increase over 2014. Per-share cash flows advanced 28 percent, which quite neatly supported a 27 percent dividend increase. The dividend is up 42 percent since the company split from Abbott in 2013.

A healthy combination of organic growth and acquisitions will keep revenues rising at about a 15 percent clip through 2017, with profits exceeding that pace into a 15–20 percent growth range.

Reasons to Buy

Research pharma companies are quite often too complex for our simple minds and tastes, so we venture into this sector carefully (as we did last year with the relatively straightforward diabetic drug maker Novo Nordisk).

Here, we find a bit more complexity since yes, as stated, AbbVie specializes in the treatment of complex and advanced diseases. We won't pretend to understand how its products actually work.

What we do like and think we understand is the underlying business strategy. AbbVie focuses on a few key drug platforms like Humira and Imbruvica, making the most of them while offering extendable solutions for other complex oncological, immunological, and neurological indications as well. While it's unfortunate that there are so many of these complex diseases around to treat, we like AbbVie's focus on this relatively more profitable, defensible end of the market.

The financial track record speaks for itself—any company with a 33 percent net profit margin that shares its success with its shareholders comes as pretty good medicine for us.

Reasons for Caution

Complexity is probably our number one issue—this company could fail miserably in one or more of its markets and we laymen would probably be none the wiser. The dependence on Humira naturally raises the specter of patent expirations, from which the company appears to position itself quite well to minimize the potential damage. Finally, we do see and worry a bit about the growth-by-acquisition tendencies, though we do think acquisitions so far make sense and are done *on top of* a pretty sound and successful business.

SECTOR: **Healthcare** ❑ BETA COEFFICIENT: **1.49** ❑ 10-YEAR COMPOUND EARNINGS PER-SHARE GROWTH: **NM** ❑ 10-YEAR COMPOUND DIVIDENDS PER-SHARE GROWTH: **NM**

	2008	2009	2010	2011	2012	2013	2014	2015
Revenues (mil)	—	—	—	—	—	18,790	19,960	22,839
Net income (mil)	—	—	—	—	—	5,066	5,375	7,060
Earnings per share	—	—	—	—	—	3.14	3.32	4.29
Dividends per share	—	—	—	—	—	1.60	1.66	2.02
Cash flow per share	—	—	—	—	—	3.44	3.62	4.64
Price: high	—	—	—	—	—	54.8	70.8	71.2
low	—	—	—	—	—	33.3	45.5	45.4

Website: www.abbvie.com

Aetna Inc.

Ticker symbol: AET (NYSE) ❑ S&P rating: A ❑ Value Line financial strength rating: A ❑ Current yield: 0.9% ❑ Dividend raises, past 10 years: 5

Company Profile

Founded in 1853, Aetna is one of the nation's longest-lived insurers and a leading provider of health insurance benefits. The company's three distinct businesses are operated in three divisions. Healthcare provides a full assortment of health benefit plans for corporate, small business, and individual customers, including PPO, HMO, point-of-service, vision care, dental, behavioral health, Medicare/Medicaid, and pharmacy benefits plans. The Group Insurance business provides group term life, disability, and accidental death and dismemberment insurance products primarily to the same sort of businesses that might sign up for its health plans. The Large Case Pensions business administers pension plans for certain existing customers.

The healthcare business is by far the largest segment and the focal point of our selection of this company. The business touches some 46 million individuals; of $60 billion in 2015 revenues, about 40 percent is Government including Medicare Advantage and Medicaid; 32 percent is Large Group Insured; and 18 percent is Small Group and Individuals. Driven in part by the Affordable Care Act, the Government segment has risen rapidly from 22 percent since 2010.

Obviously, the company is a big player in the Affordable Care Act and its related reforms. While future outcomes are uncertain, much of its majority base in providing employer coverage is left relatively intact. Prior to the ACA, as now, Aetna has proven itself to be a pacesetter among insurance providers, mainly through its support and innovations in the area of consumer-directed healthcare and preventative medicine.

For example, Aetna has led the industry in developing tools, such as the Aetna Navigator price transparency tool designed to help patients evaluate the cost and outcomes of procedures in different geographies. The company also has championed patient- and doctor-accessible medical records and other techniques for making healthcare delivery more efficient—as they put it, "Industry-leading use of patient data and new connections [to help] you play a greater, more informed role in your own health." The company estimates that now 60 percent of patients want to "take charge" of their care, and 80 percent believe that "consumerism in healthcare is good for Americans."

Aetna is a big believer in the use of analytics—using a "big data" approach to predict the types of medical conditions their covered clients are likely to encounter in the coming years based on correlations among contributing factors in their large data pool. More generally, the company follows an industry trend to focus less on "episodic" care at a medical facility toward more long-term wellness—a "health plus healthcare" model. Obviously, being able to tell a particular patient how to avoid a predicted condition is a big win for both parties. In 2015 Aetna took a big step toward becoming a more dominant player in the industry by offering $37 billion to acquire rival health insurer Humana, one of the "big five" in the marketplace. A similar move by Anthem to acquire Cigna for $45 billion would leave three major players in the health-coverage space (*100 Best Stocks* pick UnitedHealth Group is the third). That would expand Aetna's reach and bring economies of scale, but there is a lot of resistance to the merger, and it must be agreed to in all states in which the company does business.

Financial Highlights, Fiscal Year 2015

FY2015 revenues rose a moderate 4 percent, while cost containment drove earnings a healthier 15 percent higher despite a bit of subpar performance from the self-insured Affordable Care Act ("Obamacare") segment of the business. Without Humana, the company projects another 4 percent revenue gain in FY2016 and about 6 percent in FY2017. Earnings rises may take a pause in FY2016 due to higher cost in the aforementioned ACA segment but should be up 4–8 percent each year. The company has actively raised its dividend and has steadily retired shares—about 33 percent of them in ten years—and should continue along this path.

Reasons to Buy

We feel that Aetna continues to pace the pack in terms of both business and technology innovation and as such will lead the way more generally in information-driven healthcare and healthcare utilization. The company has its strategies right, is positioned to lead the way, and has declared its intentions to evolve from an "insurance" company to a "healthcare" company providing more integrated, efficient, cost-effective solutions as we move through the decade ("Managing Risk → Managing Health"). If the Humana merger goes through, the additional marketplace clout and probable economies of scale should help further.

Reasons for Caution

It now appears—as feared—that the ACA could be bringing a more expensive base of new customers into the fold—with a lag in ability to recover that cost. Public and governmental scrutiny of health insurers has never been higher, and burgeoning healthcare costs can be difficult for even a company of Aetna's capability and influence to manage. That said, new utilization management initiatives like Medicare's efforts to reduce unnecessary admissions and procedures will have collateral benefits for private insurers as well. The Humana merger could prove challenging and be—if nothing else—a distraction.

SECTOR: **Healthcare** ❏ BETA COEFFICIENT: **0.73** ❏ 10-YEAR COMPOUND EARNINGS PER-SHARE GROWTH: **127.0%** ❏ 10-YEAR COMPOUND DIVIDENDS PER-SHARE GROWTH: **55.0%**

	2008	2009	2010	2011	2012	2013	2014	2015
Revenues (mil)	30,951	34,765	34,246	33,700	36,596	47,295	58,003	60,355
Net income (mil)	1,922	1,236	1,555.5	1,850	1,658	2,058	2,330	2,690
Earnings per share	3.93	2.75	3.68	5.15	5.14	5.86	6.70	7.71
Dividends per share	0.04	0.04	0.04	0.45	0.73	0.80	0.90	1.00
Cash flow per share	5.07	3.83	5.20	6.25	6.43	7.24	8.49	9.64
Price: high	59.8	34.9	36.0	46.0	51.1	69.5	91.9	134.4
low	14.2	16.7	25.0	30.6	34.6	44.4	64.7	97.3

Website: www.aetna.com

CONSERVATIVE GROWTH

Allstate Corporation

Ticker symbol: ALL (NASDAQ) ❏ S&P rating: A- ❏ Value Line financial strength rating: A+ ❏ Current yield: 2.0% ❏ Dividend raises, past 10 years: 6

Company Profile

Allstate is the nation's largest publicly held, full-line "P/C" (Property/Casualty) insurance provider, offering the gamut of auto, home, renters, and business insurance, and has become a larger player in life insurance, retirement, and annuity segments as well. The company serves 16 million households through a network of 35,000 Allstate-exclusive agents with almost a billion and a half policies in force. It prides itself on its four-tiered brand and channel strategy for delivering choice and advice to customers.

The company sells its own Allstate product through 9,300 exclusive agencies and its "Encompass" sub-brand through independent agencies and estimates that the Allstate brand alone owns 19 percent of the traditional P/C market. The company owns and operates the e-commerce insurance portal Esurance and also sells its product directly, along with other insurance brands, through its "Answer Financial" phone portal for self-directed consumers looking for choices. That said, the lion's share of premiums ($26.3 billion, or 91 percent of policies in force) is earned through the Allstate brand, while Encompass and Esurance contribute about $1.1 billion, or about 3 percent for Esurance and 6 percent for Encompass. By product line, auto leads the way with about two-thirds of premium dollars, homeowners with 24 percent, with the rest coming from life, commercial, and other business lines. Increasingly, the company is using analytics to "microsegment" and tune the premium/cost mix.

Financial Highlights, Fiscal Year 2015

Market share gains and some price increases drove a moderate 4.8 percent gain in property/casualty revenues for FY2015; however, increases in auto-related losses due to lower gas prices and resulting increases in driving hampered earnings, which declined almost 17 percent for the year, as auto is about two-thirds of the business. The loss ratio (losses to premiums earned) notched back up to a more normal 69 percent, but this is still much lower than the low-to-mid 70s readings earlier in the decade. Revenue gains should continue in the 2–3 percent range through FY2017 with earnings up about 5 percent annually from FY2015's diminished level and could be higher if bond interest rates finally go higher. Cash payouts to shareholders look to stabilize and increase steadily, and the company has been aggressive in reducing share counts—about 8 percent in 2015 and 40 percent since 2004.

Reasons to Buy

We like the market position, brand strength, channel strategy, increased stability, and upside potential both in underwriting and in investment performance. The company has sold some underperforming operations and has gained a solid strategic foothold on its reputation, brand, and channel strategy. Esurance and other "direct" models are gaining traction, while the company is also offering a better product mix.

The Allstate brand is ever stronger, turning from a slight negative years ago to a solid positive. The company now proudly places its name on "adjacent" businesses such as Allstate Roadside Services; another branding example is the new "Package" policy, combining auto and homeowners into a single policy sold under the Encompass brand. While Allstate has improved the top line through such initiatives, there is also clearer focus on expenses, the bottom line, stability, and overall shareholder returns going forward; in our view Allstate has become a solid blue-chip performer in a difficult industry with a pretty decent upside going forward.

Reasons for Caution

Competition is stiff and another hurricane-infested year like 2005 could also hurt, although Allstate is more geographically diverse than some of its competitors. Higher auto claims rates are also a concern but should be covered by price increases eventually; they don't hit an insurer like a hurricane or other single event does. Interest rates on the industry's traditional investment instruments may continue to be weak for some time, and another major stock or bond market correction could hurt too. For years, the brand suffered from a reputation for poor claims performance and a sales-y approach. Although the company is more aware of its relatively erratic past and seems to be doing something about it, the prior volatility of its results in revenues, earnings, and especially dividends paid is hard to ignore. Finally, we'll admit that we find insurers (as most Financials) difficult to understand because of terminology and somewhat different ways of measuring and reporting financial performance; you may also find this company difficult to understand well enough to commit your capital to it comfortably. Proceed carefully.

SECTOR: **Financials** ❑ BETA COEFFICIENT: **1.10** ❑ 10-YEAR COMPOUND EARNINGS PER-SHARE GROWTH: **3.5%** ❑ 10-YEAR COMPOUND DIVIDENDS PER-SHARE GROWTH: **0.5%**

	2008	2009	2010	2011	2012	2013	2014	2015
Property/Casualty premiums (mil)	26,967	26,194	25,957	25,942	26,737	27,618	28,929	30,309
Net income (mil)	1,445	1,976	1,535	699	2,143	2,559	2,265	1,985
Earnings per share	3.22	3.47	2.83	1.34	4.34	5.70	5.42	5.21
Dividends per share	1.64	1.01	0.80	0.83	1.09	0.75	1.12	1.29
Underwriting inc. per share	(1.96)	(0.58)	(0.58)	(4.19)	2.49	4.95	4.22	4.06
Price: high	52.9	33.5	35.5	34.4	42.8	54.8	71.5	72.9
low	17.7	13.8	26.9	22.3	27.0	40.7	49.2	54.1

Website: www.allstate.com

AGGRESSIVE GROWTH

NEW FOR 2017

Amazon.com

Ticker symbol: AMZN (NASDAQ) ❑ S&P rating: A+ ❑ Value Line financial strength rating: A+ ❑ Current yield: NA ❑ Dividend raises, past 10 years: NA

Company Profile

We at *100 Best* feel a little bit old from time to time. We were well into our careers around the time Amazon was founded in 1994, and now it's the most valuable retailer in the U.S., passing Wal-Mart in market cap in 2015. This year it became the fastest company to ever reach $100 billion in annual sales. We can still remember asking ourselves, "Why are they spending so much money to sell books?"

They started their "bookstore" (our favorite type of store, by the way) at a time when the commercialization of the World Wide Web (pro tip: the "www" at the beginning of every URL) was in its infancy. The product mix grew relatively slowly, but Amazon eventually added CDs, DVDs, computer software, and electronics as their primary offerings, and they are now far and away the go-to retailer for these high-margin, in-demand lines. In the process of becoming an online juggernaut, they developed some very sophisticated inventory management, data management, and logistics practices, and they have leveraged these into products now offered to other businesses as Amazon Web Services. Amazon currently operates the retail websites for over a dozen major retailers, including Sears and Marks & Spencer.

Amazon was not the only online retail presence on the early web, but they were arguably the best funded and best managed. As such, they had the vision (and the resources) to acquire either whole or partial interests in competitors or similar businesses when the opportunities arose. Since their founding, they have been very active acquirers, having made over sixty major deals, some more successful (Zappos) than others (Pets.com). Some of the combinations are operational—in 2013 they partnered with the U.S. Postal Service to begin delivering Amazon packages on Sunday; delivering packages when people are actually home to accept them—what a concept!

Amazon continues to sell media such as books, movies, and music (representing about 20 percent of its sales). But today, consumer electronics accounts for the bulk of its 2016 online sales—a full 70 percent, in fact. Of their retail sales, their third-party Marketplace accounts for about 20 percent, which includes some of the consumer electronics and media sales cited previously.

All in all, the online retail presence has grown from a distraction in the retail industry to a true competitive threat to the likes of Walmart, Target, Macy's, Best Buy, and almost all others. Amazon brings *choice* (for example, almost 2 million items of clothing versus a few tens of thousands for a retail chain like Macy's) and *convenience* (one-stop, one- click shopping and even "free" two-day delivery with the new $99 annual Amazon Prime service). This combination of selection and service is rapidly being soaked up by the population at large and Millennials in particular and is dictating a considerable landscape shift in the retail industry at present.

The growth of "AWS"—Amazon Web Services, however, is the development to watch at Amazon. Conversations with their competitors have confirmed the strength of this business and its prospects for market expansion. Considering AWS is already bigger than Amazon was after ten years, the view forward is very encouraging.

Financial Highlights, Fiscal Year 2015

Amazon produced very strong growth in both revenues and earnings in FY2015. The top line grew 22 percent, with earnings up just a shade over 300 percent. Increased unit sales, expansion in international markets (now 33 percent of Amazon's business) and the increased profitability of AWS played a large part here, though FY2014 earnings were saddled with significant expenses for technology infrastructure.

Amazon Prime, the company's $99 premium shopping service, is simply crushing it. Based on a membership of 10 million subscribers in 2014, the aggressive projections were for a total enrollment of perhaps 25 million by 2017. In fact, market researchers estimate that this service has already captured 54 million members as of 2016. At $99 per year, this represents $5.3 billion in revenue just in the form of fees. Prime members spend well over twice what non-members spend, pulling a significant level of business from the competition.

Over the next few years, the company expects to convert this considerable investment and market penetration into revenues and profits, with revenues advancing 20–25 percent annually and net income quadrupling in FY2016 and quadrupling again by the end of the decade.

Reasons to Buy

Jeff Bezos, the company's founder (and owner of just over one-sixth of its shares), maintains that there's nothing in their business model that a competitor couldn't copy, given enough time. And he's right—they're not curing cancer at Amazon (yet). They're a retailer. But what Bezos has done is to focus on operational excellence to a nearly unheard-of degree. The company did not target profitability at all for the first five years of its existence, choosing instead to build strong relationships with suppliers and customers. Their credo with regard to operations was to make mistakes, make them quickly, and learn from them, plow what they did earn back into R&D, and then out-build their competitors on an enormous scale. This is not how a traditional retail business is grown, and many very well-regarded industry watchers at the time openly questioned Bezos's strategy.

Those critics are harder to find these days. Amazon's early big bets on their business model have paid off handsomely, and the company that made its first dime in FY2001 is on course to earn $2.5 billion in FY2016. Innovations like the customer-centric Amazon Prime membership are being copied throughout the industry. Amazon's content delivery venture has spawned a content development business that has produced a number of critical and commercial successes. Amazon's eBook delivery innovations led to the development of the Kindle eBook reader. Some have said that this is an "impulse" retailing approach that will only work in the U.S., but fully one-third of Amazon's $130 billion revenue in FY2016 will come from outside the U.S.

Finally, the Amazon Web Service deserves special attention. Accounting for just 8 percent of revenues in 2016, the business is growing at a tremendous pace; revenues in this division were up 64 percent last year, and margins here are now over 28 percent, well ahead of the rest of the company. AWS is funding much of the expansion and innovation in retail. And Amazon is not making things easy for its competitors here either; in 2015 AWS launched 722 new services, while at the same time reducing prices on AWS for the fifty-first time since the product launched.

Amazon's relentless focus on operational excellence and technical innovation is unique in the retail sector, and we think there's still a lot of room for growth. We're excited about adding it to the list for this year.

Reasons for Caution

There is some risk here—and more than we typically take on with a *100 Best* stock. But we think Amazon is not only "where the puck is going," particularly with Millennials, but has the unique position of being able to *define* where the puck is going.

When you lose $250 million in 2014 and earn $2.6 billion in 2016, you're going to attract a lot of pundits and naysayers. Amazon has seen its share price double over that same period from the low 300s to the mid 600s. Obviously, we don't think the stock has run its course, but $675 per share does give one pause. The company's aggressive development gambles do not always pay off, and there have been some less-than-wildly successful products coming out of its hardware R&D center. The company has hinted at going after other markets with the same aggressiveness—like supply chain logistics—but has backed off from that "threat"; FedEx and UPS can breathe a sigh of relief. Finally, the company has acknowledged that spending is not entirely in check and that we can expect to see some adjustments over time.

SECTOR: **Retail** ❑ BETA COEFFICIENT: **1.05** ❑ 10-YEAR COMPOUND EARNINGS PER-SHARE GROWTH: **-4.0%** ❑ 10-YEAR COMPOUND DIVIDENDS PER-SHARE GROWTH: **Nil**

	2008	2009	2010	2011	2012	2013	2014	2015
Revenues (bil)	24.5	34.2	48.1	61.9	74.5	89.0	107.0	130.0
Net income (mil)	902	1,152	631.0	130.0	274.0	(241.0)	596.0	2.485
Earnings per share	2.04	2.53	1.37	0.29	0.59	(0.52)	1.25	5.20
Dividends per share	—	—	—	—	—	—	—	—
Cash flow per share	2.88	3.81	3.77	5.04	7.68	9.70	14.60	18.60
Price: high	145.9	185.6	246.7	264.1	405.6	408.1	696.4	685.5
low	47.6	105.8	160.6	172.0	245.8	284.0	285.3	474.0

Website: www.amazon.com

AGGRESSIVE GROWTH

Apple Inc.

Ticker symbol: AAPL (NASDAQ) ❑ S&P rating: AA+ ❑ Value Line financial strength rating: A++ ❑ Current yield: 1.9% ❑ Dividend raises, past 10 years: 4

Company Profile

The Apple story of excellence and of transition from high-flying growth stock to cash-generating value stock continues into 2017. The company remains an admired bellwether for consumer innovation and design for a wide swath of consumers from preteen to seniors (and a growing number of commercial customers); we hardly need to review what the company makes and sells, but we will anyway.

Apple designs, manufactures, and markets personal computers, tablet computers, portable music players, cell phones, and related software, peripherals, downloadable content, and services. The company added the digital watch to its portfolio in mid-2015. It sells these products through its own retail stores, online stores, and third-party and value-added resellers. The company also sells digital content through its iTunes store. The company has become a big player in the "digital wallet" mobile payment space, with its Apple Pay apps and network. And finally, and perhaps most remarkably of all, the company continues to flirt with a move into the automobile business.

The company's products have become household names: The iPhone, iPod, iPad, and MacBook are just some of the company's hardware products. While the software may be less well-known, iTunes, QuickTime, OSX, and the emerging iCloud are important segments of the business, each with its own revenue stream. And who knows—is there an iCar just around the corner?

It's hard to imagine the current consumer tech landscape without Apple's presence at the top of the heap. Its product line, while comparatively narrow, is focused on areas where the user interface is highly valued. The company has leveraged this focus to become one of the most profitable companies in history and hence, as of this writing, the most valuable company in the world.

Apple is the flagship case study in creating extraordinary value through innovation, innovative leadership, and marketing excellence. That core competency came into question with the passing of leadership from Steve Jobs to the more subtle, more operationally minded Tim Cook. Indeed, the innovations have slowed in scale over the years but the company has improved its fundamentals nonetheless and is starting to once again define and dominate new markets. It is doing this not so much with new hardware products but new services such as Apple Pay, iCloud, Apple Music, and perhaps they'll finally hit the market sweet spot with Apple TV. As a result of these initiatives, and the financial and operational results recently delivered, we no longer worry so much about slippage into techno-mediocrity under Mr. Cook. And there may still be an iCar waiting in the wings—we'd bet that would be executed in some sort of partnership with an automaker, but who knows? Apple likely has many juicy "iSecrets" waiting in the wings.

Financial Highlights, Fiscal Year 2015

Once again, and likely for a long time to come, Apple's numbers remain the envy of the corporate world. FY2015 revenues advanced 22 percent on a huge $183 billion revenue base—a monstrous achievement. And that did not come at the expense of earnings, which advanced 34 percent on a 2.2 percent gain in operating margins (operational focus *does* pay off). The company has been quietly—but aggressively—returning cash to shareholders while depleting its massive share count acquired after the recent 7-for-1 split, having bought back 228 million shares in 2015, a massive $25 billion buyback. As such, per-share earnings advanced 34 percent.

Going forward, the shift to a cash-generating value play continues. Dollar strength, China softness, and a bit of a topping out of iPhone and tablet sales has most predicting fairly flat sales into 2016, with next generation iPhones, the 7 and 6SE, leading the way to a 6–8 percent revenue gain for 2017. Per-share earnings are likely to pause in 2016 and resume as well into 2017, with double-digit dividend and per-share cash flow increases likely. Results could be better than these forecasts with a moderating dollar, strengthening China, and faster-than-expected rollout of new services such as iPay—the miss is likely to be on the upside as we've seen in the past. Aggressive buybacks of 100 million shares or more annually are likely to continue as well.

Reasons to Buy

Innovation. Market leadership. Brand strength. Growth. Profitability. Cash flow. Cash returns. Best in class across the board. How could Apple *not* be a *100 Best* stock? We certainly like the results, but mostly we continue to admire (and believe in) the business and innovation excellence that got Apple there.

Apple's best-known product, the iPhone, seems ubiquitous. You probably have one. Everyone you know has one. They're everywhere, and you can be forgiven for thinking that the market for this product is saturated. Everyone thought it was getting too expensive as lower-priced Android products started to flood the market. And everyone wondered what would happen in China. But the truth is, by lowering prices, improving quality, and gradually improving feature sets, Apple is once again gaining share in the smartphone market. Better yet, we see it (and iPads as well) as the ubiquitous front-end device for everything from Apple Pay–driven commerce to music and video services.

And that's just shipment volumes—the profitability and cash-flow story is even better. Net profit margins of over 22 percent for a company of this size alone are remarkable, and suggest that the company's products are far from becoming commoditized. Margins are expected to grow slightly through the end of the decade. On the shareholder-return front, new emphasis on returning cash to shareholders has plenty of distance to go.

While many are concerned about Apple's ability to innovate, and while there has been somewhat of a slowdown in the creation of whole new businesses, like iPods and tablets, we haven't given up on such innovations. We continue to feel that Apple still has room to create some blockbusters in the "wearable" technology space—smartphone technology integrated into clothing, for example, and in flexible display technologies (see Corning, another *100 Best* pick). Apple Pay, the company's venture into the financial transaction space, could also be huge, and a big driver for sales of compatible hardware as well. We foresee other major "vertical" applications of iPhone form and technology in cars (check out "CarPlay") and in the healthcare space for remote patient monitoring and such. Breakthrough technologies in the TV space have been talked about for some time; while not gaining much traction to date, we could still tune in to some upside in that lucrative space. Finally, we'd like to remind readers that we consider operational improvements to be innovations as well.

Recently, we feel the stock price hasn't kept up with the success story; there may well be good entry points in the upcoming "flat" year. Shares were selling recently for less than 12 times earnings—a discount for a company that would normally command a premium. This isn't a guarantee, but does reduce the risk—as always, choose entry points carefully.

Reasons for Caution

Concerns continue about competition and price erosion in the smartphone and tablet spaces, but the market remains huge and growing, and there's plenty of opportunity for everyone. Too, production efficiencies and scale will continue to provide a tailwind.

In the main, we continue to admire Apple's ability to generate income, and now, to distribute it to shareholders. The franchise is the world's most valuable in market capitalization—and deservedly so. But nobody can sit on their laurels, especially when their laurels are this high off the ground and in plain sight of every competitor. Apple must continue to feed the innovation machine.

SECTOR: Consumer Discretionary ▫ BETA COEFFICIENT: 1.01 ▫ 10-YEAR COMPOUND EARNINGS
PER-SHARE GROWTH: 55.0% ▫ 10-YEAR COMPOUND DIVIDENDS PER-SHARE GROWTH: NM

		2008	2009	2010	2011	2012	2013	2014	2015
Revenues (bil)		32.5	36.5	65.2	108.2	156.5	170.9	182.8	233.7
Net income (bil)		4.8	5.7	14.0	25.9	41.7	37.0	39.5	53.4
Earnings per share		0.77	0.90	2.16	3.95	6.31	5.66	6.45	9.22
Dividends per share		—	—	—	—	0.38	1.63	1.82	1.98
Cash flow per share		0.85	1.02	2.35	4.26	6.85	6.96	8.09	11.59
Price:	high	28.6	30.6	46.7	61.0	100.7	82.2	119.8	134.5
	low	11.3	11.2	27.2	44.4	58.4	55.0	70.5	92.0

Website: www.apple.com

GROWTH AND INCOME

Aqua America Inc.

Ticker symbol: WTR (NYSE) ▫ S&P rating: A+ ▫ Value Line financial strength rating: A ▫ Current
yield: 2.3% ▫ Dividend raises, past 10 years: 10

Company Profile

If you're like most people, by the time you landed on Water Works as you
circled the Monopoly board, you had already deployed your investment capital elsewhere and weren't so excited about its modest growth and yield prospects. You can't build houses or hotels on Water Works, and the monopoly
power for owning it in tandem with the Electric Company doesn't seem as
powerful as other investments on the board. So you may have passed it up.

Well, times have changed since Monopoly was created. The strategic
importance of water, the efficiencies of operating water utilities across a wide
geography, and their stability as investments (we didn't care so much about
that in Monopoly), have made water utilities a more desirable investment,
one for which you might just have plunked down $150 as you circled the
board.

"Water Works," in this case, is Aqua America Inc., a U.S.-based publicly
traded water and wastewater utility, serving approximately 3 million
customers in eight states: Pennsylvania, Ohio, North Carolina, Illinois,
Texas, New Jersey, Indiana, and Virginia, operating 1,447 public water
and 187 wastewater treatment systems. Pennsylvania is the centerpiece,
accounting for just over half of the business. Like many modern utilities,
the company also owns a nonregulated subsidiary supplying industrial water

and services with a new and special emphasis on the Pennsylvania, Texas, and Ohio shale industries. The company has pursued growth aggressively through acquisitions, bringing in over 200 acquisitions and growth ventures in the past ten years. Another 15 small water utilities were added in 2015 following 16 additions in 2014. Over time the company has purchased some small utility services and consulting businesses as well; one example is a firm that inspects, cleans, aligns, and televises sewer and storm drain systems.

Normally we're not too thrilled with growth-by-acquisition strategies, but in this case it makes sense because a lot of local public jurisdictions and private operators see the logic in turning smaller plants over to a larger company where economies of scale and management can take effect. That, in essence, is Aqua America's strategy, and we like it—especially with the U.S. patchwork of over 50,000 operators of small water delivery systems, most of which operate at less than prime efficiency.

Financial Highlights, Fiscal Year 2015

Acquisitions and a few divestitures make true revenue and earnings trends hard to capture, but overall the company grew revenues 4.3 percent on rate increases and a 1.8 percent growth in the customer base. Per-share earnings, which had jumped substantially in FY2013 mostly due to new unregulated sales to the shale energy industry, actually dropped about 5 percent reflecting a 12 cent per share write-down in one of the unregulated shale industry supply businesses; without that event, per-share earnings would have been up 6 percent. Despite weakness in the shale industry, favorable pricing and continued economies of scale work the other way; revenues are projected ahead in the 5–6 percent range in both FY2016 and FY2017 with stronger 10–15 percent growth in core earnings. The company has raised its dividend for 24 straight years. Increases look to be in the high single digits for the next few years, strong for a utility company but well supported by cash flows.

Reasons to Buy

In the midst of a long-term bull market, we continue to keep Aqua on our *100 Best* list in defense against the next pullback. The stock barely budged in the early 2016 market correction, and we always like to have a few choices that seem relatively immune to such events. That safety, plus an interest in steadily growing cash returns, fuels our interest in Aqua America. The company is a relatively small and simple business compared to a lot we look at. It occupies a strategic position in a key utility area, especially as more water works entities become available as public sector operations are trimmed. The company is earning the maximum return on equity allowed by regulators, suggesting a "best in class" operating effectiveness; it is also beginning to expand the use and strength of its brand. The stock has a low beta of 0.39, indicating stability. The payout percentage—dividends as a percent of net profits—has trended downward, and that, along with strong cash flow, suggests continued strength on the dividend front.

Reasons for Caution

Water distribution requires a lot of expensive infrastructure, and a lot of the current infrastructure is old; in fact, the need to replace infrastructure is one reason some smaller utilities are selling out to Aqua America. Such replacement costs, particularly with the severe winters we've been having, could be high and a drag on earnings in the short term, but the company has managed them well as evidenced by the steadiness of long-term debt as a portion of total capitalization despite these capital expenditures. Big plans made to deliver water to shale operators have been attenuated by energy price declines as well.

Overall, we chose this investment in part due to its relatively inelastic demand and steady earnings and cash flow into the future even in bad economic times; however, Aqua may participate less in economic growth and rising equity markets than other stocks we choose. Too, recent share prices may have reflected some of the optimism, leaving little room to turn on the faucet for bubbly share prices.

SECTOR: **Utilities** ❑ BETA COEFFICIENT: **0.39** ❑ 10-YEAR COMPOUND EARNINGS PER-SHARE GROWTH: **8.5%** ❑ 10-YEAR COMPOUND DIVIDENDS PER-SHARE GROWTH: **8.0%**

		2008	2009	2010	2011	2012	2013	2014	2015
Revenues (mil)		627.0	670.5	728.1	712.0	757.8	768.6	780.0	814.0
Net income (mil)		97.9	104.4	124.0	144.8	153.1	205.1	213.9	202.0
Earnings per share		0.58	0.62	0.72	0.83	0.87	1.15	1.20	1.14
Dividends per share		0.41	0.44	0.47	0.50	0.54	0.58	0.63	0.69
Cash flow per share		1.14	1.29	1.42	1.45	1.51	1.82	1.89	1.87
Price:	high	17.6	17.2	18.4	19.0	21.5	28.1	28.2	31.1
	low	9.8	12.3	13.2	15.4	16.8	20.6	22.4	24.4

Website: www.aquaamerica.com

Archer Daniels Midland Company

Ticker symbol: ADM (NYSE) ❑ S&P rating: A ❑ Value Line financial strength rating: A+ ❑ Current yield: 3.0% ❑ Dividend raises, past 10 years: 9

Company Profile

ADM is one of the largest food processors in the world. It buys corn, wheat, oilseeds, and other agricultural products and processes them into food, food ingredients, animal feed and ingredients, and biofuels. It also resells grains on the open market. Rather than the finished consumer products most food processors are known for, ADM produces and distributes intermediate components for food product manufacture and is by far the largest publicly traded company in this business. Among the more important products are vegetable oils, protein meal and components, corn sweeteners, flour, biodiesel, ethanol, other food and animal feed, and now, specialty ingredients. Foreign sales make up about 53 percent of total revenue.

The company is highly vertically integrated and owns and maintains facilities used throughout the production process. It sources, transports, stores, and processes agricultural materials in more than 79 countries on six continents, with 280 processing plants and its own extensive sea/rail/road network. The company owns or leases 28,200 rail cars, 2,500 barges, 21 ocean vessels, and a fleet of trucks.

The company operates in four business segments: Oilseeds Processing (37 percent of FY2015 sales), Corn Processing (15 percent), Agricultural Services (44 percent), and newly acquired WILD Flavors and Specialty Ingredients and other (4 percent). The Oilseeds Processing unit processes soybeans, cottonseed, sunflower, canola, peanuts, and flaxseed into vegetable oils and protein meals for the food and feed industries. Crude vegetable oils are sold as is or are further refined into consumer products, while partially refined oils are sold for use in paints, chemicals, and other industrial products. The solids remaining from this processing are sold for a number of applications, including edible soy protein, animal feed, pharmaceuticals, chemicals, and paper.

The Corn Processing segment milling operations (primarily in the United States) produce food products too numerous to list but include syrup, starch, glucose, dextrose, and other sweeteners. Markets served include animal feeds and the vegetable oil market. Fermentation of the dextrose yields ethanol, amino acids, and other specialty food and feed products.

The ethanol is processed for beverage stock or industrial use as the base for ethanol-blended gasoline and other fuels.

The Agricultural Services segment is the company's storage and transportation network. This business is primarily engaged in buying, storing, cleaning, and transporting grains to/from ADM facilities and for export. It also resells raw materials into the animal feed and agricultural processing industries.

In early 2015, ADM completed the acquisition of German natural flavorings and specialty ingredients producer WILD Flavors GmbH. The expanding WILD Flavors and Specialty Ingredients segment produces many existing nutrients product lines including high-fiber and nutritional supplements like natural-source vitamin E and Omega-3 DHA. This group, and the recent acquisition of Harvest Innovations, a producer of gluten-free and minimally processed soy proteins and oils, has expanded ADM's presence in the specialty corners of the food business. The company also announced the divestiture of some of its Brazil ethanol business. There's a notable strategic shift here from commodity to higher value–add businesses.

Financial Highlights, Fiscal Year 2015

Acquisitions, spinoffs, currency effects, fluctuating prices, and fluctuating costs of agricultural commodity inputs make any yearly comparison of ADM results challenging. FY2015 was especially so, with the disposal of the cocoa business and low market prices for most of ADM's products brought on by the strong dollar, weak emerging markets, abundant global crop supplies, and the hit taken by the energy industry (most of that effect on the ethanol business). Revenues and earnings got crushed to the tune of 17 percent for the year. However, damage was limited on the per-share earnings front by a hefty 9 percent share buyback; EPS was down only 13 percent. FY2016 doesn't look too much better; the company should be able to ride improving market dynamics, operational efficiencies, and strategic acquisitions and divestitures to a modestly improved revenue and profitability picture in FY2017. Steady dividend increases and share buybacks should continue.

Reasons to Buy

Although near-term results are notably weak, we still like ADM for the longer term. Agriculture is still a key strategic business on a global basis, and increased demand for food and especially middle-class Western diets from emerging market customers bodes well. The company is and has been a strong player in the biofuels industry. While uncertainties continue in the ethanol and biofuels segment, the company's experience and scale in ethanol and biodiesel are strong positives, and the company should win as other smaller players exit the market.

There are four major suppliers that dominate the world market for commodity foodstuffs: Archer, Bunge, Cargill, and Dreyfus—the "ABCD" of world foods. Growth through selective acquisitions is an important factor to success in this business—if you miss an attractive opportunity, you can be reasonably certain one of your competitors will not. ADM continues to grow its presence in the emerging markets of Asia, South America, and Eastern Europe. Sales growth outside the United States has far outpaced domestic growth, and ADM's presence and extensive transportation capability give it a decided advantage over its smaller competitors, many of which are focused only in certain markets or certain industries. The company is fine-tuning its business mix, disposing of smaller low-margin product lines in favor of a higher value add in the food chain with the addition of WILD and other product lines; we like the increasing emphasis on this business. We like the solid track record for growth in dividends and overall shareholder value.

Reasons for Caution

We've seen how agricultural cycles and production can negatively impact this company, and we had thought the worst was over—and are surprised by recent results. Although modest by comparison to many S&P 500 peers, ADM's business and shares have become more volatile—the beta of 1.11 still suggests some safety, though compares unfavorably to 0.88 last year and 0.47 three years ago. The WILD acquisition may signal a move to the "wild" side in more specialized, less commoditized business, which seems like a good strategy but does add some risk. Also the company may be late to this party though it is well positioned as a "bulk" supplier of these key ingredients. ADM is heavily invested in the corn-ethanol-fuel processing chain. Ethanol has always existed at the very margins of the transportation fuels market, and continued softness in demand and lower prices for gasoline could have a disproportionate effect on the profitability of ethanol, although the price/cost balance remains intact so far. Federal government policy toward ethanol subsidies and ethanol imports (primarily sugar-based ethanol from Brazil) both bear watching. Finally, the company does produce that nasty-sounding but in fact relatively benign high fructose corn syrup; a pickup in nutritional health sentiment in the food and especially the beverage industry won't help.

We know we've raised more than the usual number of yellow flags this year with ADM, but we are expecting some to go away as time goes on. Again, we consider ADM a long-term play in a healthy and vital industry.

SECTOR: **Consumer Staples** ❑ BETA COEFFICIENT: **1.11** ❑ 10-YEAR COMPOUND EARNINGS PER-SHARE GROWTH: **10.0%** ❑ 10-YEAR COMPOUND DIVIDENDS PER-SHARE GROWTH: **14.0%**

	2008	2009	2010	2011	2012	2013	2014	2015
Revenues (mil)	69,816	69,207	61,692	80,676	89,038	89,804	81,201	67,762
Net income (mil)	1,834	1,970	1,959	2,036	1,496	1,342	2,248	1,849
Earnings per share	2.84	3.06	3.06	3.13	2.26	2.02	3.43	2.98
Dividends per share	0.49	0.54	0.58	0.62	0.69	0.76	0.96	1.12
Cash flow per share	3.97	4.21	4.49	4.54	3.56	3.42	4.80	4.59
Price: high	48.9	33.0	34.0	38.0	34.0	44.0	53.9	53.3
low	13.5	23.1	24.2	23.7	24.2	27.8	37.9	33.8

Website: www.adm.com

GROWTH AND INCOME

AT&T Inc.

Ticker symbol: T (NYSE) ❑ S&P rating: BBB+ ❑ Value Line financial strength rating: A++ ❑ Current yield: 5.1% ❑ Dividend raises, past 10 years: 10

Company Profile

Measured by revenue, AT&T continues to be the largest telecommunications holding company in the U.S. Although known for years as the center of the wireline local and long-distance telecom service, it has evolved to be the largest provider of wireless, commercial broadband, and Wi-Fi services in the United States and has become a large player in consumer broadband services with its ISP service and U-verse bundle product.

With the addition of DirecTV, the company is now organized around four operating units, with Business Solutions being by far the largest, accounting for 50 percent of the $140 billion in total revenues. Entertainment and Internet Services (which is where DirecTV landed) and Consumer Mobility each accounted for another 24 percent, while the remainder is from the International segment.

Business Solutions offers both wireless and wireline services to business customers and some individual subscribers. Previously, all wireless services had been concentrated in the AT&T Wireless subsidiary, but these are now split between the business and consumer segments.

The Entertainment segment offers AT&T's U-verse, DirecTV, and legacy DSL services to residential customers. They also provide legacy copper and IP-based voice services through AT&T's existing networks.

The Consumer Mobility segment provides nationwide wireless service to consumers, as well as wholesale and resale subscribers. This is the well-known consumer phone market, which offers services such as voice, text, and video.

The company estimates that more than 50 percent of its network traffic *today* is video, and you can see where this puck is going with the DirecTV acquisition. The company has also acquired Nextel Mexico; with DirecTV and other acquisitions, the company will become a major player in the Latin America market.

Financial Highlights, Fiscal Year 2015

Overall, the company's results were about in line with most estimates, with organic business growth basically flat. Incremental growth was mainly through acquisitions. Given the company's reorganization (and acquisitions), year/year comparisons of the business segments are not revealing. Although the wireless voice/data subsegment is promising, given the saturated nature of the market this type of company will never experience double-digit growth. But even slow, steady, single-digit growth makes for good business when you're this big and you generate this much cash—some $85 billion in the most recent year alone.

The company is very optimistic about its expansion into Mexico. It now claims coverage of 355 million potential subscribers in the U.S. and Mexico, and being able to provide service in both countries will be very attractive to frequent travelers. The unit operated at a minor loss in its first year on a $4.8 billion base.

Share buybacks should continue but at a more moderate pace as DirecTV is absorbed; the dividend should increase at its very predictable 4 cents per share per year pace. The company expects $2.5 billion in cost synergies with DirecTV by 2018 and, in fact, SG&A fell 17 percent subsequent to the acquisition.

Reasons to Buy

We had some concerns last year regarding the DirecTV acquisition. We wanted to see AT&T get this done without a loss of focus and with a clear message around the direction of the company. Happily, by most accounts the DirecTV acquisition has been handled well. Partly due to the fact that DirecTV had been co-marketed with U-verse by AT&T prior to the purchase, there were few operational issues at switchover and the DirecTV brand has not suffered. Customer growth in the DirecTV unit has increased, in part due to the company's emphasis on DirecTV sales over U-verse's competing product, as margins for this service via U-verse are lower.

The acquisition of satellite-based technology via DirecTV will, we think, pay large dividends down the road as we see aggressive growth in space vehicle launch capability (SpaceX and others) and the proliferation of low-cost, low-latency satellites. Nationwide, high-speed network coverage is what these emerging technologies promise, and AT&T's move in that direction is encouraging.

"The Phone Company" has for some time now been the phone, Internet, and television company. Ma Bell today looks nothing like the staid, regulated operation whose stock used to be part of the "Utilities" sector, along with power companies and municipal water districts. Nor does it look like the company broken up by the federal government in 1984 for acting too much like the monopoly it effectively was. Over the course of many decades of service, significant technological evolution, and enormous regulatory upheavals, AT&T remains the largest telecommunications provider in the U.S.

This is not new news, obviously, but it's worth keeping in mind as you look over this and other stocks in this book. We've collected the companies that are well positioned to provide value going forward. Many investors will consider AT&T and will dismiss it as old school—too tied to old wireline operations and other traditional markets and crippled by its own size and reliance on crusty declining markets. In fact, though, AT&T has managed to innovate its way into new markets and succeed against a field of competitors who were thought to be far more nimble. The company is on a growth path that leverages its strength in broadband, mobile communications, and satellite operations. Perhaps more than any other *100 Best* company, AT&T has weathered massive changes in its business environment and has formed itself into an agile and forward-looking company with a clear view of its future in the information era.

And, as usual (and in spite of our worries about the acquisition), shareholder cash returns will continue to be above average, with a strong dividend payout, regular increases, and steady share buybacks all funded by strong cash flows.

Reasons for Caution

As we mention every year, competition in the telecom sector is well established and continues to be our main concern. Pricing is a key issue in AT&T's cost-sensitive consumer markets, as many of the "value" options available have, over the past year, improved their data offerings, technology, and financing options.

The shift in device ownership plans continues apace. Traditional plans that provided a new phone for free (or at a heavily discounted price) when signing up for service are becoming less popular with consumers, who are now trending to "bring-your-own-device" plans. These BYOD plans have been a mainstay of the value providers, but top-line networks are seeing their customer base move in this direction as well. While these tend to be lower-margin accounts, AT&T is competing with providers who, often as not, were buying bandwidth in bulk from AT&T anyway. As long as AT&T can service these accounts efficiently, the financial impact of the lower margins may be minimized.

SECTOR: **Telecommunications Services** ◻ BETA COEFFICIENT: **0.75** ◻ 10-YEAR COMPOUND EARNINGS PER-SHARE GROWTH: **5.0%** ◻ 10-YEAR COMPOUND DIVIDENDS PER-SHARE GROWTH: **3.5%**

		2008	2009	2010	2011	2012	2013	2014	2015
Revenues (bil)		124.0	123.0	124.4	126.7	127.4	158.8	132.4	146.8
Net income (mil)		12,867	12,535	13,612	13,103	13,698	13,463	13,056	15,188
Earnings per share		2.16	2.12	2.29	2.20	2.33	2.50	2.50	2.69
Dividends per share		1.60	1.64	1.68	1.72	1.76	1.80	1.84	1.88
Cash flow per share		5.56	5.46	5.60	5.31	5.70	6.10	6.04	6.05
Price:	high	41.9	29.5	29.6	31.9	38.6	39.0	37.5	36.4
	low	20.9	21.4	23.8	27.2	29.0	32.8	31.7	31.0

Website: www.att.com

CONSERVATIVE GROWTH

Becton, Dickinson and Company

Ticker symbol: BDX (NYSE) ❑ S&P rating: BBB+ ❑ Value Line financial strength rating: A++ ❑ Current yield: 1.8% ❑ Dividend raises, last 10 years: 10

Company Profile

Gotten a flu shot or any other "delivery" of medicine lately? Chances are the "device" used to make the delivery had a prominent "B-D" logo on the package. That doesn't stand for "Bad–Day"—but rather "Becton, Dickinson," one of the premier medical supply and technology companies on the planet.

Becton, Dickinson is a global healthcare technology player focused on improving drug delivery, enhancing the diagnosis of infectious diseases and cancers, and advancing medical lab work and drug discovery. The company develops, manufactures, and sells medical supplies, devices, laboratory instruments, antibodies, reagents, and diagnostic products through its three segments: BD Medical, BD Diagnostics, and BD Biosciences. These products are sold to healthcare institutions, life science researchers, clinical laboratories, the pharmaceutical industry, and the general public. International sales account for about 59 percent of the total. The B-D brand is found throughout the range of clinics, medical offices, and hospitals and is well recognized in the medical community.

The company now operates in two worldwide business segments: Medical (63 percent of FY2015 sales) and Biosciences (37 percent). The former Diagnostics segment was folded into Medical.

The BD Medical segment produces a variety of drug-delivery devices and supplies, including "sharps" (hypodermic needles and syringes) and related disposal products, infusion therapy devices, intravenous catheters, insulin injection systems, regional anesthesia needles, diabetes care systems, and prefillable drug-delivery systems for pharmaceutical companies. The former Diagnostics unit offers system solutions for collecting, identifying, and transporting blood and other specimens, as well as instrumentation for analyzing these specimens. Testing systems include those for sexually transmitted diseases, microorganism identification and drug susceptibility, and certain types of cancer screening. The business also provides customer training and business management services.

BD Biosciences provides research tools and reagents to accelerate the pace of biomedical discovery. Clinicians and researchers use BD Biosciences' tools to study genes, proteins, and cells to understand disease, improve technologies for diagnosis and disease management, and facilitate the discovery and development of new therapeutics. Products include reagents, fluoroscience cell-activated sorters and analyzers, monoclonal antibodies and kits, and cell imaging and reagent solutions, among others.

In mid-2014, the company took a bold step into the healthcare delivery and quality market through the announced acquisition of CareFusion, a global provider of automated tools and systems designed to reduce patient medication errors and to prevent healthcare-associated infections. The acquisition was sizeable, adding some 45 percent to the revenue and capitalization base and about 33 percent to total net income before acquisition synergies, and is now complete.

Financial Highlights, Fiscal Year 2015

Including the CareFusion acquisition, BD turned in low single-digit revenue gains in FY2015. Revenue gains in the Biosciences segment were slightly stronger than the Medical segment due to strength in emerging markets, but emerging markets overall were not a good story in FY2015. Per-share earnings, probably the best performance benchmark for the combined company since shares were issued for the acquisition, were up almost 15 percent. The company expects more lift from emerging markets going into FY2017, with sales rising 3–5 percent for the year and per-share earnings up about 7 percent reflecting a better product mix and acquisition synergies. A stabilizing dollar will also help. Dividend increases should continue, but share buybacks have paused as the company pays down debt from the acquisition.

Reasons to Buy

Becton, Dickinson continues to be a classic "blue-chip" company, as recession proof as any stock on our list. The company offered steady and substantial growth potential, especially in earnings, cash flow, and dividends. The company will continue to benefit through the broadening of healthcare offerings into developing nations. Double-digit operating and net-profit margins exceed industry benchmarks. The CareFusion acquisition looks to be a good move at this juncture.

Reasons for Caution

CareFusion was a big bet and one that lay a bit outside of the core supplies and diagnostics business presenting some additional risks, but everything seems to be going well so far. Continued strength in the dollar and continued weakness in emerging markets, especially China, could weigh on performance. Too, one must continue to be wary of the possible distortions of demand, supply, pricing, and quantity of healthcare consumed, given the Affordable Care Act and the adaptation of the healthcare community to that and subsequent legislation. The trend toward greater cost management among care providers gives another possible "nega-trend" in its core business to consider. All said, Becton continues to be one of the best, safest, steadiest, and most well-managed players in the segment.

SECTOR: **Healthcare** ❑ BETA COEFFICIENT: **0.98** ❑ 10-YEAR COMPOUND EARNINGS PER-SHARE GROWTH: **13.0%** ❑ 10-YEAR COMPOUND DIVIDENDS PER-SHARE GROWTH: **15.5%**

	2008	2009	2010	2011	2012	2013	2014	2015
Revenues (mil)	7,156	7,160	7,372	7,828	7,708	8,054	8,446	10,282
Net income (mil)	1,128	1,220	1,185	1,272	1,123	1,159	1,236	1,480
Earnings per share	4.46	4.95	4.94	5.61	5.36	5.81	6.25	7.16
Dividends per share	1.14	1.32	1.48	1.64	1.80	1.98	2.18	2.40
Cash flow per share	6.60	7.13	7.25	8.27	8.30	8.79	9.37	11.25
Price: high	93.2	80.0	80.6	89.4	80.6	110.9	142.6	157.5
low	58.1	60.4	66.5	72.5	71.6	78.7	105.2	128.9

Website: www.bd.com

CONSERVATIVE GROWTH

Bemis Company, Inc.

Ticker symbol: BMS (NYSE) ❑ S&P rating: A ❑ Value Line financial strength rating: A ❑ Current yield: 2.2% ❑ Dividend raises, past 10 years: 10

Company Profile

You open a stick of string cheese. You pull the little tab at the end and out pops the stick of cheese, which has been happily stored in its little plastic sack through thousands of miles of trucks, warehouses, more trucks, a stockroom or two, the store, your refrigerator, and now maybe your lunch bucket or bag. You enjoy the string cheese with a sandwich made from lunchmeat packaged in a little zippered plastic bag. Afterward, you take your regular dose of allergy medication, packed up in one of those 12-tablet plastic trays with a metal foil backing to tear through.

Who makes this stuff? Did you ever stop to think about it? How it makes our lives easier, as well as those of manufacturers and distributors of these products? Neither had we, until our search for strategic and vital niche holders led us to one of the other companies in Kimberly-Clark's quiet and productive original hometown of Neenah, WI.

"Where inspired packaging takes shape" is the slogan, and it goes a long way to explain their value add in the food chain. Bemis makes all kinds of fixed and flexible packaging solutions mostly out of plastic and mainly for the food, beverage, health and hygiene, building materials, and chemicals markets. Flexible packaging products include bags, wraps, and containers, many with a pressure-sensitive or zipper closure, all set up to be filled with standard packaging line equipment and all labeled for the client's products. "Raw" packaging materials roll out of 60 facilities to the end of packing lines in 11 countries. About 33 percent of sales are international; most of that is in Latin America, China, and Australia.

In 2014 Bemis sold its line of pressure-sensitive materials used in its own packaging but also sold into the printing, graphic design, and technology markets. The company had previously sold four paper-packaging plants to Hood Packaging Company—plants that make items like paper bags for pet foods. Both sales represent a sustained effort to adjust the business mix toward higher-margin businesses.

The strategy is to help customers (mostly consumer products and industrial manufacturers) find economical solutions that improve product quality, safety, shelf life, and shelf presence—they attempt to differentiate a customer's product through the package. The company believes that its leadership position "rests on its strong technical foundation in polymer chemistry, film extrusion, coating and laminating, printing and converting" and that "material science continues to be the primary instrument for creating sustainable competitive advantage."

Financial Highlights, Fiscal Year 2015

The FY2014 and FY2015 numbers still show a drop in revenues related to the divestiture of the pressure-sensitive business; however, as an indication that the move made sense, net earnings actually advanced 4 percent in FY2015 on an improved sales mix, higher margins, and cost-cutting initiatives. Reported revenues dropped 6 percent, but "organic" growth, taking out a 6 percent currency effect and divestitures, was estimated at about break even, with a slight decrease in total volume and an offsetting slight improvement in the mix. Going forward, the company targets sales gains in the 2–3 percent range through FY2017. Margin improvements and strong cash flows support the company's stated objectives to increase per-share earnings

10 percent annually through a combination of share repurchases and net earnings; they are already well on their way with an authorized purchase of 20 million shares, which would retire over 20 percent of the float. Dividends will rise slowly and steadily as well.

Reasons to Buy

This is not an exciting company, but it is a strong niche player providing critical packaging technologies to the industries it serves. New and innovative food-packaging designs are becoming more desired as convenience and quality outweigh cost as a priority in most consumer markets these days. The new packaged salads are a good example of packaging for a product not packaged before; new ziplock containers for lunchmeats, cheeses, etc., show how the package is moving up the value-add scale. The company has a significant beachhead in growing Latin American markets, China, and Australia and is investing in new technologies and applications such as package design enhancements for microwaving, easy-open packages for elderly customers (we continue to applaud this one!), and new technologies and delivery systems for the healthcare and pharmaceutical industries. We like the strategy of fine-tuning the business mix toward more profitable, higher value–add packages, and the company seems to be executing it well and getting the desired results from it. Cash flow and cash returns to shareholders have become a priority and are steady and increasing; the issue continues to have appealingly low volatility and is generally a good defensive play.

Reasons for Caution

To a degree, Bemis is exposed to price volatility in both food and energy and to the economy in general. When food prices rise, consumers get more sensitive to price and may hesitate to pay for convenience packaging—I'll choose and boil my own Brussels sprouts, thank you; no boiling bags for me. Last year we predicted that the "stock price would wake up to the contents of this package"—and indeed it has, with another nice 12 percent gain for the measurement year after an 18 percent gain in 2014. Such gains make it more important to find good entry points.

SECTOR: **Consumer Staples** ❑ BETA COEFFICIENT: **0.63** ❑ 10-YEAR COMPOUND EARNINGS PER-SHARE GROWTH: **4.5%** ❑ 10-YEAR COMPOUND DIVIDENDS PER-SHARE GROWTH: **5.5%**

	2008	2009	2010	2011	2012	2013	2014	2015
Revenues (mil)	3,779	3,515	4,835	5,323	5,139	5,030	4,344	4,071
Net income (mil)	166.2	147.2	203.3	212.4	225.3	237.0	233.1	242.0
Earnings per share	1.65	1.38	1.83	1.99	2.15	2.28	2.30	2.47
Dividends per share	0.88	0.90	0.92	0.96	1.00	1.04	1.08	1.12
Cash flow per share	3.29	2.81	3.84	3.87	3.66	4.19	4.21	4.21
Price: high	29.7	31.4	34.3	34.4	33.9	42.3	47.2	49.4
low	20.8	16.8	25.5	27.2	29.5	33.7	34.3	38.9

Website: www.bemis.com

CONSERVATIVE GROWTH

Campbell Soup Company

Ticker symbol: CPB (NYSE) ❑ S&P rating: BBB+ ❑ Value Line financial strength rating: B++ ❑ Current yield: 2.1% ❑ Dividend raises, past 10 years: 8

Company Profile

Campbell Soup Company is the world's largest, as they like to say, maker of "real food that matters for life's moments." To most of the free world, that still translates to soup and the ubiquitous pop-culture-iconic Campbell's Soup can. Few brands have enjoyed such penetration and loyalty as the core Campbell's brand, and that brand still accounts for about 25 percent of the company's sales. But there is a lot more to this story—and there should be as Campbell's shares, much to our and everyone else's surprise, were up some 40 percent for our measurement year, good for number two gainer on our *100 Best* list. Who would have thought?

After a 2015 reorganization, the company has three reporting segments: Simple Meals and Beverages (55 percent of sales), Global Biscuits and Snacks (33 percent), and Packaged Fresh (12 percent). Simple Meals includes the core Campbell's brand along with V8, Swanson, Plum Organics, and Prego. Global Biscuits contains such favorites as Pepperidge Farm, Kelsen, and Arnott's, while Packaged Fresh is built around the emerging and healthful Bolthouse Farms brand of healthy beverages, salad dressings, organic produce, and similar products. The company also acquired Garden Fresh Gourmet in 2015, bringing lines of hummus, dips, organic chips, and similar foodstuffs.

Campbell's products are distributed to 120 countries worldwide and are sold through its own sales force and through distributors. U.S.-based operations accounted for 78 percent of revenue in FY2015. Products are manufactured in 18 principal facilities within the United States and in 13 facilities outside the country. The company's growth strategy has evolved toward greater innovation in product marketing and brand recognition and new packaging designed to broaden use in today's fast-paced economy, as well as a healthy dose of internationalization. Bolthouse, purchased in 2012 and the fastest-growing segment of the business in terms of products and revenues, gives the company better exposure to Millennials, a market not well addressed by Campbell's traditional brands.

The company recognizes "seismic shifts" in its markets—not just economic shifts but big changes in consumer needs and preferences. Consumers want healthier and fresher foods. They want greater nutrition and transparency with respect to ingredients and food origins. They want to know the impact on diet and health. They want to avoid GMOs, artificial flavors and colors, preservatives, and MSG. They want greater convenience without sacrificing diet and health. And the demographics have shifted—there are 80 million so-called Millennials and 60 million Latinos in the U.S. market—all of whom amplify these trends.

Generally the company is recognizing the need for marketable innovations and is answering that challenge with these noted acquisitions and other new products such as Campbell's Skillet Sauces, Slow Cooker and Oven Sauces, and various new organic products including a full line of organic canned and boxed soups. Their market research suggests the well-known desire for better nutrition and more "natural" ingredients. They are eliminating high fructose corn syrup from some and artificial flavorings and colors from all North American products. They are investing $125 million in new healthy food offerings. But they haven't forgotten that in-home dinner meals are back on track, growing 8.3 percent annually—but only 33 percent are made from scratch and 68 percent are planned within one hour of eating (sound familiar?). With all of that, soup now accounts for only 34 percent of sales, down from 40 percent in 2011—and will go down further.

Financial Highlights, Fiscal Year 2015

Brand strength, acquisitions, diversification into the healthier segments, and a major cost-cutting initiative led to a decent 4 percent growth in earnings on flat revenues (mostly hampered by the strong dollar) in FY2015. The company will stir in more of the same for 2016 and 2017, with cost savings leading the way to 6–10 percent earnings gains as net profit margins climb into the low double digits. In the meantime, modest dividend increases and share repurchases should juice investor returns just a bit.

Reasons to Buy

Why do we like Campbell so much? Because of the stock price gains in 2015? Yes, we like that but we need to find "fundamental" reasons too. A big reason is innovation. Their approach to innovation resonates with us. We think innovation is the key to survival particularly as markets evolve to the tastes of the new Millennial generation.

Then there's the usual: core brand and brand strength. Campbell owns the number one or number two position in each of the product categories in which it participates. It dominates the $4 billion U.S. soup market and is making headway in key foreign markets too. Cash cows are always a good thing to have as you step forward into the marketing "beyond."

Campbell isn't trying to capture the remaining 40 percent of the soup market that it doesn't own; it's trying to grow the overall size of the market and letting its 60 percent share do the talking. The strategy, well-known in the food industry, is to maintain and slowly grow its core brands while generating new growth, leveraging distribution, and sales channels, and increasing brand presence through new products often not directly associated with the Campbell brand. The strategy sounds pretty tasty to us.

Reasons for Caution

Even with the recent emphasis on innovation, the company's brands and core customer base are aging, and adoption of new products may continue to prove slow, especially among the younger set. As others, like Coca-Cola, have found out over the years, there are risks inherent with tinkering with a long-established brand such as Campbell's. We would hope that Campbell succeeds with its new ventures without pulling the rug out from under the old ones. We still like Cream of Mushroom on a rainy day, even if we have no idea what it's made of. Finally, the share price could be a bit ahead of the company itself—stir Campbell's shares into your portfolio carefully.

SECTOR: **Consumer Staples** ▫ BETA COEFFICIENT: **0.39** ▫ 10-YEAR COMPOUND EARNINGS PER-SHARE GROWTH: **5.0%** ▫ 10-YEAR COMPOUND DIVIDENDS PER-SHARE GROWTH: **6.5%**

		2008	2009	2010	2011	2012	2013	2014	2015
Revenues (mil)		7,998	7,586	7,676	7,715	7,707	8,052	8,268	8,082
Net income (mil)		798	771	842	846	783	786	800	831
Earnings per share		2.09	2.15	2.45	2.54	2.44	2.48	2.53	2.65
Dividends per share		0.88	1.00	1.05	1.15	1.16	1.16	1.25	1.25
Cash flow per share		3.07	2.87	3.25	3.48	3.35	3.82	3.53	3.68
Price:	high	40.8	35.8	37.6	35.7	37.2	45.8	46.7	55.1
	low	27.3	24.8	24.6	29.7	31.2	34.8	39.6	42.9

Website: www.campbellsoup.com

AGGRESSIVE GROWTH

CarMax, Inc.

Ticker symbol: KMX (NYSE) ▫ S&P rating: NR ▫ Value Line financial strength rating: B+ ▫ Current yield: Nil ▫ Dividend raises, past 10 years: NA

Company Profile

"The Way Car Buying Should Be." That's the slogan used by this clean-cut chain of used vehicle stores and superstores and its new big-box, retail-like model for selling cars. CarMax buys, reconditions, and sells cars and light trucks at 144 retail centers in 73 metropolitan markets, mainly in the Southeast, Midwest, and California, but is gradually moving to a more nationwide footprint. The company specializes in selling cars that are under six years old with less than 60,000 miles in excellent condition; the cars are sold at a competitive price, typically in the $10,000 to $34,000 price range, for their condition in a no-haggle environment. The price is the price; the emphasis is on the condition of the vehicles and on a helpful and friendly sales and transaction process. Sales representatives are compensated for cars they sell but not in such a way that drives them to push the wrong car on a customer. The company sold some 619,936 used vehicles in 2015, up 6.5 percent from FY2014 and up 52 percent from the 408,080 sold in 2011. The average selling price for 2014 was $19,917, about unchanged from the previous year, and the average gross margin was $2,109 per vehicle.

CarMax is gaining footholds in new markets such as Denver, Minneapolis-St. Paul, the Pacific Northwest, and New England, and most reports suggest they are gaining market share in the markets they serve with a high degree of customer satisfaction. CarMax opened 15 new stores in 2015; and they plan to open 13–16 new stores in each of the next three fiscal years. From 158 stores total today, they anticipate 188 stores by 2017 and 225 stores in place by the end of the decade, including new presence in Seattle, New York City, and San Francisco, and small-format stores they're testing in markets like Harrisonburg, VA, and Jackson, TN. The overall strategy is to build a national footprint and brand, achieve economies of scale, and make the most of online marketing initiatives.

The health of the economy and consumer spending have swung car buying into a higher gear, but with newfound consumer prudence. Many of these purchases are heading to the one- to six-year-old used car sector of the business, where prices are 40–60 percent lower than comparable new cars. In addition to "retail" used car sales, CarMax is a big player in auto wholesaling, having moved about 376,000 units mostly taken in trade; the company is the world's largest used car buyer. The company also earns income through its financing unit, known as CarMax Auto Finance, or CAF. The unit finances about 42 percent of the company's sales and accounts for about 39 percent of pretax profits.

CarMax also has service operations and sells extended warranties and other products related to car ownership. The company has state-of-the-art web-based and mobile tools as well as other aids designed to make the car selection, buying, and ownership experience easier. As CarMax puts it, customers request four things when they buy a car:

1. Don't play games
2. Don't waste my time
3. Provide security
4. Make car buying fun

The company's offering is aimed at reducing these concerns and providing the right experience. The offering continues to be unique in the industry, and competitors would have a long way to go to catch up.

Financial Highlights, Fiscal Year 2015

It was a good market once again for selling cars, with new car sales running at a 17 million annual rate—at the high end of the cyclical range. For the year ending February 29, 2016, which the company calls FY2016 but we will refer to as "2015" because most activity occurred in that year, same-store used vehicle sales were up about 2.4 percent (down a bit from last year's stellar 7 percent); total unit volume was 6.5 percent higher leading to an overall revenue increase of about 6 percent. Success factors included favorable financing, a significant growth in online and mobile vehicle shopping activity, and higher conversion rates in the store with an assortment of physical and process tweaks.

The gross margin per used vehicle ticked down slightly to $2,109 from $2,179 last year as a relatively oversupplied used car market drove down prices. The oversupply is due to high levels of lease returns in the wake of the new car sales boom starting in 2012. However, favorable results from financing drove operating margins higher again, 5.4 percent versus 5.1 percent last year and 4.7 percent two years ago. That and an aggressive 7 percent share buyback led to a 14 percent gain in per-share earnings for FY2015. FY2016 forecasts call for a 7–8 percent top-line gain mostly driven by new store openings; margins will remain about constant but the share count will come down further, perhaps another 5 percent, giving toward another 12–15 percent rise in per-share earnings. Projections for FY2017 are similar. The company announced its first share buyback program in 2012 and has pursued it aggressively every year since then, clearly set up as a shareholder return vehicle in lieu of dividends; CarMax is one of only four companies on our *100 Best* list that doesn't pay a dividend. Since then they have retired 14 percent of the float and are on track to retire a third of that 2012 225-million-share count by the end of the decade.

Reasons to Buy

Quite simply, CarMax continues to be a buy if you believe the traditional dealer model is broken and if you believe people will continue to see value in late-model used vehicles. CarMax as a brand is finally gaining national recognition as a "go-to" in the car buying (and selling) process.

Additionally, CarMax brings the latest in business intelligence and analytic models to the car-marketing process, in procurement, merchandising, pricing, and selling the vehicles. Do green Jeep Cherokees sell well in Southern California? Then let's find some, put them on the lot there, and set a market-based price. KMX is well ahead of the industry in making analysis-based supply and selling decisions and has quite successfully deployed analytic tools to adjust prices and inventories quickly to market conditions, a competency that bodes well for the future.

CarMax is increasingly a big player in the 40-million vehicle used car market (versus 17 million for new cars), taking market share from traditional used car dealers, but there's fertile ground to capture more. The company estimates that it has only 5 percent of the current market for zero-to-ten-year-old used vehicles in markets in which it operates, and only 3 percent of the total nationwide—all while being the largest player and twice the size of the nearest competitor.

The company is positioned well both for organic growth through market share and for geographic growth; there is still plenty of fertile ground for new growth, especially in the Northeast and Northwest and smaller metro areas. They estimate that they currently reach only 63 percent of the U.S. population. The footprint is slowly but surely becoming a nationwide one, which will not only help volumes but also brand recognition, pricing power, buying power, and cost absorption. The small-format store test, if successful, could add to this.

Earnings momentum has been strong lately, in part due to the aggressive and consistently executed share repurchase program.

Reasons for Caution

CarMax will always be somewhat vulnerable to economic cycles, the availability of credit, and the availability of quality used vehicles to resell. Recent concerns about vehicle availability have morphed into concerns about oversupply as lease returns flood the market. Lease returns are an important source of supply for the company, so there is good news in this as well.

A new trend toward longer six- and seven-year new car financing periods may keep people in their cars longer, but it may also incentivize people to buy used to avoid the long financing period in the first place. As this company is still in the growth phase, and new dealerships involve putting lots of new cars on the ground, working capital needs are extensive, long-term debt has risen, and cash returns to shareholders have not met our norms; however, the share repurchase program takes a big step toward fixing that.

SECTOR: **Retail** ▢ BETA COEFFICIENT: **1.44** ▢ 10-YEAR COMPOUND EARNINGS PER-SHARE GROWTH: **16.0%** ▢ 10-YEAR COMPOUND DIVIDENDS PER-SHARE GROWTH: **NA**

		2008	2009	2010	2011	2012	2013	2014	2015
Revenues (mil)		6,974	7,400	8,975	10,004	10,963	12,574	14,269	15,150
Net income (mil)		59.2	281.7	380.9	413.8	425.0	492.6	583.9	628.6
Earnings per share		0.27	1.26	1.67	1.79	1.87	2.16	2.68	3.05
Dividends per share		—	—	—	—	—	—	—	—
Cash flow per share		0.52	1.52	1.95	2.19	2.00	2.70	3.35	3.93
Price:	high	23.0	24.8	30.0	37.0	38.2	53.1	68.7	75.4
	low	5.8	6.9	18.6	22.8	24.8	38.0	42.5	50.6

Website: www.carmax.com

Carnival Corporation

Ticker symbol: CCL (NYSE) □ S&P rating: BBB+ □ Value Line financial strength rating: B+
□ Current yield: 2.8% □ Dividend raises, past 10 years: 4

Company Profile

Carnival Corporation is the world's largest leisure travel company, providing cruises and cruise vacations to destinations throughout the world. The company operates under 11 individual cruise brands, or separate cruise lines in two segments—North America, and Europe, Australia, & Asia (EAA) segments. The North America segment includes Carnival Cruise Line, Princess Cruises, Holland America Line, and Seabourn cruise brands. The EAA segment includes Costa Cruises, Cunard Cruises, Ibero Cruises, AIDA Cruises, P&O Cruises (UK), P&O Cruises (Australia), and Fathom cruise brands. Together, these cruise lines operate over 100 modern ships (with 17 more on the way between now and 2020) with over 216,000 berths, and the company claims about 47 percent of the worldwide cruise market. The company operates a few port facilities, Alaska tours, and some other adjacent travel operations. About 62 percent of revenues come from the North American brands.

The ships are modern, really, floating hotels, and the travel experience is all-inclusive and easy for guests. The typical cruise is set up for all age groups, with plenty of varied activities and foods for all, including new specialty restaurants and celebrity chefs onboard and big names like Crosby, Stills & Nash in the entertainment lineup. Fares are "all-inclusive," but travelers will find plenty of add-ons like Internet service and alcoholic beverages to run up an additional tab while onboard. Cruises range from short three- and four-day "Love Boat" cruises out of Los Angeles to three- and four-week and longer passages through entire regions like the Middle East or Southeast Asia.

Customer service is paramount and has become a recent emphasis of the Carnival lines. Live agents are available before, during, and after the cruise to answer any questions (Can my 17-year-old bring his skateboard? Yes, but he'll have to stow it while onboard the ship; he can access it for ports of call.). The experience is turnkey and much simpler than the typical land-based vacation, especially if multiple destinations are involved. The company and its lines have gotten smart about attracting repeat customers through loyalty programs and "perks" for repeat customers—some wealthier retirees might spend half a year on the company's ships as a simpler, less-expensive alternative to owning a large motor home or vacation property. Retirees have always been prime targets—but the offering is becoming more attractive to families and younger customers as well—to a degree, because cruises have become more "hip."

Recent directions include "green cruising" where ships are powered by liquefied natural gas, new cruises to Cuba (the first embarked in early 2016), and more originations and availability from China to serve the growing traveling middle class there. To that point, there are an estimated 135 million outbound travelers in China today, a figure estimated to grow to 200 million by 2020—and currently only 5 percent of the company's capacity serves China.

Financial Highlights, Fiscal Year 2015

After many years of rocky seas, particularly during the Great Recession, Carnival has finally, through a combination of marketing and operational excellence, found calmer waters and steady tailwinds. Revenues were mainly flat in FY2015 (without currency effects they would have been up about 5 percent), but occupancy and yield gains, higher onboard spending, and lower fuel prices led to a handsome 39 percent gain in net income. We might see this as a calm before a storm, but with new ships and continued marketing success the company now projects a 4 percent revenue gain in 2016 and another 20 percent gain in net income as margins improve, with pretty much more of the same into 2017. A more steady and confident Carnival is also starting to return a little more cash to shareholders, both in the form of moderate dividend increases and share buybacks.

Reasons to Buy

We think cruising has come into its own as a mainstream regular travel alternative, not just a niche business providing a once-in-a-lifetime honeymoon or retirement cruise to Alaska. Cruises are more complete and easier than in past years, and there is something for everyone. The new ships are spectacular.

The marketing story is solid—strong brands, customer service, and customer loyalty leading the way. Millennials, who once probably would never have thought of a cruise, now are attracted to the activities, special meals, and entertainment, and the experience as a whole. It is no longer just for Grandma and Grandpa. As this group is more and more likely to shun material goods for experiences, cruise operators, especially those offering "interesting" itineraries, are in the right dock at the right time.

Financially, we see a long-awaited return to steadier waters and more return to shareholders—all on the right heading.

Reasons for Caution

It's hard not to think about how economic cycles can affect this industry; fancy vacations are usually the first thing to go when times turn tough. We'd counter that cruises don't have to be "exotic" and many are affordable even on a modest family budget—there's something for everyone here. High fixed costs (ships, especially today's ships, are expensive!) present some financial challenges especially in bad times. Fuel prices can be another variable, and competition in this industry is fairly intense, but we feel that Carnival has the strongest position, the best brands, and the best overall offering. You should no longer need a life jacket to buy this company, but watching the horizon is important as it is for any stock.

SECTOR: Consumer Discretionary ❑ **BETA COEFFICIENT: 0.83** ❑ **10-YEAR COMPOUND EARNINGS PER-SHARE GROWTH: -1.0%** ❑ **10-YEAR COMPOUND DIVIDENDS PER-SHARE GROWTH: 6.0%**

	2008	2009	2010	2011	2012	2013	2014	2015
Revenues (mil)	14,646	13,157	14,469	15,793	15,382	15,456	15,884	15,774
Net income (mil)	2,330	1,790	1,978	1,912	1,464	1,078	1,516	2,103
Earnings per share	2.90	2.24	2.47	2.42	1.88	1.39	1.99	2.70
Dividends per share	1.60	—	0.40	1.00	1.00	1.00	1.00	1.10
Cash flow per share	4.56	3.94	4.30	4.36	3.84	3.44	4.06	4.83
Price: high	45.2	34.9	47.2	48.1	39.9	40.5	46.5	55.8
low	14.9	16.8	29.7	28.5	29.2	31.4	33.1	42.5

Website: www.carnivalcorp.com

GROWTH AND INCOME

CenterPoint Energy, Inc.

Ticker symbol: CNP (NYSE) ❑ **S&P rating: A-** ❑ **Value Line financial strength rating: B+** ❑ **Current yield: 5.0%** ❑ **Dividend raises, past 10 years: 10**

Company Profile

"Sell when there's something better to buy" is our guiding philosophy and mantra for removing and replacing companies on our *100 Best* list each year. Last year we did just that, replacing old-line utility favorite Southern

Company with the more progressive, more diversified CenterPoint Energy. Part of that diversification was into the natural gas business with a 55 percent interest in Enable Midstream Partners, a natural gas master limited partnership. Given what happened in energy markets, we took a big hit (especially for a utility company) during 2015. But progressive moves to write down losses and possibly sell the interest, combined with strength in other businesses and a secure, best-in-class yield, brought the stock back and convinces us to hold on to CenterPoint for at least another year. Again, sell when there's something better to buy.

CenterPoint Energy is in the electricity delivery (not production, but delivery) business, serving over 2.3 million customers in a 5,000-square-mile service territory in the greater Houston area, and is in the retail gas delivery business, serving more than 3.3 million metered customers in Louisiana, Arkansas, Minnesota, Mississippi, Oklahoma, and Texas (including Houston). It is the nineteenth-largest electric utility and sixth-largest gas distribution company in the U.S. by customer base. It is also—as of this writing—in the gas production business, with a 55 percent interest in a master limited partnership called Enable Midstream Partners, which produces and distributes wholesale gas and some oil mainly from Texas and Oklahoma. Finally, the company operates an unregulated CenterPoint Energy Services arm, which sells gas to commercial, industrial, and wholesale customers throughout most of the eastern half of the U.S. and provides an assortment of consulting services for other utilities.

CenterPoint intrigues us because, first, it does not own generating assets but instead distributes electricity to its customers produced by 18 providers, some green. It owns the wires, the meters, and the customer contact, while such messy problems as fuel costs and environmental risks are left to someone else. Second, in its distribution business, the company has learned to use technology to drive efficiency and improve the customer experience, with advanced implementations of smart grids, smart metering, and other technologies from companies like Itron, Inc. (another *100 Best* pick). The company has installed smart meters for almost all its customer base—more than 2.3 million meters—automating meter reading and frequent readouts on electricity use. Customers are never left in the dark for long—these technologies manage the grid to reduce consumption, access the least expensive source, and keep the lights on more reliably—and when that fails, the company has also learned how to hook up with customer smartphones and media to quickly advise of service interruptions or other important announcements.

Finally, we liked the idea of a gas distributor acquiring some upstream assets to control costs and assure supplies—only it backfired as energy prices cratered in late 2014. The company took a $1.8 billion noncash write-down of the asset value of Midstream and is reconsidering its ownership—now that the pain has been taken we're good with either direction CenterPoint decides to go with this investment. Electricity transmission and distribution accounts for 39 percent of FY2015 revenues; gas distribution accounts for 36 percent, and the unregulated gas sales and services unit accounts for the rest.

Financial Highlights, Fiscal Year 2015

With the limited partnership interest and the large unregulated sales unit, revenues and earnings can vary more widely than with most large utilities. Reported FY2015 revenues dropped 19 percent, but the $1.8 billion impairment charge for Enable was accounted for as a revenue impairment; without that revenues would have been $9.232 billion—almost flat from FY2014. Net earnings also took a hit due to Enable.

Rate relief, a steady 1–2 percent rise in the customer base, expense control operating efficiency, and the Enable housecleaning are projected to lead to steady per-share earnings growth of 4–6 percent through FY2017 with steady dividend increases to keep up. Depletion and depreciation allowances typically keep cash flows well ahead of earnings for this type of company. As such, cash flows are well ahead of earnings and should keep the dividend secure despite the high percentage of reported earnings (90 percent) it represents.

Reasons to Buy

CenterPoint is a progressive-minded utility located in what has been a high-growth market that simply cannot do without electricity. We look at the electricity business as a key business anchor with decent growth prospects, and we like the deployment of leading-edge technologies in that business. We like their positioning as a low-cost producer and wholesaler in the gas business with a built-in outlet in the regulated business for their product. We think the Enable investment is a temporary hit—any good news in this sector, including a sale, will only help from this point forward. The dividend is high compared to peers and appears secure. We interpret the recent dividend raise as a sign of management confidence, and we expect that management will eventually return to its 8–10 percent dividend growth philosophy. CenterPoint combines the safety and yield of a quality utility with a bit of appreciation potential in the energy production and nonregulated distribution business.

Reasons for Caution

Enable is still something of a question mark, though most of the bad news seems to be behind CenterPoint. We do worry that a protracted slowdown in the energy economy could temper Houston's growth, creating a soft patch in its own right. To an extent, CenterPoint is still a bet on a recovering energy industry, albeit with a strong base in its distribution businesses to balance the risk.

SECTOR: **Utilities** ▫ BETA COEFFICIENT: **0.32** ▫ 10-YEAR COMPOUND EARNINGS PER-SHARE
GROWTH: **2.0%** ▫ 10-YEAR COMPOUND DIVIDENDS PER-SHARE GROWTH: **3.5%**

		2008	2009	2010	2011	2012	2013	2014	2015
Revenues (mil)		11,322	8,281	8,765	8,459	7,452	8,106	9,226	7,386
Net income (mil)		447	372	442	546	581	536	611	465
Earnings per share		1.30	1.01	1.07	1.27	1.35	1.24	1.42	1.08
Dividends per share		0.73	0.76	0.78	0.79	0.81	0.83	0.95	0.99
Cash flow per share		3.42	2.94	3.14	3.43	3.89	3.54	3.85	3.40
Price:	high	17.3	14.9	17.0	21.5	21.8	25.7	25.8	23.7
	low	8.5	8.7	5.5	15.1	18.1	19.3	21.1	16.0

Website: www.centerpointenergy.com

GROWTH AND INCOME

Chevron Corporation

Ticker symbol: **CVX (NYSE)** ▫ S&P rating: **AA** ▫ Value Line financial strength rating: **A++** ▫ Current yield: **4.9%** ▫ Dividend raises, past 10 years: **10**

Company Profile

Chevron has become a poster child for strong, stable, entrenched businesses in can't-lose industries suddenly rocked out of bed by the recent energy and commodity price crash. When the price of your chief product drops 70 percent, that forces tough decisions on cost cutting and particularly on sustaining the heretofore solid and rising dividend. So far, Chevron is staying the course by using debt and capital expenditure cuts to get over the hump—and the company should emerge stronger than ever and be able to pay down the debt once the crisis subsides. Therefore, we keep this bellwether on the *100 Best* list though 2016 and 2017 performances look pretty bleak by historical standards. We've faced this sort of decision with many other companies in the oil and related industries.

Chevron is the world's fourth-largest publicly traded, integrated energy company based on oil-equivalent reserves and production. It is engaged in every aspect of the oil and gas industry, including exploration and production, refining, marketing and transportation, chemicals manufacturing and sales, and power generation.

Active in more than 180 countries, Chevron (formerly ChevronTexaco via the 2001 merger) has reserves of about 7 billion barrels of oil and 22 trillion cubic feet of gas, with a production rate of 2.5 million barrels of oil equivalent and 5.1 billion cubic feet of gas per day. In addition, it has global refining capacity of more than 1.7 million barrels per day (bpd) and operates more than 16,000 retail outlets around the world. The company also has interests in 30 power projects now operating or being developed. The upstream capacity is concentrated in North America, Africa, Asia, and the Caspian Sea region, with less exposure to the Middle East than some competitors. The company is the leading producer in Kazakhstan, Thailand, and Indonesia, which rank among the highest-potential and lowest-risk non-U.S. locations.

Although it increased the overall exposure to the 2014–15 oil price swoon, Chevron is more concentrated in oil (less in gas) than some of its competitors. That said, it is active but not overly concentrated in new shale developments, particularly in gas. Chevron also has active global downstream businesses in manufactured products including lubricants, specialty chemicals and additives, specialty refining units for aviation and maritime markets, and various logistics activities, including pipelines, shipping, and a global trading unit.

The company's global refining network comprises 14 wholly owned and joint-venture facilities that process about 2 million barrels of oil per day. Gasoline and diesel fuel are sold through more than 16,300 retail outlets under three well-known consumer brands: Chevron in North America; Texaco in Latin America, Europe, and West Africa; and Caltex in Asia, the Middle East, and southern Africa.

Chevron is the number one jet fuel marketer in the United States and third worldwide, marketing 550,000 barrels per day in 80 countries. The company's fuel and marine marketing business is a leading global supplier and marketer of fuels, lubricants, and coolants to the marine and power markets, with about 500,000 barrels of sales per day.

The company's traditional emphasis in oil hurt the company as prices fell almost 70 percent in 2014–15, severely affecting the bottom line and causing the first quarterly loss in almost 30 years in the opening quarter of FY2016. While the oil price slump clearly hurt the bottom line, long term we still feel that the emphasis on oil and the diversification through downstream refining and marketing is still the right position, and an eventual recovery in oil and gas prices will only act as a plus going forward—but it may take longer than 2017 to happen.

Financial Highlights, Fiscal Year 2015

Not surprisingly, the 70 percent oil price decline led to a 35 percent crash in FY2015 revenues, with a steeper 75 percent drop in earnings as asset values were written down and operating leverage was lost. FY2016 won't be much better, with more write-downs and expensive project startups leading to another 30–40 percent drop in earnings on what may turn into an 8–10 percent revenue gain if oil prices rebound somewhat toward the $40 range as many predict. For FY2017 the company expects a rebound to $165–$170 billion in revenues and $7.5–$8 billion in net income. Cash flows and new debt still support the dividend for now, though it is possible the company will abandon its consecutive dividend increase record this year. Of course, any rebound in energy prices during late 2016 and into 2017 should dramatically improve overall results.

Reasons to Buy

Energy stocks are very difficult candidates right now in light of declining prices and worsening industry fundamentals. Not surprisingly, declining product prices, increased inventories and competition, and a relatively fixed cost picture are not features we look for in a *100 Best* pick. We must take a long-term view and must look at long-term strengths.

For exploration and production strength and geographic and technological diversity, few companies exceed Chevron's strengths. The company is most exposed to some of the best sectors and geographies in the business and has established a good brand and track record for discovery, production, and downstream operations. The company has made what we feel are prudent cuts in its exploration activities and its expenses in general. We like the diversification into refining, which generally benefits from lower input prices so long as weather trends cooperate, which they didn't so much in 2015. Long term, the company has a solid record of earnings, cash generation, and cash distribution. We think shareholders will be well rewarded with growing cash returns in the long run—especially as energy prices normalize. Recent purchase prices have been attractive, particularly in light of the steady dividend—with a little patience, we think CVX is among the best of a hard-hit and out-of-favor industry.

Reasons for Caution

Of course, recent energy price shifts have put a dent in CVX's universe. We look at the recent price shifts as an opportunity for some of the wiser—and more cash-rich—players such as Chevron to streamline operations and to provide opportunities to acquire productive assets more cheaply. Still, all that said, the Saudis and others appear determined to undermine high-cost oil production—"fracking" in layman's terms. This business may take some time to return to its previous glory and level of safety—but at this juncture we're willing to wait.

SECTOR: Energy ❑ BETA COEFFICIENT: 1.09 ❑ 10-YEAR COMPOUND EARNINGS PER-SHARE GROWTH: 13.0% ❑ 10-YEAR COMPOUND DIVIDENDS PER-SHARE GROWTH: 10.5%

	2008	2009	2010	2011	2012	2013	2014	2015
Revenues (bil)	273.0	172.6	204.9	253.7	241.9	228.8	212.0	138.4
Net income (bil)	23.9	10.5	19.0	26.9	26.2	21.4	8.9	4.6
Earnings per share	11.67	5.24	8.48	13.44	13.32	11.09	10.14	2.45
Dividends per share	2.53	2.66	2.84	3.09	3.51	3.90	4.21	4.28
Cash flow per share	16.69	10.95	15.99	19.98	20.05	18.61	19.17	13.70
Price: high	104.6	79.8	92.4	111.0	118.5	127.8	135.1	113.0
low	55.5	56.1	66.8	102.1	95.7	108.7	100.1	69.6

Website: www.chevron.com

GROWTH AND INCOME

Cincinnati Financial Corporation

Ticker symbol: CINF (NASDAQ) ❑ S&P rating: BBB ❑ Value Line financial strength rating: B++ ❑ Current yield: 3.6% ❑ Dividend raises, past 10 years: 10

Company Profile

A year after returning Cincinnati Financial to our *100 Best* list, we continue to embrace the basic property/casualty insurer model. We continue to like the way companies that follow this model make money not only in profiting from the difference between premiums collected and costs ("underwriting income") but also by being able to invest the "float" over the years for what can be enormous gains (of course, we hold Warren Buffett's Berkshire Hathaway as the obvious paradigm for this model). We think Berkshire is too pricey for the average shareholder, and further, it pays no dividend, but we decided we liked the model well enough to have two choices on our list. So we choose Cincinnati Financial and Allstate for our list once again.

Cincinnati Financial Corporation (CFC), founded in 1968, is a holding company operating several insurers engaged primarily in property/casualty insurance marketed through independent insurance agents in 39 states. The company, one of the 25 largest property and casualty insurers in the nation, operates in four segments: Commercial Lines Property Casualty Insurance, Personal Lines Property Casualty Insurance, Life Insurance, and Investments. Commercial Lines account for about 65 percent of premium revenues and are sold in 39 states; Personal Lines about 25 percent and are sold in 31 states. All insurance products are sold through independent agencies. Life insurance and other "excess/surplus" lines (specialized niche forms of insurance) are designed to allow the agents to offer a full line and account for the 10 percent remainder.

Cincinnati Financial fully or partially owns a series of subsidiary companies that actually provide and manage the insurance products marketed by the company and its agents. Its standard market property casualty insurance group includes two subsidiaries: the Cincinnati Casualty Company and the Cincinnati Indemnity Company. This group writes a range of business, homeowner, and auto policies. Cincinnati Specialty Underwriters offers the excess/surplus lines and life, disability, and annuity products to complete the insurance product picture.

The two noninsurance subsidiaries of Cincinnati Financial are CSU Producer Resources, which offers insurance brokerage services to CFC's independent agencies so their clients can access CFC's excess and surplus lines insurance products; and CFC Investment Company, which offers commercial leasing and financing services to CFC's agents, their clients, and other customers. Like all property and casualty insurers, CFC earns income from underwriting (premiums collected less casualty payouts) and from investing the vast pool of cash generated through premiums stored up until a loss occurs.

Financial Highlights, Fiscal Year 2015

Results have definitely improved since the Great Recession, which took underwriting income well into the red and put a small dent in investment income as well (that dent was only about 10 percent, showing the resiliency of CINF's investment portfolio). From losing $3.28 per share in underwriting income in 2011, the company brought that back to a positive $2.43 (pretax) for FY2015 on improved pricing and a dearth of major casualty payouts and an unusually low level of losses paid in general. Expenses were down, underwriting margins rose to almost 9 percent, and investment income ran steady with the total portfolio earning a healthy 4 percent. A modest rise in claims and turbulent markets in early 2016 are foretelling a 14 percent drop in per-share earnings in FY2016 with a rebound to previous levels and beyond in FY2017—which could be helped along a bit by higher interest rates and thus higher investment returns. Strategic rate hikes, stricter underwriting guidelines, and the addition of reinsurance products will all help. Moderate dividend growth through the period should persist.

Reasons to Buy

As mentioned at the outset, we like the basic business model. In addition, CFC enjoys both a loyal customer base and a loyal agency base. It is smaller, more nimble than Allstate and, unlike Allstate, most business is handled through agencies—with the two companies as choices, you get both ends of the spectrum. Measured by premium volume, the company is ranked as the number one or number two carrier among 75 percent of the agencies that have represented them for the past five years. The company has invested in new pricing and modeling analytics to sharpen its approach to pricing and customer relationships. CFC is on firm financial footing with a dividend covered by investment income and cash flow and a relatively low 11 percent long-term debt as a percentage of total capital. Despite the recent financial storm, dividend payouts have increased slowly and steadily each year. From here forward, the company is well positioned to benefit from interest rate increases, which will help investment income, and underwriting income should remain solid as well.

Reasons for Caution

The current pricing environment is not that favorable; there is a lot of competition in this business, although loyal customers and especially agents will help. Interest rates on the industry's traditional investment instruments could continue to stay weak for some time. A large natural catastrophe could hurt. The stock price has risen with the good news; investors should look for good entry points.

SECTOR: **Financials** ◻ BETA COEFFICIENT: **0.81** ◻ 10-YEAR COMPOUND EARNINGS PER-SHARE GROWTH: **1.5%** ◻ 10-YEAR COMPOUND DIVIDENDS PER-SHARE GROWTH: **6.5%**

	2008	2009	2010	2011	2012	2013	2014	2015
Premiums Earned (mil)	3,010	2,911	2,924	3,029	3,344	3,795	4,242	4,480
Net income (mil)	344	215	273	121	421	466	454	585
Earnings per share	2.10	1.32	1.68	0.74	2.40	2.81	2.86	3.56
Dividends per share	1.53	1.57	1.59	1.60	1.62	1.64	1.74	1.82
Underwriting inc. per share	(0.94)	(2.19)	(1.80)	(3.28)	(0.51)	0.94	0.78	2.43
Price: high	40.2	29.7	32.3	34.3	41.0	53.7	55.3	61.6
low	13.7	17.8	25.3	23.7	30.1	39.6	44.0	49.7

Website: www.cinfin.com

CONSERVATIVE GROWTH

The Clorox Company

Ticker symbol: CLX (NYSE) ◻ S&P rating: BBB+ ◻ Value Line financial strength rating: B++ ◻ Current yield: 2.4% ◻ Dividend raises, past 10 years: 10

Company Profile

A leading manufacturer and marketer of consumer cleaning and other household products, Clorox markets a broad line of highly trusted and recognized brand names, including its namesake bleach, Green Works natural cleaners, Formula 409, Liquid-Plumr, and Pine-Sol cleaning products; Fresh Step and Scoop Away cat litter; Kingsford charcoal; Hidden Valley, KC Masterpiece, and Soy Vay dressings and sauces; Brita water-filtration systems; Glad bags, wraps, and containers; and Burt's Bees natural personal care products. In the U.S., Clorox continues to own the number one or number two market share position with over 80 percent of its products, and that continues to be a key part of its long-term strategy.

The company is divided into four segments:

- Cleaning Products (32 percent of FY2015 sales, 39 percent of pretax income) includes laundry, home-care, and professional cleaning products. Home-care products include disinfecting sprays and wipes, toilet bowl cleaners, carpet cleaners, drain openers, floor-mopping systems, toilet and bath cleaning tools, and premoistened towelettes. Professional products are for institutional, janitorial, and foodservice markets and include bleaches, disinfectants, food-storage bags, and bathroom cleaners.

- Lifestyle (17 percent, 22 percent) offers Dressings and Sauces (Hidden Valley, Soy Vay, and others), Water Filtration products, and Natural Personal Care (mainly Burt's Bees).

- Household Products (32 percent, 32 percent) includes Bags, Wraps & Containers (Glad and others), Charcoal (Kingsford and Match Light brands), and Cat Litter.

- International (19 percent, 7 percent) is set up as a separate entity to market and distribute an assortment of U.S.-made and locally made brands from 39 manufacturing facilities to markets in over 100 countries.

To give an idea how far Clorox has come as a consumer company, it was founded in 1913 as the Electro-Alkaline Company. It has been known as the Clorox Company since 1957, although it was owned by archrival Procter & Gamble from 1957 until 1969 when the FTC forced divestiture to promote competition. Overall, the liquid bleach and trash bags are the largest two product families at 13 percent of sales each, followed by charcoal at 11 percent. The company positions itself not only as a brand leader but also a leader in environmental responsibility and in responding to changing demographics, as exemplified by new formulations and packages specifically targeted to the Hispanic market.

Financial Highlights, Fiscal Year 2015

Clorox is a bit less exposed to currency effects than most companies we follow but was affected nevertheless—FY2015 revenues were up only 1 percent. Favorable commodity price trends and some operational savings, however, led to a modest margin improvement and an 8 percent gain in earnings. FY2016 forecasts call for similar results, with a strengthening of revenues in FY2017 (up 2–3 percent) on the moderation of currency effects and small product enhancements—such as a "smart" Brita pitcher that, in a partnership with Amazon, will automatically order its own replacements, and an extension of the Burt's Bees product line into lip and facial care. Net and per-share earnings should rise in the 7–10 percent range, depending on share buyback activity, which has been modest of late but could pick up.

Reasons to Buy

Clorox, due to its strong and diverse brand position and market share, has proven to be resilient in the past in all phases of the economic cycle—the shares held firm even during the early 2016 volatility. Their products and brand identities are standards in the markets they serve. As a personal preference, we especially like the Green Works products, which, unlike many "green" products, seem to actually work and to have become a standard on store shelves.

That said, many consumers have switched away from name-brand products; just how many remains to be seen. Offsetting that, the company seems to be placing more emphasis on innovation.

Clorox has proven itself to be a strong, well-managed, cash-flow and shareholder-oriented defensive player. Dividend raises have been strong and persistent—currently in the 5 percent range—and while the company has slowed its share repurchases (because of the high stock price?) it has reduced share count 40 percent since 2004. The stock has tended to trade in a very tight range even with negative news; with a beta of 0.39 for our *100 Best* portfolio it remains mostly a safety and stability play.

Reasons for Caution

The commodity price tailwind could go away, and we remain concerned that the company could be tempted again into poor acquisitions to spur growth, as it's pretty challenging to grow demand and market share for bleach, trash bags, and charcoal. That said, we applaud their current emphasis on operational improvements and brand extension (as opposed to expansion—acquiring *more* brands). Finally, the stock has posted some strong gains in past years; the current share prices leave little room for error.

SECTOR: **Consumer Staples** ❑ BETA COEFFICIENT: **0.39** ❑ 10-YEAR COMPOUND EARNINGS PER-SHARE GROWTH: **5.5%** ❑ 10-YEAR COMPOUND DIVIDENDS PER-SHARE GROWTH: **10.5%**

		2008	2009	2010	2011	2012	2013	2014	2015
Revenues (mil)		5,273	5,450	5,534	5,231	5,468	5,623	5,591	5,655
Net income (mil)		461	537	603	258	543	574	562	606
Earnings per share		3.24	3.81	4.24	2.07	4.10	4.31	4.26	4.57
Dividends per share		1.66	1.88	2.05	2.25	2.44	2.63	2.67	2.99
Cash flow per share		4.82	5.22	5.68	3.51	5.56	5.80	5.76	6.03
Price:	high	65.3	65.2	69.0	75.4	76.7	96.8	106.4	131.8
	low	47.5	59.0	59.0	60.6	66.4	73.5	83.7	102.9

Website: www.clorox.com

CONSERVATIVE GROWTH

The Coca-Cola Company

Ticker symbol: KO (NYSE) ❑ S&P rating: AA ❑ Value Line financial strength rating: A++ ❑ Current yield: 3.1% ❑ Dividend raises, last 10 years: 10

Company Profile

The Coca-Cola Company is the world's largest beverage company. For more than 100 years, the company has mainly produced concentrates and syrups, which it then bottles or cans itself or sells to independent bottlers worldwide. Then in 2010 it took a big step to "own" the supply chain with the acquisition of bottler Coca-Cola Enterprises' North American operations; CCE still handles distribution for Europe. Independent bottlers add water (still or carbonated, depending on the product), sugar, and other (often local) ingredients, then bottle and distribute the products to restaurants, retailers, and other distributors. The company operates in more than 200 countries and markets nearly 500 brands of concentrate and finished beverages. These concentrates are used to produce more than 3,500 different branded products, including Coca-Cola. In a strategic reversal we'll describe further, the company has chosen to sell off that U.S. distribution business acquired in 2010—actually, to "refranchise" it in the company's current vernacular. That will return Coca-Cola to its original state of owning, maintaining, marketing, and growing the brand but not the downstream physical distribution of the product.

The company continues to strive to expand its beverage offerings beyond the traditional carbonated soda drinks. Major brands besides Coke include Minute Maid and Simply Orange juices; Dasani and Evian bottled waters; Odwalla fruit beverages, protein shakes, and fruit bars; Powerade and Full Throttle sports beverages; Nestea Gold Peak and FUZE iced teas; Glaceau VitaminWater; and ZICO Coconut Water. Major international brands include Ayataka Green Tea and I Lohas water in Japan, Del Valle in Latin America, and others similarly local to their markets. The total numbers are staggering: 3,800 products worldwide, 500 brands, 20 of which have reached $1 billion in sales, 29.2 billion cases worldwide, which equates to 637 billion servings per year, 1.9 billion beverages consumed per day, and 21,990 servings per second, all processed through more than 250 bottlers serving 200 countries and 24 million retail outlets, and all handled through the world's largest beverage distribution system. In terms of unit case volume, 79 percent of all sales are overseas—29 percent in Latin America, 15 percent in Eurasia/Africa, 21 percent in the Pacific, and 14 percent in Europe. In revenue terms, the company counts about 54 percent as overseas sales.

As traditional carbonated drinks continue to go flat with today's Millennial generation, the company is moving forward in the "new world" of beverage consumption, with a recent investment in Keurig Green Mountain, which has now been sold to Germany's JAB Holding Co. Keurig had been working on K-Cup single servings for a recently introduced "Keurig KOLD" machine that makes single-serve soda and other chilled beverages using K-Cup servings of Coke products. It remains to be seen what will happen to this partnership and technology, but it is an indicator of one way Coca-Cola intends to expand its markets through technology and partnerships. The company has also invested in Monster Beverage and others. Some 18 of their top 20 brands have low- or no-calorie alternatives. The line of "still" (versus sparkling) beverages, which includes specialty juices, waters, and teas is expanding and now accounts for 27 percent of global sales. The new "Freestyle" machine found in a growing number of fast-food restaurants allows drinkers to customize their drinks. It's fun, and remember—customization is one of today's biggies. And did you know? It now collects data so that Coca-Cola can see what tastes are preferred; what a laboratory! (The dispenser team has its own website—check out www .coca-colafreestyle.com.) Other innovations include mass-customized cans and bottles with people's names on them, and something we've all awaited: a return to the original Coke bottle shape and format where possible.

As mentioned previously, the company is reversing its strategy to own its U.S. distribution channel—specifically its bottling network. Coca-Cola is embarking on a "21st Century Beverage Partnership Model," essentially a franchising model, where the company works closely with its bottling franchisees but does not carry the asset base, employee base, or the headaches of that relatively low-margin business. Commodity price risks also move over to the franchisees. The impact on margins is significant, raising operating margins some 8 percent (to about 36 percent) when fully implemented, which is supposed to occur by late 2017.

Financial Highlights, Fiscal Year 2015

The strong dollar and weak emerging markets impaired sales and earnings in FY2015 to the tune of a 3 percent drop in reported revenues and a 2 percent drop in per-share earnings; however, on an organic (constant currency) basis, revenues actually advanced 4 percent with a 6 percent advance in per-share earnings. Worldwide unit case volume increased 2 percent. Net profit margins remain in the 19–20 percent range, which is huge for a company this size (the company also boasts of an 18 percent free cash flow margin—also huge). Projections call for a fairly similar year in 2016; then in 2017 the effects of the refranchised bottlers kick in for a 25 percent decrease in revenues and a 25–30 percent increase in gross margins, which will actually grow net profits somewhere in the 5 percent range (not a bad trick on such a revenue drop). The new lean, mean format combined with product innovations and expansion should bring profits to record levels in subsequent years. Cash returns to investors are decent on both the buyback and dividend front, with dividends growing in the mid to high single-digit range and share buybacks reducing share counts in the 1–2 percent range annually.

Reasons to Buy

"I like to bet on sure things," Warren Buffett said, referencing why he'll never sell a single one of the 400 million shares of Coca-Cola stock he owns. That pretty much sums it up, and the reasons to buy Coke continue to be solid. The company has category leadership, especially globally, in soft drinks, juices and juice drinks, and ready-to-drink coffees and teas. They're number two globally in sports, energy, water, and ready-to-drink teas. In Coca-Cola, Diet Coke, Sprite, and Fanta, they own four of the top five brands of soft drink in the world.

The Coca-Cola name is probably the most recognized brand in the world and is almost beyond valuation. Indeed, Mr. Buffett once uttered the classic line about its brand strength and intangibles: "If you gave me $100 billion and said take away the soft drink leadership in the world from Coke, I'd give it back to you and say it can't be done."

That's all pretty old news now; what's important is that Coca-Cola has also shown us, in today's world, that it isn't just going to sit around and go flat while we investors sit around and cry in our beer. We see signs that the company "gets it" and will not only adapt, but eventually has a chance to remain the number one brand even with a full new mix of beverages and packages for the modern world. Coca-Cola has traditionally been a steady hedge stock and offers a solid dividend with a constant track record of dividend growth. The company boasts—quite rightly—about having raised dividends in each of the past 54 years, and returned some $8.0 billion out of $10.8 billion in cash generated to shareholders in 2015. It is also as close to a pure play on international business as you'll find in a U.S. company. Finally, the low beta of 0.52 continues to confirm its low-volatility credentials.

Reasons for Caution

Coca-Cola is under our constant scrutiny for relevance in today's increasingly Millennial-dominated market. Sales of traditional sparkling beverages in established markets—the U.S. and Europe, and now Latin America—are in a slow decline, probably caused in part by interest in health and reducing obesity.

For the future, these market changes could provide some speed bumps. One wonders how the Coke culture will resonate with today's Millennial beverage requirements—less sugar, fewer artificial ingredients, more customization and transparency—and one wonders further whether the new-age consumer will adapt well to healthy or fun drinks sold by Coca-Cola. Therein lies the 64-ounce question: Can they deliver change? Fast enough? Can they get the message out? In time to make a difference as traditional sugary beverages decline? Right now, our bet is "yes."

The distribution restructuring could prove distracting, too. Overall, this is a slow, steady growth story, which may be too slow for many, with new risks the company didn't face when Mr. Buffett bought in years ago.

SECTOR: **Consumer Staples** ◻ BETA COEFFICIENT: **0.52** ◻ 10-YEAR COMPOUND EARNINGS PER-SHARE GROWTH: **7.0%** ◻ 10-YEAR COMPOUND DIVIDENDS PER-SHARE GROWTH: **9.5%**

	2008	2009	2010	2011	2012	2013	2014	2015
Revenues (mil)	31,944	30,990	35,123	46,554	48,017	46,854	45,998	44,294
Net income (mil)	7,050	6,824	8,144	8,932	9,019	9,374	9,091	8,797
Earnings per share	1.51	1.47	1.75	1.92	1.97	2.08	2.04	2.00
Dividends per share	0.76	0.82	0.88	0.94	1.02	1.12	1.22	1.32
Cash flow per share	1.79	1.75	2.09	2.41	2.46	2.58	2.53	2.49
Price: high	32.8	29.7	32.9	35.9	40.7	43.4	45.0	43.9
low	20.1	18.7	24.7	30.6	33.3	36.5	36.9	36.6

Website: **www.coca-colacompany.com**

Colgate-Palmolive Company

Ticker symbol: CL (NYSE) □ S&P rating: AA- □ Value Line financial strength rating: A++ □ Current yield: 2.2% □ Dividend raises, past 10 years: 10

Company Profile

Every now and then, even the most stable and secure of companies runs into some bad news—in this case, a major write-down of Venezuelan operations gone sour. The numbers, as a consequence, look awful (you can see for yourself in the following). But, in considering the company for renewal on the *100 Best* list, we always ask ourselves: Has the business fundamentally changed? Have the strengths that got the company here in the first place gone away? In the case of Colgate-Palmolive, the numbers beneath the numbers, the fact that dividend raises continued unabated, and the core strength of the business and brands all cry out: "No change." So we keep CL on the *100 Best* list for another year without reservations as yet another good test of our fundamental selection principles.

Colgate-Palmolive is the second-largest global producer of detergents, toiletries, and other household products. The company manages its business in two straightforward segments: Oral, Personal, and Home Care; and Pet Nutrition. The Oral, Personal, and Home Care division produces and markets a number of familiar brands and products: Ajax, Palmolive, Irish Spring, Softsoap, Fabuloso, Mennen, and Speed Stick, as well as the familiar Colgate brand of oral care products. These brands are strong with substantial market share in most markets: Colgate owns 47 percent of the worldwide oral care market, 20 percent of personal care, 19 percent of the home care, and 14 percent of the total pet nutrition markets.

Although it hurt during this most recent period of dollar strength, Colgate's real strength is in international consumer products markets, with a presence in more than 200 countries and territories. About 80 percent of its business is international—and more than 50 percent of *that* business is in emerging markets.

Financial Highlights, Fiscal Year 2015

Once again, Colgate's international exposure, while an asset long term, led to more currency exposure and risk than most of its brethren, which of course, we think to be a cycle, not a long-term negative—and ultimately a positive. Add to that the Venezuela write-down; these together made for a lousy FY2015. Reported revenues declined 7 percent, per-share earnings dropped 35 percent. Are we broken? No. The Venezuela write-off was $1.18 per share; without that, earnings would have advanced 14 percent and revenues, without a nearly 12 percent currency hit, would have advanced close to 5 percent. You can clearly see the "story beneath the story."

With the Venezuela problem largely behind it, with brand and operational improvements and expanding margins, and with continued aggressive (2–3 percent) share buybacks, Colgate expects to return to a track of 3–5 percent revenue growth and 8–10 percent per-share earnings growth by FY2017 and beyond. A faster currency turnaround would strengthen this picture. Dividend increases should continue in the 5 percent range.

Reasons to Buy

"Focused on Global Growth" is the company's slogan—and it's an appropriate one. Colgate's brands are market leaders in most of the markets in which they operate, particularly in overseas markets where they are especially strong. They have a 45 percent share of the global toothpaste market and 33 percent of the manual toothbrush market. They're number one or number two with many of their other brands, including Ajax and Softsoap, and have many other well-established brands. They were recently given the title of "the number one brand purchased in the world" and their products are estimated to be in half the world's households. The company's "first to market" global strategy has given them a formidable foothold in emerging markets such as China, India, and Latin America. Colgate is in a great position to benefit from the increased acceptance and use of dental care products and other toiletries in these markets, and is actively marketing to build this opportunity.

Colgate is a conservatively run company that prefers slower organic growth over quick (but expensive) acquisitions. It plows money back into the company and achieves profitability through operational excellence, rather than paying for gross margins at any price. This is a solid defensive play with a good dividend, real earnings growth, and real earnings predictability. Looking at the bigger picture, Colgate is less prone to reach for new, rapidly changing markets, such as cosmetics, and less apt to try to grow through acquisitions than, say, a Procter & Gamble (another *100 Best* stock). This company is about slow, steady returns with little risk and little market volatility in bad times. The company touts not just ten but 52 consecutive years of dividend increases. Finally—perhaps a little thing—we find their annual report is more interesting and informative than most.

Reasons for Caution

Colgate participates in an increasingly competitive market, requiring more frequent new-product rollouts and related marketing expenses just to keep up. As we've seen, the international exposure brings currency exposure, and sometimes pure and simple business risk, as evidenced by the Venezuela exit. The Colgate business will not stimulate more aggressive investors.

SECTOR: **Consumer Staples** ▫ BETA COEFFICIENT: **0.50** ▫ 10-YEAR COMPOUND EARNINGS PER-SHARE GROWTH: **5.0%** ▫ 10-YEAR COMPOUND DIVIDENDS PER-SHARE GROWTH: **11.0%**

		2008	2009	2010	2011	2012	2013	2014	2015
Revenues (mil)		15,330	15,327	15,564	16,734	17,085	17,420	17,277	16,034
Net income (mil)		1,957	2,291	2,203	2,431	2,472	2,241	2,180	1,384
Earnings per share		1.83	2.19	2.16	2.47	2.58	2.38	2.36	1.52
Dividends per share		0.78	0.86	1.02	1.14	1.22	1.33	1.42	1.50
Cash flow per share		2.27	2.64	2.57	2.97	3.10	2.91	2.89	2.05
Price:	high	41.0	43.7	43.1	47.4	55.5	66.5	71.3	71.6
	low	27.2	27.3	36.6	37.4	43.6	52.6	59.8	50.5

Website: www.colgate.com

AGGRESSIVE GROWTH

NEW FOR 2017

Columbia Sportswear Company

Ticker symbol: **COLM** (NASDAQ) ▫ S&P rating: **NR** ▫ Value Line financial strength rating: **B++** ▫ Current yield: **1.3%** ▫ Dividend raises, past 10 years: **10**

Company Profile

In the course of producing our annual refresh of *The 100 Best Stocks to Buy*, we read a lot of corporate histories among the many types of material we use as sources. In qualifying Columbia Sportswear for our 2017 list, we read one that pretty much tops them all:

Born and raised in Portland, Oregon, Columbia Sportswear Company has been making gear so that Pacific Northwesterners can enjoy the outdoors for more than 70 years. At the helm for over 40 years has been our Chairman, Gert Boyle. Her Tough Mother persona has grown Columbia into the global sportswear company that it is today—still based in Portland, still making no-nonsense apparel and footwear to keep you WARM, DRY, COOL and PROTECTED no matter what. Our unique Pacific Northwest heritage and Boyle family irreverence is what sets us apart from the competition.

Now we don't usually lift content verbatim from such corporate writings. But this one not only describes Columbia's colorful past, but also quite aptly describes what the company has become today. It is our job to try to project this image into the future for investment purposes.

As described—and still led by the 92-year-old Ms. Boyle and her son—Columbia makes a line of practical, functional, and tastefully styled activewear that is increasingly used for non-active situations. Most of you have seen a Columbia vest or jacket or two on the streets or in the woods during your daily travels. Rainwear is a specialty—given its Portland roots—but the company makes and distributes high-quality, conservatively designed shirts, pants, hoodies and fleecewear, tops and bottoms for women, shoes, and accessories among other products. The clothing and shoes are designed for outdoor wear and for skiing/snowboarding and other rugged activities, but they are casual enough and of high enough quality to fit in well for Casual Friday at work and casual anything outside of work; you won't get turned away at your favorite nice restaurant if you show up wearing Columbia. You probably won't notice Columbia—until you notice it. It's all about one of our favorite themes: "elegant simplicity."

Apparel, accessories, and equipment accounted for about 78 percent of 2015 sales, with footwear making up the rest. The company has expanded its own direct-to-consumer channel through Columbia-branded stores and through its website. It has also expanded into more specialty lines, like yoga clothing. Columbia also owns and distributes Mountain Hardwear, a respected line of high-end performance outerwear, and other "lifestyle" brands including Sorel (women's wear), prAna ("stylish, sustainable activewear"), and Montrail (high-performance running footwear). On the innovation front, a new performance technology called "OutDry Extreme" has received excellent reviews in the rainwear category.

Financial Highlights, Fiscal Year 2015

Although hampered a bit by currency and a warm 2015 winter, Columbia Sportswear has been successful on all fronts. After a 25 percent rise in sales in FY2014, sales for FY2015 rose another 11 percent (15 percent in constant currency). The growth rate was closer to 21 percent in the U.S., spearheaded by strong direct-to-consumer sales. Net profit margins advanced from the mid-5 percent range to the mid-7s, healthy for a clothing business, and earnings advanced 27 percent on top of a 46 percent advance in FY2014.

Although sales momentum is expected to slow a bit to the 5 percent range into 2017, earnings growth is projected to exceed that and come in in the high single digits. We think these forecasts are typically Oregonian conservative.

Dividends have been ascending to the summit slowly but surely, while share buybacks remain mainly in base camp but took a short $70 million (1 percent) hike last year to test the weather.

Reasons to Buy

We were looking for a company to replace the stumbling Ralph Lauren on our *100 Best* list, and we think we found it in Columbia Sportswear. The brand has slowly but surely expanded its international reputation for functionality, performance, good design, quality, and value. It has the conservative, enduring qualities of Ralph Lauren products without being showy or pretentious; its understated elegance has resonated with Millennials much better than Ralph, and its appeal is much wider than just Millennials. Go out on a rainy day and see what people are wearing.

As the brand has solidified and gone global, the company has woken up out of the financial doldrums, too. Sales, margins, and profits are all on a solid uptrend as the products become more standard and are distributed more widely in varying retail channels (you must no longer trek to REI to buy Columbia).

Reasons for Caution

The clothing business is by nature notoriously cyclical and trendy, and we don't pretend to be able to follow these trends, let alone pick the companies that will ride ahead of them. That's why we like Columbia—it is trendy because it isn't trendy. That said, even this strength can fall on its ear as it has with Ralph Lauren, Eddie Bauer, and many of its brethren. (We think those two names experienced other problems, namely Ralph's hoity-toity snob appeal and Eddie's poor quality that Columbia may not experience if it stays on track.) Competition from the likes of Patagonia and Marmot is also substantial, but neither produces as complete a line nor has achieved as wide a distribution as Columbia. Oh, and about distribution—channel partners can be fickle too—losing a big one like Macy's could spell trouble, as could too much extension into the low end like Walmart just to boost volumes, which would cheapen the brand. Extension into barely adjacent product categories, like golf shirts, also worries us. There are a lot of possible mistakes in this industry; we hope Columbia emulates the successes of Nike and avoids the failures of many other passé clothing brands.

SECTOR: **Consumer Staples** ◻ BETA COEFFICIENT: **1.08** ◻ 10-YEAR COMPOUND EARNINGS PER-SHARE GROWTH: **1.5%** ◻ 10-YEAR COMPOUND DIVIDENDS PER-SHARE GROWTH: **24.5%**

	2008	2009	2010	2011	2012	2013	2014	2015
Revenues (mil)	1,318	1,244	1,483	1,694	1,670	1,685	2,100	2,326
Net income (mil)	106	67	77	103	100	94	137	174
Earnings per share	1.54	0.99	1.13	1.52	1.47	1.37	1.94	2.45
Dividends per share	0.32	0.33	0.37	0.43	0.44	0.46	0.57	0.62
Cash flow per share	2.03	1.53	1.71	2.19	2.07	1.95	2.74	3.33
Price: high	24.7	23.2	31.1	35.3	29.2	39.7	45.9	74.7
low	13.0	12.3	19.1	20.6	21.6	23.9	34.3	41.1

Website: www.columbia.com

AGGRESSIVE GROWTH

Comcast Corporation

Ticker symbol: CMCSA (NASDAQ) ◻ S&P rating: A- ◻ Value Line financial strength rating: A ◻ Current yield: 1.7% ◻ Dividend raises, past 10 years: 6

Company Profile

Comcast is one of the nation's leading providers of communications services and information and entertainment content passed through those services. The core business is Comcast Cable, the familiar cable TV network that has evolved into a conduit for delivering bundled high-speed Internet services, phone services, scheduled TV, and on-demand content. This business serves some 23 million subscribers in 39 states.

The company has been evolving its information and entertainment business gradually through its ownership of regional sports networks and national channels such as the Golf Channel, E! (an entertainment channel), Fandango (a moviegoer's website), and others. The company took a major leap forward as a content provider with the early 2011 closing of the acquisition of 51 percent of NBCUniversal, almost instantly turning the company into not only a connectivity powerhouse but a media powerhouse as well through its ownership of Universal Pictures and other assets. In March 2013, Comcast completed the purchase by acquiring the remaining 49 percent of NBCUniversal from General Electric, the previous parent corporation. With that acquisition, Comcast became the largest integrated content development and distribution business in the United States.

The company has been building its Xfinity Internet portal brand to compete with satellite operators and such offerings as AT&T U-verse and Verizon FiOS. Customers can buy bundles of services including TV, on-demand video, and, as an emerging offering, on-demand TV through the Hulu application. With Xfinity, customers can also get up to 105 mbps Internet service, and their 30 percent connect rate makes Xfinity the largest high-speed broadband service in the U.S. In short, Comcast has evolved from being a lackluster cable TV service to a full-scale communications utility with some of the highest-performance products on the market, using the Xfinity platform to draw customers in for the rest of its service bundle. The company now has nearly as many Internet service customers (22 million) as it does cable subscribers (23 million), with more than 11 million phone service connections thrown in for good measure.

Comcast breaks down its business into two major segments: Cable Communications and NBCUniversal. In FY2015, Cable Communications accounted for 66 percent of total revenues and 80 percent operating income. NBCUniversal, in turn, breaks down into Cable Networks (including the national and regional sports networks), Broadcast Television, Filmed Entertainment, and Theme Parks (the noted "Universal" theme parks in Florida and Hollywood, California). The vast majority of Comcast customers are residential, although the company also offers a business class service, including fiber end-user connections and cloud storage, to meet the needs of small and midsized organizations. That business segment grew 20 percent to $4.7 billion (up 45 percent over the past two years). The company also owns the Philadelphia 76ers (NBA basketball) and Flyers (NHL hockey). In early 2016 the company launched a bid to acquire content developer DreamWorks Animation SKG for $3.6 billion.

Financial Highlights, Fiscal Year 2015

The company turned in results that surprised some in the current "cord-cutting" environment, turning in a 4 percent increase in residential video services and a 10 percent increase in high-speed Internet connections. Average monthly revenue per connection grew 4 percent to $142.74. Non-cable business grew "only" 9.6 percent, as Universal had a slow year for releases. Total revenues increased 8.3 percent, an improvement over the prior year's well-received numbers. Operating cash flow increased 7.7 percent, with operating margins holding steady. Per-share earnings rose 14 percent, inclusive of a $6.75 billion share buyback. The company announced plans to repurchase another $10 billion in stock, with $5 billion to be spent in 2016.

The company's strong cash position will likely lead to further acquisitions in the next few years.

Reasons to Buy

The addition of Comcast to the 2013 *100 Best* list was one we debated out of concern about cable companies in general. However, it continues to pay off handsomely; the shares have more than doubled since our decision. We like the company's strategic and operational focus—the acquisitions make sense, and the metrics they present truly describe what's important in the business—not just size and volume, but making customer relationships better and more profitable. The different pieces of the company fit together well.

The DreamWorks Animation acquisition holds promise. DreamWorks created and owns several popular children's franchises, including "Shrek" and "Kung Fu Panda." We expect the Universal arm to capitalize on these properties, including them in featured theme parks and resort properties. Universal pictures has done well marketing other children's content (such as "Minions") so we see this as a good fit. The acquisition also opens up opportunities for NBCUniversal, as DreamWorks has an existing television content network. Comcast has recently unveiled a working application for "boxless" cable installation, where content can be streamed to platforms such as Roku and others without them requiring a Comcast set-top box. There is work to do here, but the FCC is motivating all cable providers to open up their environments, and Comcast is the first to do so. The appeal of a "Comcast-ready" third party box should open up many additional customer opportunities.

Comcast (and its competitors) are becoming a larger version of what the big three television networks used to be. They own content development and marketing, but also the content delivery infrastructure. There are no franchises or distributors to deal with, and they are free to develop independent content and compete with their own live and streamed content as they see fit. This is an extremely dynamic market model and Comcast is uniquely positioned to establish and define the leadership position.

The growth in market dominance, improved branding, and new revenues from the increased adoption of Xfinity all bode well, as does what we think will become the eventual reality of on-demand content as a standard—and profitable—product from suppliers such as Comcast.

Reasons for Caution

Although Comcast is certainly big enough to survive on its own, the trend toward industry consolidation either brings the usual risks associated with an acquisition, or risks that it could be left out and that another player combination overtakes Comcast's leadership position or some of its niches. While recent decisions on net neutrality now look to be a positive, they aren't a done deal, and we could be left with an Internet that can't charge any extra for handling heavy loads, which with the expected expansion of such loads, could become a problem.

The company faces extreme competition in most of its markets, although it may have at least a temporary bandwidth advantage at present. It's a lucrative and growing market; there will always be competing technologies and services for what Comcast has to offer.

SECTOR: **Telecommunications Services** ❑ BETA COEFFICIENT: **1.05** ❑ 10-YEAR COMPOUND EARNINGS PER-SHARE GROWTH: **32.0%** ❑ 10-YEAR COMPOUND DIVIDENDS PER-SHARE GROWTH: **23.5%**

	2008	2009	2010	2011	2012	2013	2014	2015
Revenues (mil)	34,256	35,756	37,937	55,842	62,570	64,657	68,775	74,510
Net income (mil)	2,701	3,638	3,535	4,377	6,203	6,816	8,380	8,171
Earnings per share	0.91	1.26	1.29	1.58	2.29	2.56	2.93	3.25
Dividends per share	0.25	0.27	0.38	0.45	0.60	0.78	0.90	1.00
Cash flow per share	3.10	3.57	3.89	4.44	5.26	5.59	6.48	6.90
Price: high	22.5	17.3	21.2	27.2	38.2	52.1	59.3	65.0
low	12.1	10.3	14.3	19.2	24.3	37.2	47.7	50.0

Website: www.comcast.com

GROWTH AND INCOME

ConocoPhillips Company

Ticker symbol: COP (NYSE) ❑ S&P rating: A ❑ Value Line financial strength rating: A+ ❑ Current yield: 3.0% ❑ Dividend raises, past 10 years: 9

Company Profile

We said it last year, and we'll say it again. Ouch! With an exclamation point this time.

When a company faces a 70 percent decline in the price of their product in just over a year, bad things happen to their finances. What happens from here forward depends a lot on (1) the future of oil prices and (2) how well they manage those finances. We're not sure when (not if, when) oil prices will return to previous levels or even the $60 per barrel most majors declared they could prosper with. But we do think ConocoPhillips has managed the situation well, and like other quality companies in this embattled sector, when the smoke clears they will have made good operating adjustments and will prosper even more than if the price plunge hadn't happened. So we're keeping COP on our list.

By spinning off refiner Phillips 66, ConocoPhillips became a pure play in the "E&P" (exploration and production) sector. Although lower oil and gas prices have turned ConocoPhillips from a $54 billion multinational "E&P" company into a $31 billion one (with the refining unit, it was once a $240 billion company), COP is still one of the world's largest E&P enterprises. Headquartered in Houston, TX, the company operates in 30 countries with about 19,100 employees.

The company's E&P operations are geographically diverse, producing most of its resources in the United States, including a large presence in Alaska's Prudhoe Bay. The company also has a large presence in U.S. shale "fracking" regions, including Eagle Ford and Permian regions in Texas and the Bakken region in North Dakota. (Fracking was once "good"; now it is considered "bad" because of its relatively high cost. We think it will be "good" again as great strides in efficiency are expected to lower the break-even cost.) As well, the company produces in Norway, the United Kingdom, western Canada, Australia, offshore Timor-Leste in the Timor Sea, Indonesia, Malaysia, China, Vietnam, Libya, Senegal, Nigeria, Algeria, and Russia.

Over the years, ConocoPhillips had become a strong natural gas play and a strong domestic energy player, with some 59 percent of its crude and 40 percent of gas coming from the U.S. (including Alaska). Recently the company has been selling non-producing gas assets and has been slowing deepwater exploration—all to optimize the balance sheet and cash flow. A two-thirds cut in the dividend followed these moves, and more asset sales are likely into 2017. COP has stated that it is positioning itself for "an extended period of lower, more volatile prices" and *had* said that "dividend remains a top priority for capital allocation." Although we don't like surprises, we think it's a good sign that management can admit its mistakes instead of digging in on its promises to the detriment of the company.

Financial Highlights, Fiscal Year 2015

We don't need to delve into the details of oil prices; the story is familiar. Lower oil and gas prices resulted in a 42 percent drop in 2015 revenues to $30.7 billion and a dip into the red for net earnings (which had been some $6.2 billion in 2014—what a difference a year makes!). As mentioned, the dividend was cut from $2.94 to $1.00 in early 2016. After missing its FY2015 forecasts badly, the company is giving a revenue forecast just 3.3 percent ahead of 2015, with per-share earnings predicted at a $1.00 deficit based on $30/barrel oil. As asset write-downs account for a good share of the loss, cash flows are still projected in the $6.00–$7.00 range per share, a positive sign. The company is currently expecting a full recovery and more by 2020.

Reasons to Buy

More than most others in the sector, COP has taken its medicine by selling assets, curbing non-core exploration, and cutting its dividend—in contrast to many of its peers who are borrowing to bridge the gap, including the dividend payment. For a company of Conoco's size, we think this is the right move.

It's highly unusual to include a company posting a ten-year decline in sales and recent losses on the *100 Best* list. However, COP is strong enough to sustain itself through these tough times, and management has a good handle on the situation and the various scenarios and risks. We do think oil prices will recover, perhaps a little faster than today's conservative forecasts, as supply and demand naturally correct the current glut. We like the domestic slant on the production mix; it is lower cost and more stable than most. We don't have to add a measure of geopolitics into the long list of risk factors. With these factors plus the likelihood of a "leaner meaner" company emerging from the downturn, plus a still-decent dividend likely to rise substantially upon any favorable oil price movement, we think the present situation is more of a buying opportunity than a cause for concern. Drill carefully.

Reasons for Caution

The story of ConocoPhillips has been a story of change over the past four years. The company successfully divested the refining operations to gain focus—only to gain focus on the most volatile part of the business—which has become far more volatile of late. E&P is risky by nature even with a steady oil price (although COP's domestically oriented portfolio reduces this risk); when you add in price volatility it makes for . . . well, a volatile mix. COP has taken its pain in stride, but a continuation of $30 oil (or even less, driven, say, by Iranian exports) would present some challenges.

SECTOR: Energy ❑ BETA COEFFICIENT: 1.28 ❑ 10-YEAR COMPOUND EARNINGS PER-SHARE GROWTH: 5.0% ❑ 10-YEAR COMPOUND DIVIDENDS PER-SHARE GROWTH: 13.0%

	2008	2009	2010	2011	2012	2013	2014	2015
Revenues (bil)	240.8	149.3	189.4	244.8	62.0	54.4	52.5	30.7
Net income (bil)	15.9	4.9	8.8	12.1	7.4	8.0	6.2	(1.7)
Earnings per share	10.68	3.24	5.92	8.76	5.91	6.43	4.96	(1.39)
Dividends per share	1.88	1.91	2.16	2.64	2.64	2.70	2.84	2.94
Cash flow per share	16.80	9.58	12.50	15.63	11.47	12.57	11.79	5.97
Price: high	96.0	57.4	68.6	77.4	78.3	74.6	87.1	70.1
low	41.3	34.1	48.5	68.0	50.6	56.4	60.8	41.1

Website: www.conocophillips.com

AGGRESSIVE GROWTH

Corning Incorporated

Ticker symbol: GLW (NYSE) ❑ S&P rating: A- ❑ Value Line financial strength rating: B++ ❑ Current yield: 2.6% ❑ Dividend raises, past 10 years: 5

Company Profile

When you think of Corning, you think of glass. All kinds of glass—drinking glasses, glass tableware, and that sort of thing. If you were around in the 1960s, you may remember that well-known white cookware with the little blue flowers on the side.

But things change, and so has Corning. Today's Corning is a premier technology company, more precisely, a technology materials company. If you use a smartphone, a tablet, a laptop PC, or a flat-panel television, chances are pretty good that the glass on the screen comes from Corning. A good amount of the data you see on that screen may have come through glass-based fiber-optic materials supplied by—guess who—Corning.

In fact, Corning operates in five segments, all centered on the glass business. Display Technologies (34 percent of FY2015 sales) makes a lot of those screens, actually referred to as "glass substrates for liquid crystal displays." Optical Communications (formerly Telecommunications) (33 percent) makes fiber-optic cable and an assortment of connectivity and other products related to fiber for telecommunications companies, LAN, and data center applications. Specialty Materials (12 percent) provides a wide assortment of high-tech, glass-based materials, including those specialty glass screens for smartphones, tablets, etc., which it has cleverly branded as Corning Gorilla Glass for its endurance characteristics. This product is even gaining traction in automotive and architectural markets. Also out of this division comes a new bendable display substrate known as "Willow Glass" and a host of glass and ceramic products and formulations used in the semiconductor industry, precision instruments, and even astronomy and ophthalmology. The Environmental Technologies segment (12 percent) makes ceramic substrates and filters for emission control systems, mostly for gasoline and diesel engines. The Life Sciences segment (9 percent) makes laboratory glass and plastic wares.

The company competes with a number of suppliers, mostly Japanese, on a variety of fronts, and acquired the remaining 50 percent interest in a joint venture with Samsung (Samsung Corning Precision Materials) during 2014 to make it a wholly owned subsidiary with lower-cost production facilities in Korea. Corning also has had a 50–50 joint venture with Dow Chemical for years, known as Dow Corning, a leader in silicon products and technologies producing high-quality sealants, lubricants, etc., from silicon materials. Promising innovations include the adaptation of its Willow Glass, thinner than a dollar bill, for ultrathin, ultrasensitive touchscreens to improve size and weight characteristics of mobile devices. Eventually this will evolve into bendable, curved, and curvable glass displays, allowing us to literally wear our devices—an exciting prospect. During 2015 Corning also launched the fourth generation of Gorilla Glass and new enhancements to other display glasses and technologies. The extension of Gorilla Glass beyond electronic devices into architectural and automotive designs is on track—such as the company's new "Dynamic Windows"—architectural glass panels that automatically darken, reducing energy consumption.

Financial Highlights, Fiscal Year 2015

Currency strength and weakness in the flat-panel TV displays melted down Corning's prospects for a good FY2015; as CEO Wendell Weeks put it, "We understand that growth is an ongoing process and is rarely linear." So true—revenues slumped 7 percent, and earnings dipped a steeper 46 percent. With firming prices in the weak display segment, improved volumes and margins, and continued strength from the communications and specialty segments, the company expects to return to its higher margins and recover most of its net income decline through the end of FY2017. Per-share earnings should return to the $1.50–$1.60 range by FY2017 with plenty of upside if currency conditions improve and new technologies take hold.

Reasons to Buy

As Corning puts it, we are now in the "Glass Age"—many promising new technologies are built on a foundation of high-tech glass products, and Corning is the best pure play in this niche. We like companies that stand to benefit no matter how a market plays out. Our CarMax pick benefits whether Ford or Toyota or Hyundai wins; CarMax sells used cars no matter what. At least for glass displays, Corning is in the same position—whether Samsung or Apple comes out on top of the smartphone contest, Corning wins. The explosion in smart devices and the new technologies Corning is likely to bring to that space create some excitement down the road. We think the inevitable advent of wearable mobile computing devices will be a big spark for this company.

Aside from the short-term speed bump in display technologies, the core businesses like fiber optics are doing well, and we expect some of the new technologies like Gorilla Glass and the self-darkening glass products to become core businesses. Across the board, Corning continues to differentiate their products through innovation. The presence of competition, especially Japanese competition, reminds us from time to time that Corning doesn't own the "glass" niche outright, but it is close to owning the innovation in this area; for those who like pure plays in a strong and profitable technology segment, Corning is a good bet.

Finally, Corning has returned plenty of cash to shareholders both in the form of dividends and the share buybacks and appears positioned to do so going forward, especially on the buyback front.

Reasons for Caution

While its product portfolio is broader than it was 15 years ago, supplying well beyond the telecom industry, the company is still subject to business and inventory cycles. Glass, without the right amount of innovation, is a commodity business. There is plenty of foreign competition, and while many of their innovations are differentiated right out of the gate, the struggle is always to keep those products differentiated and to keep the pace of innovation moving.

SECTOR: **Information Technology** ❑ BETA COEFFICIENT: **1.44** ❑ 10-YEAR COMPOUND EARNINGS PER-SHARE GROWTH: **11.5%** ❑ 10-YEAR COMPOUND DIVIDENDS PER-SHARE GROWTH: **NM**

		2008	2009	2010	2011	2012	2013	2014	2015
Revenues (mil)		5,948	5,395	6,632	7,890	8,012	7,819	9,715	9,111
Net income (mil)		2,424	2,114	3,275	2,620	1,728	1,961	2,472	1,339
Earnings per share		1.53	1.35	2.07	1.76	1.15	1.34	1.73	1.00
Dividends per share		0.20	0.20	0.20	0.23	0.32	0.39	0.52	0.36
Cash flow per share		2.01	1.86	2.64	2.49	1.85	2.12	2.79	2.15
Price:	high	28.1	19.5	21.1	23.4	14.6	18.1	23.5	25.2
	low	7.4	9.0	15.5	11.5	10.6	11.6	16.5	15.4

Website: www.corning.com

AGGRESSIVE GROWTH

Costco Wholesale Corporation

Ticker symbol: COST (NASDAQ) ❑ S&P rating: A+ ❑ Value Line financial strength rating: A+ ❑ Current yield: 1.2% ❑ Dividend raises, past 10 years: 10

Company Profile

At this time last year we were musing about whether retailing behemoth Costco had run its course, had any room to grow, whether it was long in the tooth as a retailing concept, too small in the margins, too expensive to buy as a stock, and too "mass" intensive to appeal to today's variety of custom-demanding Millennials. We almost ditched our four-wheel flatbed and headed for the exits—but we instead went down one more aisle and were most pleasantly surprised. Apparently Costco still has plenty of appeal to cost-conscious Millennials—and a whole lot of us cost-conscious "old folks" as well. We're keeping the company on our 2017 shopping list.

Costco Wholesale Corporation operates a multinational chain of membership warehouses, mainly under the Costco Wholesale name, that carry brand-name merchandise at substantially lower prices than are typically found at conventional wholesale or retail sources. The warehouse sales model was designed to help small to medium-sized businesses reduce costs in purchasing for resale and for everyday business use, but as most know, the individual consumer has been their big growth driver. The company capitalizes on size and operational efficiencies, like "cross-docking" shipments directly from manufacturers to stores, to deliver attractive pricing to its customers. Based on sales volume, Costco is the largest membership warehouse club chain and second-largest general retailer in the world.

Costco carries a broad line of product categories, including groceries, appliances, television and media, automotive supplies, toys, hardware, sporting goods, jewelry, cameras, books, housewares, apparel, health and beauty aids, tobacco, furniture, office supplies, and office equipment. The company also operates self-service gasoline stations at a number of its U.S. and Canadian locations. Approximately 57 percent of sales comes from food, beverages, alcohol, sundries, and snacks. Another 16 percent comes from hardlines—electronics, appliances, hardware, automotive, office supplies, and health and beauty aids—and 11 percent from softlines—primarily clothing, housewares, media, jewelry, and domestics. The rest, including gasoline, pharmacy, optical, and other services, form a catchall "other" category. The emergence of Costco as a grocer of choice cannot be missed, and the company reports particular strength in its Fresh Foods lines (meats, produce, deli, and bakery), indicating appeal to the more cost-conscious set of trend-conscious food consumers.

Additionally, Costco Wholesale Industries, a division of the company, operates manufacturing businesses, including special food packaging, optical laboratories, meat processing, and jewelry distribution. A wide and growing variety of products are sold under its "Kirkland" private label.

Costco is open only to members of its tiered membership plan, the higher "Executive" tier at $110 annually (versus $55 for the standard membership) gaining access to reward points and other perks and discounts. Executive members account for about one-third of the base and two-thirds of the sales. In all, there are 81 million members (up 6 percent), with a 91 percent membership renewal rate in the U.S. and Canada.

As of early 2016 Costco has 702 locations: 492 in the United States and Puerto Rico (up from 474), 90 in Canada (versus 89), 36 in Mexico (from 34), 27 in the U.K. (versus 26), 24 in Japan (versus 20), 12 in Korea, 11 in Taiwan, 8 in Australia, and 2 in Spain. The company also has a significant and growing e-commerce presence at www.costco.com. Though it still accounts for only 3 percent of revenues, it grew 20 percent again in FY2015.

Financial Highlights, Fiscal Year 2015

Same-store sales increased about 3 percent in the U.S. but currency effects hurt international sales; the worldwide figure was 1 percent (without currency effects and gasoline, the company estimates a 7 percent worldwide same-store sales gain). For FY2015, total revenues increased 3.2 percent, while lower input costs especially in the fresh food category improved operating margins about 0.3 percent to 4.1 percent; that was good enough for a

13 percent gain in net profit and per-share earnings—and as it turned out, a 13 percent dividend raise as well. For FY2016 Costco expects top-line growth in the 3 percent range on comparable same-store sales growth and the addition of about 30 new warehouses. Margins may attenuate just a bit as a new entry-level wage hike takes effect; forecasts call for a 1–2 percent rise in net earnings, which would have been about 2.5 percent without the wage hike (we support this gesture of good corporate citizenship; the new entry-level wage will be a respectable $13–$13.50/hr.). For FY2017 the picture brightens to a 10 percent net earnings increase fed by lower credit card fees (the switch from AMEX to Visa is described in the following), more house-brand distribution, and growth in more profitable pharmacy, optical, and hearing aid sales. Revenues are slated to rise about 8 percent assuming that currency effects subside.

Membership revenues increased 4 percent to about $2.4 billion annually—an obviously large driver of Costco's $2 billion-plus annual net profit.

Reasons to Buy

Costco is in an attractive best-of-both-worlds niche: It is a price leader consistent with the attitudes of today's more frugal consumer, yet it enjoys a reputation for being more upscale than the competition. We've all heard the boast "I got it at Costco" from even our most affluent and high-minded friends. And of course, there's everybody else.

We also continue to like the international expansion and think the formula will play well overseas—although their ambitious European and Asian plans may be tempered a bit by local preferences for small package sizes and the general lack of storage space. Any U.S. resident who has hosted a visitor from abroad knows that Costco is a favored destination during the visit. We expect international expansion will be one of the company's primary growth drivers over the next ten years. We also applaud the recent move to switch exclusive credit card use from American Express to a co-branded Citigroup Visa credit card (in addition to accepting ordinary Visa and MasterCard debit cards). This card is less expensive and more accessible to most members, and should broaden sales appeal. Costco also gets high marks for employee pay, satisfaction, and loyalty, and for corporate citizenship in general.

In all, the company has a strong brand in a highly competitive sector, reports excellent same-store comps (excluding currency and gasoline, which are both likely to reverse), is gaining market share, and has a strong management track record. Although the 1.2 percent yield isn't that much of an attraction, the company has raised its dividend consistently in double digits since initiating it in 2004.

Reasons for Caution

One concern is the dependence on low-margin food and sundry lines. That said, food does get customers into the store and gets them there more than once a week (overall visit frequency indeed rose 4 percent in 2015). More store traffic means more and more regular store sales overall.

Our biggest concerns continue to be the high share price, low margins, and dependence on membership fees for profitability. All three bring a measure of vulnerability to the stock—a misstep could be costly. On the flip side, management has shown its ability to navigate through difficult periods, the brand is strong, and the prospects for a global footprint, above all else, are encouraging for the future. In light of those three items, we're keeping Costco on our shopping list for 2017.

SECTOR: Retail ▫ BETA COEFFICIENT: 0.58 ▫ 10-YEAR COMPOUND EARNINGS PER-SHARE GROWTH: 10.5% ▫ 10-YEAR COMPOUND DIVIDENDS PER-SHARE GROWTH: 20.5%

	2008	2009	2010	2011	2012	2013	2014	2015
Revenues (mil)	72,483	71,422	77,946	88,915	99,137	105,156	112,640	116,119
Net income (mil)	1,283	1,086	1,307	1,462	1,741	1,977	2,058	2,334
Earnings per share	2.89	2.57	2.93	3.30	3.97	4.49	4.65	5.27
Dividends per share	0.61	0.68	0.77	0.89	1.03	1.17	1.33	1.51
Cash flow per share	4.48	4.25	4.85	5.34	6.13	6.69	7.05	7.90
Price: high	75.2	61.3	73.2	88.7	106.0	126.1	146.8	169.7
low	43.9	38.2	53.4	69.5	78.8	98.6	109.5	117.0

Website: www.costco.com

CONSERVATIVE GROWTH

CVS Health Corporation

Ticker symbol: CVS (NYSE) ▫ S&P rating: BBB+ ▫ Value Line financial strength rating: A+ ▫ Current yield: 1.7% ▫ Dividend raises, past 10 years: 10

Company Profile

Stanley and Sid Goldstein were distributing health and beauty products in the early 1960s when they decided to branch out into retailing, opening their first Consumer Value Store in Lowell, MA, in 1963. The CVS chain had grown to 40 outlets by 1969, the year they sold the business to Melville Shoes. Melville underwent a restructuring in the mid-1990s, spinning off CVS and other retail units.

Stan and Sid should be proud. CVS is now the largest pharmacy healthcare provider in the United States and ranks tenth on the *Fortune* 500 list. In keeping with its mission, two years ago it changed its name from "CVS Caremark" to "CVS Health." Its flagship Retail Pharmacy domestic drugstore chain operates 9,655 retail and specialty pharmacy stores in 40 states, the District of Columbia, and now Brazil. The company holds the leading market share in 88 of the 100 largest U.S. drugstore markets, more than any other retail drugstore chain. Over time, it has expanded through acquiring other players in the category—Osco, Sav-On, Eckerd, and Longs Drugs. CVS's purchase of Longs Drugs in 2008 vaulted the company into the lead position in the U.S. drug retail market, ahead of Walgreens.

Stores are situated primarily in strip shopping centers or free-standing locations, with a typical store ranging in size from 8,000–13,000 square feet. Most new units being built are based on either a 10,000-square-foot or 12,000-square-foot prototype building that typically includes a drive-thru pharmacy. Prescriptions generate over 70 percent of Retail Pharmacy sales, which in turn makes up about 36 percent of the company's total sales and is far more profitable, generating 81 percent of gross profits. The company estimates it owns 21.8 percent of the overall retail pharmacy market.

The Caremark acquisition in 2007 transformed CVS from strictly a retailer into the nation's leading manager of pharmacy benefits, the middleman between pharmaceutical companies and individuals with drug benefit coverage. The Caremark acquisition forms the core of the company's Pharmacy Benefits Management (PBM) operations, which have some 65,000 pharmacy outlets including hospitals and clinics as well as the previously mentioned retail stores. The company now manages about 1.7 billion prescriptions a year to 65 million plan members, and the Pharmacy Services segment now makes up about 64 percent of sales—but only 19 percent of gross profit. This is a low-margin business, with gross profit of about 5 percent of revenue versus more than 30 percent for the Retail Pharmacy segment.

Part of the Retail Pharmacy segment, the company's MinuteClinic concept is especially interesting in today's climate of managing healthcare costs. CVS now has 1,135 clinics (including 80 new clinics in Target stores—see following) in 33 states and D.C., offering basic health services like flu shots given by 2,200 nurse practitioners and physician's assistants in a convenient retail environment. The company opened 161 new stores and closed 31 in 2015. Plans are to grow MinuteClinic into 1,500 locations in 35 states by 2017. The concept gradually is gaining mainstream acceptance with 28 million patient visits to date—and of course, those clinics located in CVS stores bring traffic to those stores. The company also operates mail order and online pharmacies for regular and chronically ill patients.

Finally, CVS made two key acquisitions in 2015. First, it became the operator of more than 1,600 pharmacies located in Target stores, filling some 100 million prescriptions annually. There is also a network of 80 health clinics within these stores. That transition will be finished by mid-2016, with new strategies designed to convert Target shoppers to the embedded CVS-operated pharmacies. Second was the purchase of Omnicare to serve the skilled nursing and long-term care markets, also to be completed by mid-2016.

Financial Highlights, Fiscal Year 2015

Continued negative effects of discontinued tobacco sales, another less-severe flu season, and certain provisions of the Affordable Care Act were offset by strong performance in pharmacy benefits, retail pharmacy, and acquisitions to bring a 10 percent top-line gain for the second year in a row, substantial for a company of this size. Likewise, net earnings were up 10 percent, and per-share earnings, on the back of a 39 million share buyback, were up 15 percent. Acquisitions will help propel revenues ahead 17–18 percent in FY2016 with per-share earnings ahead 11–14 percent (another $4 billion is earmarked for buybacks). Revenue growth will attenuate to a still-healthy 8–9 percent in FY2017 with per-share earnings up 12–15 percent. The company is on track to retire all the shares issued since the Caremark acquisition—some 600 million of them—having retired approximately 380 million to date.

Reasons to Buy

CVS is clearly a smartly diversified market leader and knows how to take advantage of that position without alienating customers or key healthcare payers. What's more, its "retail" location in the healthcare food chain positions it perfectly to capitalize on the initiatives of the Affordable Care Act: more patients getting more and lower-cost services. This, of course, all comes on top of favorable demographics: an aging population, one also ever more willing to pay for convenience, and a growing acceptance of CVS as a local convenience store for needs beyond health and personal care products. We like the fact that the company made a tough decision in 2014 to discontinue tobacco and came through with stellar financials.

The overall strategy seems to be to grow market share and scale both with its retail operations and with its pharmacy benefits businesses. Cross-selling of prescriptions, retail products, and health services all seems to be working well and is an important part of the strategy.

These moderate and steady gains have turned into plenty of return for shareholders in the form of cash dividends, steady and large share buybacks, and resulting share price appreciation, and CVS continues to be one of the surer bets on our list to continue this trend.

Reasons for Caution

The business model is intact and positioned for growth as the ACA becomes standard and as demographics shift in CVS's favor. That, of course, could change dramatically if political forces undermine ACA or force big changes in it. The stock continues to rise steadily, and while we can see the reasons why, it does force new investors to find good entry points. A lot of the good news has already been factored in.

SECTOR: Retail ▫ BETA COEFFICIENT: 0.85 ▫ 10-YEAR COMPOUND EARNINGS PER-SHARE GROWTH: 15.0% ▫ 10-YEAR COMPOUND DIVIDENDS PER-SHARE GROWTH: 22.0%

	2008	2009	2010	2011	2012	2013	2014	2015
Revenues (mil)	87.5	98.7	98.0	107.2	123.1	126.7	139.4	153.2
Net income (mil)	3,589	3,803	3,700	3,766	4,394	4,902	5,255	5,810
Earnings per share	2.44	2.63	2.67	2.80	3.43	4.00	4.51	5.16
Dividends per share	0.26	0.30	0.35	0.50	0.65	0.90	1.10	1.40
Cash flow per share	3.37	3.73	3.75	4.10	4.99	5.74	6.30	7.18
Price: high	44.3	38.3	37.8	39.5	49.8	72.0	98.6	113.6
low	23.2	23.7	26.8	31.3	41.0	49.9	64.9	81.4

Website: www.cvs.com

AGGRESSIVE GROWTH

Daktronics, Inc.

Ticker symbol: DAKT (NASDAQ) ▫ S&P rating: NR ▫ Value Line financial strength rating: B+ ▫ Current yield: 4.8% ▫ Dividend raises, past 10 years: 7

Company Profile

You're driving down the highway. You're thinking about getting rid of a month's worth of grime and dirt and crud from your car. Suddenly, in vivid Technicolor, you see a billboard ahead on your right. Not just any old indifferent and ignorable billboard displaying the same old thing months on end. It's brightly lit. It flashes an offer. Five Star Car Wash, at this exit, has a "Today Only—25 Percent Off" special. A few minutes ago you passed an electronic sign flashing "Road Work Ahead—Current Delay 30 Minutes." So, you tap the brakes, hit the right lane, and off the interstate you go. A win-win—you have a clean car, and the car wash, having a lighter day than usual and temporarily pricing its services accordingly, gets another unit through their system.

Hockey great Wayne Gretzky made famous the idea of "skating where the puck is going," and it's still one of our favorite investing maxims. Like it or not, we think such real-time, highly visual signage is where the puck is going in marketing—real-time visual displays to complement your real-time mobile devices. Give it time, and it will come. Give it time, and there will be real-time visual graphic displays on park benches and subway entrances. Give it time, and there will be "digital street furniture" and such just about everywhere. So how do you invest in this looming megatrend? There's a small company located almost literally in the middle of nowhere—Brookings, South Dakota—that makes this stuff. Chances are this company made both of the signs mentioned previously. "Digital Street Furniture" is actually one of their product lines. Their core and founding business is really the large multimedia scoreboards in place in a growing number of sports arenas. The company, Daktronics, has a hand in an assortment of places where digital display technology can make a difference in outdoor environments, from $40 million scoreboards to the variable dollars-and-cents-per-gallon digital displays outside your local gas station.

Daktronics is the world's leading supplier of electronic scoreboards, large electronic display systems, digital messaging solutions, and related software and support services for sporting, commercial, and transportation applications. The company offers everything from small signs and scoreboards costing under $1,000 to the large $40 million sports-complex scoreboards mentioned previously.

Business segments include Commercial, Live Events, High School Parks and Recreation, Transportation, and International: These groups are organized around customer segments and are all set up to create and sell unique applications of the core product lines of the company, which include video display systems, scoring and timing systems, digital billboards, digital street furniture, and simpler message displays like price, time, and temperature displays. Most of the company's products are based on LED technology with low to high resolution and embedded digital controllers. Here is a bit more "color" on the five segments:

- Commercial (27 percent of 2015 revenue) sells a variety of digital signage to auto dealer, restaurant, gaming, retail petroleum (gas stations, mainly), and shopping center markets. Vivid video displays used for architectural or commercial purposes as part of the full building design is another emerging subsegment of this business.
- Live Events (38 percent of revenue, 18 percent growth) produces the traditional and some highly customized scoreboards, as well as signs for entertainment venues, including programmable displays, parking information signs, and even specialized signs for places of worship.
- High School Park and Recreation (11 percent). Included here are not only digital-age marquee signs for theaters and other venues but also for the box office, merchandise sales areas, and others.
- Transportation (8 percent). You've seen the freeway signs; there is also plenty of digital signage in airports, train stations, and other mass transit facilities.
- International (17 percent) sells all applications into international markets.

Overall, Daktronics has about a 30 percent share of the LED video display market, making it the number one player. In early 2016 the company acquired Canadian digital media solutions provider ADFLOW Networks, signaling a greater emphasis on providing complete solutions, not just LED hardware. That move, and new ultra-high definition and outdoor products reflect a greater depth and breadth of offerings in this market.

The company has about 2,750 employees—including, somewhat unusually, about 400 interns and students on the payroll mostly from the local South Dakota State University. Retired cofounder and chairman Aelred

J. Kurtenbach, a PhD electrical engineer and professor at SDSU, owns 5.1 percent of the shares. His son, Reece A. Kurtenbach, runs the company. The website, at www.daktronics.com, is a fun and instructive ride.

Financial Highlights, Fiscal Year 2015

Several crosscurrents affected the business again in FY2015—mostly negatively. The strong dollar hurt (the good news is that the International segment topped $100 million for the first time). The overall business mix shifted toward large sports arena installations, which are less profitable due to subcontracting, tight deadlines, and in 2015, higher-than-expected warranty expenses. Relatively flat volumes in other segments, in part due to competition, reduced throughput, which increased unit costs. Revenues declined just over 4 percent, while net income dropped about 50 percent. FY2016 and FY2017 bring higher backlogs and decent prospects in all businesses. Revenues should rise in the 8–10 percent range annually. More volume to absorb fixed costs, less subcontracting, improved mix, and reduced warranty costs should bring FY2016 earnings back to previous levels, with a 20 percent improvement to $25 million in FY2017 as operating and net profit margins recover. The dividend, already generous for a company of this size, may be in for ongoing 20 percent raises if these earnings numbers materialize; the company has strong cash flows and manages them carefully.

Reasons to Buy

Since beaches and surf weren't part of the landscape when we were growing up in the Midwest, like any normal kids we were fascinated with signs of all kinds. Daktronics takes signs to a new level.

We continue to feel that such digital signage is a big part of the future of mass, real-time marketing communications—a "system" including your mobile device plus electronic signage—like it or not. Overall, we like situations where a core technology is applied successfully to an ever-larger number of end markets. Too, we think as such digital signage becomes more mainstream, the company will be able to produce in larger volumes, even mass-produce more of their applications, which should drive down unit costs and increase profitability. We see advantages in the location, too—a dedicated work force and low cost of doing business. Too, the company has virtually no debt.

All this said, Daktronics hasn't performed as well as hoped for when we added it to our *100 Best* list in 2015 in an attempt to get a bit of niche technology and small-cap growth "energy" into the mix. The company just hasn't hit its stride (nor its own production capacity) with its business, though backlogs and order flows remain fairly strong. Our patience is paid for in part by the attractive dividend, and we hope for an eventual "breakout" in this enticing market. We may not be wrong, just early.

Reasons for Caution

While the company is the top player in its market, there is plenty of product and price competition in the form of major Japanese firms like Mitsubishi (and if you've been to Tokyo, you know how mainstream digital signage can be). We do also wonder if environmental movements will rise up to quell what could easily become overstimulating visual "pollution," but so far to our knowledge this hasn't happened on a large scale.

More conventionally, Daktronics clearly has a riskier profile than most of our picks. Order flow and delivery timing can vary considerably especially in the Live Events segment, but we continue to think the business will smooth out considerably once electronic commercial signage becomes more mainstream.

SECTOR: **Information Technology** ❑ BETA COEFFICIENT: **1.40** ❑ 10-YEAR COMPOUND EARNINGS PER-SHARE GROWTH: **2.5%** ❑ 10-YEAR COMPOUND DIVIDENDS PER-SHARE GROWTH: **20.0%**

	2008	2009	2010	2011	2012	2013	2014	2015
Revenues (mil)	582	393	442	489	518	552	616	590
Net income (mil)	26.4	(7.0)	14.2	8.5	22.8	22.2	20.9	10.0
Earnings per share	0.64	(0.17)	0.34	0.20	0.53	0.51	0.47	0.20
Dividends per share	0.09	0.10	0.10	0.22	0.23	0.39	0.40	0.40
Cash flow per share	1.25	0.37	0.81	0.62	0.91	0.85	0.82	0.60
Price: high	23.1	10.5	17.3	16.7	11.9	16.1	15.6	13.2
low	5.7	5.9	7.1	8.0	6.3	9.4	10.8	7.2

Website: www.daktronics.com

AGGRESSIVE GROWTH

Deere & Company

Ticker symbol: DE (NYSE) ❑ S&P rating: A ❑ Value Line financial strength rating: A++ ❑ Current yield: 3.1% ❑ Dividend raises, past 10 years: 10

Company Profile

Every year several stocks test our mettle and conviction as long-term investors. This year (and last year for that matter, and perhaps next year as well),

Deere & Co. falls into that category. The business right now—plain and simple—sucks! We don't use that word very often but sometimes there is no better word to describe current business conditions—and, importantly, what we think is the bottom of a cycle. Farm incomes dropped 38 percent last year, sales dipped 22 percent in FY2015 (and perhaps as much as 8 percent further in FY2016), the strong dollar has cut into foreign sales, and inventories are piling up at dealerships. What's to like? Has the business changed forever? We think not. Agriculture will always be important and will expand in importance as populations grow and become more affluent. The cycle will turn back upward. And if it helps alleviate our doubts, Warren Buffett has raised his stake by a third, the largest new acquisition in 2015, to a 5 percent stake in DE's shares. Such endorsements cannot be ignored.

Founded in 1837, Deere & Company grew from a one-man blacksmith shop into a worldwide corporation that today does business in more than 160 countries and employs more than 57,000 people around the globe. Deere has a diverse base of operations reporting into three segments: Agriculture and Turf, Construction and Forestry, and Financial Services.

Deere has been the world's premier producer of agricultural equipment for nearly 50 years. The Agriculture and Turf segment produces and distributes tractors, loaders, combines, harvesters, seeding, mowers, hay baling, tilling, crop care and application, and other equipment. If it's used on a farm and requires an engine, Deere likely offers it.

Additionally, over the years, the company has developed and expanded lines of turf and utility equipment, including riding lawn equipment and walk-behind mowers, golf course equipment, utility vehicles, and commercial mowing and snow-removal equipment. Deere also offers a broad line of associated implements; integrated agricultural management systems technology and solutions; precision agricultural irrigation equipment and supplies; landscape and nursery products; and other outdoor power products.

With the Construction and Forestry segment, Deere is also the world's leading manufacturer of forestry equipment and a major manufacturer of heavy construction machines (Caterpillar is still the market leader in this segment). Major lines include construction, earthmoving, material-handling, and timber-harvesting machines including but not limited to backhoe loaders; crawler dozers and loaders; four-wheel-drive loaders; excavators; motor graders; articulated dump trucks; landscape loaders; skid-steer loaders; and log skidders, feller bunchers, log loaders, log forwarders, log harvesters, and related attachments.

As the company reports it, revenue for the Agriculture and Turf segment is about 75 percent of the $26 billion in FY2015 revenue; the Construction and Forestry segment makes up the remainder. The Financial Services segment rolls its revenue into the other segments, and only segment profits are reported, but that segment produces about 20 percent of total net profit.

The Financial Services segment includes John Deere Credit, which is one of the largest equipment finance companies in the United States, with more than 1.8 million accounts. Overall, international sales continue to account for 37 percent of the total.

Financial Highlights, Fiscal Year 2015

We've already noted the near-disastrous sales trends. Indeed, the company does not expect to recover to 2014 sales levels even by the end of the decade. The better news lies in earnings and cash flow. While obviously hurting, with per-share earnings down some 50 percent since 2013, they are still substantially positive at a projected $4.25 per share in FY2016 and should regain footing in FY2017 and beyond, as we think sales will too. Per-share cash flows are still in the $6–$7 range, the balance sheet is strong, and the dividend is still rising. Although buybacks have slowed, the company has retired 20 percent of its float since 2011. Deere may become a classic case study in managing a down cycle for better days ahead. We'll see.

Reasons to Buy

As the saying goes, "Everything is a cycle"—and we're placing our bets that this, too, shall pass and the aforementioned heavy use of Deere machinery, coupled with the inevitable long-term growth in agriculture will put the company back on top of its game in a few years. Who can argue about the long-term growth in agriculture, since the global population is predicted to increase 50 percent by 2050 and as global standards of living increase on top of that? Indeed, the company reminds us that global grain demand has already increased 40 percent just from 2000 through 2014. And then, there's the Buffett factor. There you have it: our reasons for keeping Deere on our list despite the stumble.

We're also big fans of the brand and historic excellence. "Nothing runs like a Deere" is the company's apt slogan, and as far as industrial companies go, Deere continues to be a poster child for U.S. industrial ingenuity and excellence. It has an outstanding brand (and one of the most popular logos for hats, jackets, and so on, worn by people who have barely seen a farm field!) and reputation in the agriculture industry, and we see the ag industry as strong and strategic far into the future as global living standards improve and emerging markets develop.

Longer term, farm incomes should rise worldwide, and the company continues to invest in developing markets. Too, we think that innovation is a plus—Deere leads its competitors in R&D investment (more than 5.5 percent of sales), bringing the Internet and GPS to farming and farming machines; new engines also promise greater fuel economy and reduced emissions.

Beyond its products, Deere has established an almost unassailable brand leadership with its services and customer-centered innovations. Deere, more than others, puts its people in the field (literally) to figure out what agriculture professionals really need, and they work with their customers closely to sell their products through a solid dealer network.

Finally, the company continues to show commitment to shareholders by returning more than 50 percent of cash generated over the past ten years to shareholders in the form of dividends and share buybacks.

Reasons for Caution

Clearly, the company is plowing through an extraordinarily difficult period—and as we said, our commitment to the long term is being severely tested. The company is, and always will be, vulnerable to cycles in the farm sector. The normal cycle, and in particular indelible memories of 1980s farm difficulties, can cause the farmers who buy this stuff to get cautious pretty quickly. All in all, farming will always be with us, both in the U.S. and overseas, and there will always be a demand for machines and especially smarter, more efficient ones—Deere has an enormous brand and long-term track record. "Sell when there's something better to buy"—and we see nothing better to buy in this strategically important segment of the economy.

SECTOR: **Industrials** ▫ BETA COEFFICIENT: **1.12** ▫ 10-YEAR COMPOUND EARNINGS PER-SHARE GROWTH: **13.0%** ▫ 10-YEAR COMPOUND DIVIDENDS PER-SHARE GROWTH: **15.5%**

	2008	2009	2010	2011	2012	2013	2014	2015
Revenues (mil)	25,804	20,756	23,573	29,466	33,501	34,998	32,961	25,775
Net income (mil)	2,053	1,198	1,865	2,799	3,065	3,533	3,162	1,937
Earnings per share	4.70	2.82	4.35	6.63	7.64	9.08	8.53	5.76
Dividends per share	1.06	1.12	1.16	1.52	1.79	1.99	2.22	2.40
Cash flow per share	6.01	4.05	5.72	8.34	9.56	11.45	11.45	8.62
Price: high	94.9	56.9	84.9	99.8	89.7	95.6	94.9	98.2
low	28.5	24.5	46.3	59.9	69.5	79.5	76.9	71.9

Website: **www.deere.com**

E. I. du Pont de Nemours and Company (DuPont)

Ticker symbol: DD (NYSE) ❑ S&P rating: A ❑ Value Line financial strength rating: A++ ❑ Current yield: 2.4% ❑ Dividend raises, past 10 years: 7

Company Profile

"When in doubt, reorganize." This popular satire about Corporate America could certainly apply to DuPont, which withstood a rancorous proxy fight early in 2015 calling for a breakup of the company only to take on a bigger shakeup thereafter. The management structure stayed intact but was convinced to shed some low-margin commodity businesses. If that wasn't enough, later in the year it announced a mega-merger with rival chemical producer Dow Chemical. And if *that* wasn't enough, it announced plans to split the combined company into three separate businesses, more or less accomplishing what Nelson Peltz's Trian Fund had imagined in the first place—although on a much larger scale than he probably imagined. It took us a while to come to this conclusion, but we feel DuPont and its ultimate spinoffs will create shareholder value and provide some attractive investment choices, some and maybe all of which will qualify independently as entries in *100 Best Stocks*. So we'll keep DuPont on our list and wait to see what ultimately shakes out.

"The miracles of science" is the slogan and rallying cry of this now-$25 billion-plus science and technology juggernaut, originally founded in 1802 to make gunpowder. The spinoff of the Performance Chemicals business into a separate company called "Chemours"—which took refrigerants, titanium dioxide pigments, a number of other chemical commodities, and about $6.5 billion in revenue out of the picture—took place in mid-2015. The numbers presented do not include the Chemours business, which was spun off to shareholders, and also reflect an earlier spinoff of the Performance Coatings business.

Although the company is still known to many as a cyclical diversified chemical company making a host of lifeless chemical products and ingredients, many by the tank car–load, with recent changes today's DuPont continues to reawaken as a world leader in science and technology with important end-product ingredients in a range of disciplines, including biotechnology, electronics, materials and science, safety and security, and synthetic fibers.

The company has always been a technology leader with such well-known inventions as Nylon and Rayon in earlier years, and Teflon and Kevlar more recently. The vision and guiding philosophy for the core DuPont business is still "market- driven science," and it has delivered successfully on that vision.

Today's DuPont looks at itself as a leader in three fields: Agriculture & Nutrition, Industrial Biosciences, and Advanced Materials.

- Within the Agriculture & Nutrition segment is the Agriculture business unit itself. Agriculture delivers a portfolio of products and services specifically targeted to achieve gains in crop yields and productivity, including Pioneer brand seed products and well-established brands of insecticides, fungicides, and herbicides. Pioneer develops, produces, and markets corn hybrid and soybean varieties and sells wheat, rice, sunflower, canola, and other seeds under the Pioneer and other brand names. DuPont also sells a line of crop protection products for field and orchard agriculture. The smaller Nutrition and Health unit consists of the recently acquired Danisco's specialty food ingredients business and Solae, a majority-owned venture with Bunge Limited, which is engaged in developing soy-based technologies. The unit provides solutions for specialty food ingredients, health, and safety. Products include cultures, emulsifiers, gums, natural sweeteners, and soy-based food.

- The Industrial Biosciences unit is engaged in developing and manufacturing a wide range of enzymes, the biocatalysts that enable chemical reactions, on a large scale. The segment's enzymes add value and functionality to a broad range of products and processes, such as animal nutrition, detergents, food manufacturing, ethanol production, and industrial applications.

- The Advanced Materials segment is made up of Electronics and Communications, which makes a line of high-tech materials for the semiconductor industry, including ceramic packages and LCD materials. E&C supplies differentiated materials and systems for photovoltaics (solar), consumer electronics, displays, and advanced printing. It also includes the Performance Materials business unit, which supplies high-performance polymers, films, plastics, and substrates to a variety of industries from automotive to aerospace and consumer durable goods manufacturers and many others, and the Safety and Protection unit, maker of protective fibers and clothing, including bulletproof apparel; disinfectants; and protective building surfaces—Tyvek house wrap is one of the bigger brands here.

Ordinarily the story would stop here, and we would move on with the financial presentation. But not in this case. As mentioned previously, the deck was reshuffled again in a big way, with the announcement of a blockbuster merger with rival Dow. At first, we did not understand this merger, for it seemed to bring back many of the commodity chemical businesses DD had just rid itself of, and we're still concerned about regulatory scrutiny. But the company shortly afterward proposed a split of the combined company into a focused Agriculture business, a Materials Science business, and a Specialty Products business. We think these focused businesses have promise both from an innovation and from a size and scale perspective; in the meantime, the combined company will clean house to the tune of $3 billion in expenses and be able to better tap into growth and growth synergies once the split takes place. That's the plan, anyway.

Financial Highlights, Fiscal Year 2015

With all of these changes in the air, a review of FY2015 performance seems almost anticlimactic, and projections forward are difficult to make as well. Softness in the agriculture business and general manufacturing worldwide led to a slight drop in revenues and a more pronounced drop in net earnings, although an aggressive 4 percent share buyback moderated the per-share earnings slide somewhat. With limited visibility, revenues are expected to stay generally flat through 2017 (with some spinoffs possible due to antitrust concerns) with earnings recovering upward 15–20 percent from current levels. A lot, of course, has to do with the timing of the reorganization; faster would be better for both revenues and expenses. Projections through the end of the decade are much stronger, which is one reason why we've held onto this issue.

Reasons to Buy

The transformation, long waiting in the wings, looks anything but tentative and should allow DuPont (and its brother Dow) to settle into an effective alignment for the long term. The product pipeline continues to be full, individual product margins remain strong, the product mix is improving, and the company's biggest moneymakers still dominate their markets. Exits from commodity businesses, lower commodity costs, and a large slate of cost cuts should help the bottom line.

The company—and its descendants—will continue to capitalize on "global megatrends": population growth, alternative energy production, and so forth. The improvement of worldwide food production is at the center of its new growth initiatives. The combined businesses have brand leadership in many important categories and have been committed to total shareholder returns with a solid dividend track record and an aggressive share buyback program.

Reasons for Caution

Mergers and reorganizations are complex, and DuPont is taking on both in a big way. Things could change or fall apart, and the list of possible distractions is long—there is some risk here. DuPont is no longer a "quiet" stock suitable for buying and putting away for the long term. While we do think there is unrealized value down the road, new and existing shareholders will have to keep track of the situation as it develops. It's way too soon to declare "success."

SECTOR: **Materials** ◻ BETA COEFFICIENT: **1.76** ◻ 10-YEAR COMPOUND EARNINGS PER-SHARE GROWTH: **5.5%** ◻ 10-YEAR COMPOUND DIVIDENDS PER-SHARE GROWTH: **2.5%**

	2008	2009	2010	2011	2012	2013	2014	2015
Revenues (mil)	30,529	26,109	31,505	37,961	34,812	35,734	34,723	25,130
Net income (mil)	2,477	1,853	3,032	3,698	3,137	3,632	3,703	2,503
Earnings per share	2.73	2.04	3.28	3.93	3.33	3.68	4.01	2.77
Dividends per share	1.64	1.64	1.64	1.64	1.70	1.78	1.84	1.72
Cash flow per share	4.33	3.70	4.80	5.67	5.19	5.65	5.87	4.54
Price: high	52.5	35.6	50.2	57.0	57.5	65.0	75.8	80.6
low	21.3	16.0	31.9	37.1	41.7	45.1	59.3	47.1

Website: www.dupont.com

CONSERVATIVE GROWTH

Eastman Chemical Company

Ticker symbol: EMN (NYSE) ◻ S&P rating: BBB ◻ Value Line financial strength rating: A ◻ Current yield: 3.1% ◻ Dividend raises, past 10 years: 6

Company Profile

Spun off in 1993 from the bankrupted Eastman Kodak, Eastman Chemical is one of those "better living through chemistry" companies with a history of solving problems and providing standard, high-tech, and high-precision materials to industries ranging from food and beverage to toys to medical equipment to computers and electronics. The Eastman mission could be almost be refined into "better living through *polymer* chemistry"—the chemical building blocks, mostly sourced from petroleum and other feedstocks known as hydrocarbons that turn into all things useful such as plastics, paints, coatings, inks, and the like. Many of their products are "intermediaries," used to manufacture *other* chemicals and products. When speaking the language of the company you quickly pick up expressions like "olefin cycle" and "phthalate," among the more difficult concepts and spelling challenges, like "ophthalmology." We've encountered these before in the *100 Best Stocks* space.

The company is organized into five product segments, all of which have something more or less to do with petrochemicals:

- *Advanced Materials* (24 percent of 2015 sales) produces and markets specialty plastics, interlayers, and films, including copolyesters, cellulose esters, and safety glass, plastic, and window film products for the automotive and transportation, building materials, LCD and display manufacturing, health and wellness, and durable goods industries.
- *Additives & Functional Products* (19 percent) produces chemical products for the coatings industry and for tires, paints, inks, building materials, durable goods, and consumables markets. Key technology platforms include rubber additives, cellulosic polymers, ketones, coalescents, polyester polymers olefins, and hydrocarbon resins.
- *Fibers* (15 percent) produces acetate tow, triacetin, and solution-dyed acetate yarns for the apparel, filtration, tobacco (filters), fabric, home furnishings, medical tape, and other industries.
- *Additives & Plasticizers* (14 percent) produces intermediary products, mainly adhesive resins and plasticizers, sold into the consumables, building materials, health and wellness, industrial chemicals, and durable goods markets.
- *Specialty Fluids and Intermediates* (27 percent) is a catchall for other products that don't fall into the other segments, including new or custom-made polymer-based products for key customers. Acetic acid, ethylene, paint and building materials intermediaries, agrichemicals, and aviation hydraulic fluid are among the many products in this group.

Obviously there could be considerably more detail in these descriptions, but it would probably only be meaningful to those with a strong chemistry or materials background. Bottom line: Eastman makes a lot of strategically important materials that support a lot of manufacturing processes for common and fairly high-volume items, such as beer bottles, automotive glass, and LCD displays. Additionally, these materials are used in considerable amounts in overseas manufacturing. Eastman has adapted by setting up plants in 16 countries and driving foreign sales to 57 percent of the total. By region, sales are 46 percent from North America, 27 percent Asia-Pacific, 22 percent EMEA, and 5 percent Latin America.

Financial Highlights, Fiscal Year 2015

The strengthening dollar and a slowdown in global manufacturing activity, especially in the U.S. and China, led to lackluster results in FY2015 and most likely FY2016. Strength was noted in the Additives & Plasticizers and Advanced Materials businesses while the Fibers and Specialty Fluids lines showed weakness—likely reflecting stronger pricing environments and demand for more specialized niche products. FY2015 revenues rose a very modest 1 percent and are expected to remain flat through FY2016. Net earnings, on the other hand, rose a healthy 13 percent on reduced input costs, efficiency measures, and new strength from recent acquisitions. For FY2017 the company expects improvements in overseas volumes, particularly from emerging economies, and from a (we hope) stabilization of the dollar. Share counts should remain fairly constant over the next few years as the company pays down debt related to acquisitions; however, healthy dividend increases in the low double-digit range appear likely.

Reasons to Buy

Eastman is currently in a holding pattern as it digests acquisitions and waits for the worldwide manufacturing economy and the dollar to turn around. Like many *100 Best* picks, this well-managed enterprise has used the lag period to increase efficiency and gain ground on weaker players and should emerge quite well eventually.

Although Eastman lies on the edge of the "buy businesses you understand" test, the company really does produce things vitally important to manufacturing mainstream and advanced products. Successful product development has always been a key strength for Eastman. Eastman will benefit from the continued strength in domestic manufacturing, although its international operations, particularly in Asia, are also a source of strength. Eastman continues to position itself for continued moderate organic growth with a strong base of repeat business, a more favorable cost structure, and excellent cash flow. Recent share prices and increasing dividends indicate a buying opportunity.

Reasons for Caution

Eastman's fortunes will follow those of the larger manufacturing sector in general and, to a lesser extent, the feedstock (petroleum) market more specifically. Too, their fourth-largest end market by sales volume is tobacco (filter materials) at 15 percent of sales—although it is getting replaced by other product categories, it will be a drag on growth. There is also some concern about the health effects of phthalates, one of their key plasticizer products, although they do sell a line of non-phthalate plasticizers.

Eastman did take on a lot of debt with the Solutia and other acquisitions but is deploying cash actively to pay down this debt. That said, the debt payments, projected in the billions over the next few years, has taken share repurchases off the table for the time being. We are a bit more concerned with the debt level (at 65 percent of total capital recently, down from 68 percent last year) than we were, but projections call for that to be reduced to 46 percent, closer to its long-term norm. The acquisitions nearly doubled the size of the company in five years—such a big bite does produce some management risks in our opinion. That said, Eastman has all the earmarks of a well-managed company.

SECTOR: Materials ❑ BETA COEFFICIENT: 1.65 ❑ 10-YEAR COMPOUND EARNINGS PER-SHARE GROWTH: 22.0% ❑ 10-YEAR COMPOUND DIVIDENDS PER-SHARE GROWTH: 3.5%

	2008	2009	2010	2011	2012	2013	2014	2015
Revenues (mil)	6,720	5,047	5,842	7,178	8,102	9,350	9,527	9,648
Net income (mil)	342	265	514	653	802	1,008	751	848
Earnings per share	2.25	1.82	3.48	4.56	5.38	6.45	4.95	5.66
Dividends per share	0.88	0.88	0.90	0.99	1.08	1.25	1.40	1.60
Cash flow per share	4.20	3.72	5.62	6.76	7.55	9.45	8.08	9.60
Price: high	39.1	31.0	42.3	55.4	68.2	83.0	90.6	83.9
low	12.9	8.9	25.9	32.4	39.2	63.5	70.4	62.8

Website: www.eastman.com

GROWTH AND INCOME

Empire State Realty Trust

Ticker symbol: ESRT (NYSE) ❑ S&P rating: NR ❑ Value Line financial strength rating: NR ❑ Current yield: 1.9% ❑ Dividend raises, past 10 years: 1

Company Profile

The Empire State Building is a national treasure. Beautifully designed, it is an emblem of New York business well known to the world. It is such an emblem that more than 4 million people came to visit it last year, just to go up to the observation deck; 65 percent of them were from overseas. That observation deck is a $112 million annual icing on the cake for what we still think is an exciting new REIT built around the Empire State Building. But is this REIT just the Empire State Building? No—it has diversified to hold 14 office buildings in key locations across the New York area, nine in Manhattan and five others in or near major transportation hubs in White Plains, NY, and Stamford and Norwalk, CT. ESRT also owns six standalone retail properties, four in Manhattan and two in Connecticut. The Empire State Realty Trust is a pure play on real estate in the most dynamic and sought-after real estate market in the world.

The Empire State Realty Trust was formed in 2011 and went public in October 2013. As a REIT, ESRT is relatively small in comparison to other real estate trusts, but they make up for that in their strengths, which they call out quite clearly in their presentations:

- *Unique, irreplaceable properties.* ESRT is a pure play in the New York area, one of the world's most prized office markets; the cornerstone of their base, the Empire State Building, is one of the most recognized icons in the world. Another concentration of office properties is in the revitalizing 34th Street and Broadway area, home of the Macy's flagship store.
- *Expertise in reconditioning such properties.* The Empire State Building is beautiful, particularly for you fans of classic Art Deco architecture. But it needed a facelift—and got a big one from ESRT. In addition to managing properties, ESRT has a construction arm specializing in reconditioning and repurposing buildings and spaces for tenant use. The Empire State Building got a major energy retrofit; it is a showcase project and is estimated to save some tenants 38 percent and as much as 57 percent on energy costs (check out www.esbsustainability.com for

details); it got a new fitness center for tenants also. ESRT will lease you "white box" space—or spaces tailored to your needs. ESRT is performing energy and functionality upgrades to other vintage buildings as well. It is part of their strategy to increase attractiveness . . . and of course, rents.

In area, ESRT owns and manages about 10 million rentable square feet; 74 percent of that is Manhattan office space, 19 percent is Greater New York space, and 7.2 percent is dedicated retail, mostly in Manhattan. The Empire State Building itself is about 2.7 million square feet, or about 27 percent of the rentable space in the trust. The client list is a corporate who's who, with older companies like Macy's, Bank of America, Johnson Controls, and Bulova mixed in with latter-day names like LinkedIn, Expedia, and Shutterstock. The client base is diverse, with just 18 percent being the "typical" New York financial industry names. About 94 percent of current office space is leased; 93 percent of retail is also rented. Most clients sign long-term leases of ten years or so, and the company is trying to move to large block or entire floor leases.

For 2015, the roughly $658 million in annual revenue breaks down as follows: 60 percent Manhattan office, 12 percent Greater New York Metro office, and 11 percent retail. What about the other 17 percent? you may ask. Look up, please. It's from the Observatory, split between the 86th and 102nd floor of the Empire State Building. We mentioned it at the beginning of this narrative—the Observatory brought in $112 million in FY2015, a nice "kicker" to the business, one that most REITs don't have.

Financially, ESRT touts what they refer to as "embedded, derisked growth." The "embedded" part refers to loyal tenants and a carefully managed "laddering" of lease expirations; the company attempts to have 5–10 percent of its lease base expire each year. Those expirations will be renewed at higher rates, to include not just inflation but also to cover improvements. ESRT estimates that rents will grow overall 12–27 percent per year through 2020 as leases expire. "Derisked" refers to this smooth steady upward path but also to the location and desirability of the properties they own. They also present "best in class" financial fundamentals, with Manhattan leasing spreads (roughly comparable to gross margin—lease less mortgage obligations) of 37 percent versus 18.1 percent for their peer group. Notably the spread advanced substantially from 23 percent last year. The "debt to enterprise value" ratio is 25 percent versus 40 percent for peers. Only about

41 percent of the portfolio is encumbered by mortgages—down from 99 percent at IPO. Less debt, less leverage, greater profitability.

As investments REITs are typically good income producers, since they are required by law to pay a substantial portion of their cash flow to investors. The accounting rules are different, and REIT investors should focus on Funds From Operations (FFO), which is analogous to operating income; net income figures have depreciation expenses deducted, which can vary in timing and not always be realistic. Funds From Operations (FFO) support the dividends paid to investors.

Financial Highlights, Fiscal Year 2015

As ESRT only went public in the fall of 2013, we still do not have a well-developed financial presentation for the company or its financial history. Total Funds From Operations (FFO) increased 17 percent to $258 million. FY2015 results include the execution of 245 new leases with a substantial 73.7 percent increase in rents for those leases; of that total, 177 of those were Manhattan office leases with an average rent increase of 43.3 percent (again, some of that rent increase is "organic," some reflects building improvements). Occupancy rates dropped slightly to 87.3 percent; the drop was mainly attributed to space being renovated. Observatory revenue grew 0.6 percent over FY2014. The REIT estimates that it has completed 94 percent of a $700 million spending plan to redevelop and restore its Manhattan buildings (the largest, of course, being the Empire State Building). The completion of that spend should enhance net income going forward—and in turn, shareholder payouts, since REITs are legally required to pay out 90 percent of reported income.

As yet, we have not been able to obtain projections into FY2016 and FY2017.

Reasons to Buy

ESRT exhibits most of the traits we like to see when we consider buying a real estate investment trust. It has good real estate, yes, but it isn't just the real estate—it's a good business, too. It adds value in the form of redevelopment services, and the observation deck is a nice bonus. We don't depend solely on the rising value of the underlying real estate, and we don't depend too much on increasing the rent. That said, the prime locations they own and the exclusive focus on the New York area make for an excellent opportunity to raise rents—which is, in fact, happening at a good pace.

And who wouldn't want to own a piece of the Empire State Building? The energy and whole-building retrofit of the Empire State Building has won considerable acclaim with green building advocates and others; a search on "empire state building energy retrofit" gives several angles to this story. The building was once felt to be in an irreversible decline; the retrofit, energy, and publicity around it have returned it to its classic status as a prestige address. ESRT is using it wisely as a brand centerpiece for events, social media, and general marketing.

In short, not only do we like the fundamentals, we also admire the overall value creation strategy. As retrofits and other investments in the portfolio are completed across the portfolio (they are expected to wind down after 2016), ESRT will become a much stronger cash machine, and with REIT rules, that cash will end up in the pockets of shareholders in the not too distant future.

Reasons for Caution

ESRT is new and far less proven than most of our choices, although it has a seasoned management team from its roots as a private equity trust. We can't give you as much historical analysis as we would with most *100 Best* stocks investments. Too, the short-term future of commercial real estate in general is not too bright, as many major tenants are reviewing their space commitments—that said, we don't think this concern affects New York real estate so much. All in all, ESRT still appears an opportunity to "get in on the ground floor" of what we think will be a strong investment for years to come.

SECTOR: **Real Estate** ❑ BETA COEFFICIENT: **0.60** ❑ 10-YEAR COMPOUND FFO PER-SHARE GROWTH: **NM** ❑ 10-YEAR COMPOUND DIVIDENDS PER-SHARE GROWTH: **NM**

	2008	2009	2010	2011	2012	2013	2014	2015
Revenues (mil)	—	—	—	—	—	—	635.3	657.6
Net income (mil)	—	—	—	—	—	—	26.7	33.7
Funds from operations per share	—	—	—	—	—	—	0.84	0.97
Real estate owned per share	—	—	—	—	—	—	8.42	8.55
Dividends per share	—	—	—	—	—	—	0.34	0.34
Price: high	—	—	—	—	—	15.6	18.1	19.0
low	—	—	—	—	—	12.6	14.1	14.6

Website: www.empirestaterealtytrust.com

AGGRESSIVE GROWTH

Fair Isaac Corporation

Ticker symbol: FICO (NYSE) ❑ S&P rating: NR ❑ Value Line financial strength rating: B++ ❑ Current yield: 0.1% ❑ Dividend raises, past 10 years: 1

Company Profile

"Making Every Decision Count" is the motto of the Fair Isaac Corporation, which provides decision support analytics, software, and solutions to help businesses improve and automate decision making and risk management. The most well-known and best example of these solutions is the FICO score—an analytic single-figure estimate of a consumer's creditworthiness used in the credit industry and for other purposes such as employment and insurance.

FICO provides its analytic solutions and services to a variety of financial and other service organizations, including banks, credit-reporting agencies, credit card–processing agencies, insurers, telecommunications providers, retailers, marketers, and healthcare organizations. It operates in three segments: Applications, Scores, and Tools. The Applications segment provides decision and risk management tools, market targeting and customer analytics tools, and fraud detection tools and associated professional services, all now under an umbrella called Enterprise Fraud Management. (If you've had a credit card fraud alert recently, it probably came from FICO's "Falcon" suite of fraud prediction and protection services.) The Scores segment includes the business-to-business scoring solutions; myFICO solutions, delivering FICO scores for consumers; and associated professional services. The Tools segment provides software products and consulting services to help organizations build their own analytic tools. Many of these analytics and scores are packaged to be available through the "cloud" as "SaaS"— Software as a Service—applications, providing a steady revenue stream tied to their use.

The company actively works with customers in a variety of vertical markets to identify and apply their tools and applications; these analytics go beyond traditional financial applications into marketing and operational optimization. The company promotes its vertical applications in the grocery, retail, pharmaceutical and life sciences, insurance, financial services, and consumer packaged goods industries.

Financial Highlights, Fiscal Year 2015

Total revenues advanced 6 percent in FY2015. The largest segment, Applications (at 63 percent of the business) grew at 4 percent. The Scores segment, which contributes 25 percent of the business, grew 11 percent, while the Tools business, accounting for 13 percent of the business, moved forward at a 7 percent rate. Earnings have flattened due to R&D expenses and some competitive pressure but are expected to resume their upward path to $3.00 per share in FY2016. The company should profit from a broadening base of applications outside the financial services industry.

We should note that the company's apparently "stingy" dividend policy is offset by aggressive share buybacks; the company has reduced share counts some 50 percent since 2005 and has plans to reduce them another 10–15 percent over the next few years. Few companies on our *100 Best Stocks* list have such a deliberate and aggressive share count reduction policy.

Reasons to Buy

In an otherwise pretty lousy year for investing, Fair Isaac has clearly bucked the trend and has shown how patient investing can pay off. We'll continue to ride this slow, steady horse another year as others continue to fade.

"Big data" and related analytics are hot right now as more vertical industries (banking, retail, utilities, pharma, medical devices, health insurers, etc.) learn how to use them more efficiently and effectively to manage different parts of their business. There are a number of companies, large and small, in the analytics business, but few have the brand reputation, product packaging, and leadership enjoyed by FICO. The company is a pure play and is considered to be the gold standard for this type of product. It is more turnkey and easy for customers who don't have advanced mathematicians and software engineering staffs to buy. As a consequence, and with the brand recognition of the FICO score, the company has attained a pretty large moat on its brand and is a good example of how packaging and market definition can be as important as the product.

We also think a stabilizing financial industry with new rules, fewer workers, more services provided over the Internet, and a greater recognition for risk and risk management will bode well for the FICO product suite. Financial and other decision-making FICO products offer a good combination of streamlining and sophistication. Long term, we can easily see their modeling approaches being further extended to analyze customer behavior and provide decision support for insurability, employability, acceptance into schools, and even customer behaviors in stores or online, other areas well beyond a consumer's ability to repay extended credit. International demand for FICO's products continues to grow, too, notably in China, where fraud protection continues to be a big business.

The dividend remains inconsequential, but it doesn't take a genius (or analytics) to appreciate the company's policy of providing shareholder returns in the form of share buybacks.

Reasons for Caution

There continues to be some competition on the scoring front, but the forefront FICO brand keeps serious competition at bay. Software companies always run a certain amount of technology risk. The ability to sell in a "cloud" environment and to maintain or increase margins by selling the right mix of products and channels will be key. There is some public concern that scoring models oversimplify lending and insurability decisions and should not be used or relied on so heavily. And, as we saw in the Great Recession, the company is vulnerable to economic downturns.

In all, we feel the company will continue to succeed on the basis of its brand, reputation, and market leadership. The stock has performed well against a weak market backdrop, but we wonder if it's too much given the midrange growth levels and even considering the aggressive buybacks. "Score" your purchases carefully.

SECTOR: Business Services ❑ BETA COEFFICIENT: **1.45** ❑ 10-YEAR COMPOUND EARNINGS PER-SHARE GROWTH: **5.0%** ❑ 10-YEAR COMPOUND DIVIDENDS PER-SHARE GROWTH: **10.0%**

	2008	2009	2010	2011	2012	2013	2014	2015
Revenues (mil)	744.8	630.7	605.6	619.7	676.4	743.4	789.0	839.0
Net income (mil)	81.2	65.1	64.5	71.6	92.0	90.1	94.9	86.5
Earnings per share	1.64	1.34	1.42	1.79	2.55	2.48	2.72	2.65
Dividends per share	0.08	0.08	0.08	0.08	0.08	0.08	0.08	0.08
Cash flow per share	2.49	2.15	2.36	2.58	3.20	3.54	3.98	3.85
Price: high	32.2	24.5	27.0	38.5	47.9	63.5	74.4	97.6
low	10.4	9.8	19.5	20.0	34.6	41.3	50.3	69.4

Website: www.fico.com

FedEx Corporation

Ticker symbol: FDX (NYSE) ❑ S&P rating: BBB ❑ Value Line financial strength rating: A++
❑ Current yield: 0.7% ❑ Dividend raises, past 10 years: 9

Company Profile

FedEx Corporation is the world's leading provider of guaranteed express delivery services and a major player in the overall small shipment and small-package logistics market. The corporation is organized as a holding company, with four individual businesses that compete collectively and operate independently under the FedEx brand, offering a wide range of express delivery services for the time-definite transportation of documents, packages, and freight:

- The familiar FedEx Express operation offers overnight and deferred air service to 57,000 drop-off locations, operating 650 aircraft through ten air express hubs, and approximately 150,000 ground vehicles to support this business.
- FedEx Ground offers overnight service from 500 pickup/delivery terminals for up to 400 miles anywhere in the United States for packages weighing up to 150 pounds.
- FedEx Freight offers standard and priority LTL (less than truckload) service across North America mainly for business supply-chain operations with 370 terminals and service centers.
- FedEx Services, which includes 1,800 former Kinko's copy and office centers, now operates under the FedEx/Office brand, and FedEx Tech-Connect provides solutions to integrate supply chain management IT tools with FedEx's systems.

The company has about 340,000 "team members"—employees and contractors. They serve more than 375 airports in over 220 countries. Except for the number of countries served, all of these figures are slightly attenuated from previous years as the company weeds out unproductive and redundant locations in a drive for efficiency.

In FY2015, the Express segment accounted for 57 percent of revenues, Ground 27 percent, Freight 13 percent, and Services 3 percent, representing yet another slight annual increase in the overall mix for the Ground and Freight services and a more sizeable increase for Services. The company estimates that over 96 percent of its customers use two or more of these services, attesting to the fact that FedEx's business is increasingly tuned to providing a total and flexible logistics solution.

Recent strategic acquisitions include international small-package logistics provider TNT Express, which, when complete, will add to the international network and will in particular give the company a ready-made ground network in 40 European countries to handle e-commerce expansion. The acquisition of GENCO, a reverse logistics provider, provides a key stronghold in the growing consumer e-commerce business. A new FedEx SameDay City branded service is being offered in 23 cities.

Financial Highlights, Fiscal Year 2015

Although global trade and manufacturing have been weak recently, e-commerce on the revenue side and dramatic cost savings from lower fuel prices and process initiatives led to a strong year, especially for profits, in FY2015 and going forward. FY2015 revenues advanced 4 percent in FY2015 with earnings up a full 22 percent (per-share earnings were up 32 percent). A price increase and continued lower costs will bring another 10–15 percent annual earnings gain through FY2017 on continued moderate 4 percent revenue increases. These figures do not include TNT Express. Cash flows are very strong; some share buybacks and moderate dividend hikes are likely.

Reasons to Buy

FedEx has several tailwinds now—lower fuel costs, the customer-driven logistics fine-tuning just mentioned, and the growth of e-commerce. The company estimates that e-commerce shipments will double to the $1.3 trillion range in the five-year period 2012–2017.

A strong tailwind of e-commerce business and greater need for a complete, economical, and partially time-sensitive logistics mix is the right place to be as American manufacturing activity and local sourcing increase—although this will dampen international shipments, a trend we've already seen. The company is optimizing "SmartPost" cooperation with the U.S. Postal Service with its own Ground network for "last mile" distribution. With SmartPost and other business expansions, the Ground segment is approaching a 30 percent market share for such services, a position from which it can start to call the shots in the marketplace for lucrative e-commerce and time-sensitive ground business. Indeed, of late, the company has been able to raise prices while also gaining market share.

The continued resurgence in the economy and growth in online shopping and delivery will certainly help volumes and pricing, and the continuing shift to e-commerce gives a boost to this recovery. The logistics business is always ripe for innovation, and FedEx has long been an innovator in the transportation and small-package shipment business, not only with new transportation services, but also with new tools to help customers track shipments and manage their supply chains in real time; we expect this to continue. Given solid profit gains and cash flows, recent share prices would seem to indicate a good entry point.

Reasons for Caution

The company is always vulnerable to economic downturns and fuel prices, particularly if cost increases come faster than they can be recovered in rates and fuel surcharges—as is often the case. Export traffic—which fills empty outbound planes—continues to be hampered by the strong dollar. While cash flows are strong, this company must occasionally purchase or lease aircraft, and this and other capital expenditures can put a big dent in cash flows. While the company has done a good job of carving out its "full service" niche, it is always vulnerable to competition in both domestic and overseas markets; that said, its size and scale are an advantage in most cases.

We like the fact that the company has raised the dividend every year (except 2009 during the Great Recession) since starting to pay dividends in 2002, and while payouts are increasing, they are still less than we think they could be.

SECTOR: **Transportation** ▫ BETA COEFFICIENT: **1.27** ▫ 10-YEAR COMPOUND EARNINGS PER-SHARE GROWTH: **7.0%** ▫ 10-YEAR COMPOUND DIVIDENDS PER-SHARE GROWTH: **10.5%**

		2008	2009	2010	2011	2012	2013	2014	2015
Revenues (mil)		37,953	35,497	34,734	39,204	42,680	44,287	45,567	47,453
Net income (mil)		1,821	1,173	1,184	1,452	2,032	1,561	2,097	2,572
Earnings per share		5.83	3.76	3.76	4.90	6.41	6.23	6.75	8.95
Dividends per share		0.40	0.44	0.44	0.48	0.52	0.56	0.60	0.80
Cash flow per share		12.13	10.09	10.01	11.13	13.08	12.41	16.32	18.35
Price:	high	99.5	92.6	97.8	98.7	97.2	144.1	183.5	185.2
	low	53.9	34.0	69.8	64.1	82.8	90.6	128.2	130.0

Website: www.fedex.com

CONSERVATIVE GROWTH

Fresh Del Monte Produce Inc.

Ticker symbol: FDP (NYSE) ▫ S&P rating: NR ▫ Value Line financial strength rating: B++ ▫ Current yield: 1.2% ▫ Dividend raises, past 10 years: 3

Company Profile

Founded in 1892, Del Monte originated as a brand for coffee packaged for the prestigious Del Monte hotel in Monterey, CA. The original firm expanded its business and selected Del Monte as the brand for a new line of canned peaches, and the rest, as they say, is history. The company has grown—in a large part based on acquisitions particularly of tropical fruits and food producers—into one of the largest vertically integrated producers and distributors of fresh and fresh-cut fruits and vegetables, as well as prepared fruits and vegetables, juices, beverages, and snacks, in the world.

The company has 90,000 acres in production, and its products are available in 100-plus countries. Products include bananas (the largest product line at 46 percent of sales), an all-important "other fresh produce" category (45 percent of sales), and prepared food (9 percent). The "other fresh produce" category deserves further breakout, and in some cases, description:

- Gold pineapples (13 percent)—the branding is "Del Monte Gold Extra Sweet."
- Fresh-cut produce (12 percent)—this is the category we're most excited about, and is the fastest-growing segment (was 10 percent last year). It offers fresh-cut fruits—pineapples, melons, grapes, citrus, apples, mangos, kiwis, and others—and vegetables for salads packed in convenient, safe, and branded plastic containers; so far sold only in the U.S., Canada, U.K., Japan, and the Middle East. These products are gaining traction in foodservice and convenience store end markets.
- Nontropical fruit (7 percent)—the biggest contributor is avocados, but also includes grapes, apples, pears, peaches, plums, nectarines, cherries, citrus, and kiwis.
- Melons (3 percent)
- Tomatoes (3 percent)
- Vegetables (1 percent)
- Other fruit, products, and services (3 percent)

A big part of why we like Fresh Del Monte is that it's not just a producer but is also a logistics company specializing in fresh packaging and transport, really for all parts of the fresh-food supply chain. It runs from farm to store shelf, including sophisticated refrigerated storage and transport, all the way to helping end-store operators with market research, promotion, display, stocking decisions, and other logistical support. The company owns a fleet of 20 ocean-going refrigerated vessels and manages a network including 4,500 refrigerated containers, refrigerated port facilities, and 40 distribution and "fresh cut" centers. Too, the company has innovated in such areas as Controlled Ripening Technology for bananas, which it licenses to other producers.

As an example of what this brings, for its largest category, bananas, 50 percent of sales are in North America, 20 percent in Europe, 17 percent in Asia, and 13 percent are in the Middle East. In fact, overall sales outside North America account for 45 percent of the business: 18 percent in Europe, 14 percent in the Middle East and Africa, and 11 percent in Asia. This supply-chain leadership gives the company a distinct advantage and a laboratory within which they can produce and distribute all sorts of new products and packages to a large part of the world, a big advantage over the world's many, many small producers. See a market for fresh fruit snacks in special packages in Japan? Fresh Del Monte can produce it and get it there.

Financial Highlights, Fiscal Year 2015

Historical revenues, profit margins, and profits have been somewhat volatile for Fresh Del Monte, but the increase in scale, diversity of offering, and diversity of market are starting to smooth things out. It is no longer just a banana and pineapple grower and distributor.

FY2015 showed favorable volume trends in most key segments but some price softness particularly in bananas (volumes were up 7 percent but prices were down 3 percent in that segment). Overall, pineapples and the fresh-cut product lines have been strongest. In total, revenues advanced 3.5 percent, but margins slipped slightly mainly due to banana "softness"; earnings dropped 9.5 percent. For FY2016 and FY2017, strength in the fresh-cut segment, new production facilities, market share gains, and stronger international sales should bring another 3–4 percent sales advance in FY2016 with a similar advance in earnings and a 5–10 percent earnings gain on another 3–4 percent top-line advance in FY2017. Operating and net profit margins should stay in the 5.5–6 percent range and 3–4 percent range through the period and should be more consistent as worldwide scale grows. After a large 8 percent share buyback in 2014 the pace has been more modest but steady at about 1 percent. We feel that all of these forecasts are conservative, particularly as the fresh-cut product lines gain traction in a widening set of markets.

Reasons to Buy

What brought us to Fresh Del Monte two years ago wasn't just the pineapple, or even the bananas. It is their emerging leadership in healthful and especially innovative and modern fresh packaged foods, items we think will play well with today's demographic, who demand fresh, convenient, natural, unique, and customizable foods and "fresh-cut" food packages. More fundamentally, we're attracted to the brand, the logistics network, "fresh-cut" opportunities, increased scale, and operating efficiency. We like the vertical integration, which gives it control of its supply chain, and most of all, we like Fresh Del Monte's competitive advantage in distribution, and we see this playing well with what we expect to be a growing demand for smartly packaged fresh and fresh-cut food offerings, which are currently only 12 percent of the business. We think this could take off, and combined with packaged salads and such, become a major category in groceries and mass distributors of food products. People want convenience and variety, and these prepackaged items fit in—and when you take into account storage and spoilage, they actually become cheaper than their unpackaged equivalents. They can be mixed any way the markets want, as we've seen with prepackaged salads. Like pineapples, blueberries, and mangos together? Fresh Del Monte can produce and distribute just such a medley. You don't have to buy a pineapple, cut it up, buy a bag of blueberries; you get the idea.

All of that, plus a helping of financial strength (debt is only 13 percent of total capital) and a bias toward shareholder returns, makes this mid-cap offering a worthwhile recipe to play emerging trends in the food industry.

Reasons for Caution

Past results have been volatile, and the thin margins reflect a company that is more of a "commodity" producer than anything else. We think the "fresh-cut" offerings will grow Fresh Del Monte out of this category. As a logistics company, particularly one with a moderate amount of air cargo in its mix, it is vulnerable to fuel price shocks. There is also strong competition in most parts of this industry.

SECTOR: **Consumer Staples** ◻ BETA COEFFICIENT: **0.44** ◻ 10-YEAR COMPOUND EARNINGS
PER-SHARE GROWTH: **3.5%** ◻ 10-YEAR COMPOUND DIVIDENDS PER-SHARE GROWTH: **NM**

	2008	2009	2010	2011	2012	2013	2014	2015
Revenues (mil)	3,531	3,496	3,552	3,590	3,421	3,684	3,928	4,057
Net income (mil)	158	144	62	93	143	87	144	131
Earnings per share	2.48	2.26	1.02	1.56	2.46	1.54	2.73	2.49
Dividends per share	—	—	0.05	0.30	0.40	0.50	0.50	0.50
Cash flow per share	3.82	3.58	2.40	2.87	3.69	2.79	4.12	3.87
Price: high	39.8	26.7	25.2	28.6	26.9	30.8	35.0	47.5
low	12.9	12.2	19.2	21.3	21.6	24.7	24.0	32.0

Website: www.freshdelmonte.com

GROWTH AND INCOME

General Electric Company

Ticker symbol: GE (NYSE) ◻ S&P rating: AA+ ◻ Value Line financial strength rating: B++
◻ Current yield: 3.0% ◻ Dividend raises, past 10 years: 8

Company Profile

Everyone knows GE, and most know the recent story of GE—the colossal conglomerate built mostly around things that use or produce electricity and a few other things like jet engines and railroad locomotives. Oh yes, and built around that colossal finance arm—GE Capital—that morphed into a $300 billion giant that dominated the business and—almost—took down the company in the Great Recession. A giant colossal conglomerate that a colleague and pundit rightfully and painfully described as "a hedge fund that makes jet engines."

The tide has turned. GE has transformed—or at least has reached the latter stages of that transformation. Today's GE now describes itself, quite aptly, as the "Digital Industrial" company. Industrial at its core, for it makes all kinds of capital equipment and end products mostly sold to industrial customers but some for consumers, too. And "digital" because of a growing emphasis on products and machines controlled by software and by the Internet. Oh, and GE Capital? About three-quarters of it is gone now, sold off to better and greener pastures like Wells Fargo and Blackstone where good and not-so-good financial assets belong. Good riddance. And back to the main story, which we think is a good one . . .

With or without its finance unit, General Electric is still colossal. Formed in 1892 as a major producer of all things electric in the wake of the commercial harnessing of electricity, the company evolved over the years into a massive conglomerate producing aircraft engines, power generation, railroad locomotives, household appliances, energy infrastructure, alternative energy equipment, medical imaging equipment, oilfield service equipment, and a vast array of other mostly industrial products—in addition to its departing General Electric Capital Services, or "GE Capital" financial arm.

In total, the company has seven operating industrial segments. By segment and percent of FY2015 revenues, they are: Power & Water (17 percent), Oil & Gas (14 percent), Energy Management (5 percent), Aviation (19 percent), Healthcare (15 percent), Transportation (5 percent), Appliances & Lighting (7 percent), and 3 percent other. GE Capital accounts for about 15 percent but once produced 30 percent of revenue and a third of profits . . . and a lot of headaches and risks that both management and investors—for the most part—are glad to be rid of.

International sales account for about 55 percent of revenues, a number that is likely to rise steadily with the return to the industrial base. The GE Capital divestiture is estimated to be about three-quarters complete; the remaining $50 billion on the table, to be closed by 2017, will fund more share buybacks acquisitions and strengthening of business in other segments. During 2015 the company completed the acquisition of French international power production and distribution systems business Alstom, which will build up the Power business with a 60 percent increase in GE-supplied installed base worldwide. The company also sold most of its appliance business to Haier. (The deal was originally with Electrolux but that deal fell through and the eventual sale to Haier fetched a higher price—$5.4 billion.) These changes will further simplify the remaining business mix, change the segment balance described previously, and increase focus on the key markets of Power, Healthcare, and Aviation while awaiting a cyclical recovery in Oil & Gas. Really, these changes amount to a return to its value "roots"—changes we've felt long to be coming.

Financial Highlights, Fiscal Year 2015

The seas of change continue to make comparisons and forward estimates difficult. In general, while earnings and revenues have declined sharply starting in FY2015 due to the GE Capital divestitures, they should stabilize by 2017. Per-share amounts should remain fairly comparable due mostly to the buybacks in store.

Consistent with the changes, FY2015 revenues dropped 16 percent, with some weakness in the Oil & Gas segment and a pretty hard currency hit mixed in. The strongest businesses in 2015 included Power & Water, Energy Management, Aviation, and Transportation, while Oil & Gas and to a lesser degree Healthcare were laggards. Revenues and profits going forward are still hard to predict: Current projections call for flat to 3 percent higher revenues and much more robust 10–15 percent increases in earnings going forward as operational improvements take hold. Steady and large buybacks and dividend increases are clearly in the cards.

Reasons to Buy

At heart, the company is simplifying and returning to its roots as a top-grade industrial infrastructure play. It is downsizing, rightsizing, and trimming businesses all over—not just its financial services arm—and happily, that process is approaching completion so far as the Finance business is concerned. The value unlocked—not to mention the reduction of risk and the decreased consumption of management bandwidth—should be huge pluses in our view. We should note again that the company will keep some of its financial business intact—the part that finances acquisition of GE products—a move that makes a lot of sense to us.

Beyond the finance divestiture, the company continues to tout its "look of a simpler company." It is nearing the end of a five-year plan to increase operational efficiency by such actions as reducing HQ operations and reducing the number of resource planning software systems (by 77 percent was the goal for that one). Now the goal shifts to reducing production costs and increasing operating margins by a half percent each year (huge for a $130 billion company)—and also to integrating certain cross-functional services like engineering and plant capacity between the various businesses.

Cash returns to shareholders will remain significant as divestitures continue, regulation subsides, and profitability and cash flows increase. These factors will likely eliminate hundreds of millions more shares from the share count and get the dividend back up to its historical levels approaching 5 percent.

All in all, we think the company is getting back to what it does best, and we also think the brand image will improve as well as it retrenches into its core businesses. There is considerable need to replace infrastructure, and GE is right at the heart of this trend. GE is a strong force in its markets, likely to get stronger without the distractions of managing one of the largest financial businesses in the world. We hope we can devote more of this narrative in the future to describing GE's *businesses*, not its business *change*.

Reasons for Caution

The efforts and distractions of the GE Capital divestiture are diminishing but are still present. The company is still active in the acquisitions market and is still complex, and now it is more exposed than ever to the vagaries of the oil and gas business—at least a temporary drag on growth and earnings. Although the company has plans to retire a billion shares, the 9 billion remaining are somewhat of a negative. It's hard to generate meaningful per-share gains when new sales and profits are divided up into so many little slices. The divestiture and its proceeds will continue to help fix this.

SECTOR: **Industrials** ❑ BETA COEFFICIENT: **1.19** ❑ 10-YEAR COMPOUND EARNINGS PER-SHARE GROWTH: **NM** ❑ 10-YEAR COMPOUND DIVIDENDS PER-SHARE GROWTH: **NM**

	2008	2009	2010	2011	2012	2013	2014	2015
Revenues (bil)	182.5	156.8	150.2	147.3	147.4	146.0	148.6	127.7
Net income (bil)	18.1	11.4	12.6	14.9	16.1	16.9	16.6	12.3
Earnings per share	1.78	1.03	1.15	1.31	1.52	1.64	1.65	1.32
Dividends per share	1.24	0.61	0.46	0.61	0.70	0.79	0.88	0.92
Cash flow per share	2.81	2.07	2.13	2.28	2.44	2.65	2.60	1.85
Price: high	38.5	17.5	19.7	21.7	23.2	28.1	27.6	31.5
low	12.6	5.7	13.8	14.0	18.0	20.7	23.7	19.4

Website: www.ge.com

GROWTH AND INCOME

General Mills, Inc.

Ticker symbol: GIS (NYSE) ❑ S&P rating: BBB+ ❑ Value Line financial strength rating: A+ ❑ Current yield: 3.0% ❑ Dividend raises, past 10 years: 10

Company Profile

As observed again in the Introduction to this year's *100 Best Stocks to Buy*, changing demographics and tastes led us to take a closer look and make some tough choices among old-line mainstays in the food and beverage world and elsewhere. Traditional breakfast cereals have struggled; today's Millennials seek health and uniqueness *in addition to* convenience. But we continue to like this company's slow, steady approach to life, and there is enough going on to meet the demographic challenge posed by the Millennial generation, in our view. As such, General Mills will remain on the *100 Best* list for 2017.

General Mills is the second-largest domestic producer of ready-to-eat breakfast cereals and the sixth-largest food company in the world. Sales are broken out into three major segments, organized by channel: U.S. Retail (60 percent of 2015 revenues), International (29 percent), and Convenience Stores and Foodservice (11 percent).

Major cereal brands, most of which bear the Big G label, include Cheerios, Wheaties, Lucky Charms, Total, and Chex (which is as much a snack base as a cereal). The company owns Pillsbury, which it acquired in 2001. Other consumer packaged food products include baking mixes (Betty Crocker and Bisquick); meals (Betty Crocker dry packaged dinner mixes); Progresso soups; Hamburger Helper; snacks (Pop Secret microwave popcorn, Bugles snacks, and grain and fruit snack products); Pillsbury refrigerated and frozen dough products, including Pillsbury Doughboy, frozen breakfast products, and frozen pizza and snack products; organic foods; and other products, including Nature Valley, Yoplait (which was acquired in 2011 along with Go-Gurt), and Colombo yogurt. The company's holdings include many other brand names, such as Häagen-Dazs ice cream and a host of joint ventures.

In the International sector, General Foods sells numerous local brands, in addition to internationally recognized brands such as Häagen-Dazs ice cream and Old El Paso Mexican foods. The company is in a 50–50 joint venture with Nestlé known as Cereal Partners Worldwide. International accounts for about $5.1 billion in sales, or 29 percent of the total, with Europe holding the largest share (41 percent) followed by Canada (22 percent), Asia-Pacific at 20 percent, and Latin America at 17 percent of the International total.

The Convenience Stores and Foodservice Sector is mainly a distribution channel targeting convenience stores, hotels, and restaurants, and wholesale and grocery store bakeries with both branded and unbranded products.

The company offers a breakdown of its U.S. Retail business by type of product to better understand this relatively diverse food business:

- 20 percent ready-to-eat cereal including the familiar brands
- 18 percent snacks, including Nature Valley, Fiber One, and Chex Mix
- 16 percent Yoplait—yogurts, including Go-Gurt and newly popular Greek yogurts
- 15 percent convenient meals including Hamburger Helper, Progresso soups, and Betty Crocker side dishes
- 10 percent baking mixes and ingredients including Betty Crocker, Pillsbury, Bisquick, and Gold Medal Flour

- 10 percent dough
- 5 percent super premium ice cream
- 5 percent vegetables

As you can see, General Mills is part of most well-stocked pantries, and it has at least a moderate amount of healthy fare to go with the traditional offerings. We kept this company on the list not just for good financial performance and a better-than-most percentage of healthful offerings, but also for the promise of innovation. The company plans to double its current sourcing of organically grown food; it is now the fourth-largest manufacturer of organic food products in the U.S. Prominent organic brands include Cascadian Farm, Annie's, and Muir Glen, now accounting for about 4 percent of total sales.

General Mills is also investing in the important and relatively more profitable gluten-free food lines. The company plans to have 90 percent of its Cheerios line gluten-free by 2016. It also expects to eliminate artificial flavors in cereal by 2017. As the company develops new products, it places emphasis not just on the Millennial group, but also the 55-and-over age groups. We like that, too!

Financial Highlights, Fiscal Year 2015

Historically General Mills has been a slow, steady climber producing single-digit business gains with generous increases and decent share buybacks—we've liked the combination. FY2015 was a mixed year, with revenues down less than 1 percent and per-share earnings up about 1 percent—a figure that would have been higher (about 8 percent) without the divestiture of Green Giant and currency. Cash flows continued strong, and the company did deliver an 8 percent dividend increase on top of a 3 percent share buyback. The company still faces some headwinds with currency and at the breakfast table—but that high-margin business seems to be bottoming out at the moment. The company will ride an uptick in cereals, efficiency measures, and a more profitable mix to higher margins into FY2017 against some pricing pressure, continued currency headwinds, and divestitures to a 6–8 percent gain in per-share earnings on a 6–8 percent *decrease* in sales. We expect decent dividend growth and share buybacks to continue.

Reasons to Buy

As Chex Mix–crunching 55-and-overs, we can hardly resist General Mills, can we? But more seriously, although the customer base is a challenging moving target, the company continues to move forward at a slow, steady, and extremely regular pace. A glance at a ten-year price chart (something we don't do that often) would bear this out. The stock's highly defensive nature came in handy during the early 2016 market jitters.

General Mills has a good mix of cash-cow businesses like flour and baking mixes to finance the necessary advancements into the Millennial realm without depriving shareholders. We wouldn't be surprised to see faster advancements into organic and other areas popular with Millennials (who, we believe, will continue to crave convenience), which should of course enhance revenue and especially profit growth through the decade.

The long-term policy aimed at share repurchases has recently brought the share count down from 758 million in 2004 to 598 million; moderate repurchases look to continue with decent dividend increases adding some icing to the cake. Finally—and once again—General Mills continues to be a notably safe and stable defensive play and "sleep at night" stock with a beta of 0.40—among the lowest on our *100 Best Stocks* list.

Reasons for Caution

The shift in consumer preferences is real and here to stay; our long-term commitment to GIS is based on their long-term commitment to avoid soggy cereal and to do something about it. While commodity prices have moderated, the company is strongly affected by commodity prices and cycles. A degree of takeover interest has emerged; the shares aren't the bargain they were a while back. Shop carefully.

SECTOR: **Consumer Staples** ◻ BETA COEFFICIENT: **0.40** ◻ 10-YEAR COMPOUND EARNINGS PER-SHARE GROWTH: **7.5%** ◻ 10-YEAR COMPOUND DIVIDENDS PER-SHARE GROWTH: **10.0%**

	2008	**2009**	**2010**	**2011**	**2012**	**2013**	**2014**	**2015**
Revenues (mil)	13,652	14,691	14,796	14,880	16,658	17,774	17,910	17,630
Net income (mil)	1,288	1,367	1,571	1,652	1,707	1,789	1,824	1,765
Earnings per share	1.78	1.99	2.30	2.48	2.56	2.69	2.83	2.86
Dividends per share	0.79	0.86	0.96	1.12	1.22	1.32	1.55	1.67
Cash flow per share	2.50	2.78	3.09	3.29	3.47	3.71	3.94	3.93
Price: high	36.0	36.0	39.0	40.8	41.9	53.1	55.6	59.9
low	25.5	23.2	33.1	34.5	36.6	40.4	46.7	47.4

Website: www.generalmills.com

CONSERVATIVE GROWTH

W.W. Grainger, Inc.

Ticker symbol: GWW (NYSE) ❑ S&P rating: AA+ ❑ Value Line financial strength rating: A++
❑ Current yield: 2.0% ❑ Dividend raises, past 10 years: 10

Company Profile

Grainger is North America's largest supplier of maintenance, repair, and operating supply (MRO) products. It sells more than 1.4 million different products from more than 4,500 suppliers through a network of 681 branches (330 in the U.S.), 33 distribution centers (19 in the U.S.), and several websites, with a catalog containing some 570,000 items (a fascinating read if you like this sort of thing). Grainger also offers repair parts, specialized product sourcing, and inventory management supplies. Grainger sells principally to industrial and commercial maintenance departments, contractors, and government customers, but the range of both customers and products is quite broad (see the 2015 Fact Book referenced as follows). The company has nearly 2 million customers, mostly in North America, and achieves overnight delivery to approximately 95 percent of them.

Its Canadian subsidiary is Canada's largest distributor of industrial, fleet, and safety products. It serves its customers through 181 branches and six distribution centers and offers bilingual websites and catalogs. Grainger, S.A. de C.V. is Mexico's leading facilities maintenance supplier, offering customers more than 84,000 products. The company also has important operations, through joint ventures, in Japan, China, and India and does business in 166 countries worldwide.

The top five product categories are Safety and Security (18 percent), Material Handling (12 percent), Metalworking (12 percent), Cleaning and Maintenance (9 percent), and Pumps, Plumbing, and Equipment (8 percent), with 15 categories in all. Although Grainger is the largest single player, the market remains quite fragmented, with Grainger itself claiming only about 6 percent of the total market in North America.

Many of Grainger's customers are corporate account customers, primarily *Fortune* 1000 companies that spend more than $5 million annually on facilities maintenance products. Corporate account customers typically sign multiyear contracts for facilities maintenance products or a specific category of products, such as lighting or safety equipment. The company also helps its customers, large and small, with inventory management, supplying a tool called "Keepstock" to help them manage their MRO inventories and place orders automatically. The Grainger strategy is quintessentially multichannel and centered on being easy to do business with; they strive to ". . . build [their] business for how [their] customers think, buy, and act, even down to the individual buyer." Customers can interact with a direct sales force, with one of the 330 distribution outlets in the United States, or order through an e-commerce website. The strategy is to expand online sales (currently 27 percent of the total) and automatic orders out of Keepstock (currently 19 percent) while decreasing reliance on phone and counter orders and downsizing branch count (49 branches were closed in 2015). It has plans to perhaps grow e-commerce beyond 50 percent of the total—making it one of the stronger e-commerce success stories out there.

Financial Highlights, Fiscal Year 2015

The strong dollar, soft domestic and international manufacturing markets, and softness in the energy industry threw a bit of a wrench into Grainger's works in FY2015. Revenues were flat and a slight decrease in margins due in part to restructuring expenses and increased smaller volume sales to smaller businesses led to an 8 percent drop in net income (share buybacks limited the drop in per-share earnings to 3 percent). Continued softness particularly in the international sector will attenuate revenue gains to the 3–4 percent range, and expansion of smaller sales will continue to flatten the bottom line into FY2017. That said, a more cooperative dollar and any rebound in manufacturing and energy will be added pluses. The company has pledged to return two-thirds of its substantial cash flows to investors through continued buybacks and likely double-digit dividend increases over the next few years. Grainger has reduced share counts from 84 million in 2006 to 58 million recently, a 31 percent drop. Notably, the company has raised its dividend 44 consecutive years—these facts all point toward long-term thinking when it comes to shareholder returns.

Reasons to Buy

"For the Ones Who Get It Done" is the subtitle of the company's excellent 2015 Fact Book (available on its Investor Relations webpage), an appropriate title and an informative and fun read, refreshingly clear, and the best of its sort we've found. Grainger is far and away the biggest presence in the MRO world—and we think the story is still intact.

The only broadline competitor is one-quarter its size, and as noted previously the rest of the market is highly fragmented. The company also has the deepest catalog by far. It's estimated that 40 percent of purchases in the MRO market are unplanned, so having the broadest inventory, fastest delivery, and friendliest service is a big advantage for Grainger. Likewise, the small market share across the globe offers a good growth opportunity. Recent sluggish business results and the lofty stock price had us questioning Grainger's viability as a *100 Best Stock* once again for 2017, but its marketplace strength, positioning for a manufacturing rebound, solid customer interface strategies, and strong cash flow kept us "maintained" for another year.

Reasons for Caution

Grainger will always be vulnerable to economic cycles and manufacturing displacement, especially so long as it remains concentrated on U.S. soil. Grainger's international expansion should have helped alleviate this concern, but that sector has softened of late as well, leaving the company with some unused capacity in once-hot manufacturing regions. We've looked for entry points for years, and it appears the next two years may provide a few.

SECTOR: **Industrials** ❑ BETA COEFFICIENT: **0.75** ❑ 10-YEAR COMPOUND EARNINGS PER-SHARE GROWTH: **14.5%** ❑ 10-YEAR COMPOUND DIVIDENDS PER-SHARE GROWTH: **17.5%**

	2008	2009	2010	2011	2012	2013	2014	2015
Revenues (mil)	6,850	6,222	7,182	8,075	8,950	9,438	9,965	9,973
Net income (mil)	479	402	502	643	690	824	838	793
Earnings per share	6.09	5.25	6.81	9.04	9.52	11.52	12.26	11.94
Dividends per share	1.55	1.78	2.08	2.52	3.06	3.59	4.17	4.59
Cash flow per share	8.28	7.60	9.40	11.33	12.22	14.51	15.81	16.46
Price: high	94.0	102.5	139.1	193.2	221.8	276.4	269.7	257.0
low	58.9	59.9	96.1	124.3	172.5	201.5	223.9	189.8

Website: www.grainger.com

AGGRESSIVE GROWTH

Honeywell International

Ticker symbol: HON (NYSE) ❑ S&P rating: A ❑ Value Line financial strength rating: A++ ❑ Current yield: 2.1% ❑ Dividend raises, past 10 years: 9

Company Profile

Honeywell is a diversified international technology and manufacturing company operating in four business segments, engaged in the development, manufacturing, and marketing of aerospace products and services; control technologies for buildings, homes, and industry; automotive products; and specialty materials. The company groups these activities into three segments: Aerospace and Automotive (39 percent of FY2015 sales), Automation and Control Solutions (37 percent), and Performance Materials and Technologies (24 percent).

The Aerospace and Automotive segment's aerospace-related businesses include cockpit controls, power-generation equipment, and wheels and brakes for commercial and military aircraft and for airports and ground operations. It also makes jet engines for regional and business jet manufacturers. Products include avionics, auxiliary power units (APUs), aircraft lighting, and landing systems. The automotive business consists of a portfolio of parts and supplies for the automotive, railroad, and other industries. Products include cooling system components, turbochargers, and an assortment of other items. In 2014 the company sold its "friction materials" business (mainly brake components) and had previously sold its retail consumer automotive brands to focus on OEM components.

Honeywell's Automation and Control Solutions segment is best known as a maker of home and office climate-control equipment. It also makes home automation systems; thermostats; sensing and combustion controls for heating, A/C, and other environmental controls; lighting controls; security systems and sensing products; and fire alarms. This segment produces most of the components of what is known in the trade and advertising lingo as a "smart building," along with devices that play well with the new "connected" homes, data analytics, and "Internet of Things" concepts. Indeed, the company is looking at itself as ever more a software company and is investing management time, effort, and new hiring in improving the software development cycle. Honeywell estimates that its products are at work in some 150 million homes and 10 million commercial buildings worldwide. This part of the business also produces a number of factory automation products. The company estimates that it holds the number one market-share position in environmental and combustion controls, security and fire-protection systems, and industrial safety products and systems.

The Performance Materials and Technologies operation makes a wide assortment of specialty chemicals and fibers, plastics, coatings, and semiconductor and electronics materials, which are sold primarily to the food, pharmaceutical, petroleum-refining, and electronic packaging industries. Carbon fiber materials are among the more important and fastest-growing products in this segment.

The company has a considerable international footprint, with technology and manufacturing centers located outside the U.S.; five such centers are located in China along with a similar number in India. The company estimates 54 percent of its business to be done outside the U.S.

Citing "compelling industrial logic," Honeywell has made several overtures to acquire fellow industrial and aviation conglomerate and *100 Best* stock United Technologies in recent years and most recently in early 2016. The "logic" included $3.5 billion in "cost synergies," a unified management and marketing approach, and other factors. UTX has so far rejected these offers citing "regulatory concerns" but it appears that management "doesn't want to engage." Given that UTX's management (and business structure too) are in a state of flux, we think this acquisition could still happen—and if nothing else, it shows where Honeywell is going: more toward aggressive acquisitions to become more of a dominant player in its markets. "Great positions in good industries" is one of its strategic slogans.

Financial Highlights, Fiscal Year 2015

Foreign exchange, the friction materials divestiture, turmoil in the energy industry, and general economic softness all contributed to a 4 percent drop in FY2015 revenues; however, operational and mix improvements led to a substantial 2.5 percent gain in operating margin to 20 percent even, resulting in a net income gain of almost 8 percent. With modest buybacks, per-share earnings advanced 9.5 percent. Going forward, strategic acquisitions and a sharp focus on operating initiatives are expected to boost sales back to 2014 levels in FY2016 and another 3–5 percent in FY2017; earnings will continue to grow faster, with per-share net up 10–12 percent each year. The company has been reducing long-term debt and increasing the dividend at a double-digit rate while also executing modest share buybacks; these trends look to continue.

Reasons to Buy

A bet on Honeywell is a bet on a well-managed "best in class" producer of a wide variety of business and consumer products with an underlying technology theme—not really "high tech" but using advanced technologies to deliver a solution. The company shows many of the traditional signs of being well managed, with a strong and strategic focus on profitability, cash flow, and operational efficiency and a healthy respect for transparency, as evidenced by its informative annual reports, investor presentations, and other corporate materials.

Honeywell has outlined its key growth vectors as technology, innovation, globalization, and expanded presence in key markets like home and business energy management. It is now expanding its focus to complete solutions through "connectivity" and "adjacency" opportunities, many being software driven, within many of their platforms; software sales are expected to grow by a factor of four over the next five years. We like this diverse but timely set of focal points. Honeywell also has a valuable distribution network and existing customer base in all of its businesses. The company has a solid balance sheet and participates almost exclusively in high-margin businesses, particularly with the divestiture of the consumer auto and brake lining business, and looks for market leadership and complimentary market strength in its current acquisitions.

Reasons for Caution

Many of the industries Honeywell sells to can be cyclical and/or low-growth businesses: e.g., aviation, automotive, and even the well-regarded energy management businesses. Also it's easy to question the reliance on acquisitions to fuel growth. However, as we've seen, the focus on efficiency and profitability will make the most of cyclically sensitive businesses. Too, the company seems to have a knack for making acquisitions that make strategic sense. While a UTX acquisition also makes strategic sense in our view, it will no doubt burn a lot of energy—as it has even in the discussion phase. The stock has been on a long run, more than doubling since 2011; new investors are advised to be patient.

SECTOR: **Industrials** ◻ BETA COEFFICIENT: **1.16** ◻ 10-YEAR COMPOUND EARNINGS PER-SHARE GROWTH: **12.5%** ◻ 10-YEAR COMPOUND DIVIDENDS PER-SHARE GROWTH: **9.5%**

	2008	2009	2010	2011	2012	2013	2014	2015
Revenues (mil)	36,556	30,908	33,370	36,500	37,665	39,055	40,306	38,581
Net income (mil)	2,792	2,153	2,342	2,998	3,552	3,965	4,422	4,768
Earnings per share	3.75	2.85	3.00	3.79	4.48	4.97	5.56	6.04
Dividends per share	1.10	1.21	1.21	1.37	1.53	1.68	1.87	2.15
Cash flow per share	5.03	4.07	4.27	5.11	5.72	6.32	6.83	7.34
Price: high	63.0	41.6	53.7	62.3	64.5	91.6	102.4	107.4
low	23.2	23.1	36.7	41.2	52.2	64.2	82.9	87.0

Website: **www.honeywell.com**

CONSERVATIVE GROWTH

Illinois Tool Works Inc.

Ticker symbol: ITW (NYSE) □ S&P rating: A+ □ Value Line financial strength rating: A++ □ Current yield: 2.3% □ Dividend raises, past 10 years: 10

Company Profile

Illinois Tool Works is a longstanding multinational conglomerate involved in the manufacture of a diversified range of industrial products, mainly components, fasteners, and other "ingredients" for manufacturers. Customers include the automotive, machinery, construction, food and beverage, and general industrial markets. The company currently operates some 89 divisions in 57 countries, employing approximately 49,000 people. Some of the products are branded and familiar, like Wolf and Hobart kitchen equipment and Paslode air power tools; most are obscure and only known to others in their industries. Sales outside North America account for about half the total.

The remaining segments are presented as follows with approximate revenue percentages:

■ Automotive OEM (18 percent) includes transportation-related components, fasteners, and polymers, as well as truck remanufacturing and related parts and service for the automotive manufacturer market. Important brands include Drawform ("high volume, highly toleranced deep drawn metal stampings"), and Deltar Interior Components, which makes things like interior door handles.

■ Test & Measurement and Electronics (15 percent) supplies equipment and software for testing and measuring of materials and structures, solder, and other materials for PC board manufacturing and microelectronics assembly. Brands include Brooks Instrument, Buehler, Chemtronics, Instron, Magnaflux, and Speedline Technologies.

■ Polymers & Fluids (13 percent) businesses produce adhesives, sealants, lubrication and cutting fluids, and hygiene products for an assortment of markets. Their primary brands include Futura, Krafft, Devcon, Rocol, and Permatex and such brands as Rain-X and Wynn's for the automotive aftermarket.

■ Food Equipment (12 percent) produces commercial food equipment and related services, including professional kitchen ovens, refrigeration, mixers, and exhaust and ventilation systems. Major brands include Hobart, Traulsen, Vulcan, and Wolf.

▪ Construction Products (12 percent) concentrates on tools, fasteners, and other products for construction applications. Their major end markets are residential, commercial, and renovation construction. Brands include Ramset, Paslode, Buildex, Proline, and others.

▪ The Welding segment (13 percent of revenues) produces equipment and consumables associated with specialty power conversion, metallurgy, and electronics. Their primary products include arc-welding equipment and consumables, solder materials, equipment and services for electronics assembly, and airport ground support equipment. Primary brands include AXA Power, Hobart, and Weldcraft.

▪ Specialty Products (14 percent) is a hodgepodge of brands and businesses that includes Diagraph (industrial marking and coding systems), Fastex (engineered components for the appliance industry), and ZipPak reclosable plastic packaging.

In 2012, the company embarked on a five-year "Enterprise Strategy" program aimed at simplifying the business and applying sound customer-driven operating principles to fine-tune its base of customers, markets, products, facilities, and supply chains. Emphasis is placed on removing customer pain points, reducing complexity by applying the "80–20" rule (focusing on the 20 percent of customers, products, and processes that deliver 80 percent of the results), and by fine-tuning the relationships between headquarters and the operating entities. Growing organically (instead of by acquisition) and improving margins are the chief business objectives; the main strategy is to focus on businesses with strong sustainable differentiation. We normally don't bring too many such strategic initiatives to light, but we will in this case because (1) it's working, as gross margins have improved from the 19–21 percent range to a projected 26 percent in FY2017; and (2) such focus is needed in a company with such size and operating complexity; otherwise, it quickly becomes an uncoordinated conglomerate jumble, as many others before it have. We continue to appreciate ITW's efforts and look forward to the completion of this initiative in 2017.

Financial Highlights, Fiscal Year 2015

By removing about $2.5 billion in annual revenue, the 2014 Industrial Packaging divestiture clouds the comparison somewhat, but sharper business focus and the economic recovery have helped ITW's results. Comparable revenues rose about 10 percent in FY2015, driven by strength across the board and particularly in the Automotive OEM segment. Despite currency effects and some weakness in the industrial segments, earnings also rose 10 percent on a continuing business basis helped along by a 1.3 percent increase in operating margin to 24.8 percent.

Projections call for sales gains in the 2–4 percent range through FY2017, with per-share earnings up closer to 7 percent due to margin improvements and steady aggressive 2–6 percent share buybacks each year. The company commits half its profits each year to shareholder returns through dividends and buybacks.

Reasons to Buy

Buying shares of ITW continues to be like buying a mutual fund of medium-sized manufacturing businesses you've probably never heard of but would definitely like to own. Indeed, think of it as the Berkshire Hathaway of manufacturing companies if you will—we do. We enjoy doing this presentation every year; it's a good tour through how to run a modern conglomerate effectively, and they present themselves well to investors.

ITW is well diversified and serves many markets, some with end products, some with components, some in cyclical industries such as automotive and construction, some in steady-state industries like food processing. The company has solid models for making acquisitions and seems to do better than most conglomerates historically in choosing candidates and then managing them once they're in the fold. The new "Enterprise" initiative appears to be doing a good job of turning opportunity into cash flow and using that cash flow to enhance shareholder returns. The balance sheet is strong and net profit margins are projected to rise quite nicely for this type of business. The company is slowing down its acquisitions, which should reduce distractions and costs in absorbing new businesses.

Reasons for Caution

ITW is by nature tied to some of the more volatile elements of the business cycle, so it may not be the best pick for investors living in fear of the next downturn. In particular, we worry a bit about the Automotive segment going forward, although recently the unit has been gaining share in the automotive market. Conglomerates are notoriously difficult to manage (it's hard enough to manage one business, let alone 89 of them); that said, the company is working to streamline management structure and is also putting fewer new acquisitions on its plate.

SECTOR: **Industrials** ❑ BETA COEFFICIENT: **1.18** ❑ 10-YEAR COMPOUND EARNINGS PER-SHARE GROWTH: **8.5%** ❑ 10-YEAR COMPOUND DIVIDENDS PER-SHARE GROWTH: **12.0%**

	2008	2009	2010	2011	2012	2013	2014	2015
Revenues (mil)	15,869	13,876	15,870	17,787	17,924	14,135	14,484	13,405
Net income (mil)	1,583	969	1,527	1,852	1,921	1,629	1,890	1,886
Earnings per share	3.05	1.93	3.03	3.74	4.06	3.63	4.67	5.13
Dividends per share	1.15	1.24	1.27	1.38	1.46	1.60	1.75	2.07
Cash flow per share	4.56	3.27	4.17	5.06	5.55	5.20	6.25	6.50
Price: high	55.6	51.2	52.7	59.3	63.3	84.3	97.8	100.1
low	28.5	25.6	40.3	39.1	47.4	59.7	76.3	78.8

Website: www.itwinc.com

AGGRESSIVE GROWTH

International Flavors & Fragrances, Inc.

Ticker symbol: IFF (NYSE) ❑ S&P rating: BBB+ ❑ Value Line financial strength rating: A+ ❑ Current yield: 2.1% ❑ Dividend raises, past 10 years: 10

Company Profile

"We are the catalyst for discoveries that spark the senses and transform the everyday" crows the well-crafted website for International Flavors & Fragrances—a company that passes our smell tests after several years of indecision. IFF is a leading manufacturer of "sensorial experiences"—natural and artificial flavoring and fragrance chemicals for the food and beverage and consumer products industry, including cosmetics, perfumes, soap and detergents, hair care, pharmaceuticals, and a wide variety of other products. Fragrances accounted for about 53 percent of 2015 sales; flavorings the other 47 percent.

Not surprisingly, the company's value proposition and strategy is to create a differentiated and high value add for its customers by providing critical, unique, and highly researched ingredients. Many of the thousands of flavorings and fragrances are custom made for clients. For the food and beverage industry, the company estimates that its flavorings cost only 1–5 percent of the product's total cost, but generate 45 percent of the motivation to purchase it and to purchase it repeatedly.

The company is truly "international," with 78 percent of sales originating outside the U.S.; in fact, 50 percent of sales originate in emerging markets. Recognizing that flavor and fragrance preferences are very local in nature, the company has established an operational presence in 32 countries and lab facilities in 13 of them, including the U.S. Still, it estimates only a 16 percent share of the global flavorings and fragrances market and holds the number two position behind Swiss flavorings maker Givaudan.

Research and development is a big part of what IFF does—researching consumer tastes and preferences, how flavors and aromas work and hold up in different environments, and how to manufacture their products and develop the best delivery system to make them work over the desired life cycle. Research includes things like study of the "psychophysics of sensory perception" and the genetic basis for preferences in flavor and fragrance. New products and concepts include a proprietary encapsulation technology, which coats individual fragrance droplets with a polymeric shell to enhance life-cycle performance, and a product called "PolyIFF"—a solid-fragrance technology embedding scent into molded plastic. The company collaborates with chefs, fashion designers, filmmakers, and other trendsetters to evolve new ideas. R&D accounted for 8.2 percent of sales in 2015.

Financial Highlights, Fiscal Year 2015

IFF projects that the $18 billion market for flavors and fragrances will grow about 3–4 percent annually, with fully 75 percent of the growth coming from emerging markets, as taste and aroma become more important product components in China, Latin America, Africa, and the Middle East. With its strong international footprint, currency was a leading headline for IFF in FY2015. Net sales were off 2 percent for the year but up 5 percent on a constant currency basis. The strong international manufacturing footprint resulted in better results on the earnings front, with net income up about 3 percent for the year. The dollar and emerging economies remain rather large unknowns for FY2016, but currently sales are projected to rise about 4 percent in FY2016 and another 2 percent in FY2017 with 4–5 percent earnings increases both years as margins expand somewhat on moderating input costs. Moderate share buybacks make the per-share results look better. If the dollar weakens, these figures could be much stronger.

IFF has accelerated its dividend increases into the low double-digit range annually. They do make small acquisitions and pay for them with debt, which they pay down pretty quickly afterward. Their capital is allocated primarily for this purpose, capital expenditures, and for dividend increases.

Reasons to Buy

IFF we had only put this company on our list a few years ago when we first considered it . . . but we can't make a big stink about that now. We added it to the list for 2016—only to hit an off year due to currency and emerging markets. We'll keep it in better hopes for 2017 and beyond.

We still like this company a lot. It has a strong niche and produces elements critical in differentiating products in the fairly undifferentiated food and consumer products businesses. That should play better over time as people's tastes become more trained and more demanding—both in the rich world and especially in developing nations, which is an important trend right now. Not only does the company produce many of the world's leading flavorings and fragrances, it also has the market research and know-how to give it a competitive advantage—a moat—both with its customer insights and knowing how to make and deliver the stuff. We also like the relatively recession-proof nature of this business; we doubt that they will take the flavoring out of your favorite foods anytime soon, although we suppose that a greater uptake of generic products, such as cleaning products, could put a bit of a dent in this business. But remember, flavorings only account for 1–5 percent of the cost of your favorite beverage, and we Coke drinkers all know what happens when a company monkeys with that.

Reasons for Caution

The cost and availability of key ingredients like vanilla (a large portion of which comes from unstable regions in West Africa) can affect IFF adversely. The strong overseas footprint is probably an advantage most of the time, but today's strong dollar and volatile emerging markets like China and Brazil attenuate that advantage; also, it's hard to keep up with changing consumer tastes in so many places. Intellectual property protection is also a challenge; many try and some succeed in reverse engineering key ingredients.

SECTOR: **Consumer Staples** ▫ BETA COEFFICIENT: **0.94** ▫ 10-YEAR COMPOUND EARNINGS PER-SHARE GROWTH: **8.0%** ▫ 10-YEAR COMPOUND DIVIDENDS PER-SHARE GROWTH: **9.0%**

		2008	2009	2010	2011	2012	2013	2014	2015
Revenues (mil)		2,389	2,326	2,623	2,788	2,821	2,953	3,089	3,023
Net income (mil)		221	214	264	306	328	368	416	430
Earnings per share		2.76	2.69	3.26	3.74	3.98	4.47	5.08	5.25
Dividends per share		0.96	1.00	1.04	1.16	1.30	1.46	1.72	1.97
Cash flow per share		3.77	3.70	4.27	4.71	4.95	5.54	6.25	6.45
Price:	high	48.0	42.6	56.1	66.3	67.8	90.3	105.8	123.1
	low	24.7	25.0	39.3	51.2	52.1	67.5	82.9	97.6

Website: www.iff.com

AGGRESSIVE GROWTH

Itron, Inc.

Ticker symbol: ITRI (NASDAQ) □ S&P rating: NR □ Value Line financial strength rating: B+ □ Current yield: Nil □ Dividend raises, past 10 years: NA

Company Profile

We've been very patient with Itron—it was the worst performer on our 2014 *100 Best Stocks* list, and it doesn't pay a dividend to boot. But we've long liked the company, and we like the business they're in, so we stuck with it through sickness. Now, perhaps, we've turned the corner to—finally—enter a period of lasting health. We hope we're right.

Itron is the world's largest provider of standard and intelligent metering systems for residential and commercial gas, electric, and water usage, primarily to the utility industry. Intelligent meters, in addition to tracking raw usage over time, can also measure at the point of use operating parameters such as pressure, temperature, voltage, phase, etc. This information can be extremely valuable to the supplying utility but has in the past been difficult and expensive to obtain.

Itron supplies a range of products from basic meters that are read manually to meters that act as network devices and transmit their data in real time to the managing utility and/or to the consuming customer. Products and systems are produced and sold in three groupings:

- Standard metering—basic meters that measure electricity, gas, or water flow by electrical or mechanical means, with displays but no built-in remote reading or transmission capability.
- Advanced metering—these units, depending on the country and the communications technologies available—transmit usage data remotely through telephone, cellular, radio frequency (RF), Ethernet, or power line carrier paths. Among other value adds, these meters transmit usage data for billing, thereby eliminating the need for onsite meter reading—a big savings for utility companies.
- Smart metering—smart meters collect and store interval data and other detailed info, receive commands, and interface with other devices through assorted communication paths to thermostats, smart appliances, and home network and other advanced control systems.

Itron also sells a range of software platforms for utilities and building managers for the management of the installed base and the analysis and optimization of usage, and it is active in developing so-called "smart grid" solutions for utilities and utility networks. The company also markets advanced metering initiative (AMI) contracts to utilities, where it installs devices and monitors and optimizes power usage for a utility. At present, electric meters represent about 43 percent of the business, gas meters about 29 percent, and water meters the remaining 29 percent. The company has about 8,000 customers in 100 countries, and about 55 percent of the business comes from outside the U.S. and Canada. The company has become a major player in the emerging "Smart City" energy use concept, and sees long-term benefit from the growing electrification of transport. Itron products are also frequently mentioned in "Internet of Things" circles.

Pretty smart stuff, don't you think? The question has always been—can they make money?

Financial Highlights, Fiscal Year 2015

Up until now, Itron has suffered on multiple fronts. First, there's the universal headwind of currency, the impact of which is magnified by the concentration of international sales. Then, utilities went through some belt tightening as capital was consumed to convert from coal to gas, as fuels became cheaper overall, and as pending interest rate increases dampened enthusiasm to spend. Some large installation contracts ended, also. But a combination of good technology, greater demand in the water segment, and operational efficiencies may get Itron around the corner.

FY2015 revenues continued to stagnate. But an uptick in margins due to efficiencies and an improved ("smarter") mix led to a near doubling of net profit, and continued share buybacks in the 2–3 percent range helped earnings per share to its best level since 2012.

Better news shows in the company's backlogs. It's "book to bill" (orders to shipments) ratio was 1.7 recently—a strong figure for this type of industry—and total backlog is up 11.5 percent and now exceeds $1.5 billion. The company expects revenues to pick up to about $2 billion by FY2017, with earnings doubling again to about $60–$70 million—or $1.60–$1.90 per share—a figure that could go higher as more efficiencies and operating leverage play in with greater volumes. The company continues to return cash to shareholders through healthy buybacks in lieu of cash dividends.

Reasons to Buy

Can you picture a day when you might manage your energy consumption, device by device, in your home using your smartphone? Even if you're away from the home? And the day when utilities can monitor usage in real time to shift supply of a resource such as electricity that cannot be easily stored? A day when you (or your apps) work together with your utility to optimize energy use from all sources at all times of the day? A day when solar energy generated from one locale on a sunny day is moved to another with clouds and rain?

If you believe that the need for managed energy efficiency will only grow in the future, Itron is a good place to be. As utilities modernize, reduce costs, and replace infrastructure, Itron products and networks will be in the sweet spot. Internationally, utilities are adding infrastructure, as well as replacing it, and Itron is positioned well for that, too. Public policy will provide some tailwinds too. Recent droughts will probably bode well for water conservation and smart metering. Worldwide, only about 15 percent of 2.5 billion meters are "smart" or "advanced," while in the U.S. that figure is approaching 50 percent. Smarter, more advanced meters are where the puck is going.

While Itron has guided optimistically and missed before, we think things might finally be "switched on" for a good run. We hope we're right.

Reasons for Caution

Companies that sell good ideas don't always grow, particularly if the size of their markets is limited or they are particularly conservative about spending money; that might describe the utility industry, which has been spending money on a lot of other things lately, including new gas-fired plants. Energy credits and subsidies are always subject to change. The next two years will be a test of whether the company can size its business properly to the conditions, bring more good ideas to more markets successfully, and execute in general.

If not—we may just run out of patience.

SECTOR: Information Technology ▫ BETA COEFFICIENT: **1.72** ▫ 10-YEAR COMPOUND EARNINGS PER-SHARE GROWTH: **1.5%** ▫ 10-YEAR COMPOUND DIVIDENDS PER-SHARE GROWTH: **NA**

	2008	2009	2010	2011	2012	2013	2014	2015
Revenues (mil)	1,909	1,687	2,259	2,434	2,178	1,949	1,971	1,878
Net income (mil)	117.6	44.3	133.9	156.3	128.5	15.0	13.7	24.8
Earnings per share	3.36	1.15	3.27	3.85	2.71	0.36	0.35	0.64
Dividends per share	—	—	—	—	—	—	—	—
Cash flow per share	4.96	2.53	4.85	5.56	4.84	2.60	2.93	2.90
Price: high	109.3	69.5	81.9	64.4	50.3	48.4	43.7	42.7
low	34.3	40.1	52.0	26.9	33.3	37.0	32.3	27.9

Website: www.itron.com

Johnson & Johnson

Ticker symbol: JNJ (NYSE) ❑ S&P rating: AAA ❑ Value Line financial strength rating: A++ ❑ Current yield: 2.9 percent ❑ Dividend raises, past 10 years: 10

Company Profile

"Caring for the world, one person at a time" is the slogan of Johnson & Johnson, one of the largest and most comprehensive healthcare "family of companies" in the world. JNJ offers a broad line of consumer products, over-the-counter drugs, and various other medical devices and diagnostic equipment.

With total FY2015 sales of over $70 billion, the company has three reporting segments: Pharmaceuticals (about 44 percent of revenues), Medical Devices and Diagnostics (about 37 percent), and Consumer Healthcare (about 20 percent). Across those segments, Johnson & Johnson has more than 250 operating companies in 60 countries, selling some 50,000 products in more than 175 countries. Among Johnson & Johnson's premier assets are its well-entrenched brand names, which are widely known in the United States as well as abroad. As a marketer, JNJ's reputation for quality has enabled it to build strong ties to commercial healthcare providers.

In the Consumer segment, the company's vast portfolio of well-known trade names includes Band-Aid adhesive bandages; Tylenol; Stayfree, Carefree, and Sure & Natural feminine hygiene products; Mylanta; Pepcid AC; Motrin; Sudafed; Zyrtec; Neosporin; Neutrogena; Johnson's baby powder, shampoo, and oil; Listerine; and Reach toothbrushes. Names in the Pharmaceutical segment are less well-known but include major entries in the areas of antiseptics, antipsychotics, gastroenterology, immunology, neurology, hematology, contraceptives, oncology, pain management, and many others distributed both through consumer and healthcare professional channels. Medical Devices and Diagnostics products include professionally used cardiovascular, orthopedic, diabetic, neurologic, and surgical products among others.

The company is typically fairly active with acquisitions, acquiring small niche players to strengthen its overall product offering.

Financial Highlights, Fiscal Year 2015

Johnson & Johnson continues to own a dominant and stable franchise in a secure and lucrative industry. We like the model of steady, recurring income from solid consumer brands such as Tylenol combined with more aggressive and lucrative ventures into pharmaceuticals and surgical products. However, currency effects—as forecasted—and some competitive headwinds in the Pharmaceuticals segment led to a 5 percent decline in the top line for FY2015, with a similar drop in the bottom line. Without currency, sales were ahead about 2 percent.

Future guidance, always conservative for J & J, now calls for a slight 1–2 percent increase in FY2016 revenues and a more moderate 5.3 percent increase into FY2017; per-share earnings, on the back of moderate buybacks, are slated to rise 6–7 percent in FY2016 and again in FY2017.

The company has raised its dividend for 53 straight years. As a testimonial to the company's exceptional financial strength, it is one of three industrial companies to earn an "AAA" Standard & Poor's rating.

Reasons to Buy

A term we don't hear as much anymore in the investment arena is "blue chip." A name taken from the highest-value poker chip on the table, it was used to describe a stock into which you could put your money without fear. A blue-chip stock was where you put money that you would normally put in a bank, if banks would only pay dividends and occasionally offer you more than a toaster as an incentive to stick around. Johnson & Johnson has been a blue chip for as long as there have been blue chips.

JNJ continues to be a conservatively run company whose growth prospects are on the lower end of this book's scale, but clearly the company has great appeal in the investment community especially in periods of market volatility. Even if it's more often unexciting for the growth and momentum investor, JNJ's business model reminds us of the blue chips—steady earnings and cash flow combined with a healthy dividend and share repurchases, leading to very gratifying total shareholder returns. It's a "sleep at night" stock with a decent track record for shareholder "raises."

Reasons for Caution

While we still think JNJ is a good, steady horse for a relatively long race, it has picked up some speed of late, increasing the chance of getting winded somewhere along the way. The P/E, a figure we don't rely on heavily but do look at, has expanded from 14–15 to the 17–18 range, adding a bit of downside risk to the mix. That said, a good bit of this increase has to do with the impact of currency on earnings and not matters related to the business itself.

SECTOR: **Healthcare** ▫ BETA COEFFICIENT: **0.62** ▫ 10-YEAR COMPOUND EARNINGS PER-SHARE GROWTH: **7.5%** ▫ 10-YEAR COMPOUND DIVIDENDS PER-SHARE GROWTH: **10.5%**

	2008	2009	2010	2011	2012	2013	2014	2015
Revenues (mil)	63,747	61,897	61,587	65,030	67,224	71,312	74,311	70,074
Net income (mil)	12,949	12,906	13,279	13,867	14,345	15,576	16,323	15,409
Earnings per share	4.57	4.63	4.76	5.00	5.10	5.52	5.70	5.50
Dividends per share	1.80	1.93	2.11	2.25	2.40	2.59	2.76	2.97
Cash flow per share	5.70	5.69	5.90	6.25	6.45	7.10	7.26	6.90
Price: high	72.8	65.9	66.2	66.3	72.7	96.0	109.5	106.5
low	52.1	61.9	56.9	64.3	61.7	70.3	86.1	81.8

Website: www.jnj.com

GROWTH AND INCOME

Kimberly-Clark Corporation

Ticker symbol: KMB (NYSE) ▫ S&P rating: A ▫ Value Line financial strength rating: A++ ▫ Current yield: 2.7% ▫ Dividend raises, past 10 years: 10

Company Profile

Kimberly-Clark develops, manufactures, and markets a full line of personal care products, mostly based on paper and paper technologies. Well-known for its ubiquitous Kleenex brand tissues, KMB also is a strong player in consumer bath tissue, diapers, feminine and incontinence products—and in industrial and professional markets as well all primarily paper-based cleaning and sanitation products. The company was founded in 1872 and is headquartered today near Dallas, TX, with a historical, technology, and manufacturing base in the Fox River Valley in Wisconsin. There are manufacturing facilities in 38 countries serving customers in 175 countries; about 49 percent of the company's sales originate outside North America.

After a major spinoff described shortly, the company now operates in three segments: Personal Care, Consumer Tissue, and K-C Professional & Other. The Personal Care segment (now 50 percent of FY2015 revenues) provides disposable diapers, training and youth pants, and swim pants; baby wipes; and feminine and incontinence care products, and related products. Brand names include Huggies, Pull-Ups, Little Swimmers, GoodNites, Kotex, Kotex Lightdays, Depend, and Poise. Baby care is the single largest business category with $6 billion in revenues—about 28 percent of the business—mostly sold under the Huggies brand. The diaper brands, including adult versions Poise and Depend, are among the faster-growing businesses.

The Consumer Tissue segment (now 33 percent) offers facial and bathroom tissue, paper towels, napkins, and related products for household use under the Kleenex, Scott, Cottonelle, Viva, Andrex, Scottex, Hakle, and Page brands. Ah (choo), there's Kleenex, a $2 billion business in itself, almost 10 percent of the total. But Scott is no softie either, accounting for another 10 percent.

The K-C Professional & Other segment (17 percent) provides paper products for the away-from-home, that is, commercial/institutional marketplace under Kimberly-Clark, Kleenex, Scott, WypAll, Kimtech, KleenGuard, Kimcare, and Jackson brand names.

On the innovation front, KMB is working on personalized "MyKleenex" tissue packaging (yes, you can create your own Kleenex boxes with your own name, pictures, and designs), fast-dissolving Scott toilet tissue, new Kleenex Balsam tissues to soothe sore noses, and new Huggies sun care lotions and dispensers for "little swimmers."

Financial Highlights, Fiscal Year 2015

Currency headwinds, the 2014 Halyard healthcare spinoff, and an $835 million (net) pension settlement made yearly comparisons once again difficult. Revenues came in about 6 percent lower but with a 10 percent currency loss, so "organic" growth was closer to 5 percent positive. Net earnings, helped along by the "FORCE" cost-savings initiative described as follows, would have been as much as 35 percent ahead of FY2014 if not for the pension adjustment and a small write-down for Venezuelan operations. New product developments, international expansion, and the successful cost-reduction and restructuring program known as "FORCE" will be with us through FY2017, with $400 million in cost savings on tap for FY2016 alone. Revenues are projected flat for FY2016 and ahead 3 percent for FY2017; earnings should recover to previous levels in FY2016 and advance 10–15 percent in FY2017 with a better product mix and higher margins. Cash returns to investors should continue to grow into FY2017. The company will probably repurchase $600 million–$1 billion in stock this year: 1–2 percent of total shares outstanding. The share count is down 20 percent in the past ten years.

Reasons to Buy

Despite recent numbers, the story hasn't changed. Kimberly-Clark has shown itself to be a steady and solid business and investment performer in all kinds of economic climates. The relatively high yield and strong track record of raising dividends and buying back shares is a definite plus. Strong cash flow has financed strategic business investments, including international expansion in emerging markets, product innovations, and strategic marketing. The company continues to be rock solid, with a low beta of 0.32 (and solidarity during the early 2016 volatility) and with shareholder interests a consistent priority.

The company has stellar brands and should do well expanding them into overseas markets. Also, compared to some peers, especially Procter & Gamble, the company is less inclined to go for "glamour" markets such as cosmetics, choosing instead to add to margins through operating efficiencies and scale. Safety-oriented investors may find this approach preferable, and the company gets top ratings for financial strength and price stability.

Reasons for Caution

While the paper products business is steady, it isn't too easy to see where additional growth will come from, even with more innovation and brand-strengthening activity. The company, rightly so, is targeting international expansion, but competition and currency fluctuation make the results far from certain. The cost of pulp and paper raw materials will always be volatile. Companies like KMB have sometimes come to rely on acquisitions for growth; KMB has, so far, largely resisted this temptation but that could change. Finally, investors and the markets have recognized KMB's consistent excellence and once again have bid up the share price in response to all the good earnings news.

SECTOR: **Consumer Staples** ❑ BETA COEFFICIENT: **0.32** ❑ 10-YEAR COMPOUND EARNINGS PER-SHARE GROWTH: **1.5%** ❑ 10-YEAR COMPOUND DIVIDENDS PER-SHARE GROWTH: **8.0%**

		2008	2009	2010	2011	2012	2013	2014	2015
Revenues (mil)		19,415	19,115	19,746	20,846	21,063	21,182	19,724	18,591
Net income (mil)		1,698	1,884	1,843	1,591	1,750	2,142	1,476	1,013
Earnings per share		4.14	4.52	4.45	3.99	4.42	5.53	3.91	2.77
Dividends per share		2.27	2.38	2.58	2.76	2.92	3.24	3.36	3.52
Cash flow per share		5.98	6.40	6.53	6.78	6.70	7.89	6.40	4.67
Price:	high	69.7	67.0	67.2	74.1	88.3	111.7	118.8	125.0
	low	50.3	43.1	58.3	61.0	70.5	83.9	102.8	103.0

Website: www.kimberly-clark.com

CONSERVATIVE GROWTH

The Kroger Company

Ticker symbol: KR (NYSE) ❑ S&P rating: BBB ❑ Value Line financial strength rating: A ❑ Current yield: 1.2% ❑ Dividend raises, past 10 years: 9

Company Profile

Kroger is the nation's largest retail grocery store operator, with about 2,778 supermarkets and multi-department stores, 784 convenience stores, and 323 specialty jewelry stores operated around the country. Supermarket operations account for about 94 percent of total revenue and are located in 35 states with a concentration in the Midwest (where it was founded) and in the South and West, where it grew mostly by acquisition. The company is dominant in the markets it serves, with a number one or two market share position in 42 of its 49 major markets.

Kroger operates through a series of store brands many of you will be familiar with but probably did not associate with the Kroger name, including King Soopers, City Market, Fred Meyer, Fry's, Ralphs, Dillons, Smith's, Baker's, Food 4 Less, Harris Teeter, and an assortment of others totaling about two dozen business names. In late 2015 Kroger made the rather interesting acquisition of Roundy's, parent company of the urban upscale supermarket chain Mariano's which operates 34 stores in the Chicago area and 117 other stores mainly in Wisconsin. The Mariano's footprint is urban and somewhere between a traditional grocery and Whole Foods—an interesting new style of store that should play well with urban and Millennial consumers, and naturally could be expanded elsewhere.

The typical Kroger supermarket is full service and well appointed with higher-margin specialty departments such as health foods, seafood, floral, and other perishables. The Fred Meyer stores carry a large assortment of general merchandise in addition to groceries, turning them into modern-era big-box department stores; the company has 132 stores in all that meet this format, mostly in the West. There are also 131 "price impact warehouse" stores under the Food 4 Less, Foods Co. and Ruler Foods brands and 117 "marketplace" stores—"Kroger Marketplace," "Fry's Marketplace," "King Soopers Marketplace," and so forth—with expanded offerings similar to Fred Meyer to complement the supermarkets. About 1,387 "supermarket fuel centers" and 1,950 pharmacies round out the supermarket picture. Finally, the company has a considerable presence in manufacturing its own store-branded food items, with 38 such plants located around the country and estimates that 26 percent of revenues and 40 percent of unit volumes come from in-house brands. The company also plays well in the organic subsegment, growing natural and organic sales roughly 15 percent annually compared to an overall growth of 10 percent in this market U.S. wide. Kroger is also a leader in applying the latest smartphone technologies to the grocery-shopping experience; they estimate that their shoppers spend 43 percent more time on their mobile apps than other grocery shoppers.

The company's appealingly simple operating philosophy is summed up in three words: "Simple. Consistent. Differentiator." The mantra continues: "Products I want, plus a little. Great people. Good prices. 'I want to return.'" We usually don't go too far with slogans and mantras found on websites and investor presentations, but we liked this one a lot.

Financial Highlights, Fiscal Year 2015

Kroger boasts that same-store supermarket sales have grown for 45 consecutive quarters, and this is a good track record particularly in light of the Great Recession and more recently, heightened competition from the likes of Wal-Mart, Target, and others. While same-store comps continue to grow, the rate has slowed a bit from the 4–5 percent range to the 2–3 percent range in 2016 and beyond—in part due to lower inflation in general and meat prices in particular. Another bit of good news: We can chuck the line "hurt by currency headwinds"—Kroger is 100 percent U.S. based. FY2015 revenues in total grew about 1.3 percent, slower than the comp growth mostly due to lower fuel prices, which aren't included in the comp figures. Slightly improved margins, due to operational efficiencies, critical mass, more house-brand sales, and a leveling off of commodity food prices gave considerable strength to net earnings, which rose a full 15 percent. With the Roundy's acquisition and continued "comp" increases revenues should rise in the 7–8 percent range in 2016 and 4–5 percent range in 2017, while earnings should rise in the 8–10 percent range both years. Kroger's own shares continue to top its own shopping list; they have now retired a third of their float since 2005. The dividend, which commenced in 2006, should also continue to rise, perhaps a bit faster as the company slows its share repurchases in 2016.

Reasons to Buy

Kroger has done a good job in a tough market. Major discount retailers like Wal-Mart and Target have stepped into the grocery business with a fairly significant price advantage, yet so far Kroger has been able to fend them off by focusing on product breadth, the shopping experience, and strategic price reductions. We also like the Fred Meyer–quality grocery-plus-department-store format, a more pleasant and balanced shopping experience than either Walmart or Target and a format that Kroger would do well to roll out nationwide. We also see the recently acquired Mariano's as a good expansion model. The company also has a good toehold on the low-price warehouse food business with Food 4 Less. In short, the company has a good dog in every grocery and marketplace store "fight" around the country.

This success has finally been recognized in the share price and last year's two-for-one split, which too has been helped along by the dramatic share buybacks. Kroger has surprised us by becoming something of a momentum stock in today's market. All told, this is a well-managed company that continues to dominate its niches.

Reasons for Caution

You can't think "full-service grocer" without raising the fear of competition from discounters, and the recent recession trained a lot of shoppers to look for the lowest possible prices, even if they had to go to two or three stores to complete a week's shopping. If the conventional grocery store format is condemned to the dustbin of retail history, Kroger could be vulnerable, but we feel it has enough clout and experience in new formats to adapt. The razor-thin 1.5 percent profit margins characteristic of this industry leave little room for error, though they did tick up to 1.6 percent in 2014 and 1.9 percent recently—a sign that competitive pressures aren't *too* strong. The market has finally recognized Kroger's success and has made the shares more volatile and less of a bargain—shop carefully.

SECTOR: **Retail** ❑ BETA COEFFICIENT: **0.76** ❑ 10-YEAR COMPOUND EARNINGS PER-SHARE GROWTH: **11.5%** ❑ 10-YEAR COMPOUND DIVIDENDS PER-SHARE GROWTH: **10.5%**

		2008	2009	2010	2011	2012	2013	2014	2015
Revenues (bil)		76.0	76.7	82.1	90.4	96.7	98.5	108.5	109.8
Net income (mil)		1,249	1,122	1,118	1,192	1,423	1,445	1,757	2,039
Earnings per share		0.95	0.87	0.87	1.00	1.32	1.43	1.76	2.06
Dividends per share		0.18	0.19	0.20	0.22	0.27	0.32	0.35	0.41
Cash flow per share		2.07	2.08	2.19	2.52	2.99	3.15	3.81	4.27
Price:	high	15.5	13.5	12.1	12.9	13.5	21.9	32.5	42.8
	low	11.1	9.7	9.5	10.5	10.5	12.6	17.8	27.3

Website: www.kroger.com

Macy's, Inc.

Ticker symbol: M (NYSE) ❑ S&P rating: BBB+ ❑ Value Line financial strength rating: B++
❑ Current yield: 3.8% ❑ Dividend raises, past 10 years: 8

Company Profile

Talk about markdowns. Macy's was our fourth-biggest loser on the *100 Best 2016* list with a 33 percent loss for our measurement year. That's not a good place to be, particularly when you don't have the backstory of the energy and commodity bust to rely on as an excuse. We had to take a hard look at Macy's and what got it onto the list in the first place—dominance in the department store niche, strong initiatives in omnichannel marketing to appeal to today's modern shopper, and excellent shareholder returns. Are these features still intact? Despite the movement away from mall stores and bricks and mortar in general, we think they are. So here once again, we will parade Macy's onto the 2017 *100 Best* list, for another year anyway. We hope our Macy's balloon doesn't get stuck on a light pole.

Macy's is now by far the largest operator of department stores in the U.S. The company operates mainly under two brand names, Macy's and Bloomingdale's, and operates, after 410 store closures, 870 stores total (730 Macy's stores) in 45 states, Puerto Rico, and Guam. Macy's has been assembled over the years from a large assortment of famed department store predecessors including Marshall Field, May, and a portfolio of names once under ownership of Federated Department Stores, including Lazarus, Weinstocks, Dillard, Abraham & Straus, I. Magnin, and others, and now the newly acquired Bluemercury skincare shops and spas. The company, in current form, was assembled after Federated emerged from bankruptcy in 1992.

In addition to department stores, Macy's operates its own credit card operations and an internal merchandising group that, among other things, develops or licenses and markets a number of familiar proprietary brands such as Charter Club, Club Room, Hotel Collection, Tommy Hilfiger, Ellen Tracy, the Martha Stewart Collection, and more recently, Finish Line activewear. Private label brands continue to account for 20 percent of sales. The company has also embarked on a deliberate strategy to target the "Millennial" age group (born between 1982 and 2001) with selected styles and brands—an important growth strategy as the department store demographic typically leaves this group out. Macy's has unabashedly declared that it is focused on an "upscale niche," with greater emphasis on the "hottest" brands and special "customer amenities" such as personal shoppers, "outstanding" fitting rooms and lounges, and international visitors centers.

The company also operates 90 specialty stores including outlets and furniture stores. The sales mix for Macy's and Bloomingdale's is approximately 23 percent feminine apparel; 38 percent feminine shoes, cosmetics, intimate apparel, and accessories; 23 percent men's and children's; and 16 percent home and miscellaneous. Macy's acquired luxury beauty products and spa retail chain Bluemercury in 2015 with 80 outlets in 19 states, and now plans to co-locate some of these stores in their larger mall stores. International expansion is also a growth vector, with a Bloomingdale's store in Dubai and more to come in that region; Macy's online ships to 100 countries.

The online presence, macys.com, continues to grow and is strategically more integrated with the sales process, what it calls "omnichannel" shopping. It's easy to shop online, then see the product, pick it up, and importantly, pay the online price at the store. Such store pickups are thought to lead to more sales when customers are at the store picking up merchandise. Also, omnichannel shopping expands available stock, colors, and sizes and produces logistical and supply-chain efficiencies, as orders can be flexibly filled from nearby stores if that makes sense; all stores support each other and the online channel, too.

Financial Highlights, Fiscal Year 2015

In FY2015 Macy's broke a long and enviable five-year string of same-store comp increases to report a 2.5 percent drop for the year and a 4 percent drop in the second half. Several factors including warm weather and port disruptions led to an overstocked retail channel U.S. wide; store closures also factored into both revenues and profits. Sales dropped about 3.5 percent for the year; net earnings fell a more substantial 21 percent on lower margins due to discounting and poor fixed-cost absorption on lower volumes.

As the company continues to consolidate stores and merchandise, sales and earnings will remain largely flat to slightly lower through 2017, while cash flows will continue to improve on a per-share basis, as write-downs subside and share counts decrease. Dividend growth has been and will be solid, and share buybacks have dropped the share count 40 percent in the past 10 years and 25 percent in the past four—a good bargain for current shareholders.

Reasons to Buy

Justifiably perhaps, most investors would perceive Macy's and the department store business to be yesterday's news, as big-box retailers and the

Internet have taken over. True, those players have snatched important parts of the retail business, but the company's motto, espoused on its annual report and elsewhere, is "The Agility to Adapt." Indeed, and even though it faces persistent headwinds from online, big-box, and specialty retailers, the department store idea has made something of a comeback with more affluent, brand-conscious, and experience-conscious shoppers. The stores have been upgraded, merchandise assortments made more exciting and targeted to younger buyers, and service has improved. Merchandise assortments have been localized and are now more exciting and edgier and more aimed at the younger set. Department stores aren't just for grandma any longer; more and more they're being tuned for the Millennial generation. The integration of online and physical stores into a unified experience continues to be one of the best such efforts we've seen. New technologies, such as large-screen digital displays and tablets in the hands of store personnel, are expanding the sales experience. Merchandise localization efforts (referred to by the company as "My Macy's") are working well, as is the "omnichannel" integration of inventories across the physical and online systems. The company has learned a lot from the past eight years of experimentation with both initiatives and is starting to reap the rewards as all stores and store inventories are now online with the omnichannel strategy. We also like the idea of incorporating smaller stores (and spas) inside the larger ones, starting with Bluemercury but eventually leading to other "outside" brands, much as Apple has its stores inside of Best Buy. Plans are to open 42 Bluemercury stores, 18 inside existing Macy's stores. Why not make the best use of the real estate and give shoppers more reason to set foot into the stores?

In sum, we find a lot to like about the company's strategy and its execution—but clearly 2015 was an off year. Cash flow continues to almost double reported per-share earnings and, through dividend increases and large share buybacks, Macy's continues to lure investors through its front doors.

Reasons for Caution

The economy, of course, is always a risk, and any return to higher levels of unemployment, foreclosures, taxes, or any other factors that would make customers feel less flush will hurt. Declining mall traffic and continued migration to online shopping are concerns, although the omnichannel model protects Macy's from online sales erosion better than many of its competitors. Macy's still relies heavily on promotional discounts and special sale events, which have probably become habitual shopping practice among many customers; we suspect that relatively few customers actually pay full price for most of what they buy. That, of course, puts a limit on achievable top-line growth.

SECTOR: **Retail** ❑ BETA COEFFICIENT: **0.78** ❑ 10-YEAR COMPOUND EARNINGS PER-SHARE GROWTH: **7.0%** ❑ 10-YEAR COMPOUND DIVIDENDS PER-SHARE GROWTH: **16.0%**

	2008	2009	2010	2011	2012	2013	2014	2015
Revenues (mil)	24,892	23,489	25,003	26,405	27,686	27,931	28,105	27,079
Net income (mil)	543	595	867	1,238	1,410	1,539	1,591	1,255
Earnings per share	1.29	1.41	2.03	2.88	3.45	4.00	4.40	3.77
Dividends per share	0.20	0.20	0.20	0.35	0.80	0.90	1.13	1.35
Cash flow per share	4.33	4.29	4.77	5.61	6.34	7.01	7.71	7.46
Price: high	28.5	20.6	26.3	33.3	42.2	54.1	66.6	73.6
low	5.1	6.3	15.3	21.7	32.3	36.3	50.1	34.1

Website: www.macysinc.com

CONSERVATIVE GROWTH

McCormick & Company, Inc.

Ticker symbol: MKC (NYSE) ❑ S&P rating: A- ❑ Value Line financial strength rating: A+ ❑ Current yield: 2.1% ❑ Dividend raises, past 10 years: 10

Company Profile

McCormick manufactures, markets, and distributes spices, herbs, seasonings, flavors, and flavor enhancers to consumers and to the global food industry. It is the largest such supplier in the world. Customers range from retail outlets and food manufacturers to foodservice businesses.

McCormick's Consumer business (about 61 percent of sales), its oldest and largest, manufactures consumer spices, herbs, extracts, proprietary seasoning blends, sauces, and marinades. Spices are sold under an assortment of recognizable brand names: McCormick, Lawry's, Zatarain's, Thai Kitchen, Simply Asia, Club House, Billy Bee, Produce Partners, Golden Dipt, Old Bay, and Mojave. The company estimates its retail market share to be four times the nearest competitor.

Industrial customers include foodservice, food-processing businesses, and retail outlets. The Industrial segment was responsible for 39 percent of sales.

Many of the spices and herbs purchased by the company, such as black pepper, vanilla beans, cinnamon, and herbs and seeds, must be imported from countries such as India, Indonesia, Malaysia, Brazil, and the Malagasy Republic. Other ingredients such as paprika, dehydrated vegetables, onion, garlic, and food ingredients other than spices and herbs originate in the United States.

The company was founded in 1889 and has approximately 10,000 full-time employees in facilities located around the world. Major sales, distribution, and production facilities are located in North America and Europe. Additional facilities are based in Mexico, Central America, Australia, China, Singapore, Thailand, and South Africa. There are innovation centers in 14 countries. The biggest sales components are Americas Consumer (40 percent), Americas Industrial (26 percent), EMEA Consumer (13 percent), EMEA Industrial (8 percent), and Asia-Pacific Consumer (8 percent). The company's products reach consumers in 140 countries. China is now the second-largest market, thanks to the 2013 acquisition of Wuhan Asia-Pacific Condiments (WAPC), and it grew 9 percent last year. The recent acquisition of Italian spice maker Drogheria & Alimentari serves to both expand its international footprint and to bring a few more interesting flavors into the domestic market. The acquisition of Stubb's adds to McCormick's presence alongside your grill.

McCormick has been innovating both on the product and on web and media fronts, including more informative print and web content with recipes and other information to spur cooking with spices. Last year, the company was ranked fifth out of 114 food brands in the U.S. market for its "Digital IQ" index. The company has expanded the digital portion of its advertising budget from 11 percent in 2011 to 38 percent last year. Examples of innovative brand and Internet marketing include an initiative to map your spice tastes by giving you a personalized "FlavorPrint"—then e-mailing you weekly recipes with spice recommendations tailored to that map. Flavor and flavor trend innovations include a new packaging initiative—called Recipe Inspirations—to sell prepackaged spices set to cook a particular meal. Too, they have a place on their website to enter in a singular spice, one that you might like and/or have an abundance of in your pantry; they shoot back recipes for that spice (something we amateur hash slingers have longed for in cookbooks; give me a selection of recipes that use allspice, for instance). All of these initiatives broaden the market to reach the millions of plain folks like us who weren't born with a wooden spoon in our mouths. For those who were born with such a spoon, or who acquired one through years of training and experience, there is also a "McCormick for Chefs" page. In short, we like this recipe: dominant brand, effective digital marketing to spice it up. McCormick is one of the best examples we've seen.

Financial Highlights, Fiscal Year 2015

Overall, business continues to respond nicely to new trends for more interesting foods and to a greater likelihood of eating at home after the recession. Growth has slowed somewhat, but looks more attractive without currency effects; FY2015 revenues grew only 1 percent but grew 6 percent on a constant dollar basis, mostly on brand marketing, distribution expansion, and product and packaging innovations (8 percent of sales came from products launched in the past three years). A few small acquisitions and some price increases also figured in. Margins remained about the same; net earnings also increased about 2 percent but about 3 percent on a per-share basis.

A fine-tuning of the product mix toward higher-margined offerings and moderate productivity improvements should bring a modest 1–2 percent sales gain for FY2016 and a 3–4 percent gain in earnings; these figures accelerate to a 7–8 percent earnings gain on a 4–5 percent revenue gain into FY2017 as margins expand and dollar effects (hopefully) diminish. Dividend increases, which have occurred for 30 straight years now, should continue, as should modest but steady share buybacks.

Reasons to Buy

Simply put, McCormick dominates its food business niche. As a strong pure play in the seasonings business, McCormick is the largest branded producer of seasonings in North America and one of the largest in the world. It is the largest private-label producer of seasonings as well, giving the company a substantial level of price protection. McCormick is not just a producer, it is also an innovator and a marketer, and we feel they've done the right things to build interest in their products and in their brand. They also do well in specialized niche markets, like Mexico and China. We think they're in the right place as new, fresher, and more tailored, customized, interesting, and international food trends all emerge. We also think they're in a pretty good place with Millennials, who want new, different, healthy, and customizable approaches to almost everything—including food—and who want to source their information about food and culinary excellence from the Internet.

On the consumer side, as amateur cooks ourselves we continue to feel that people would use more spices if they only knew how to use them. The website and its recipe offerings and the prepackaged Recipe Inspirations meal kits will get the less experienced cooks using spices more effectively in their own cooking. Doesn't that prepackaged Country Herb Chicken & Dumplings, which deploys six prepackaged McCormick spices, sound good? In our view, these initiatives, combined with continuing growth in the health-conscious segment by learning to replace fat flavoring with spice flavoring, will add to a solid business base for the company.

McCormick estimates the spice market to be growing at 6 percent annually, and with its 22 percent share of the global market, there is plenty of opportunity. That mixes well with the profitability, stability, and defensive nature of the company; it continues to present an attractive combination for investors.

Reasons for Caution

Downsides include the rising cost of ingredients and the sourcing of many of these ingredients in geopolitically unstable regions. Top-line growth is likely to remain moderate except by acquisition; and projections seem muted in contrast to their view of global spice market growth (maybe they're just being conservative?). While earnings and share-price growth have been steady, the price of the stock has been spiced up a bit by its success. All that said, we don't see people's tastes in taste diminishing anytime soon.

SECTOR: **Consumer Staples** □ BETA COEFFICIENT: **0.51** □ 10-YEAR COMPOUND EARNINGS PER-SHARE GROWTH: **8.0%** □ 10-YEAR COMPOUND DIVIDENDS PER-SHARE GROWTH: **10.5%**

	2008	2009	2010	2011	2012	2013	2014	2015
Revenues (mil)	3,177	3,192	3,339	3,650	4,014	4,123	4,243	4,396
Net income (mil)	282	311	356.3	380	408	418	442	450
Earnings per share	2.14	2.35	2.65	2.80	3.04	3.13	3.37	3.48
Dividends per share	0.88	0.96	1.04	1.12	1.24	1.36	1.48	1.60
Cash flow per share	2.83	3.08	3.39	3.55	3.85	4.00	4.24	4.36
Price: high	42.1	36.8	47.8	51.3	66.4	75.3	77.1	87.5
low	28.2	28.1	35.4	43.4	49.9	60.8	52.6	70.7

Website: www.mccormick.com

McKesson Corporation

Ticker symbol: MCK (NYSE) ❑ S&P rating: BBB+ ❑ Value Line financial strength rating: A++
❑ Current yield: 0.8% ❑ Dividend raises, past 10 years: 7

Company Profile

In turbulent markets, sometimes even your surest bets hit a rough patch; such is the case with McKesson, one of our steadiest healthcare performers—and winners—over the years. The business hasn't changed much—but the valuation did, with a P/E ratio falling from the low 20s to the low teens on some pricing weakness in generic lines and some weakness in the international sector. In emotional markets, often the business is just fine; the pricing of the stock gets out of whack. We'll keep McKesson on the *100 Best* list as the solid fundamentals are barely changed.

McKesson Corporation is America's oldest and largest healthcare services company and engages in two distinct businesses to support the healthcare industry. Pharmaceutical and medical-surgical supply distribution is the first and by far the largest business: The company is the largest such distributor in North America, delivering about a third of all medications used daily. The company delivers to approximately 40,000 pharmaceutical outlets as well as hospitals and clinics throughout North America from 28 domestic and 17 Canadian distribution facilities, and has just added a major distribution stronghold for Europe. The distribution business accounts for about 98 percent of sales.

Second, and not to be ignored, is a technology solutions business that provides clinical systems, analytics, clinical decision support, medical necessity and utilization management tools, electronic medical records, physical and financial supply-chain management, and connectivity solutions to hospitals, pharmacies, and an assortment of healthcare providers. The strategically important information technology business is a $3.2 billion business all by itself. McKesson's software and hardware IT solutions are installed in some 76 percent of the nation's hospitals with more than 200 beds and 52 percent of hospitals overall.

The company offers products and services covering most aspects of pharmacy and drug distribution, including not only physical distribution and supply-chain services but also a line of proprietary generics and automated dispensing systems, record-keeping systems, and outsourcing services used in retail and hospital pharmacy operations. The central strategies are to provide a one-stop distribution solution for pharmaceuticals, generics, and surgical supplies, and to provide technology solutions to deliver higher-quality and more cost-effective care at the hospital and clinical levels.

In line with those strategies, McKesson continues along the path of acquiring significant healthcare businesses—large and small—to add to its core offering and to expand globally. In early 2014, the company completed the acquisition of German pharmaceutical distributor Celesio, gaining a strong entry into the international wholesale, retail, and generic distribution markets, particularly in Europe.

Financial Highlights, Fiscal Year 2015

You'd think that with a 30 percent drop in the share price, revenues and earnings would be marching backward at a rapid rate. Not the case—in FY2015 the company logged an 8 percent gain in both revenues and net earnings. Pricing and international weakness will attenuate revenue gains to the 3–4 percent range in FY2016, resuming to the previous 7–8 percent range for FY2017. Net earnings should rise in the 8 percent range both years, and per-share earnings will rise something closer to 10 percent annually. The company will continue with moderate dividend increases and share buybacks, and has retired 25 percent of its shares in the past ten years. MCK has also deployed cash to pay off long-term debt from recent acquisitions.

Reasons to Buy

The distribution business continues to be solid and relatively recession-proof. Demographics and the addition of millions to the insured healthcare rolls will keep demand moving in the right direction, and acquisitions have strengthened that position in domestic and especially international markets. McKesson dominates its niches and is a go-to provider of much of what hospitals and clinics need to operate. It holds market leader position in several important market categories, including number one in pharmaceutical distribution in the United States and Canada, number one in generic pharmaceutical distribution, number one in medical management software and services to payers—you get the idea.

Additionally, hospitals and other healthcare providers are starting to get the memo that it is time to improve utilization and operational efficiency, and McKesson's technology solutions are hard to ignore, although many might do so at first glance, as they are only 2 percent of the business. As most distributors do, McKesson operates on very thin margins; the expansion of technology services and generic-equivalent drugs should eventually become a growth driver as efficiency measures continue to catch on.

The company has a strong track record of stability and operational excellence and is well managed; for long-term investors the recent share price weakness would seem to signal a buying opportunity; a recent P/E of 11.5 seems too low for a company of this strength and track record.

Reasons for Caution

McKesson does operate on thin margins and as such has a low tolerance for mistakes or major changes in the healthcare space, changes that could be brought on by legislation, regulation, or competition. While we applaud the aggressive buyback strategy, we'd like to see a bit more return to shareholders in the form of cash dividends; that said, the company has quintupled the indicated dividend since 2007 and appears to be poised to continue on that path.

SECTOR: Healthcare ◻ BETA COEFFICIENT: 0.96 ◻ 10-YEAR COMPOUND EARNINGS PER-SHARE GROWTH: 15.0% ◻ 10-YEAR COMPOUND DIVIDENDS PER-SHARE GROWTH: 14.0%

	2008	2009	2010	2011	2012	2013	2014	2015
Revenues (bil)	106.8	106.7	112.1	122.7	122.5	137.6	179.5	193.5
Net income (mil)	1,194	1,251	1,316	1,463	1,516	1,947	2,614	2,830
Earnings per share	4.28	4.58	5.00	6.05	6.33	8.35	11.11	12.70
Dividends per share	0.48	0.48	0.72	0.76	0.80	0.88	1.04	1.12
Cash flow per share	6.03	6.37	7.18	8.40	9.30	11.50	15.68	17.30
Price: high	68.4	65.0	71.5	87.3	100.0	166.6	214.4	243.6
low	28.3	33.1	57.2	66.6	74.9	96.7	96.7	160.1

Website: www.mckesson.com

AGGRESSIVE GROWTH
Medtronic, PLC

Ticker symbol: MDT (NYSE) ◻ S&P rating: A ◻ Value Line financial strength rating: A++ ◻ Current yield: 2.0% ◻ Dividend raises, past 10 years: 10

Company Profile

Medtronic is the world's largest manufacturer of implantable medical devices and is a leading medical technology company, providing lifelong solutions to "alleviate pain, restore health, and extend life," primarily for people with chronic diseases. FY2015 was a year of major change for the company, as it completed a $50 billion acquisition of "rival" device maker Covidien, expanding sales by almost 50 percent mostly by gaining market share internationally and in three key segments: Surgical Solutions, Vascular Therapies, and Respiratory and Monitoring Solutions. Through the acquisition of Covidien, Medtronic also acquired an offshore headquarters in Dublin, Ireland, reducing tax rates and increasing net profit margins about 25 percent in the process. The dust is still settling on the acquisition; what follows is our best glimpse at the combined company.

Post-acquisition, Medtronic continues to operate mainly in the areas of cardiovascular, neurological, and other surgeries and therapies and in diabetes management. There are four business segments:

- Cardiac and Vascular Group (46 percent of FY2015 sales). Businesses include Cardiac Rhythm & Heart Failure, Coronary & Structural Heart, and Aortic & Peripheral Vascular. This group as a whole develops products that restore and regulate a patient's heart rhythm as well as improve the heart's pumping function. This segment markets implantable pacemakers, defibrillators, Internet and non-Internet–based monitoring and diagnostic devices, and cardiac resynchronization devices. A new implantable cardiac monitor about a third the size of an AAA battery and 80 percent smaller than competing products was recently approved by the FDA, exemplifying the company's R&D leadership in this industry, as do new efforts to automate remote monitoring and management of heart rhythm patients, a promising expansion of the "Internet of Things" concept into healthcare. Products also include therapies to treat coronary artery disease and hypertension, including balloon angioplasty catheters, guide catheters, diagnostic catheters, guidewires, and accessories. Another line of products and therapies treats heart valve disorders and repairs/replaces heart valves, some through catheters without chest incisions. The unit also markets tools to assist heart surgeons during surgery, including circulatory support systems, heart positioners and tissue stabilizers, ablation tools, stent graft, and angioplasty solutions.
- The Minimally Invasive Technologies Group (12 percent of sales) produces an assortment of products under its Surgical Solutions and Patient Monitoring and Recovery business units.
- The Restorative Therapies Group (33 percent of sales) includes Spine, Biologics, Neuromodulation, Surgical Technologies, and Neurovascular business units. The Spine unit develops and manufactures products that treat a variety of disorders of the cranium and spine, including

traumatically induced conditions, deformities, herniated discs and other disc diseases, osteoporosis, and tumors. The Biologics business is the global leader in biologics regeneration and pain therapies across a variety of musculoskeletal applications including spine, orthopedic trauma, and dental. The Neuromodulation unit employs many technologies used in heart electrical stimulation to treat diseases of the central nervous system. It offers therapies for movement disorders; chronic pain; urological and gastroenterological disorders, including incontinence, benign prostatic hyperplasia (BPH), enlarged prostate, and gastroesophageal reflux disease (GERD); and psychological diseases. The Surgical Technologies unit develops and markets products and therapies for ear, nose, and throat–related diseases and certain neurological disorders; among them are precision image-guided surgical systems.

- The Diabetes Group (9 percent of sales) offers advanced diabetes management solutions, including insulin pump therapy, glucose monitoring systems, and treatment management software.

The pre-Covidien company operated in 140 countries, with about 46 percent of revenues coming from outside the U.S. and 11 percent from emerging markets. Research and Development expenses are about 9 percent of sales. At the time of this analysis we do not have comparable figures for the combined company.

Financial Highlights, Fiscal Year 2015
The Covidien acquisition, begun in mid-2014 and completed in early 2015, added about $10 billion in sales, 7 points to the net profit margin due to tax savings and operational efficiencies, and about $3.5 billion to net profits. "Organic" sales gains are harder to know, but the company estimates on an apples-to-apples basis. With Covidien figures included for 2014 and 2015, sales rose about 3.6 percent. The company still expects substantial synergies—almost $1 billion annually in a few years—to evolve from the merger, and it projects continued sales growth in the low single digits but earnings growth in the 6–7 percent range in FY2016, slowing a bit to the low single digits in FY2017. A moderating dollar and resumed growth in emerging markets could improve all of these figures for FY2017.

Reasons to Buy
The name Medtronic continues to be synonymous with medical technology; the company remains one of the pure plays in the healthcare technology

space. The company was already a "best in class" player in the markets and technologies it was engaged in, and over time its technologies have become more mainstream. Too, we are big supporters of its investments in remote medicine, its investments in emerging markets, and its involvement with new products and breakthroughs, especially in neuromodulation and diabetes management. In the short term, cardiovascular procedures once deferred due to the weak economy are starting to happen on a more normal schedule. Finally, while the merger adds some acquisition risk and long-term debt, we expect the company to gradually retire the 400 million shares issued for the acquisition and to continue its steady track record of dividend increases.

Reasons for Caution

Our previous concerns had to do with exposure to new trends in healthcare cost containment and utilization, particularly in the U.S. Adding Covidien's geographic and product line diversity tempers these concerns somewhat. Still, Covidien is an aggressive move, and carries with it some acquisition risk in size, complexities, and unknown outcomes particularly with the Ireland relocation. Public and U.S. government pressure to "repatriate" some of the tax savings might become an issue as well. That said, Medtronic still appears to be a strong, entrenched leader in medical technology, and well positioned to get stronger still.

SECTOR: Healthcare ❑ BETA COEFFICIENT: 1.02 ❑ 10-YEAR COMPOUND EARNINGS PER-SHARE GROWTH: 9.5% ❑ 10-YEAR COMPOUND DIVIDENDS PER-SHARE GROWTH: 15.0%

	2008	2009	2010	2011	2012	2013	2014	2015
Revenues (mil)	14,599	15,817	15,933	16,184	16,590	17,005	20,261	28,800
Net income (mil)	3,282	3,576	3,647	3,447	3,857	3,878	4,937	8,750
Earnings per share	2.61	2.92	3.22	3.46	3.75	3.82	4.45	5.15
Dividends per share	0.63	0.82	0.90	0.97	1.04	1.12	1.22	1.52
Cash flow per share	3.45	3.96	4.16	4.13	4.60	4.73	5.15	7.15
Price: high	57.0	44.9	46.7	43.3	44.6	58.8	75.7	79.5
low	28.3	24.1	30.8	30.2	35.7	41.2	53.3	55.5

Website: www.medtronic.com

Microchip Technology, Inc.

Ticker symbol: MCHP (NASDAQ) ❑ S&P rating: BB+ ❑ Value Line financial strength rating: A
❑ Current yield: 3.0% ❑ Dividend raises, past 10 years: 9

Company Profile

Your washing machine senses the load, adjusts the wash time and temperature accordingly, and tells you when it's done. Your refrigerator expands or contracts its power cycle according to outside temperature and the time of day to save on peak power costs. Security systems show you what's happening in all parts of your home—and in other homes, such as that of your aging elders. Asset monitors keep track of inventory and key business equipment. It's all connected, always on, all the time.

Ready or not, this "Internet of Things," this Star Wars world of all of our stuff connected to all our other stuff and doing our thinking for us is really coming. The application possibilities are almost endless. But not every electronic product is connected to the Internet; many, many other products have intelligence and/or ease of use features like touch sensitivity to make life easier; Microchip Technology products provide the "distributed intelligence" for many of the smart, feature-rich products we use every day.

Microchip Technology is a leading manufacturer and supplier of specialized semiconductor products primarily embedded as controllers, processors, or memory into products, mostly products other than computers. The company's devices, many of which are customizable, custom-made, or programmable, sense motion, temperature, touch, proximity, and other environmental conditions, process the information, and control the device accordingly. Applications number literally in the thousands but are concentrated in automotive, communications, consumer product, appliance, lighting, medical, safety and security, and power and energy management products. Microchip products are typically small in size (the smallest is 1.3 × 2.4 millimeters), low power, low cost, and capable of operating reliably in extreme conditions. The company offers a full suite of design assistance, tools, and consulting services to help customers, usually OEM manufacturers, develop the best applications. They position these services as "low-risk product development" resources for their customers.

Microchip owns most of its manufacturing capability in four plants: two in Arizona, one in Oregon, and one in Thailand, as part of a deliberate strategy to increase process yields and shorten cycle times (the list of facilities will grow somewhat at least short term with acquisitions—see following). Most but not all products are shipped "off the shelf" with short cycle times or as a scheduled production. R&D accounts for about 16 percent of revenues. As the company sells primarily to other OEM electronic product manufacturers, about 84 percent of sales are to international customers; about 29 percent are to China. Technology licensing accounts for about 5 percent of revenues.

Microchip has more clearly aligned itself and its branding behind the concept of embedded control solutions, and now calls itself "The Embedded Control Solutions Company"—a clear and well-defined business position. The company continues to be an active acquirer as the semiconductor industry consolidates; the latest in early 2016 is the $3.4 billion acquisition of microcontroller and touch technology supplier Atmel. Previous good-sized acquisitions in 2014–15 include communications device maker Micrel; Taiwan-based ISSC, a provider of semiconductors and solutions for the Bluetooth and wireless markets; Supertex, a medical and industrial lighting products company; and Belgian high-speed data and video transceiver maker EqcoLogic.

Financial Highlights, Fiscal Year 2015

With all of the acquisitions it is pretty hard to separate the "organic" growth, which has been hampered by sluggish overall semiconductor demand. FY2015 results were largely flat both on the top and bottom lines. Going forward though 2017, excluding Atmel for now, top-line growth is projected in the 8–10 percent range, with earnings up in the 5–8 percent range, acquisition costs no doubt impacting the earnings and dividend growth in the near term.

Reasons to Buy

Distributed intelligence and the Internet of things are upon us. One doesn't have to look hard to find "smart" products; they're almost everywhere. Not just your smartphone, but your appliances, car, climate-control system, alarm system, in elevators, airplanes, airports, hospitals—you name it. As their functionality improves, they will become a standard part of daily life, just as compact discs, Bluetooth, flat-screen TVs, smartphones—heck, the Internet itself—have all become in the past few decades. Manufacturers will *have* to embrace these new technologies and build them in just to stay in the market.

We like companies that make the Things that make things work, and Microchip seems well positioned as a leading supplier of all this intelligence as "smart" moves far beyond the "smartphone." We remain hesitant about semiconductor companies in general—development and manufacturing costs are high, especially if a company owns its own "fabs" (manufacturing facilities) and product cycles are short. There is plenty of competition everywhere for most products, much of it from lower-cost producers in Asia. Inventory cycles can also play havoc with semiconductor producers, who do best by producing in large quantities. Microchip, in our view, has overcome a lot of that by choosing high-value-add niches and by offering plenty of design and technical support "value add" to go along with the product—and now with its acquisitions, by becoming a more dominant player in its niche.

All that said—and for many of these reasons—it has also become a tradition for capital-intensive semiconductor companies to not pay dividends or much else in the way of cash returns to shareholders. Capital is gobbled up internally for what seems to be endless new investments in fab capacity, design tools, and ever more expensive materials and supplies. Microchip has bucked that trend—how many semiconductor firms have paid a dividend, let alone raised it, for nine consecutive years?

Reasons for Caution

The growth-by-acquisition strategy makes us a little nervous, although we see the logic in niche dominance and in efficiency and scale. Once again, semiconductor makers will always endure the burdens of high capital requirements, short product cycles, inventory cycles of OEMs and distributors, and to no small degree the economy as a whole. Competition, especially from low-cost foreign suppliers, is keen in all semiconductor markets. Unfortunately, that competition includes at least a measure of "illegal" competition through pirated or reverse-engineered technologies, which the company vigorously fights. To address all forms of competition, Microchip has worked hard to make its offering more "whole" with design assistance and short lead times, both of which have pleased its customers.

SECTOR: **Information Technology** ❑ BETA COEFFICIENT: **1.08** ❑ 10-YEAR COMPOUND EARNINGS PER-SHARE GROWTH: **11.0%** ❑ 10-YEAR COMPOUND DIVIDENDS PER-SHARE GROWTH: **4.0%**

	2008	2009	2010	2011	2012	2013	2014	2015
Revenues (mil)	903	948	1,487	1,383	1,606	1,920	2,150	2,180
Net income (mil)	206	213	430	337	389	531	594	590
Earnings per share	1.11	1.14	2.21	1.65	1.89	2.45	2.65	2.65
Dividends per share	1.35	1.36	1.37	1.39	1.41	1.42	1.43	1.43
Cash flow per share	1.66	1.63	2.83	2.26	3.02	3.60	4.32	4.25
Price: high	38.4	29.6	36.4	41.5	38.9	44.9	50.0	52.4
low	16.3	16.2	25.5	29.3	28.9	32.4	36.9	37.8

Website: **www.microchip.com**

Monsanto Company

Ticker symbol: MON (NYSE) □ S&P rating: BBB+ □ Value Line financial strength rating: A+ □ Current yield: 2.5% □ Dividend raises, past 10 years: 9

Company Profile

Monsanto was once a major chemical company with a broad pedigree ranging from saccharine to sulfuric acid to Agent Orange and DDT. Monsanto was absorbed into Pharmacia & Upjohn in 2000, which kept its pharmaceutical products and spun off the agricultural products business into a "new" Monsanto in 2002. Today's Monsanto provides a set of leading-edge, technology-based agricultural products for use in farming in the United States and overseas. The company broadly views its business as providing a system of seeds, biotechnology trait products, herbicides, and now, data, mainly to farmers to produce better-quality and healthier foods and animal feedstocks while expanding yields and reducing the costs of farming.

The company has two primary business segments: Seeds and Genomics, and Agricultural Productivity. The Seeds and Genomics segment (68 percent of FY2015 revenues) produces seeds for a host of crops, most importantly corn and soybeans, but also canola, cotton, and a variety of vegetable and fruit seeds. Most of the seed products are bioengineered to provide greater yields and to be more resistant to insects and weeds. Familiar to many consumers, especially those who travel in the Midwest, is the DeKalb seed brand, but there are many others.

The Agricultural Productivity segment (32 percent) offers glyphosate-based herbicides, known as Roundup to most of us, for agricultural, industrial, and residential lawn and garden applications. Beyond this market-leading product, the division also offers other selective herbicides for control of pre-emergent annual grass and small-seeded broadleaf weeds in corn and other crops. Monsanto owns many of the major brands in both seed and herbicide markets.

In recent years, the company underwent some upheaval as patents on its flagship Roundup herbicide system expired, almost immediately followed by reports that certain weeds were developing immunity to it anyhow and cheaper foreign competitors were starting to invade its garden. Beyond that, Monsanto alienated some of its farmer base with pricing and marketing practices for its seed and herbicide systems. These reports and a sag in earnings brought the share price from the 70s to the mid-40s in mid-2010.

Since then, the company has taken steps to modernize its herbicide offerings and become less dependent on them, to develop the core seed businesses further especially in soybeans and cotton, and to focus on developing markets like Latin America and China, making it less dependent on the "one-trick" Roundup pony. That said, it has introduced new and more effective (and more profitable) versions of this product, choosing not to rely on its expired patent base and technology laurels here, either.

Innovation is a big part of the general Monsanto story. New products are aimed at stabilizing the production of cotton, a big deal especially since Monsanto already plays big in cotton-growing countries such as India, China, and Pakistan. New insect-resistant "Intacta" soybean seeds are gaining traction particularly in international markets.

Among the many positive moves, the company also diversified into the agricultural consulting, analytics, and decision support business by acquiring the Climate Corporation. We continue to applaud these moves.

It looked like the big news for Monsanto in 2015 would be the acquisition of Swiss global agribusiness giant Syngenta, a leader in agrichemicals and pesticides as well as a player in many of Monsanto's traditional markets. Monsanto withdrew the bid but may be considering another one.

Financial Highlights, Fiscal Year 2015

Three years past the major U.S. drought of 2012, the farming business suffers from weaker farm incomes but also a glut in agricultural production; falling commodity prices hurt farmers and thus Monsanto. Demand for farm products in the rest of the world continues to increase but has leveled off somewhat. Even in this environment, U.S. farmers seek Monsanto solutions to reduce costs and produce efficiently, and more farmers in more regions of the world are adopting Monsanto solutions as demand for farm products increases. It just isn't happening very quickly, and many farmers have worked to get by on less input cost.

All of that, plus a stronger dollar, kept company revenues flat in FY2015 with only a modest increase slated for FY2016. Net earnings are also flat, but continued share buybacks totaling some 10 percent in FY2015–FY2016 have driven per-share earnings and cash flows nicely higher with decent dividend increases.

Reasons to Buy

Monsanto will provide business schools with an excellent case study in becoming too dependent on one product and watching that product decline—and responding by retrenching to its core strengths for a resurgence. The company continues to lead in innovation and technology applied to agricultural use and continues to advance in biotech applications in its Seeds and Genomics segment while advancing its products in the Agricultural Productivity segment with glyphosate-related products and analytics and consulting services as well. All of this is working in the backdrop of growing food demand from growing middle classes on a growing global scale. Monsanto doesn't own the "agriculture tech" space outright but clearly plays a leadership role; the company has stated a goal to double corn, soybean, cotton, and canola yields by 2030, thus becoming a leading agent of efficiency and change. When that formula is also profitable, great things can happen, and they have up to now—revenues, margins earnings, cash flow, and dividends are all moving in the right direction at an accelerating pace. Recent share prices leave considerable room for growth once the commodity bust subsides and the whole story regains traction.

Reasons for Caution

Not everyone—including its customer base of farmers—is happy with Monsanto. Many have been outspoken for years about the power and practices of the company, and some of that angst has turned into possible legal headwinds. More recently—and a bit more concerning—is the global movement against "GMO" foods, that is, genetically modified food products. The movement has strengthened markets for organically grown products and created an upswell of negative perceptions about the Monsanto system (and those of competitors as well). Adding fuel to the fire, the World Health Organization released a study listing glyphosate as a "category 2A" probable carcinogen, although many outside agencies have questioned this report.

To date, these issues collectively are presenting little more than a PR challenge for the company, which has started to incorporate "health" into its research and marketing messages, but it all bears watching. Aside from that, of course, an acquisition the size of Syngenta would present some risks and challenges.

SECTOR: Industrials ❑ **BETA COEFFICIENT: 1.19** ❑ **10-YEAR COMPOUND EARNINGS PER-SHARE GROWTH: 20.0%** ❑ **10-YEAR COMPOUND DIVIDENDS PER-SHARE GROWTH: 20.0%**

		2008	2009	2010	2011	2012	2013	2014	2015
Revenues (mil)		11,365	11,724	10,502	11,822	13,516	14,861	15,855	15,001
Net income (mil)		1,895	2,448	1,327	1,615	1,997	2,450	2,787	2,758
Earnings per share		3.39	4.41	2.41	2.93	3.70	4.54	5.19	5.73
Dividends per share		0.83	1.01	1.08	1.14	1.28	1.56	1.78	2.01
Cash flow per share		4.50	5.49	3.57	4.07	4.90	5.79	7.06	7.42
Price:	high	145.8	93.4	87.1	78.7	94.8	116.8	128.8	126.0
	low	63.5	66.6	44.6	58.9	69.7	94.0	104.1	81.2

Website: www.monsanto.com

AGGRESSIVE GROWTH

The Mosaic Company

Ticker symbol: MOS (NYSE) ❑ S&P rating: BBB ❑ Value Line financial strength rating: A ❑ Current yield: 4.4% ❑ Dividend raises, past 10 years: 4

Company Profile

The Biggest Loser. No, this isn't a reference to our favorite (?) TV dieting show. It's a reference to Mosaic—our biggest investment loser for FY2016. The stock lost almost 40 percent for the measurement year. And yet—you're reading a narrative now for the company as part of our 2017 *100 Best* list. What gives?

Indeed. As with most commodity producers, crop nutrient producer Mosaic had a miserable year. We've generally shied away from commodities producers anyway for lack of competitive advantage and for the inevitable down cycles they suffer. The reason Mosaic is still on the list is that we think it has been beaten up too much and offers good value going forward. We hope we're right—and if we are, we'd anticipate a healthy rebound to its former glory on our *100 Best* list in 2017. If we're wrong—well we've just offered up a big bag of fertilizer.

As mentioned, we generally shy away from commodities producers because of the difficulties in establishing a brand or a competitive advantage. Typically the business becomes a race to the bottom, where the low-cost producer wins. But if you're the low-cost producer, you probably aren't making much money—and you probably won't stay the low-cost producer for long.

We prefer companies that have other routes to establishing—and maintaining—a competitive advantage. But then, there are commodities, and then there are *strategic* commodities. What do we mean by that? Well, some commodities are more important—and in more constrained supply—than others. If a company can invest itself wholly in these commodities, can own the largest and most efficient mines and establish a dominant market share and position, it will establish a competitive advantage. That's the main idea behind the Mosaic Company.

"Helping the World Grow the Food it Needs" is the website headline for plant nutrient miner and producer Mosaic Company. Formed in 2004 through a merger of Cargill's fertilizer operations with IMC Global, Mosaic is the dominant world producer in the so-called "P+K" market—that's phosphorus and potassium, for those of you who shied away from high school chemistry. And in case you're not clear on why P and K are important, they are vital fertilizer ingredients and hence essential to most of the world's agriculture production. Plants require more potassium than any other nutrient besides nitrogen, and it is important to root-system development and many processes that form plant starch and proteins. Potassium is mined and sold in its oxide form known more popularly as potash. Phosphorus is a vital component of photosynthesis for plant metabolism and growth.

Mosaic is the largest combined—and among the most efficient—P+K producers in the world. About two-thirds of the business is phosphorus and a third potash. Both minerals are produced commercially in a limited number of places in the world. Mosaic has interests in the important locations in North and South America, notably Florida phosphorus mines and potash mines in Saskatchewan, Michigan, New Mexico, and Peru. Through a network of processing and packaging plants in several countries, the company sells its product in approximately 40 countries. As a percentage of FY2015 sales, North America accounted for 51 percent, Asia 31 percent, Latin America 15 percent, and the rest 3 percent.

The "strategic commodity" idea introduced previously got tarnished a bit by a market disruption in 2013. In 2013 Russia's Uralkali, a major producer, got into a tiff with Belarus's Belaruskali, another major producer, and broke their cartel agreement. Uralkali announced a new business strategy emphasizing volume over price, leading to stiff 25–40 percent declines in world potash prices, undercutting Mosaic. (Actually Mosaic has its own potash cartel formed with Potash Corp of Saskatchewan and Agrium known as "Canpotex.") That disruption was followed by a number of factors consistent with the worldwide commodity price slowdown and a few affecting the nutrient industry and Mosaic in particular. But as a low-cost producer, Mosaic has learned to survive, even thrive, in this lower-priced environment. We think global potash markets will eventually recover, although not to 2007–2008 levels where potash approached $1,000 a ton (versus today's $300), as higher-cost producers take product off the market and as Uralkali reevaluates its strategy.

Financial Highlights, Fiscal Year 2015

As expected, the 2013 market disruption started the slide, and a number of other factors exacerbated it in FY2015: weak agriculture prices, a resulting glut in channel inventories, weakness in Brazil, where Mosaic had made a significant investment in 2014, weakness in China, the stronger dollar, and a new resource tax levied by Canada affecting Saskatchewan potash mining. All together, revenues dropped 2 percent (there was some volume increase in the phosphate market despite these factors), and earnings were off 3 percent. Not too bad, but the inventory imbalance in particular and some mine cutbacks and continued price weakness will affect 2016 results further, with a projected 10 percent drop in FY2016 revenues and a 30–35 percent drop in earnings. Yuck! We'd ordinarily close the book there, but most in the industry project a recovery in 2017 gaining strength into the end of the decade based on a better balance of supply and demand and a return of strength in the ag industry. For now, we're going along with that bet, and are also attracted by strong cash flow, significant buybacks, and dividend raises while we wait. (Mosaic bought back 15 million shares—about 4 percent—at bargain prices during 2015.)

Reasons to Buy

Obviously, a lot depends on what happens from here, as the markets balance and prices and production recover. We're betting on Mosaic's long-term industry leadership in a long-term strategic industry. Demand for food will only increase over time, and Mosaic is the largest of ten world producers of P+K. The combination of prime mining sites, size, and operational efficiency in its processing and distribution operations should lead to at least maintaining, if not expanding, market share. We enthusiastically applaud the dividend hikes and the dedication to returning cash to shareholders in general, whatever form that may take.

Reasons for Caution

A lot of negatives have piled up for this company, and how they sort out over time will matter, although the company has enough financial strength and management savvy to deal with them in the best way possible. Commodity markets and commodity producers are inherently volatile, and any reduction in planting or backup in inventory, not to mention overall global economic weakness or short-term droughts as experienced in the U.S. in 2012, can drive prices down in a heartbeat. Low crop prices, while often driven by larger plantings (using more fertilizer) also strain farm budgets; this mixed effect is hard to predict and can cause short-term inventory disruptions. Worse, a commodity volume and price war such as the one that erupted during FY2013 can be particularly damaging if it blows the assumptions of the most carefully laid business plans and strategies. We think the Uralkali disruption will eventually dissipate (with Mosaic having learned a lot from it), and the natural economics of world food demand and supply will take over; Mosaic is a long-term story as well as an opportunity for short-term investment success if and when market conditions improve.

SECTOR: Materials ▫ BETA COEFFICIENT: 1.46 ▫ 10-YEAR COMPOUND EARNINGS PER-SHARE GROWTH: 11.5% ▫ 10-YEAR COMPOUND DIVIDENDS PER-SHARE GROWTH: NM

	2008	2009	2010	2011	2012	2013	2014	2015
Revenues (mil)	9,812	10,298	6,759	9,937	11,108	9,974	9,056	8,895
Net income (mil)	1,962.2	1,909.7	862.8	1,942.2	1,930	1,744	1,029	1,000
Earnings per share	4.38	4.28	1.93	4.34	4.42	4.09	2.68	2.78
Dividends per share	—	0.20	0.20	0.20	0.28	1.00	1.00	1.08
Cash flow per share	5.20	5.11	2.94	5.35	5.73	5.51	4.64	4.94
Price: high	103.3	62.5	76.9	59.5	62.0	64.6	51.3	53.8
low	21.9	31.2	37.7	44.9	44.4	39.8	40.3	27.0

Website: www.mosaic.com

GROWTH AND INCOME

NextEra Energy, Inc.

Ticker symbol: NEE (NYSE) ▫ S&P rating: A- ▫ Value Line financial strength rating: A ▫ Current yield: 3.0% ▫ Dividend raises, past 10 years: 10

Company Profile

NextEra is a full-service utility, power-generating unit, and utility services provider built around the utility stalwart Florida Power & Light, which formally changed its name to NextEra in 2010. NextEra not only represents an evolution in name but also a hint about how the company does business and expects to do business in the future as a leading user and innovator in clean and large-scale alternative energy sourcing for the power market.

Headquartered in Juno Beach, FL, FPL Group's principal operating subsidiaries are NextEra Energy Resources, LLC, and the original Florida Power & Light Company, one of the largest rate-regulated electric utilities in the country. FP&L serves 8.9 million people and 4.8 million customer accounts in eastern and southern Florida. Through its subsidiaries, NextEra collectively operates the third-largest U.S. nuclear power generation fleet and has a significant presence in solar and wind generation markets. NEE is the world's largest user of wind and sun resources to generate electricity. As proof that such leadership works, customer electricity rates in its operating territories are 30 percent below the national average.

As a nonregulated subsidiary, NextEra Energy Resources, LLC (or "NEER"), is a wholesale energy provider and a leader in producing electricity from clean and renewable fuels and, unlike many other alternative energy–driven businesses, is a viable standalone business entity. It has 4,700 employees at 115 facilities in 25 states and has solar and wind farms, nuclear energy facilities, and gas infrastructure operations not just in Florida but in 22 states and Canada. NEER's energy-producing portfolio includes 9,300 wind turbines on 100 farms in 19 states and four Canadian provinces which is estimated to comprise 17 percent of the entire wind power–generating capacity in the U.S., 14 percent of utility-scale solar power production, and 6 percent of total U.S. nuclear power production. All told, the combined fuel mix of alternative energy and natural gas not only reduces fuel costs (33 percent of revenues, compared to 40s and 50s in much of the industry), but it also produces levels of sulfur dioxide (the cause of acid rain) some 97 percent below the average for the U.S. electric industry, a nitrous oxide emission rate 79 percent below the industry, and a carbon dioxide (CO_2) emission rate 55 percent below industry averages—these numbers are still improving. The NEER subsidiary accounts for nearly a third of NextEra's total revenue—and nearly half of its profits—a healthy return for an alternative energy–based operation.

The company has a few small but promising nonregulated subsidiaries, offering design and consulting services for other alternative and conventional utility providers, and it also operates a fiber-optic network. NextEra is a regular winner of awards for most green, most ethical, and most admired companies—in fact, it made a Top 10 position on *Fortune*'s 2015 list of World's Most Admired Companies.

Finally, in December 2014 the company announced an agreement to acquire the electric-generating business of Hawaiian Electric for about $4.3 billion. Hawaiian Electric faces more challenges than most from individual solar panel installation; the merger appears to be an attempt to lead the development of a "new era" for electric utilities integrating individual with centralized generation. NEE will likely set a path for optimized, integrated grids while also satisfying the state's desire to move to alternative energy platforms. Stay tuned—the merger has run into some recent opposition—but it should be an interesting show of NEE's global leadership in the electric industry.

Financial Highlights, Fiscal Year 2015

Revenues advanced a modest 2.7 percent in FY2015, while lower fuel costs and expanded use of renewables led to a 12 percent gain in net earnings. Continued expansion of the renewables and non-utility businesses should lead to annual top-line growth in the 4 percent range through FY2017, with earnings advancing in the 5–6 percent range, depending in part on regulatory cooperation. Dividends should continue to grow in the high single-digit range annually.

Reasons to Buy

Every year we look forward to evaluating and writing about NextEra; they are leading so many initiatives in what's really a pretty boring industry otherwise, and their website and presentation materials do a good job describing them.

For those who believe that alternative energy is the future for large-scale power generation, NextEra continues to be the best play available. The company continues to grow alternative energy capacity on all fronts, particularly wind and solar, and continues to make money on these efforts. All of this adds to the solid and traditional FP&L regulated utility base; this company has the steady feel of a traditional utility with a bit more interest in the form of alternative energy plays and leading-edge power utility technology. As mentioned previously, NEE will lead the way into figuring out the grid of the future, utilizing an optimized mix of centralized and distributed alternative and conventional generating resources. Cash flow is very strong and supports both hearty dividend increases and continued investments in alternative energy production but hasn't been used to reduce share counts.

Reasons for Caution

The company's FP&L subsidiary is still a regulated utility and may not always receive the most accommodating treatment. Additionally, alternative energy tax credits may diminish over time. Alternative energy innovations and nuclear power carry some risk, and the merchant energy business has fallen on hard times of late. Too, the low price of natural gas makes some of the alternative energy offerings less attractive in the short run. Growth prospects lead to a relatively high share price and low yield for the industry—this is not your Grandma's utility stock—but NEE also is a clear leader in the industry, a trendsetter rather than a trend follower.

SECTOR: **Utilities** ▫ BETA COEFFICIENT: **0.32** ▫ 10-YEAR COMPOUND EARNINGS PER-SHARE GROWTH: **8.0%** ▫ 10-YEAR COMPOUND DIVIDENDS PER-SHARE GROWTH: **8.0%**

	2008	2009	2010	2011	2012	2013	2014	2015
Revenues (mil)	16,410	15,646	15,317	15,341	14,256	15,136	17,021	17,465
Net income (mil)	1,639	1,615	1,957	2,021	1,911	2,062	2,469	2,761
Earnings per share	4.07	3.97	4.74	4.82	4.56	4.83	5.60	6.06
Dividends per share	1.78	1.89	2.00	2.20	2.40	2.64	2.90	3.08
Cash flow per share	8.03	8.75	9.60	9.29	8.70	10.65	12.10	12.90
Price: high	73.8	60.6	56.3	61.2	72.2	89.8	110.8	112.6
low	33.8	41.5	45.3	49.0	58.6	69.8	84.0	93.7

Website: www.nexteraenergy.com

AGGRESSIVE GROWTH

Nike, Inc.

Ticker symbol: NKE (NYSE) ▫ S&P rating: AA- ▫ Value Line financial strength rating: A++ ▫ Current yield: 1.1% ▫ Dividend raises, past 10 years: 10

Company Profile

Nike's principal business activity is the design, development, and worldwide marketing of footwear, apparel, equipment, and accessory products. Nike is the largest seller of athletic footwear and athletic apparel in the world, but a big part of the story is how it is extending beyond traditional footwear and apparel. Its products are sold through retail accounts, Nike-owned retail outlets (of which there are 339 in the U.S. and 592 overseas), its website, and a mix of independent distributors and licensees in more than 190 countries around the world. Recently, the company has added specialized destination "Running Stores" and has expanded reach with more "Direct-to-Consumer," or DTC or "factory" outlets, carrying its traditionally strong product innovation to the channel and retail marketplace.

Nike does no manufacturing—virtually all of its footwear and apparel items are fashioned by independent contractors outside the United States, while equipment products are produced both in the United States and abroad.

Nike's shoes are designed primarily for athletic use, although a large percentage of them are worn for casual or leisure purposes. Shoes are designed for men, women, and children for running, training, basketball, and soccer use, although the company also carries brands for casual wear. The company has been very successful with its offerings for the women's market.

Nike sells apparel and accessories for most of the sports addressed by its shoe lines, as well as athletic bags and accessory items. Nike apparel and accessories are designed to complement its athletic footwear products, feature the same trademarks, and are sold through the same marketing and distribution channels. The new buzzword is "athleisure," and Nike is there front and center. All Nike-branded products are marketed with the familiar "swoosh" logo, one of the most recognized and successful branding images in history.

Nike has a number of wholly owned subsidiaries, or "affiliate brands," including Converse, Hurley, Jordan, and Nike Golf, which variously design, distribute, and license dress, athletic, and casual footwear, sports apparel, and accessories.

Nike-branded products account for about 94 percent of 2015 revenues. Of the total $28.7 billion in Nike-branded revenues (excluding subsidiaries), about 64 percent of it comes from footwear, 30 percent from apparel, and the remainder from equipment. Footwear remains the fastest-growing segment of the business at 13 percent, although the much smaller Converse subsidiary grew at 18 percent for the year albeit only representing 7 percent of total revenues. Approximately 45 percent of sales come from North America, 19 percent from Western Europe, 10 percent from China, 5 percent from central and eastern Europe, 2.5 percent from Japan, and 13 percent from other emerging markets. FY2015 growth came from Western Europe (21 percent), China (19 percent), North America (12 percent), central and eastern Europe (15 percent), Japan (9 percent), and emerging markets (8 percent). Strength in Europe is real and reflects increasing market share over local favorites Adidas and Puma, and is particularly impressive, given currency effects.

Financial Highlights, Fiscal Year 2015

FY2015 revenues continued to burn up the track despite currency effects. Sales rose 10 percent—and 14 percent on a constant currency basis. While labor and material costs rose again, the company also leveraged newer, higher-margined products, firm pricing, DTC sales, and some operating efficiencies into another 0.5 percent increase in operating margins (to 15.6 percent) to cross the finish line with an Olympic-class 22 percent gain in net income. That and a 1.5 percent share buyback combined to strengthen per-share earnings by 22.5 percent.

Direct-to-consumer channels—mainly factory stores and online—continue to be a strong story, with growth in that category in North America of about 17 percent (8 percent same-store sales growth) to $3.5 billion, or almost 25 percent of the business, while DTC in Europe grew 40 percent (24 percent same store) to account for 22 percent of the total Western Europe business. DTC was particularly strong in China, with 28 percent same-store sales growth and 27 percent of the business.

The company stands in good position in all markets, and we should see largely more of the same for the next two years, with revenues up 7–8 percent and net income up 14–16 percent annually over the two-year pull through 2017. Double-digit dividend increases and 1–3 percent share buybacks should also persist through the period.

Reasons to Buy

Why buy Nike? In a word, brand—and brand extension. The Nike brand and its corresponding swoosh continue to be one of the most recognized—and sought after—brands in the world. It is a lesson in simplicity and image congruence with the product behind it. Nike doesn't sit still with it; rather, the company is learning to leverage it into more products outside the traditional athletic wear circuit—golf clubs, golf balls, even a new line of GPS watches and apps to find, say, a new route for your run and to track your performance right on your phone. The company continues to invest in innovation in all of its segments, including new fabrics, colors, uniform materials, and digital linkages to make active lifestyles more productive and fun—and it is now extending this innovation further into marketing and retail. As well, Nike doesn't just limit the brand appeal to athletes: Slogans like "Just Do It" and "If you have a body, you're an athlete" emphasize the appeal and lifestyle across all segments of the population. We continue to think this is drop-dead smart.

Of course, solid brand and brand reputation lead to category leadership and, hence, higher revenue and profitability, and Nike has finished far ahead of the pack in this area, too. The company reached $30 billion in sales just four years after it reached $20 billion, a figure that took 40 years to achieve.

The company also posted double-digit sales gains (in constant currency) across all world regions, more solid evidence of worldwide strength and growth opportunity. The brand and the moat created by the brand seem to have nowhere to go but forward, and improved manufacturing efficiencies, strong channel relationships, and international exposure all keep the company moving faster in the right direction. Despite its size, the company continues to deliver double-digit earnings, cash flow, and dividend growth. We continue to like the combination of protected profitability through brand excellence, operational excellence, and a clean conservative balance sheet, all providing a good combination of safety and growth potential.

Reasons for Caution

A few things could put hurdles in Nike's path. The first is higher labor and commodity input prices. Second, the company has occasionally been in the news—and the rumor mill—for unfair labor practices and child labor violations in some of its foreign manufacturing plants. The company doesn't actually own or operate these plants, but the rumors can stick nonetheless. Too, we think Nike gets today's more trendy, fashion-conscious, variety-seeking consumer, but we have also noticed what we feel is a degradation in value to achieve variety and offer lots of bright colors. We hope the company doesn't steer too far off the track to be "trendy." As well, while we think its image and marketing extend well into a direct-to-consumer selling strategy, the potential for conflict with existing channels is always a cause for concern. Finally, the stock price continues to rise at full speed; we'd recommend looking for good entry points before getting into the starting blocks.

SECTOR: **Consumer Discretionary** ❑ BETA COEFFICIENT: **0.52** ❑ 10-YEAR COMPOUND EARNINGS PER-SHARE GROWTH: **13.5%** ❑ 10-YEAR COMPOUND DIVIDENDS PER-SHARE GROWTH: **17.5%**

	2008	**2009**	**2010**	**2011**	**2012**	**2013**	**2014**	**2015**
Revenues (mil)	18,627	19,176	19,014	20,862	24,128	25,313	27,799	30,601
Net income (mil)	1,734	1,727	1,907	2,133	2,223	2,464	2,693	3,273
Earnings per share	0.86	0.88	0.97	1.10	1.18	1.35	1.49	1.85
Dividends per share	0.22	0.25	0.27	0.30	0.35	0.41	0.47	0.52
Cash flow per share	1.04	1.06	1.15	1.30	1.42	1.62	1.85	2.26
Price: high	17.7	16.7	23.1	24.6	28.7	40.1	49.9	68.2
low	10.7	9.6	15.2	17.4	21.3	25.7	34.9	45.3

Website: www.nikeinc.com

CONSERVATIVE GROWTH

Norfolk Southern Corporation

Ticker symbol: NSC (NYSE) ❑ S&P rating: BBB+ ❑ Value Line financial strength rating: A ❑ Current yield: 3.2% ❑ Dividend raises, past 10 years: 10

Company Profile

Norfolk Southern Corporation was formed in 1982 as a holding company when the Norfolk & Western Railway merged with the Southern Railway. Including lines received in the split takeover (with CSX) of Conrail, the current railroad operates 21,000 route-miles of track in 22 eastern and southern states. It serves every major port on the East Coast of the United States and has the most extensive intermodal network in the east.

Company business in FY2015 was about 17 percent coal (down from the low 20s in previous years), 50 percent carload industrial products, and 23 percent intermodal. Major gateways include ports in the eastern half of the U.S., Great Lakes ports, and major interchange points with the two major Western systems, Union Pacific (another *100 Best* stock) and Burlington Northern Santa Fe. The company estimates that its networks reach 65 percent of U.S. manufacturing and 55 percent of U.S. energy consumption. In the late 1990s, the company split the acquisition of northeastern rail heavyweight Conrail with rival CSX Corporation, so it has considerable operations in the Northeast and Midwest in addition to its traditional southern base. The heaviest traffic corridors are New York–Chicago; Chicago–Atlanta; Appalachian coalfields to the port of Norfolk, VA, and Sandusky, OH; and Cleveland–Kansas City. The company has a diverse base of large Midwestern factories and large and smaller southern factories and basic materials producers in the coal, chemical, automotive, and lumber industry, giving a well-diversified traffic base.

The company provides a number of logistics services and has substantial traffic to and from ports and overseas destinations. The opening of the widened Panama Canal appears poised to give some lift to southern and East Coast ports, which NSC serves well. The company has an active program to attract line-side customers to build freight volumes.

In 2015, Canadian Pacific, operator of the trans-Canada system and subsidiaries in the north central U.S., launched a hostile takeover attempt for NSC, which has fought hard against it. Such a merger would be less natural than an end-to-end combination with western U.S. lines Union Pacific or BNSF, which we think would make better sense for Norfolk Southern. We think there could also be regulatory issues—anyway, it is unlikely to happen but could spur a more favorable combination.

Financial Highlights, Fiscal Year 2015

Continued shifts in the energy market, which first reduced coal and now oil shipments, are hitting NSC hard at present. Coal volumes were down as much as 22 percent in FY2015, with coal revenues down 33 percent. Coal is now 17 percent of revenues, down from 31 percent in 2011. Oil, which had made up some of the shortfall, is now in decline as well as the recent oversupply has cut into domestic production. Really, all commodities have been off; automotive is the only bright spot, and the strong dollar has reduced export traffic. As such, FY2015 revenues dipped almost 10 percent while earnings derailed 22 percent. The company expects flat earnings on another small revenue decline in FY2016, with a slightly stronger FY2017. "Near-term visibility is low" according to the company. NSC is making some adjustments to labor costs and capital improvement budgets to help cope. Due to lower volumes, the key "operating ratio" measure—the ratio of variable to total costs—rose to 72.6 from 69.2 in 2014 and 71.0 percent in FY2013 although not to the higher 75.4 experienced in 2011.

Reasons to Buy

NSC and its competitors have all been hurt, first by the coal slowdown, then the slowdown in exports due to the dollar, and finally, by a slowdown in oil shipments and fracking supplies necessary to support oil production. But as we've said for other companies involved, this appears to be in part a cycle—demand for these commodities should recover, and NSC, like other companies, is well positioned to ride out the storm and emerge even stronger. While the stronger dollar and weaker export market are short-term drags, the ports NSC serves will clearly benefit from the Panama Canal widening, as customers will opt for longer sea and shorter land passages. Last year's West Coast port strike pushed more traffic this way short term, but most industry analysts suggest that at least some of this traffic will continue to avoid the less-dependable West Coast port system.

Additionally, NSC serves some of the more dynamic and up-and-coming manufacturing markets in the United States, namely, Asian and other foreign-owned manufacturing facilities found particularly in the Southeast. The company has created a Heartland Corridor time freight and double-stack container routing between Chicago and the East Coast, reducing distance by 250 miles and, more importantly, transit time is down from four to three days. Similar improvements have occurred on its Crescent Corridor between Louisiana and New Jersey. Such innovations will further assert the company's leadership. Additionally, we like the strength and diversity coming from serving the domestic and especially the foreign-owned auto industry—the company serves plants for (in alphabetical order) BMW, Chrysler, Ford, General Motors, Honda, Isuzu, Mazda, Mercedes-Benz, Mitsubishi, Nissan, Subaru, Suzuki, and Toyota.

Finally, cash flow continues to be strong, dividend raises are consistent, and the company will continue to chug down the share repurchase track once the downturn subsides—recent prices indicate an attractive entry point.

Reasons for Caution

The decline in coal traffic, which mostly supports electric utilities, also exposes the company more to general economic downturns as the remaining mix is more economically sensitive. Oil-related traffic may take a while to come back if energy prices stay low. Too, increased oil shipments expose the company to headline risk and accidents.

Finally, in the railroad industry, as in other capital-intensive, high–fixed-cost industries, it's hard to have just the right amount of capacity. Too much volume can actually be a bad thing as it overtaxes physical plant and causes service disruptions. The tendency is to overreact and spend too much on capital improvements—then the next downturn hits. We're in that mode now. While NSC has proven capable and fairly agile in managing such swings, they always pose a risk.

SECTOR: **Transportation** ❑ BETA COEFFICIENT: **1.27** ❑ 10-YEAR COMPOUND EARNINGS PER-SHARE GROWTH: **10.5%** ❑ 10-YEAR COMPOUND DIVIDENDS PER-SHARE GROWTH: **19.0%**

		2008	2009	2010	2011	2012	2013	2014	2015
Revenues (mil)		10,661	7,969	9,516	11,172	11,040	11,245	11,624	10,513
Net income (mil)		1,716	1,034	1,498	1,853	1,749	1,850	2,000	1,556
Earnings per share		4.52	2.76	4.00	5.27	5.37	5.85	6.39	5.11
Dividends per share		1.22	1.36	1.40	1.68	1.94	2.04	2.22	2.36
Cash flow per share		6.88	5.07	6.48	8.22	8.49	8.96	9.57	9.76
Price:	high	75.5	54.8	63.7	78.4	78.5	93.2	117.6	112.1
	low	41.4	26.7	46.2	57.6	56.1	62.7	87.1	72.1

Website: www.nscorp.com

Novo Nordisk A/S

Ticker symbol: NVO (NYSE) ❑ S&P rating: AA- ❑ Value Line financial strength rating: A++ ❑ Current yield: 1.7% ❑ Dividend raises, past 10 years: 10

Company Profile

Unfortunately, diabetes is a huge and growing disease as more people around the world live to an older age and eat higher-calorie diets. Novo Nordisk, which started out in the early 1920s as two separate diabetes medicine producers, merged in 1989 and now garners almost 80 percent of its current $16 billion in revenues supplying diabetes medicine and care products. The company estimates that it owns 47 percent of the world market and 36 percent of the U.S. market for insulin; and 28 percent of the worldwide diabetes care market overall—up from 27 percent last year.

And, unfortunately, diabetes as a disease continues to grow. Although diabetes is a complex disease for which the many treatments aren't easy to understand, it does break down into two "types" (really, three, if you include the rarer gestational diabetes occurring only in pregnant women): Type 1, in which the pancreas fails to produce enough insulin (and regular insulin supplements are required), and Type 2, a condition whereby cells fail to absorb insulin properly, often called "adult onset" diabetes. NVO estimates that 415 million people (about 6 percent of the world population) have diabetes of one type or another—and that only about half of them have been diagnosed. On top of that, NVO estimates that 600 million live with obesity, which has a tendency to bring on diabetes. The company estimates that its products are used by about 25 million people worldwide today, and plans to grow this to 40 million by 2020.

Major products include traditional human-based insulin and protein-related products for Type 1 diabetes treatment, which are being replaced by higher-performance "modern" and "new generation" insulins. The company is now rolling out several new-generation insulins. One is Tresiba, which lasts 42 hours or more; as with many such rollouts the product became well established abroad before attaining U.S. FDA approval. Another treatment called Ryzodeg for both Type 1 and Type 2 diabetes is manufactured artificially. It is absorbed faster and lasts longer than traditional human insulin and has recently launched in Japan. Another called Xultophy for Type 2 diabetes and hypoglycemia treatment, which has been rolled out in Europe, awaits FDA approval. Another product, with the rather non-descript moniker "NN218" delivers a faster-acting insulin for both diabetes types and is up for approval in both Europe and the U.S. Another recently approved new treatment called Saxenda addresses obesity and overweight adults with Type 2 diabetes or cardiovascular problems. You can see the pattern: The company develops new, more effective formulas and delivery systems (including new oral delivery systems) and typically gets them approved in non-FDA-controlled markets first. By the time they hit the U.S., they are both proven and more profitable. These new therapies are growing at a 20–35 percent clip annually and deliver both sales growth and higher margins.

We shouldn't ignore the 20 percent of Novo Nordisk devoted to diseases outside the diabetes space. The Biopharmaceuticals segment targets hemophilia and other bleeding disorders, hormone-replacement therapies, and human growth hormone markets. The model is similar—pioneering approvals outside the U.S., then migrating them into U.S. markets. The company spends about 15 percent of revenues on R&D; about 48 percent of sales in total come from the U.S., which the company indicates is currently responsible for 62 percent of its top-line growth.

Financial Highlights, Fiscal Year 2015

Strong adoption of new products was offset by another 11 percent depreciation of the native kroner versus the dollar; still, FY2015 revenues advanced a healthy 9 percent, although well short of earlier 15–20 percent forecasts Again, the dollar was the main culprit as sales advanced 22 percent in local kroner. Earnings advanced a healthier 19 percent with a record net profit margin of 32.6 percent helped along by favorable tax conditions and an improved product mix. Forecasts call for 5–10 percent revenue gains through FY2017, which could be better than that with less of a dollar headwind. As the "new" diabetes products grow and mature, net margins will continue to improve, and earnings are forecast up 10–12 percent each of the next two years. Meanwhile, NVO has plans to retire about 10 percent of its shares over the next few years and grow the dividend at something around 10 percent; to that end it raised the dividend 28 percent and approved a $2 billion buyback for 2016. Also worth noting: the company has zero long-term debt and, since domiciled outside the U.S., enjoys a tax rate in the low 20s versus low 30s for most U.S.-based corporations.

Reasons to Buy

Novo Nordisk appears to be an excellent growth story in what is, unfortunately, a healthcare market that is only going to grow over time. It is the closest thing to a pure play in this market. Steady revenues and profits from a traditional insulin treatment base fund new research and releases of more effective, more tailored, easier-to-use diabetes treatments. On top of that, it has diversified into other related and key disease segments—obesity, hemophilia, and growth disorder medicines. We feel very comfortable with this course, and the strong international footprint allows them to gain regulatory and market acceptance long before they enter the prized U.S. market. Financials, too, are excellent.

Reasons for Caution

Taking all this growth into account, shares sell for a premium to earnings that may make some investors uncomfortable; it is more a growth story and less of a shareholder cash–return story than most stocks on our list, although cash returns are catching up. Naturally, we are concerned about regulatory approvals, attempts to control prescription drug costs, and the potential aggressiveness of competitors, who could want their bigger slice of this lucrative market. Some regulatory bodies are holding prices to less-than-acceptable levels—the blockbuster Tresiba was taken off the market in Germany recently as a consequence because the price was held by regulators to the level of ordinary insulin, something the company refers to as an "extreme" case. Finally, even though Novo presents itself well, it is in a complex business on a complex international stage; it continues to push our "buy businesses you understand" mantra to its limits.

SECTOR: **Healthcare** ❑ BETA COEFFICIENT: **0.83** ❑ 10-YEAR COMPOUND EARNINGS PER-SHARE GROWTH: **21.5%** ❑ 10-YEAR COMPOUND DIVIDENDS PER-SHARE GROWTH: **28.5%**

		2008	2009	2010	2011	2012	2013	2014	2015
Revenues (mil)		8,629	9,842	10,814	11,559	13,384	15,435	14,511	15,779
Net income (mil)		1,827	2,075	2,563	2,979	3,800	4,651	4,326	5,141
Earnings per share		0.59	0.69	0.88	1.04	1.38	1.73	1.65	1.98
Dividends per share		0.19	0.22	0.27	0.38	0.50	0.62	0.83	0.73
Cash flow per share		0.75	0.87	1.05	1.24	1.58	1.95	1.88	2.19
Price:	high	14.7	14.0	22.8	26.6	34.1	38.9	49.1	60.3
	low	8.4	8.3	12.8	18.9	22.8	29.9	36.6	41.7

Website: www.novonordisk.com

Oracle Corporation

Ticker symbol: ORCL (NYSE) ❑ S&P rating: AA- ❑ Value Line financial strength rating: A++ ❑ Current yield: 1.7% ❑ Dividend raises, past 10 years: 5

Company Profile

Although the landscape of corporate IT is changing considerably, most notably with the advent of the cloud, it is still built around a foundation of data—and no company has been as synonymous with data (and databases) as Oracle. Led by tech pioneer Larry Ellison, who still owns 27 percent of the company, Oracle is a global provider of database and applications software, "engineered systems" (Oracle hardware preconfigured with Oracle software), and services. Software licenses, renewals, and support constitute roughly 72 percent of revenue, with nearly 55 percent of revenue coming from outside the United States. In detail: New software licenses account for 22 percent of FY2015 revenue, cloud services ("SaaS" and "PaaS"; see following explanation) 6 percent, software license updates and product support 49 percent, hardware systems 14 percent, and services 9 percent. Cloud software now accounts for about 15 percent of all software licenses sold.

The acquisition of Sun Microsystems in 2010 brought with it what was to become Oracle's first line of hardware products. These were basically little more than standard Sun servers with Oracle software installed. These product lines have now been pared down and customized into Oracle's "Exadata" machines, which are very large stand-alone installations with enormous storage capacity.

In the enterprise world, Oracle is ubiquitous. Its database, middleware, and applications, which include everything from sales to accounting to supply-chain to human resources management products, hold the top spots in retail, banking, manufacturing, financial services, the public sector, and several other industry segments. Increasingly, the company is offering its customers a full choice of deployment models: These products and services are being delivered through the "cloud" as SaaS (Software as a Service) and PaaS (Platform as a Service) offerings. Too, the company has acquired over 100 companies in the past decade; perhaps the most visible is the 2004 acquisition of applications software provider PeopleSoft. The ad refrain "More Enterprise SaaS Applications Than Any Other Cloud Services Provider" pretty much sums up where the company's head is at the moment. In addition, the company spent over $5.5 billion—14.5 percent of revenues—on R&D.

Financial Highlights, Fiscal Year 2015

Due mainly to persistent currency effects, FY2015 total revenues were roughly flat at $38.3 billion and would have been up about 4 percent on a constant currency basis. Software and Cloud revenues were up 5 percent on a constant currency basis (1 percent with currency), with Cloud SaaS and PaaS revenues up 35 percent on a constant currency basis, while Hardware systems were up 2 percent (down 3 percent with currency), and Services actually declined 4 percent. Earnings dropped 5 percent in total in part due to larger R&D investments in cloud platforms, while per-share earnings, on the back of a 100 million share buyback dropped 3 percent. Currency will continue to be a headwind in FY2016, with a rosier picture set for FY2017 as the cloud business matures and some new database products gain traction. We should note that although net earnings growth is modest, the *net profit* margin is fully 33 percent—software is a very profitable business.

Reasons to Buy

For many years people viewed Oracle as a company that just didn't get it. Why design and market an Exadata machine for a data center when no one builds their own data center anymore? Why not just use Amazon Web Services? Why continue to market a giant database that requires a large staff of expensive professionals to configure? Everybody knew the sexy part of the market is in small, targeted application software.

These were valid questions and would have been reasons for concern if Oracle were just now getting into the business, but the simple truth is there are over 300,000 Oracle database customers, including nearly all of the *Fortune* 100. Oracle database support and licensing revenues were, and continue to be, a massive cash cow. This large installed base is a *huge* asset, and brings with it a large population of very skilled practitioners, people who have made their entire careers out of installing, configuring, and supporting this software. Understanding that, the company continues to update its namesake product with new capabilities.

However, Oracle also came to recognize the trend among small and midsized companies toward lower capital investment in data services, which has now migrated into larger enterprises. Many startups and even mature companies are moving to cloud service schemes such as SaaS and PaaS. Oracle has responded with a dual approach of internal development programs and targeted acquisitions. As a result, Oracle is now the second-largest (by revenue) SaaS vendor in the world.

We like Oracle's financials, its steady share-price growth, and its wallet—if you plan to grow by acquisition, it's good to have $52 billion in cash. Share-price increases have not been stellar over the years, but through share buybacks the company expects to reduce share counts by a billion shares—about 20 percent—in a ten-year period ending in 2016. It could reduce the share count by another 500 million in the next five years. In 2009 the company also instituted a dividend, which has grown steadily since.

Reasons for Caution

In spite of Oracle's history of steady, if not spectacular, share-price increases, questions about its future growth—and profitability—remain: Can Oracle compete effectively in an increasingly mobile and cloud-based computing environment? Is it too dependent on its cash-cow database products? Are the recently shrinking net profit margins (still 32.6 percent) a bad sign? Can the company sustain them in the competitive cloud environment? Are the company's acquisitions hitting the right segments, and is it buying at the right price? Is it moving fast enough in the cloud and SaaS space? Oracle still seems to be at an inflection point: Will it dominate the cloud as it has dominated the data center? Initial prospects are encouraging, but there are a lot of nimble competitors out there, and the technology changes rapidly.

SECTOR: **Information Technology** ◻ BETA COEFFICIENT: **1.12** ◻ 10-YEAR COMPOUND EARNINGS PER-SHARE GROWTH: **18.0%** ◻ 10-YEAR COMPOUND DIVIDENDS PER-SHARE GROWTH: **NM**

	2008	2009	2010	2011	2012	2013	2014	2015
Revenues (mil)	22,609	23,495	27,034	35,850	37,221	37,253	38,305	38,253
Net income (mil)	6,799	7,393	6,494	11,385	12,520	12,958	13,214	12,489
Earnings per share	1.30	1.44	1.67	2.22	2.46	2.68	2.87	2.77
Dividends per share	—	0.05	0.20	0.20	0.24	0.30	0.48	0.51
Cash flow per share	1.37	1.53	1.75	2.32	2.65	2.91	3.10	3.04
Price: high	23.6	25.1	32.3	36.5	34.3	38.3	46.7	45.3
low	15.0	13.8	21.2	24.7	25.3	29.9	35.4	35.1

Website: www.oracle.com

Ormat Technologies

Ticker symbol: ORA (NYSE) □ S&P rating: NA □ Value Line financial strength rating: C++
□ Current yield: 1.2% □ Dividend raises, past 10 years: 2

Company Profile

Ormat Technologies is the largest geothermal energy pure play in North America. Relatively small by comparison to most of the companies selected for this year's book, Ormat is nonetheless in an attractive place at an attractive time. A renewed interest in baseline "green" power, combined with a growing need for electrification far from traditional grid-based solutions puts Ormat in a unique position as a provider of clean, always-on baseline electricity at the lowest operating cost of any solution.

The company operates in two segments: In the Electricity segment, they build, own, and operate geothermal power plants, selling the electricity; in the Product segment, they sell power plant equipment utilizing their proprietary geothermal technology to geothermal operators and to industrial users for use in remote power generation and recovered energy applications. The company's total worldwide installed capacity is just about 700 megawatts, concentrated mainly in the state of Nevada, with an additional 1,300 megawatts owned and operated by third parties. Their geothermal plants (63 percent of revenue in 2015) top out at about 35MW each and are located in approximately 50 thermally active locations in the western United States, the Pacific Rim, and the Mediterranean. The power generation products are particularly attractive for harsh, remote locations as the technology requires very little in the way of management or maintenance. The company also produces recovered energy installations, which produce electricity from nearly any form of waste heat. The vast majority of these units are currently sold outside of the United States and are commonly used in gas pipeline compressor stations, but are suited to any process which generates significant waste heat, including refineries.

The company owns over 100 patents on its very efficient energy conversion process. Their products do not require exotic manufacturing processes or materials, and the company builds almost all of its own products at its plants in Nevada and Israel.

Financial Highlights, Fiscal Year 2015

The Electricity segment recorded 1.7 percent year/year decline, attributed mainly to the lower price of oil and natural gas. The company has fixed-cost purchase agreements in place for 86 percent of its production, with the balance tied to the price of replacement fuels for some contracts. The company has since taken steps to hedge this exposure, with an expected savings of $1.2 million. The Product segment revenue grew 23 percent year/year, driving its contribution to overall revenue to 37 percent from 31 percent in the prior year. A large (nearly $1 per share) tax benefit (compared to the prior year) helped drive EPS up nearly 105 percent, but without this benefit it was still a good year for Ormat, with solid gains in revenues and very strong growth in real cash flow.

Reasons to Buy

In our earlier book *The 100 Best Aggressive Stocks You Can Buy 2012* we recommended Ormat as a somewhat speculative play in the emerging green energy sector. For 2017 we see that it has transitioned from a good idea to a good business, and we still like the company. We're happy to see it has paid off for the brave souls who bought in at $16.

Ormat is far less of a speculative play now; this sector still relies on governmental incentives for a significant chunk of its financial lifeblood, but those incentives are far broader now, taking the form of well-established long-term carbon credit swaps and carbon reduction mandates at both the state and federal level. Global incentives are also taking shape, following an agreement at the UN Climate Change Conference and several other Eurozone initiatives. The State of Nevada, long a friend of Ormat, may well lead the nation in clean energy implementation, recently passing legislation requiring the elimination of at least 800MW of coal-fired generating capacity by the end of 2019. In short, compared to 2011, in 2017 there are even more reasons for optimism about the future for renewable energy in general and Ormat in particular.

In 2011 we wrote that Ormat is a stock you buy partly on facts and partly on faith. And although Ormat is still an outlier in this year's guide with regard to earnings predictability, we're far less cautious than we were six years ago. The stock's P/E ratio is about average for the market, and the company is confident in their prospects. They recently announced a doubling of the dividend (to a 3.1 percent yield at current price) on a 7 percent projected increase in revenues.

Ormat is still a beneficiary of DOE cash grants and ARRA loan guarantees for geothermal projects, but their need for these funds is beginning to dwindle as private sector financing has become more significant in the past two years. There are three facilities online and under development in Kenya and five such facilities in Turkey. There are ten privately held facilities in New Zealand generating 350 MW, some with over twenty years of operation.

Incentives are important for geothermal installations. Geothermal plants are quite a bit more expensive to bring online than, say, a gas turbine plant. A geothermal plant will cost approximately $2,500 per kW of installed capacity versus $1,000 per kW for a gas turbine facility. Operating costs, however, are where the geothermal plant shines—generation costs are in the range of $0.01–$0.03 per kilowatt hour. Coal, the next cheapest alternative, yields costs of $0.02–$0.04 per kilowatt hour. Geothermal plants are also extremely reliable, with 24/7 availability (a big differentiator from solar and wind power) and near 98 percent uptime, with very little maintenance and near zero environmental impact. Coal plants, on the other hand, average about 75 percent availability and come saddled with massive environmental costs that are rarely subsidized directly by ratepayers (for now). These geothermal plants are very good solutions for particular needs in particular locations, but cannot be plopped down just anywhere as they require a source of geothermal heat. Fortunately, the Department of Energy estimates there are a very large number of potential sites in the western United States, and developing nations without access to coal or oil can create baseline electrical capacity with extremely low rates with appropriate levels of investment.

Finally, we need to call out Ormat's annual report. We love data, and Ormat delivers—the annual report is 220 pages of whole-grain goodness, without a single photograph. The company brings transparency to a new level.

Reasons for Caution

The company occupies a space that is somewhat at the fringes of the rapidly growing renewable energy market. Because its installations are only possible in certain geographies, geothermal production may not be front-of-mind when renewable legislation is penned unless actively lobbied. Also, some of the areas in which the company operates are politically unstable, and the company's installations may be the largest outside investment for hundreds of miles around. There have been few problems to date, but the annual report is worth reading on this topic.

SECTOR: **Energy** ◻ BETA COEFFICIENT: **1.00** ◻ 10-YEAR COMPOUND EARNINGS PER-SHARE
GROWTH: **10%** ◻ 10-YEAR COMPOUND DIVIDENDS PER-SHARE GROWTH: **NA**

	2008	**2009**	**2010**	**2011**	**2012**	**2013**	**2014**	**2015**
Revenues (mil)	344.8	415.2	373.2	437.0	514.4	533.2	559.5	594.4
Net income (mil)	49.8	68.9	10.4	(43.1)	(51.1)	37.3	54.2	119.6
Earnings per share	1.12	1.51	0.22	(0.95)	(1.12)	0.81	1.18	2.43
Dividends per share	0.20	0.25	0.27	0.13	0.08	0.08	0.21	0.26
Cash flow per share	2.42	2.93	2.14	1.17	1.13	2.87	3.40	4.62
Price: high	57.7	44.1	38.8	31.2	22.2	28.2	30.5	40.9
low	21.8	22.8	25.8	14.1	16.0	18.8	24.0	25.9

Website: www.ormat.com

GROWTH AND INCOME

Otter Tail Corporation

Ticker symbol: OTTR (NASDAQ) ◻ S&P rating: BBB ◻ Value Line financial strength rating: B+
◻ Current yield: 4.4% ◻ Dividend raises, past 10 years: 4

Company Profile

Otter Tail Corporation is a holding company and a mini-conglomerate operating primarily in the upper Midwest. The conglomerate is centered on and stabilized by the Otter Tail Power Company, a regulated utility serving about 130,000 customers in rural western Minnesota, the eastern half of North Dakota, and the eastern quarter of South Dakota. (In case you're wondering, these areas just miss the vast energy exploration territories of western North Dakota—maybe a good thing as it turns out.) About 50 percent of electric revenues come from Minnesota, 41 percent from North Dakota, and 9 percent from South Dakota. After some 2014 divestitures primarily in the electric utility construction business, the utility accounted for about 49 percent of the total revenues in FY2015 (and 74 percent of profits), while the Manufacturing & Infrastructure unit, a group of four businesses engaged in metal parts, plastic pipe, and infrastructure products manufacturing make up the other 51 percent (26 percent of profits); these non-utility businesses are further described (following).

Extensive use of wind generation and hydro power, and lower grades of coal available in the region, have driven fuel costs down to 15.5 percent of revenues (from 16.6 percent in FY2014), a very low figure for the industry. (By comparison, Xcel Energy, which supplies electricity to surrounding areas in North Dakota and Minnesota as well as other Great Plains locations, Colorado, and Texas, spends 49 percent of revenues on fuel, and most conventional utilities run in the 35–50 percent range.) Approximately 21.4 percent of power generation is from wind and hydro sources, and the company has made its first investments in solar to meet a Minnesota state requirement by 2020. Regulatory recovery of this investment, and another investment in two new high-voltage transmission lines, which also broadened the service area, should help earnings going forward.

Beyond the utility, the company has sold eight fairly good-sized businesses in the past four years in order to sharpen its focus. The remaining four businesses within its Manufacturing & Infrastructure segment include:

- BTD Manufacturing is a metal-stamping, fabricating, and laser-cutting shop supplying custom parts for agriculture, lawn care, health and fitness, and the RV industry.
- T.O. Plastics supplies thermoformed packaging and handling products for the horticultural, medical, food, electronics, and other consumer industries, including medical device packaging, plastic trays, housings and enclosures, and food and plant containers.
- Northern Pipe Products produces PVC water and sewer pipes up to 24 inches in diameter for pressurized applications and drainage.
- VinylTech, a producer of a similar line of utility-grade PVC products in Arizona, serves customers mostly in the Southwest.

In 2015 the company sold the Foley Company, a specialty contractor involved in industrial power, water and wastewater, and other complex construction projects. The remaining non-utilities activities include Manufacturing (BTD), which generated $215 million in revenues in FY2015 and $4.2 million in profits; and the Plastics group, which includes the other three businesses and generated $12 million in income on $157 million in revenues.

The company takes a very hands-off approach to managing its Manufacturing & Infrastructure subsidiaries; in fact, each has its own unique website with links within the Otter Tail Corporation site. In total, the company has 2,005 employees, and most operations are centered in the upper Midwest, VinylTech being the exception.

Financial Highlights, Fiscal Year 2015

Because of the divestitures over the years, sequential numbers continue to be difficult to compare. Once again the company showed a small gain in net earnings despite a slight decline in revenues, a modest reaffirmation of the divestiture strategy. Results were helped along in part by cost recovery from recent utility infrastructure upgrades and lower input costs for some of its manufactured product lines—and hurt by soft PVC product pricing and BTD's dependence on the energy industry, scrap metal pricing, and weak sales to agricultural equipment manufacturers. While Otter Tail intends to retain and improve the non-utility businesses, it has stated that it will focus capital investment on the utility operations for the time being.

Forecasts call for modest 3–4 percent gains in the top line over the next two years with a 10–12 percent gain in the bottom line over the period. Like many utilities, the company has been issuing a few shares to "deleverage," probably a smart move with impending interest rate increases, but earnings and cash-flow improvements will support a steadily growing dividend, something we weren't sure about when Otter Tail first came to our *100 Best* list.

Reasons to Buy

When we first added Otter Tail to the 2012 *100 Best Stocks* list, admittedly we were taken by its Berkshire Hathaway–like construct of a basic business around a steady core, the electric utility. Some of the other businesses may have been a bit too far-flung to manage effectively—so the company has retrenched, trimmed the branches, so to speak, first with windmill construction and transportation, then with other businesses that didn't fit so well. After the pruning, the company is still more or less constructed around this diversified and well-anchored model. The non-utility core is centered on infrastructure construction and materials—which we like—and is managed much in the Berkshire Hathaway style of hands-off, autonomous, you-supply-the-management-not-us style, which we also like.

Although the returns have been a bit below our standards, we like the steady yield, safety, and diversification inherent in this issue. The manufacturing and plastics businesses offer a potential upside "kicker" when the energy and manufacturing cycle recovers. Otter Tail remains a "small town" company in contrast to "big city" corporate America.

Reasons for Caution

The utility is stable but not likely to be helped along by population growth, and the manufacturing and construction businesses are cyclical. The company is on much more solid footing than it was a few years ago, but it still doesn't have the reserve strength of larger companies. We compared Otter Tail to Berkshire Hathaway but should note that Berkshire is more diversified and has much larger anchor businesses.

SECTOR: **Energy** ❑ BETA COEFFICIENT: **0.73** ❑ 10-YEAR COMPOUND EARNINGS PER-SHARE
GROWTH: **-0.5%** ❑ 10-YEAR COMPOUND DIVIDENDS PER-SHARE GROWTH: **1.0%**

	2008	2009	2010	2011	2012	2013	2014	2015
Revenues (mil)	1,311	1,040	1,118	1,078	859	893	799	780
Net income (mil)	35.1	26.0	13.6	16.4	39.0	50.2	56.9	58.6
Earnings per share	1.09	0.71	0.38	0.45	1.05	1.37	1.55	1.56
Dividends per share	1.19	1.19	1.19	1.19	1.19	1.19	1.21	1.23
Cash flow per share	2.81	2.76	2.82	2.39	2.71	3.03	3.09	3.14
Price: high	46.2	25.4	25.4	23.5	25.3	31.9	32.7	33.4
low	15.0	18.5	18.2	17.5	20.7	25.2	26.5	24.8

Website: www.ottertail.com

AGGRESSIVE GROWTH

Patterson Companies, Inc.

Ticker symbol: PDCO (NASDAQ) ❑ S&P rating: NR ❑ Value Line financial strength rating: A
❑ Current yield: 1.9% ❑ Dividend raises, past 10 years: 6

Company Profile

Patterson Companies is a value-added distributor now operating in two segments—Dental Supply and Veterinary Supply. The Medical Supply unit, which comprised about 12 percent of the business, was sold for $725 million in 2015.

Dental Supply provides a complete range of consumable dental products, equipment, and software; turnkey digital solutions; office design and setup; and value-added services to dentists and dental laboratories primarily for the North American market. Veterinary Supply will likely be the nation's largest distributor of consumable veterinary supplies, equipment, diagnostic products, vaccines, and pharmaceuticals to companion-pet veterinary clinics. The Veterinary Supply business doubled in 2015 with the $1.1 billion purchase of distributor Animal Health International. We haven't seen a full year's operational results with Medical gone and AHI integrated but believe from company presentations that the two business segments are about the same size now while the Dental side generates most of the profits. Patterson has one-third of the North American dental supply market. Sales in the dental market break down as follows: 56 percent consumables, 33 percent total equipment, 11 percent technical services and other.

As one of the lead dogs, Patterson has the clout to negotiate a number of exclusive distribution deals. It is sole distributor for the industry's most popular line of dental chairs and also has an exclusive on the CEREC 3D dental restorative system, an increasingly popular alternative to traditional dental crowns. Patterson is also the leading provider of digital radiography systems, which create instant images of dental work, superior to the images generated by traditional x-ray equipment. The company also supplies and supports dental practice financial and supply-chain management software and offers physical and system design and consulting services to dentists seeking to build or remodel dental offices. The company positions itself as a one-stop shop for its customer dentists and dental clinics, and identifies "Digital Dentistry" as a key trend in its marketing presentations and product mix.

The recent focus and additions to the Veterinary Supply segment reflect industry trends toward greater "companion animal" ownership and spend rates; the company estimates a 43 percent growth in pet owner expenditures since 2007 alone. Before the AHI acquisition the company enjoyed a 21 percent market share in the veterinary supply business; that figure should rise substantially.

Financial Highlights, Fiscal Year 2015

The dental business has continued to lag due to postponement of elective and semi-elective procedures, better preventative care, and more competition. More of today's growth comes from the Veterinary side, and the acquisition is creating costs synergies besides. The timing of the acquisition and divestiture make for a bit of a murky FY2015, but revenues were up 23 percent due to AHI coming onboard for part of the year; net earnings were actually down due to acquisition costs. FY2016 and FY2017 will present a cavity-free picture, with revenues up in the 5–7 percent range and net earnings up roughly 10-12 percent not including the one-time dip in FY2015 as a base. Patterson continues to buy back shares aggressively, retiring 6 percent of its float in 2015 and 40 percent since 2006.

Reasons to Buy

We think "dental lag" could decline and bring better-than-expected results, as the population has grown older, in addition to the dental ailments already put off. Dental procedures, capital investment, and inventory replenishment will all return to more normal levels—and perhaps then some. When this happens, it may not be too much to expect a "hockey stick"–shaped trajectory for sales, earnings, cash flow, and yes, the stock price—although some would probably prefer to avoid using the hockey stick analogy to describe a dental supply stock!

While there have been some improvements in the art of long-term dental care, such as more widespread fluoride use, we also see a growing need for more expensive procedures, including replacement crowns as well as more expensive and material-intensive implant restorations continuing, if not growing, as the population ages and as dental care becomes a bigger industry overseas.

But the real change and kicker are the company's moves into the companion-pet veterinary and rehabilitative markets, both of which are driven by a growing and profitable demographic. The company estimates that 68 percent of households own a pet, compared to 56 percent in 1988, another of several favorable demographic trends. The company can leverage its already established dental industry expertise to become the preferred vet supplier.

Today the company is primarily focused on the North American market, with promised 24- to 48-hour delivery for most items. International growth presents another large opportunity, with recent acquisitions gaining a foothold in Western Europe, especially in the veterinary business.

As we mentioned, Patterson continues to aggressively return cash to its investors, making significant share repurchases and now, larger dividend increases. Patterson is one of a small handful of mid-cap companies on our *100 Best Stocks* list, so it may be of interest to investors looking for something in that size range to complement our mostly large-cap-dominated list.

Reasons for Caution

Competition in this arena is strong, and the company will have to stay sharp to take advantage as dental lag subsides; otherwise, it could lose share to competitors. We believe that the number of companies offering good dental insurance is declining, and any factor that makes dental procedures more "elective" will likely work against Patterson. Though it is the higher growth part of the business, the veterinary distribution business is relatively low margin; an issue if its portion of Patterson's total business becomes too large.

While the wait for an upside may be longer than some, we also believe this stock has less downside than most.

SECTOR: **Healthcare** ❑ BETA COEFFICIENT: **0.89** ❑ 10-YEAR COMPOUND EARNINGS PER-SHARE GROWTH: **7.0%** ❑ 10-YEAR COMPOUND DIVIDENDS PER-SHARE GROWTH: NM

	2008	2009	2010	2011	2012	2013	2014	2015
Revenues (mil)	3,094	3,237	3,415	3,536	3,637	4,064	4,375	5,405
Net income (mil)	200	212	225	213	210	214	223	180
Earnings per share	1.70	1.78	1.91	1.92	2.03	2.10	2.40	1.80
Dividends per share	—	0.10	0.42	0.50	0.58	0.68	0.82	0.94
Cash flow per share	2.00	2.04	2.20	2.31	2.43	2.54	2.42	2.65
Price: high	37.8	28.3	32.8	39.9	37.6	44.4	49.5	53.1
low	15.8	16.1	24.1	26.2	29.0	34.3	37.0	38.5

Website: www.pattersoncompanies.com

AGGRESSIVE GROWTH

Paychex, Inc.

Ticker symbol: PAYX (NASDAQ) ❑ S&P rating: NR ❑ Value Line financial strength rating: A ❑ Current yield: 3.3% ❑ Dividend raises, past 10 years: 8

Company Profile

Paychex, Inc. provides payroll, human resources, and benefits outsourcing solutions for small- to medium-sized businesses with 10–200 employees. Founded in 1971, the company has more than 100 offices and serves over 590,000 clients in the United States as well as about 2,000 clients in Germany and a new base through a partnership in Brazil. Some 85 percent of its customers are the small- to medium-sized businesses previously mentioned. The company has two sources of revenue: service revenue, paid by clients for services, and interest income on the funds held by Paychex for clients.

Paychex offers a one-stop shop portfolio of services and products (and consequently, employees), including:

- Payroll processing
- Payroll tax administration services
- Employee payment services, including expense reporting, reimbursements, etc.

- Regulatory compliance services (new-hire reporting and garnishment processing)
- Comprehensive human resource outsourcing services
- Retirement services administration
- Workers' compensation insurance services
- Health and benefits services
- Time and attendance solutions
- Medical deduction, state unemployment, and other HR services and products

The company's products are marketed primarily through its direct sales force, the bulk of which is focused on payroll products. In addition to the direct sales force, the company uses its relationships with existing clients, CPAs, and banks for new client referrals. Approximately two-thirds of its new clients come via these referral sources.

Larger clients can choose to outsource their payroll and HR functions or to run them in-house using a Paychex platform. For those clients, the company offers what it calls "Major Market Services" (MMS) products, which can be run locally or on a web-hosted, SaaS environment.

In addition to traditional payroll services, Paychex offers full-service HR outsourcing solutions; custom-built solutions including payroll, compliance, HR, and employee benefits sourcing and administration; outsourcing management; and even professionally trained onsite HR representatives. The company also manages retirement plans and other benefits, including pretax "cafeteria" plans, and has a subsidiary insurance agency offering property and casualty, workers' comp, health, and auto policies to an employer's employee base.

The company is the nation's number one provider of payroll services to small businesses (1–50 employees) and number two for midsized businesses (50–500 employees). About 31,000 of the 590,000 Payroll clients use the full Human Resource Services offering, with a total employee count of 858,000, and it accounts for about 35 percent of Paychex's revenues. The company has recently made a push to implement web-based and mobile versions of its key products, adding to convenience and reducing paperwork for its clients. Through the Retirement Services Group, the company administers 70,000 retirement plans, achieving the number one spot nationwide by number of plans.

The company has increased its R&D spend to fund the development of new online user interfaces and SaaS (Software as a Service) client delivery.

The company acquires small companies both vertically to offer new services and horizontally to expand market presence, as it did in 2015 with the acquisition of temporary staffing industry provider Advance Partners.

Financial Highlights, Fiscal Year 2015

As the global economy continues to strengthen after the Great Recession, employment expansion helps Paychex's business, and the company has done well expanding the breadth of its services, too. The payroll base expanded only 2 percent again in FY2015, but gains in the breadth of services and some pricing gains led to a 9 percent revenue gain in FY2015 with a projected 8 percent gain to follow in FY2016. Net income increased 8 percent in FY2015 and, due to a more profitable mix and price strength, income is expected to rise 13 percent in FY2016. Results would have been better if short-term interest rates on deposits were higher than last year's 1 percent— and it's anybody's guess when this might actually happen going forward. Higher net interest rates would only be a bonus to the already strong performance.

Reasons to Buy

A bet on Paychex is a bet on three things: (1) continued improvement in the economy, (2) continued adoption of broader platform services, and (3) an eventual increase on interest rates (so they can make money on the float). In the meantime, you get a decent yield and little downside risk if you own the stock.

Paychex's primary market is companies with fewer than 100 employees. In the aftermath of the Great Recession, small business is leading the way while larger businesses are focused on reducing cost, which also helps Paychex as a provider of outsourced services. Beyond that, the cost of switching and good client relationships have made for a loyal client base. We continue to think the trend to outsource payroll and HR activities will not only continue but accelerate as easier Internet-based solutions come more into favor.

The company is conservatively run, well managed, and well financed. It isn't just a "service" company, it is an IT company with a lot of innovation in its DNA. Margins are significantly higher than its closest competitor, Automated Data Processing (ADP). It carries no long-term debt—zero— and should have little difficulty funding the generous dividend, even at its current payout level of 80 percent of earnings. Fragmentation in the market and Paychex's extremely strong financial position will allow the company to continue to grow market share through acquisition. Finally, sooner or later short-term interest rates must tick upward; when that happens the company will once again be able to profit from the float (the company has $3–$4 billion of its customers' money held for payroll at any given time). Such an increase in interest income would likely fund greater dividend increases and share repurchases; this is one of the few stocks on our list that can tangibly benefit from *moderate* interest rate increases. We like that defensive characteristic.

Reasons for Caution

This company will always be vulnerable to economic swings, such as those brought on by *large* interest rate increases. The company's acquisition strategy makes sense, as those acquisitions will increase market share, but they do come with costs and risks.

SECTOR: **Information Technology** ❑ BETA COEFFICIENT: **0.35** ❑ 10-YEAR COMPOUND EARNINGS PER-SHARE GROWTH: **7.5%** ❑ 10-YEAR COMPOUND DIVIDENDS PER-SHARE GROWTH: **12.5%**

		2008	2009	2010	2011	2012	2013	2014	2015
Revenues (mil)		2,066	2,083	2,001	2,084	2,230	2,326	2,519	2,739
Net income (mil)		576	534	477	516	548	569	627	675
Earnings per share		1.56	1.48	1.32	1.42	1.51	1.56	1.71	1.85
Dividends per share		1.20	1.24	1.24	1.24	1.27	1.31	1.40	1.52
Cash flow per share		1.82	1.72	1.56	1.67	1.78	1.83	2.02	2.16
Price:	high	37.5	32.9	32.8	33.9	34.7	45.9	48.2	54.8
	low	23.2	20.3	24.7	25.1	29.1	31.5	39.8	41.6

Website: www.paychex.com

AGGRESSIVE GROWTH

Perrigo Company

Ticker symbol: PRGO (NASDAQ) ❑ S&P rating: BB+ ❑ Value Line financial strength rating: A ❑ Current yield: 0.5% ❑ Dividend raises, past 10 years: 10

Company Profile

Perrigo is the world's largest manufacturer of over-the-counter pharmaceutical products for the store-brand market. They also manufacture generic prescription pharmaceuticals, nutritional products, and active pharmaceutical ingredients (APIs).

Consolidation is the name of the game in the pharmaceutical business and especially in the lucrative generics segment. In 2014, Perrigo acquired Elan, an Irish maker of mostly prescription pharmaceuticals, broadening their offering in this subsegment and acquiring an Irish headquarters base for tax advantages. The company also added another generic marketer to its portfolio—Omega Pharma—mostly to build the generics business in European markets and 35 countries in all.

Both acquisitions added considerably to the size and profitability of the company. However, while digesting these acquisitions, Perrigo received an offer of $205 per share from rival pharma maker Mylan, which management thought undervalued the company. That takeover attempt—and the rumors around it—drove Perrigo's stock price to new highs, only to retreat to, and really below, previous valuations when that acquisition failed. We had to examine Perrigo closely to figure out whether the 40 percent decline in Perrigo's shares reflected a real change in business prospects and decided that it didn't. For now, Perrigo is "business as usual"; we still like the business, and it remains on the *100 Best* list for 2017.

Perrigo operates in four segments: Consumer Healthcare, Nutritionals, Rx Pharmaceuticals, and API. With Elan blended in, but Omega not quite yet, Consumer Healthcare is by far the largest segment, generating about 54 percent of Perrigo's FY2015 revenue, while Nutritionals brings in 13 percent, Rx Pharma 23 percent, and APIs 4 percent. Eventually, the Omega acquisition will expand the portion of sales attributable to generics.

The company's success depends on its ability to manufacture and quickly market generic equivalents to branded products. It employs internal R&D resources—which run 4 percent of sales—to develop product formulations and manufacture in quantity for its customers. It also develops retail packaging specific to the customers' needs. The company expects a greater percentage of medicines to become available over the counter (versus Rx); this has been the case with Allegra and similar medications in recent years. The company estimates that 72 percent of educated consumers choose store brands, and 91 percent of them stay with them once chosen. They also estimate that they save consumers $7.5 billion a year with more favorably priced generics.

If you have bought a store-branded over-the-counter medication such as ibuprofen, acetaminophen, skin remedies, or cough medicine at a store like Target or Walmart in the past year, there's a good chance (a 75 percent chance, in fact) that it was made by Perrigo. The company's Consumer Healthcare business produces and markets over 2,700 store-brand products in 26,000 individual SKUs of 11,000 formulations (the difference between the two is mainly different package sizes) to approximately 1,000 customers, including Wal-Mart, CVS, Walgreens, Kroger, Target, Safeway, Dollar General, Costco, and other national and regional drugstores, supermarkets, and mass merchandisers. Wal-Mart is its single largest customer and accounts for 15 percent of Perrigo's net sales (down from 19 percent a few years ago). It's a good deal, because it's a steady cash stream, and Perrigo doesn't really have to invest in marketing. The company estimates that population demographics, new store-branded products, and transitions of certain drugs from prescription to over-the-counter sales contribute about equally to an approximately 5–10 percent "organic" growth rate.

The Nutritionals segment is relatively new as a standalone segment and includes store-brand infant formula, vitamins, and minerals. The segment distributes 900 store-brand products in 3,400 SKUs to more than 150 customers.

Enlarged by the Elan acquisition, the Rx Pharma operations produce generic prescription drugs (in contrast to the over-the-counter drugs produced in the Consumer Healthcare segment), obviously benefitting when key patented drugs run past their patent protection. Rx Pharma markets approximately 800 generic prescription products, many of them topicals and creams, with over 1,300 SKUs, to approximately 350 customers, while the API division markets an assortment of active ingredients to other drug manufacturers as well as for the company's own products, including a number of active ingredients that we'd have trouble spelling correctly, so we won't even try. The company's products are manufactured in nine facilities around the world. Its major markets are in North America, Mexico, the U.K., and China. About 28 percent of sales are outside the U.S.

Financial Highlights, Fiscal Year 2015

Continued absorption of recent acquisitions and a firm 5–10 percent organic growth rate as highlighted previously led to a healthy 13 percent top-line advance in FY2015; consolidation of global HQ activities in Ireland and other organizational streamlining led the way to a stellar 35 percent gain in net income, highlighted by a 10 percent drop in the tax rate. Per-share earnings did not fare quite so well with a 13 percent gain, as additional shares were issued to fund acquisitions. Fundamentals look strong with a 25–30 percent revenue gain forecast for 2016 (again, helped along by acquisitions) and another 35 percent gain in net income; things should settle into a more normal pattern for FY2017 with revenues up 8–10 percent and earnings up

5 percent. Share buybacks are scheduled to resume in 2016 with $1.5 billion allocated to that task, which would retire about 8 percent of the float.

Reasons to Buy

Perrigo is a real success story of solid niche dominance (store-branded medications) with a couple of high-growth, high-margin businesses mixed in. Steady growth in sales combined with a steady growth in margins has a multiplicative effect, and the company has enjoyed well-above-average profit growth in this industry. The Elan and Omega mergers appear to be working out well. Not only does Perrigo currently dominate a niche, it is a growing niche. The company calls it "Quality Affordable Healthcare Products." People are becoming more sensitive to their own healthcare costs and spending in general and are opting more often for the store brand; after all, 200 mg of ibuprofen is 200 mg of ibuprofen. This all sits on top of the demographic tailwind of the aging population and the institutional tailwind of doing what's necessary to rein in costs.

Since the Mylan merger failed, the stock reflects a better value proposition and is priced more favorably with respect to fundamentals, and takeover winds are still blowing. Still, entry points must be chosen carefully.

Reasons for Caution

Perrigo broke most of our rules in making a major acquisition of a complex business, then moving to another country where accounting standards make business evaluation more difficult. Normally we would have dropped the company right then and there, but again, we like its track record and niche dominance. Then the proposed acquisition drove the stock price higher—another negative—but it also showed something of the value of this company in the pharma business. Naturally, we're not too thrilled with the company's cash returns to investors and increasing share counts, and Perrigo also is a little more acquisitive itself than we would like. But behind all this fog sits a pretty good business in our opinion, one that has become more fairly valued to boot.

SECTOR: **Healthcare** ❑ BETA COEFFICIENT: **0.80** ❑ 10-YEAR COMPOUND EARNINGS PER-SHARE
GROWTH: **24.0%** ❑ 10-YEAR COMPOUND DIVIDENDS PER-SHARE GROWTH: **13.5%**

	2008	2009	2010	2011	2012	2013	2014	2015
Revenues (mil)	1,822	2,007	2,269	2,765	3,173	3,540	4,061	4,604
Net income (mil)	150	176	263	341	411	442	739.5	1,001
Earnings per share	1.58	1.87	2.83	3.64	4.37	4.68	6.39	7.24
Dividends per share	0.21	0.22	0.25	0.27	0.32	0.35	0.39	0.46
Cash flow per share	2.35	2.67	3.69	4.78	5.84	6.41	8.21	10.60
Price: high	43.1	61.4	67.5	104.7	120.8	157.5	171.6	215.7
low	27.7	18.5	37.5	62.3	90.2	98.6	125.4	140.4

Website: www.perrigo.com

CONSERVATIVE GROWTH

Praxair, Inc.

Ticker symbol: PX (NYSE) ❑ S&P rating: A ❑ Value Line financial strength rating: A ❑ Current
yield: 2.8% ❑ Dividend raises, past 10 years: 10

Company Profile

Praxair, Inc. is the second-largest supplier of industrial gases in the world.
The company, which was spun off to Union Carbide shareholders in June
1992, supplies a broad range of atmospheric, process, and specialty gases;
high-performance coatings; and related services and technologies.

Praxair's primary products are atmospheric gases—oxygen, nitrogen,
argon, and rare gases (produced when atmospheric air is purified,
compressed, cooled, distilled, and condensed) and process and specialty
gases—carbon dioxide, helium, hydrogen, and acetylene (produced as by-
products of chemical production or recovered from natural gas). Customers
include makers of primary metals, metal fabricators, petroleum refiners, and
producers of chemicals, healthcare products, pharmaceuticals, biotech, food
and beverage, electronics, glass, pulp and paper, and environmental products.
By end market, manufacturing, metals, and energy producers account for 54
percent of 2015 sales (energy alone is 13 percent); chemicals, electronics,
and aerospace another 21 percent; and healthcare and food/beverage the
next 17 percent, with the remaining 9 percent to "other" industries.

The gas products are sold into the packaged-gas market and the merchant
market. In the packaged-gas market, bulk gases are packaged into high-
pressure cylinders and either delivered to the customer or to distributors.

In the merchant market, bulk gases are liquefied and transported by tanker truck to the customer's facility.

The company also designs, engineers, and constructs cryogenic and noncryogenic gas supply systems for customers who choose to produce their own atmospheric gases onsite. This is obviously a capital-intensive delivery solution for Praxair but results in lower delivered cost to the customer and higher returns for Praxair, as all operational costs are paid by the customer. Contracts for these installations can run to 20 years. About 28 percent of volume is packaged, 34 percent is "merchant," and 29 percent is generated on site.

Praxair Surface Technologies is a subsidiary that applies wear-, corrosion-, and thermal-resistant metallic and ceramic coatings and powders to metal surfaces in order to resist wear, high temperatures, and corrosion. Aircraft engines are a primary market, but it serves others, including the printing, textile, chemical, and primary metals markets, and provides aircraft engine and airframe component overhaul services. About 45 percent of Praxair's sales come from outside North America.

Financial Highlights, Fiscal Year 2015
Softness in energy, basic materials manufacturing such as steel, coal gasification, and select other vertical markets, weakness in emerging markets, and continued dollar headwinds blended with strength in food, healthcare, and certain refining industries to produce mixed and mostly lower results for FY2015. Total sales fell about 13 percent and are expected to remain in the $10.5–$11 billion range through FY2017. Per-share earnings fell a more moderate 6.5 percent. The company is guiding flat for FY2016 with a gradual earnings recovery to around $6 per share as operational efficiencies take effect. The company specifically aims to return about half of its cash flow to shareholders while investing the other half in the business.

Reasons to Buy
Until recently Praxair has had a steady history of high margins, growth, and few to no surprises. The "perfect storm" of energy and manufacturing weakness, emerging market problems, and a strong dollar has interrupted this steady flow. However, we don't feel that the fundamental business has changed, and like so many others, Praxair will again flourish when the cycle reverses and new efficiencies take effect. Praxair is the largest gas provider in the emerging markets of China, India, Brazil, Mexico, and Korea and continues to invest heavily in plants in these regions. In general, the international

presence is more balanced and diversified than most of its competitors, and it is not as dependent upon growth in China. The company is a big player in the re-emergence of U.S. manufacturing.

We especially like the company's high margins (31 percent and still growing) and cash-flow generation—and the willingness to share it with shareholders.

Reasons for Caution

The down cycle has hit Praxair harder than many expected. Competitors are strong, and getting stronger with the consolidation of smaller players in the industry. As hydrocarbon energy products are feedstock for many of Praxair's products, the company has enjoyed recent trends but could take a minor hit as energy prices recover. The strong international presence means that results are sensitive to currency headwinds, but those headwinds may subside or even turn into tailwinds; we expect a little help on that front in FY2017 too. We will continue to look out for fundamental changes in Praxair's business; we haven't seen anything major to this point.

SECTOR: Materials □ BETA COEFFICIENT: 0.84 □ 10-YEAR COMPOUND EARNINGS PER-SHARE GROWTH: 12.0% □ 10-YEAR COMPOUND DIVIDENDS PER-SHARE GROWTH: 17.5%

		2008	2009	2010	2011	2012	2013	2014	2015
Revenues (mil)		10,796	8,956	10,118	11,252	11,224	11,925	12,273	10,776
Net income (mil)		1,335	1,254	1,195	1,672	1,692	1,755	1,694	1,547
Earnings per share		4.19	4.01	3.84	5.45	5.61	5.87	5.73	5.35
Dividends per share		1.50	1.60	1.80	2.00	2.20	2.40	2.60	2.86
Cash flow per share		8.63	6.85	6.95	8.95	9.10	9.70	9.90	9.45
Price:	high	77.6	86.1	96.3	111.7	116.9	130.5	135.2	130.4
	low	53.3	53.3	72.7	88.6	100.0	107.7	117.3	98.6

Website: www.praxair.com

CONSERVATIVE GROWTH

The Procter & Gamble Company

Ticker symbol: PG (NYSE) ❑ S&P rating: AA ❑ Value Line financial strength rating: A++ ❑ Current yield: 3.3% ❑ Dividend raises, past 10 years: 10

Company Profile

Procter & Gamble dates back to 1837, when William Procter and James Gamble began making soap and candles from surplus animal fat from the stockyards in Cincinnati, OH. The company's first major product introduction took place in 1879 when it launched Ivory soap. Since then, P&G has continually created a host of blockbuster products, added some key acquisitions, exited the food business and a few others, and, in total, has some of the strongest, most recognizable consumer brands in the world.

P&G is a uniquely diversified consumer products company with a strong global presence. P&G markets its broad line of products to nearly 5 billion consumers in more than 180 countries.

The company is a recognized leader in the development, manufacturing, and marketing of quality laundry, cleaning, paper, personal care, and healthcare products.

To understand Procter, it's worth a look at how the company is organized:

- *Beauty, Hair and Personal Care* (24 percent of FY2015 sales, 23 percent of profits) includes shampoo, skin care, deodorant, hair care and color, and bar soap products, including such traditional brands as Head & Shoulders, Ivory soap, Safeguard, Secret, Pantene, Vidal Sassoon, Cover Girl, and Old Spice, and some newer and edgier brands like Olay, Hugo Boss, SK-II, James Bond 007 men's fragrances, Gucci, and Dolce & Gabbana, and a handful of professional brands. There are 36 brands in all.

- *Grooming* (10 percent, 16 percent) includes razors, blades, pre- and post-shave products, and other shaving products, including Gillette, Fusion, Mach3, and Prestobarba brands.

- *Health Care* (10 percent, 11 percent) is made up of two subunits, Personal Health Care and Oral Care. Personal Health Care in turn includes gastrointestinal, respiratory, rapid diagnostics, and vitamins/minerals/supplements, and includes such brands as Vicks, Metamucil, Prilosec, and Pepto-Bismol. Oral Care includes the familiar Crest, Scope, Fixodent, and Oral-B brands among others.

- *Fabric and Home Care* (29 percent, 24 percent) covers many of the familiar laundry and cleaning brands—Tide, Cheer, Dawn, Febreze, Downy, Bounce, Era, Mr. Clean, and a handful created for international markets—34 brands in all.
- *Baby, Feminine, and Family Care* (27 percent, 26 percent) markets mostly paper products like Puffs, Charmin, Pampers, Bounty, Always, and Tampax into baby care, feminine care, adult incontinence, and family care markets.

Procter has always been a hallmark example of brand management and building intrinsic brand strength—that is, strength not from the company name but through the brand's own name and reputation. It is described as a "house of brands," not a "branded house," although we're starting to see the "P&G" name more prominently in its marketing and advertising. The company tells us that its 50 "Leadership Brands" are some of the world's most well-known household names, that 90 percent of its business comes from these 50 brands, and that 25 of them are billion-dollar businesses.

The company has a strong and growing international presence, with 60 percent of sales originating outside the U.S. and Canada. The company also manufactures locally in its largest international markets, with on-the-ground operations in approximately 70 countries.

The company has begun a process of brand realignment, which will entail shrinking the portfolio from 166 brands down to just 65 by the end of 2017. The remaining brands account for approximately 85 percent of FY2015 sales and 95 percent of pre-tax profit. The company completed its sale of its Duracell batteries business to Berkshire Hathaway in March for $2.9 billion and will sell 43 of its Beauty brands to Coty for $12.5 billion. The professional grooming brands will be sold soon, and their Pet Care brands have already been divested. In all, of the 100-odd brands targeted for divestiture actions, 93 have been completed.

Financial Highlights, Fiscal Year 2015

Like many other global *100 Best* businesses, P&G experienced strong currency headwinds this past year—although organic revenue growth was up slightly, adjusted revenues declined 5 percent. Perhaps more noteworthy is the decrease in unit volumes, which fell 1 percent. The company did have a number of significant one-time charges and restructuring costs that amounted to $1.60 per share off of earnings, and even though core earnings per share were up 11 percent on a constant currency basis, the problem in the top-line growth stands out, and the company is committed to fixing it. The primary impact came from Beauty, Hair, and Personal Care, although again, foreign exchange issues drove unfavorable pricing in these cost-sensitive products and markets.

In part to address the price-sensitivity issues, a point of focus for the company in FY2015 was cost reduction and execution. Emphasis on input cost reduction has driven a $6–$7 billion decrease in cost of goods sold. These are savings that will carry forward for years to come and which will fund (in part) a large shareholder return program (more following).

Also notable was a one-time charge of $2.1 billion to "deconsolidate" (write off, basically) its Venezuelan operations due to an inability to convert currency and extract dividends from the unit.

Reasons to Buy

Regardless of developments in the world economy, people will continue to shave, bathe, do laundry, and care for their babies, and P&G is the global leader in baby care, feminine care, fabric care, and shaving products. Everyone should consider at least one defensive play in their portfolio, and P&G continues to deserve a spot at the top of the list.

P&G is extending its reach to capture share in channels and markets currently underserved. Developing markets are a huge opportunity, representing 86 percent of the world's population, and P&G feels it can be a leader in many product categories. Emerging markets now represent 38 percent of their FY2015 revenue, up from 32 percent in 2011 and 20 percent in 2002. P&G is also broadening its distribution channels to pursue opportunities in drug and pharmacy outlets, convenience stores, export operations, and even e-commerce.

We like the company's new position on brand proliferation. More is not always better, particularly when each brand carries with it a not-insignificant SG&A and Marketing overhead. Also, does a company like P&G bring anything special to the battery business? We don't think so, and we're glad they agree. As the company continues to evolve its organizational structure, it has departed from its traditional model of managing brands as wholly separate businesses with brand-specific advertising budgets, product research labs, and so forth. Synergies from combining ads and ad strategies alone should reduce total costs across the company's many portfolios. While we will miss some of the brands they are likely to cut, the business won't miss them all that much; focus, critical mass, and profitability appear to be their strategic mainstays moving forward.

Lastly, it's worth mentioning P&G's reaffirmed commitment to shareholder return. Although the share price has been flat to slightly down over the past year, the company has a plan to reward shareholders going forward. P&G has returned about $60 billion over the last five years in the form of stock buybacks and dividend increases. This is a significant amount of money, but P&G plans to up the ante to $70 billion over the next four years, nearly a 50 percent increase.

In short, we continue to like the brand, marketplace, and financial strength; sure and steady dividend growth (the company has raised its dividend 60 straight years); and short- and long-term prospects.

Reasons for Caution

Revenue growth remains a key challenge. P&G will be spending a lot of money on innovation in its core markets (one of the reasons for the 2014 reorganization), but the company has stated that gains in top-line growth won't be immediate and will likely be quite irregular. In fact they predict roughly flat organic sales through the end of FY2016.

The recent recession made consumers much more price conscious, and many switched to generics. That switch has reversed to a degree, but not everyone is coming back onboard. While commodity prices are favorable today, rising commodity costs can affect P&G, and the emphasis on the health and beauty business brings more exposure to often-fickle consumer tastes and shorter brand life than the company may be used to. Finally, the economies of Russia and Brazil are worth watching for all multinational players—no one predicts another Venezuela in either of those two countries, but their large populations and volatile currencies can make for the wrong kind of leverage for a high volume, low-margin manufacturer in uncertain times.

SECTOR: **Consumer Staples** ◻ BETA COEFFICIENT: **0.46** ◻ 10-YEAR COMPOUND EARNINGS PER-SHARE GROWTH: **7.0%** ◻ 10-YEAR COMPOUND DIVIDENDS PER-SHARE GROWTH: **10.5%**

	2008	2009	2010	2011	2012	2013	2014	2015
Revenues (mil)	83,503	79,029	78,938	82,559	83,680	85,500	83,062	76,279
Net income (mil)	12,075	11,293	10,946	11,797	11,344	11,869	12,220	11,535
Earnings per share	3.64	3.58	3.53	3.93	3.85	4.05	4.22	4.02
Dividends per share	1.45	1.64	1.80	1.97	2.14	2.29	2.45	2.59
Cash flow per share	4.97	4.65	4.87	5.21	5.20	5.33	5.57	5.31
Price: high	73.8	63.5	65.3	67.7	71.0	85.8	93.9	91.8
low	54.9	43.9	39.4	57.6	59.1	68.4	75.3	65.0

Website: www.pg.com

GROWTH AND INCOME

NEW FOR
2017

Prologis, Inc.

Ticker symbol: PLD (NYSE) ❑ S&P rating: BBB+ ❑ Value Line financial strength rating: B+
❑ Current yield: 3.6% ❑ Dividend raises, past 10 years: 2

Company Profile

In most of life, when you try something, and it works, you tend to stick with it. We're strong believers in this principle when it comes to investing, especially when there's some logic—not just sheer luck—behind the success.

And so it goes with REITs. Real Estate Investment Trusts. Specialized investments that allow you to become a landlord and to collect rents. Doesn't that sound enticing? Especially when you get a share of a diversified portfolio with professional management built in? And especially when you get a good business on top of the core real estate?

Long averse to investment "products," we dipped our toes into this pool by adding Welltower (formerly Health Care REIT) to the *100 Best* list three years ago. Good business (senior living) on top of a strong real estate asset core (high-end senior living properties). It worked and has been one of our best performers since added, especially on a "risk adjusted" basis. Then we added Public Storage two years ago, which turned out to be our number one gainer last year. Then we added the cream-of-the-office-space crop, Empire State Realty Trust, last year. Good pick, and we think this skyscraper will reach new heights this year. So we're going to the well one more time—this time with a logistics business and real estate core called Prologis.

Prologis is the global leader in industrial logistics real estate across the Americas, Europe, and Asia. "Industrial logistics real estate" is mainly distribution warehouses and specialized facilities that store goods and prepare them for shipment, sometimes with some final assembly or value-add, and are an integral component of the supply chain for many types of organizations. Major clients include third-party logistics providers, transportation companies, retail (including online), and manufacturers.

The REIT operates 3,380 properties in all across 20 countries, with 2,482 in the Americas, 768 in 13 countries in Europe, and 130 in 3 countries in Asia. The company owns and operates most of these properties mainly as standard warehouses in industrial parks or near port or airport facilities, leasing them to large and small companies either in whole or in sections according to need. Prologis also develops custom partner solutions through their "Global Customer Solutions" business which designs, builds, and operates custom distribution facilities for major accounts like Amazon, DHL, and others. In fact, their top ten customers accounted for 11.4 percent of the business; Amazon is the largest customer at 4.5 percent; Home Depot is second at 1.8 percent; and FedEx is third at 1.5 percent. Overall, however, the customer base is quite diverse with 5,200 customers in all.

Financial Highlights, Fiscal Year 2015

FY2015 was a very good year for the business, with demand exceeding supply for such kinds of facilities—a statement borne out in the numbers. Occupancy rates were up 0.8 percent to a very strong 96.9 percent. Same-store net operating income was up 5.6 percent on a 13.1 percent average rent increase on property rollovers (rentals to new tenants). Core Funds From Operations (FFO—a standard measure of true income for REITs) was up 19 percent on a 25 percent increase in revenues (which included a moderate acquisition).

Revenues should advance 5–10 percent per year through 2017; per-share FFO is expected to be ahead 10–15 percent in 2016 and a more modest 4–5 percent in 2017.

Reasons to Buy

The value proposition of modern, flexible logistics sites for today's organizations is strong, and particularly strong for e-commerce businesses—like Amazon, as previously noted. More generally, the state of the art in supply-chain management has advanced significantly in just a few years, driven by e-commerce and just-in-time production management. As supply chains become more global, and as products become more customized and have shorter life cycles, as shipments get smaller, more numerous, and more likely to have an assembly and a "reverse" component, flexible logistics solutions become far more important. Equally important is today's current business climate, with companies relying on back-end productivity rather than top-line growth to increase profits. Prologis sits right in the middle of this trend, with a solid base of real estate, skills to manage it, and skills to partner with major clients to deliver the right and often customized solution.

All major financial metrics are on a strong upward advance, pricing power is apparent, and double-digit dividend increases appear likely. Consistent with much of the REIT industry, share counts are on the rise as Prologis replaces debt with equity or uses equity to finance acquisitions. The current debt-to-equity ratio of 44 percent is very healthy.

Reasons for Caution

We've picked four REITs—in senior living, self-storage, New York real estate—and now, logistics and warehousing—Prologis. Guess which one is most vulnerable to economic downturns. Prologis? Right. A protracted economic downturn would hurt this business more than many REITs (we have avoided shopping center and hospitality REITs because in our view they're even more vulnerable). The abundance of customers in the e-commerce space could also spell trouble. As Millennials shift their focus from goods to experiences, and as most sought-after goods get smaller (like smartphones), the future global economy could simply require less physical space to operate.

SECTOR: **Real Estate** ❑ BETA COEFFICIENT: **1.42** ❑ 10-YEAR COMPOUND EARNINGS PER-SHARE GROWTH: **NM** ❑ 10-YEAR COMPOUND DIVIDENDS PER-SHARE GROWTH: **NM**

	2008	2009	2010	2011	2012	2013	2014	2015
Revenues (mil)	—	—	—	1,533	2,006	1,750	1,761	2,197
Net income (mil)	—	—	—	(153.4)	(102.4)	219.4	636.2	869.4
Funds from operations per share	—	—	—	1.10	1.19	1.65	1.88	2.23
Real estate owned per share	—	—	—	57.25	55.74	45.67	47.63	52.47
Dividends per share	—	—	—	1.12	1.12	1.12	1.32	1.52
Price: high	—	—	—	37.5	37.6	45.5	44.1	47.6
low	—	—	—	21.7	28.2	34.6	36.3	36.3

Website: www.prologis.com

GROWTH AND INCOME

Public Storage

Ticker symbol: PSA (NYSE) ❑ S&P rating: A ❑ Value Line financial strength rating: A+ ❑ Current yield: 2.5% ❑ Dividend raises, past 10 years: 8

Company Profile

You have stuff. We have stuff. We all have stuff. Stuff to store somewhere. Stuff from our families, stuff from our kids, stuff from our past. Boats, RVs, and extra vehicles. And we all need to store that stuff somewhere. But where? As more of us live in houses with smaller yards and devoid of basements, where? As more of us choose to rent rather than buy, where? As more of us, especially the younger Millennials among us, choose to live closer to the centers of larger cities, where? As the retirees among us downsize, where? As the elderly give up their primary residences, where?

You get the idea. There is more personal stuff for most of us to store, and less space to do it. That's where Public Storage comes in. And you know it's been an interesting year when a normally slow, steady REIT becomes your best-performing stock on a list of 100—up 43 percent including dividends for the 2016 measurement year.

Public Storage is a real estate investment trust owning and operating 2,277 self-storage properties in 38 states and another 216 facilities in seven countries in Europe. The company has a 49 percent interest in Europe's Shurgard, and also owns a 42 percent interest in another trust called PS Business Parks, which owns 103 rentable properties in eight states. The company points out that, based on the number of tenants, it is one of the world's largest landlords.

Most are probably familiar with the format—small, unfinished, generally not-climate-controlled lockers rentable on a month-to-month basis for personal and business use. They range in size from 25–400 square feet, and there are typically 350–750 storage spaces in each facility. Some include covered parking for vehicle, boat, and RV storage. On average the company nets about $1 per square foot per month—a rather handsome sum considering these units do not come with any of the finish or comfort of an apartment, which may rent for something similar per square foot depending on the market.

Not surprisingly, the largest concentrations are in California, Texas, and Florida (since these are centers for retirees and homes with no basements), and most are near a major U.S. or European city. The three largest markets are New York, San Francisco, and Los Angeles. Branding in the U.S. is "Public Storage"; in Europe it is "Shurgard."

The key strategies continue to be revenue and cost optimization, market-share growth in major markets, and building brand recognition. The company has a centralized call center and a website to help market its product and facilitate transactions. Acquisitions are also an important part of the strategy; the current market is fragmented with PSA only owning 10–20 percent of the market at most, and good properties come up regularly. The company expects to grow its property base a steady 1–2 percent annually.

Our principle in owning REITs remains the same; we're not looking for just real estate, we want to own a good business that *just happens* to own a lot of real estate. REITs are typically good income producers, as they are required by law to pay a substantial portion of their cash flow to investors. The accounting rules are different, and REIT investors should focus on Funds From Operations (FFO), which is analogous to operating income; net income figures have depreciation expenses deducted, which can vary in timing and not always be realistic. FFO supports the dividends paid to investors.

Financial Highlights, Fiscal Year 2015

FY2015 saw an uptick in the usually steady gains for the year mostly due to increased occupancy rates, higher rents, and the stronger margins that came as a result. Occupancy rates ended 2015 at 94.1 percent versus 93.5 percent for 2014, with a rate as high as 94.5 percent for the year—a stellar figure in any real estate venture and especially one where turnover is relatively high. Realized rents rose 6 percent, again better than 2014's 5 percent. As a consequence, revenues grew about 8.5 percent and per-share FFO grew over 10 percent, new highs for the company, as was the 44.2 percent net profit margin. Forecasts call largely for more of the same, with revenues advancing 7–10 percent annually and per-share FFO advancing 7–12 percent annually through 2017. The company has been adding a few more shares following an industry-wide trend toward deleveraging its balance sheet (more equity, less debt).

Reasons to Buy

As stated previously, our emphasis is more on the business and less on real estate, and with Public Storage, we feel we've found a good business that happens to be based on real estate. PSA has the best brand and highest operating efficiency in the business, and the core business model and need for its product is sustained and growing. No matter how easy it is to sell stuff on Craigslist, it's also too easy to acquire stuff, and we still don't see people getting out of that habit anytime soon. At the same time, real estate is trending away from large suburban McMansions with extra space and more toward city digs, patio homes, cluster homes, and the like. All point to strong, steady business prospects for providers of flexible storage solutions, and as PSA strengthens its brand and market-share foothold, more of that business will go its way. The rising rents and occupancy rates are good evidence that this is already happening. The dividend has risen at a substantial and accelerating rate in recent years and is well funded; too, there is less debt than typically found in a real estate investment business.

Reasons for Caution

The excellent performance of the stock may be a bit ahead of the performance of the company and may be due for a breather—this is the biggest negative we can think of, so we repeat last year's warning: Unlock the door and enter carefully. Beyond that, real estate is real estate, and is more subject to ups and downs than was once thought.

SECTOR: **Real Estate** ❑ BETA COEFFICIENT: **0.63** ❑ 10-YEAR COMPOUND FFO PER-SHARE GROWTH: **8.0%** ❑ 10-YEAR COMPOUND DIVIDENDS PER-SHARE GROWTH: **12.5%**

	2008	2009	2010	2011	2012	2013	2014	2015
Revenues (mil)	1,746	1,628	1,647	1,752	1,826	1,982	2,195	2,382
Net income (mil)	636	835	672	824	670	845	908	1,053
Funds from operations per share	5.17	5.03	5.22	5.93	6.31	7.53	7.98	8.79
Real estate owned per share	46.48	46.48	44.51	43.35	42.71	47.97	49.20	49.49
Dividends per share	2.20	2.20	3.05	3.65	4.40	5.15	5.60	6.50
Price: high	102.5	85.1	106.1	136.7	152.7	176.7	190.2	253.9
low	52.5	45.3	74.7	100.0	129.0	144.4	148.0	192.1

Website: www.publicstorage.com

AGGRESSIVE GROWTH

Qualcomm, Inc.

Ticker symbol: QCOM (NASDAQ) ❑ S&P rating: A+ ❑ Value Line financial strength rating: A++ ❑ Current yield: 3.9% ❑ Dividend raises, past 10 years: 10

Company Profile

Qualcomm, based in surf-friendly San Diego, is responsible for producing the hardware at the heart of most of the high-end mobile web-surfing devices in use today. Their Snapdragon processors are used in most of the "flagship" smartphones on the market, as well as many tablets. In addition to processors, the company also makes many of the modems and "front-end" hardware used at both ends of a cellular connection, as well as peripheral devices for personal computers, such as wi-fi and Bluetooth transceivers.

Integrated circuits and other tangible products account for about 68 percent of Qualcomm's revenue—the rest is derived from the company

IP (intellectual property) licensing activity. Qualcomm, founded in 1985, has been at the forefront of the development of much of the fundamental technology of cellular communications. Their CDMA, LTE, and GSM patents are at the core of the world's cellular industry and form the foundation for the bulk of the company's business, both in hardware and licensing.

Not surprisingly, the licensing arm generates the bulk of the earnings (86 percent in 2015), while the cost-heavy chip development and production arm generates the remaining 14 percent. Qualcomm began as a "front-end" and licensing business and later got into the general-purpose processor business with the advent of smartphones. The company is still investing heavily in their relatively new Snapdragon CPU development, as well as preparing 5G chipsets, while the existing fundamental IP continues to garner licensing fees.

Financial Highlights, Fiscal Year 2015

Following a six-year run over which revenues grew 205 percent, Qualcomm's FY2015 brought a 0.5 percent downturn. The bulk of the bad news was attributed to a slowdown in the growth of flagship devices such as the iPhone 6S and Galaxy Edge. As 45 percent of Qualcomm's FY2015 revenue was derived from Apple and Samsung, even a small decline in their shipments has a noticeable effect on Qualcomm's earnings. Consequently, the results were not a surprise but were disappointing nonetheless. Unit prices held firm, though, as the company's current lineup of products holds the number one or two positions in all of their markets.

The company acquired CSR plc, a fabless semiconductor design and engineering firm, for $2.4 billion. CSR has specific expertise in the IoT ("Internet of Things") and automotive markets.

Reasons to Buy

If there's a word to describe Qualcomm's presence in the mobile market, it's "ubiquitous." Qualcomm's platform, voice, and data communications devices are used in the mobile products of over 90 manufacturers. In some cases, only the front-end parts are used. In many cases, though, the manufacturer will simply copy Qualcomm's whole product reference designs for particular price points and use them without modification. This minimizes the manufacturer's development cost and time-to-market, while absolutely maximizing Qualcomm's silicon content and revenue.

As the developer (or co-developer) of many of the technologies used in modern wireless communications, Qualcomm is a major beneficiary of all licensing activity associated with cellular communication. Every cell phone produced in at least the past ten years has come with Qualcomm IP, for which the manufacturer has been (or should have been) paying Qualcomm on a per-unit basis. We mention the licensing collections issue only because there has been a growing level of attention on a number of licensees who are under-reporting device sales in order to avoid payment of fees. As the bulk of these licensees are in China, a full solution may lead to litigation, but it is being addressed.

Qualcomm is a major presence in the growing mobile automotive market. In-car communication and data services have become extremely popular with consumers, to the point where manufacturers are offering a range of those services either as standard equipment or options, even on their entry-level cars. Qualcomm's GPS and sensor technologies are already in wide use here, but plans for extended functionality in these applications hold promise for significant growth. We expect the growth of Apple's CarPlay, Android Auto, and other in-car data services to leverage strongly on Qualcomm's existing technology while, again, providing for licensing revenue regardless of the hardware employed.

Qualcomm is investing heavily in IoT. All of these interconnected devices use Bluetooth, near-field communication, or simple wi-fi to provide wireless, always-on connectivity, and all of these technologies are already in place and under further development at Qualcomm. The company's product line here includes technology for wearables, smart homes, healthcare, and other markets.

Lastly, as often happens with companies that we like, Qualcomm is using the period of slow sales to address costs company wide. The company expects to eliminate $1.1 billion in costs from a FY2015 basis of $7.3 billion over a period of two years.

Reasons for Caution

Qualcomm presents an interesting proposition for calendar year 2017. As we write this, we expect a decline in FY2016 revenues following a weaker FY2015. The decline is due to a number of factors. First, Intel is expected to make entries into the mobile market, potentially cutting into some of the Apple contracts. Second, there are some signs of saturation in the upper-tier markets (U.S. and Europe). While we recognize these developments and fully expect QCOM shares to take an "adjustment" during 2016, we feel Qualcomm will be undervalued and well positioned for calendar year 2017. Intel has yet to prove they can make a cost-competitive, low-power processor in this space; their most modern fabs are already at capacity, and their modems will not match Qualcomm's current functionality until 2020. Also, the Chinese and other developing markets still have a lot of room to grow, and Qualcomm has a broad range of low- and mid-range products that Intel will not have. Finally, for every Intel part shipped, Qualcomm will still collect licensing fees. Some comfort there.

SECTOR: **Information Technology** ❑ BETA COEFFICIENT: **0.95** ❑ 10-YEAR COMPOUND EARNINGS PER-SHARE GROWTH: **17.5%** ❑ 10-YEAR COMPOUND DIVIDENDS PER-SHARE GROWTH: **22.5%**

		2008	2009	2010	2011	2012	2013	2014	2015
Revenues (mil)		11,130	10,387	10,982	14,957	19,121	24,866	26,487	25,277
Net income (mil)		3,740	3,169	4,071	5,407	6,463	7,911	9,032	7,641
Earnings per share		2.25	1.90	2.46	3.20	3.71	4.51	5.27	4.66
Dividends per share		0.60	0.66	0.72	0.81	0.93	1.20	1.54	1.80
Cash flow per share		2.53	2.28	2.94	3.85	4.31	5.30	6.10	5.81
Price:	high	56.9	48.7	50.3	59.8	68.9	74.3	82.0	75.3
	low	28.2	32.6	31.6	46.0	53.1	59.0	67.7	45.9

Website: www.qualcomm.com

AGGRESSIVE GROWTH

Quest Diagnostics Inc.

Ticker symbol: DGX (NYSE) ❑ S&P rating: BBB+ ❑ Value Line financial strength rating: B++ ❑ Current yield: 2.3% ❑ Dividend raises, past 10 years: 5

Company Profile

If you have gone for any kind of medical test, either at the recommendation of a doctor or as required by an employer or insurance company, chances are you got that test in a lab operated by Quest Diagnostics. Quest is the world's leading provider of diagnostic testing, information, and services to support doctors, hospitals, and the care-giving process.

The company operates more than 2,200 labs and patient service centers including about 150 smaller "rapid-response" labs in the U.S. and has facilities in India, Mexico, the U.K., Ireland, and Sweden. It provides about 150 million lab test results a year and serves physicians, hospitals, employers, life and healthcare insurers, and other health facilities. The company has a logistics network including 3,000 courier vehicles and 20 aircraft, and has some 20 *billion* test results from the past decade in its databases, a rich source for medical research data.

The company offers diagnostic testing services covering pretty much the gamut of medical necessity in its testing facilities. It also offers a line of diagnostic kits, reagents, and devices to support its own labs, home and remote testing, and other labs. Employer drug testing is a big business. The company offers a series of "wellness and risk management services," including tests, exams, and record services for the insurance industry. The company also does tests and provides other support for clinical research and trials, and finally, through its information technology segment, it offers a Care360 platform to help physicians maintain charts and access data through its network, which has about 200,000 physicians enrolled. Mobile technology is another innovation front; the company has developed a mobile solution within Care360 known as "MyQuest" to help patients keep track of test results, schedule appointments and medications, and share information with physicians and other care providers.

The company has also been a leader in developing so-called "moderate complexity" direct molecular testing procedures, where more complex diagnostic tests can be performed in "moderate complexity" environments—i.e., a "retail" lab format such as Quest operates. Such a new test for encephalitis was cleared by the FDA in March 2014—a first, and a strong endorsement of this type of procedure delivery. The company is also a leader in "gene-based" and "esoteric" testing and has launched an assortment of molecular genetics tests supporting new trends in the health industry toward individualized medicine—medicine based on a patient's own unique gene makeup and characteristics.

Financial Highlights, Fiscal Year 2015

Anticipated gains in volume from the Affordable Care Act have failed to materialize, and revenues for FY2015 were up less than 1 percent partly as a consequence. Volumes throughout the industry were flat. But also a stronger value-add component with complex testing and operational improvements led to higher net margins, and this led in turn to a 16 percent profit increase in FY2015. Quest projects revenue gains in the 1–3 percent range through FY2017 and earnings gains in the 6–8 percent range through the period. Moderate share buybacks and dividend increases will continue.

Reasons to Buy

We still think the ACA will lead to a permanent volume increase. Additionally, an ever-greater emphasis on wellness and preventative care is likely to send more people for routine checkups, particularly if insurance carriers offer benefits (like free tests or lower coinsurance) to motivate such preventative care.

Even more, we're excited about the innovative new tests performed at the retail lab level for molecular-level and gene-based diagnostics, which bode well for the future; the company is advancing to higher, more profitable levels of the diagnostic food chain.

We're also fans of the ancillary businesses—clinical trials, insurance qualifications, employer testing, and IT services—which all should do well in an environment favoring greater cost control and outsourcing of distinct services such as Quest provides. The company is a leader in its industry and has a beta of 0.67 indicating relative safety. Finally, Quest has retired more than 25 percent of its shares in the past ten years.

Several factors in the ongoing evolution of healthcare and healthcare cost management seem to line up right for this company, and the cash returns give us a decent cushion if we turn out to be wrong.

Reasons for Caution

Continued pressure to contain healthcare costs may bring some additional malaise over the next few years. Offsetting that is the placement of more emphasis on preventative care, a Quest sweet spot. To a degree, the company has been forced to reach for growth through acquisitions, which don't always work out—but again, better volumes through ACA and new testing should mitigate this trend. The company may also face more competition as large-group physician practices get larger and bring some of their lab operations in-house—although that trend may be countered by hospitals and other large organizations getting *out* of this relatively easily outsourced business. In all, it's a complex and ever-changing environment with a lot of moving parts.

SECTOR: **Healthcare** ❑ BETA COEFFICIENT: **0.67** ❑ 10-YEAR COMPOUND EARNINGS PER-SHARE GROWTH: **7.5%** ❑ 10-YEAR COMPOUND DIVIDENDS PER-SHARE GROWTH: **13.5%**

	2008	2009	2010	2011	2012	2013	2014	2015
Revenues (mil)	7,249	7,455	7,400	7,511	7,468	7,146	7,435	7,493
Net income (mil)	640.0	730.3	720.9	728.7	700.0	612.0	587.0	682.0
Earnings per share	3.27	3.88	4.05	4.53	4.43	4.00	4.10	4.77
Dividends per share	0.40	0.40	0.40	0.47	0.81	1.20	1.29	1.47
Cash flow per share	4.75	5.52	5.00	6.42	6.23	6.22	6.21	6.90
Price: high	59.9	62.8	61.7	61.2	64.9	64.1	68.5	89.0
low	38.7	42.4	40.8	45.1	53.3	52.5	50.5	60.1

Website: www.questdiagnostics.com

AGGRESSIVE GROWTH

ResMed, Inc.

Ticker symbol: RMD (NYSE) ❑ S&P rating: NR ❑ Value Line financial strength rating: A ❑ Current yield: 2.0% ❑ Dividend raises, past 10 years: 3

Company Profile

Sleep disorders are a big deal among adult populations. Reading the clinical description of sleep disorders and their myriad causes could for some be a cure for such disorders, but suffice it to say (as ResMed does in its market analysis) that 26 percent of U.S. adults age 30–70, or about 46 million people, have some form of sleep apnea. That's where the story of ResMed begins.

Perhaps you know someone using a "CPAP" (continuous positive airway pressure) machine to alleviate "SDB" (sleep-disordered breathing) or "OSA" (obstructive sleep apnea). As we age and tend to gain weight, these devices are becoming a more mainstream way for folks (and their partners) to get some much-needed sleep.

Formed in 1989, ResMed develops, manufactures, and distributes medical equipment for treating, diagnosing, and managing sleep-disordered breathing and other respiratory disorders. Products include diagnostic products, airflow generators, headgear, and other accessories. The original and still largest product line of CPAP machines delivers pressurized air through a mask during sleep, to prevent collapse of tissue in the upper airway, a condition common in people with narrow upper airways and poor muscle tone—in many cases, people who are older and overweight. A great many of the estimated 46 million with sleep apnea, who exhibit the typical symptoms of daytime sleepiness, snoring, hypertension, and irritability, have yet to be diagnosed.

CPAP machines and their cousins VPAP (variable positive airway pressure) and others were at one time massive, clunky machines restricting movement and very difficult to travel with. No more: The new machines are smaller, lighter, cheaper, and easier to use. We don't like solutions that are worse than the problem, and ResMed has turned the corner on that with the new machines; they're becoming more acceptable, less expensive, and more mainstream. We think the company's four-pronged strategy is a good one: Make the machines easier to deal with (and afford), increase clinical awareness and the rate of diagnosis, expand into new applications including stroke and congestive heart failure treatment, and expand internationally. The company has executed effectively on all fronts.

The company markets its products in 100 countries, makes them in five countries outside the U.S., and invests about 7 percent of revenues in R&D.

ResMed continues to develop a holistic sleep management offering; a new "S+" non-contact sleep tracker is one new product example. The company continues to make small acquisitions to broaden its product line particularly into disease treatment and into new international markets. The 2016 acquisition of cloud software provider Brightree entered the company into the teleconnected home sleep disorder care market. Recent emphasis on consumables—sleep masks—bodes well for a strong repeatable sales base.

Financial Highlights, Fiscal Year 2015

Like most companies with large international businesses, ResMed suffered for the gains in the dollar. Sales and income gains for FY2015 were highly tempered by the strong dollar, which shaved about 6 percent off of sales (they still advanced 7 percent) and as much as 20 percent off of net earnings. Intrinsic product demand, especially for new flow generators and masks, remains strong. Going forward, the company expects revenue gains in the 7–8 percent range through FY2017 and earnings gains in the 3–4 percent range for FY2016, advancing to 10–11 percent in FY2017. Aggressive share buybacks should strengthen per-share earnings, and dividend increases should be healthy.

Reasons to Buy

We believe that the company's four-pronged strategy, previously outlined, is right on. As these machines, and the diagnosis of the condition they're designed for, become more mainstream, we expect more people in the market, lower prices, and reduced inconvenience. All these things should open up larger and larger slices of the market for the company. Demographics are a plus, too—as people get older and heavier, these machines will find more potential users. It's a niche business, and ResMed dominates the niche and is the only company solely focused on this market. While we tend not to rely on this in our selections, we feel the company has the earmarks of a good acquisition candidate for a larger provider of healthcare technology products.

Clearly ResMed's results would look better were it not for the impact of the strong dollar. Unlike most emerging companies in the healthcare technology sector, the dividend is substantial and share buybacks have already been a healthy source of shareholder return. Outstanding shares are projected to drop to 135 million in FY2017 from 152 million in 2011.

Reasons for Caution

One of the bigger issues facing CPAP and related technologies is the eligibility for reimbursement or coverage through Medicare/Medicaid and through private insurers. The current landscape is a mixed bag: Many non-Medicare health insurance plans do not cover the machines (which range from about $600–$1,900 in price), and Medicare has driven payment rates down through competitive bidding and across-the-board cuts.

Too, the market is becoming more competitive, and there have been a few legal contests on intellectual property—most of which have gone ResMed's way so far. We feel that ResMed's technology leadership (as exemplified by a new wireless control for one of its major devices), full-line offering, and experience in this market will prevail.

SECTOR: **Healthcare** ◻ BETA COEFFICIENT: **0.69** ◻ 10-YEAR COMPOUND EARNINGS PER-SHARE GROWTH: **19.5%** ◻ 10-YEAR COMPOUND DIVIDENDS PER-SHARE GROWTH: **NM**

		2008	2009	2010	2011	2012	2013	2014	2015
Revenues (mil)		835	921	1,092	1,243	1,368	1,514	1,555	1,679
Net income (mil)		114.1	146.4	190.1	227.0	254.9	307.1	345.4	352.9
Earnings per share		0.73	0.95	1.23	1.44	1.71	2.10	2.39	2.47
Dividends per share		—	—	—	—	—	0.68	1.00	1.12
Cash flow per share		1.14	1.33	1.66	1.96	2.40	2.71	2.99	3.03
Price:	high	26.2	26.7	35.9	35.4	42.9	57.3	57.6	75.3
	low	14.5	15.7	25.0	23.4	24.4	42.0	41.5	49.0

Website: www.resmed.com

AGGRESSIVE GROWTH

NEW FOR 2017

C.H. Robinson Worldwide, Inc.

Ticker symbol: CHRW (NASDAQ) ◻ S&P rating: NR ◻ Value Line financial strength rating: A ◻ Current yield: 2.4% ◻ Dividend raises, past 10 years: 9

Company Profile

C.H. Robinson Worldwide, Inc. is one of the largest third-party logistics ("3PL") providers in North America. The company provides bundled and "turnkey" freight transportation services and logistics solutions to companies of all sizes, in a variety of industries. The company is a non asset–based provider, meaning it contracts with a network of 68,000 transportation carriers (mostly trucking firms but also railroads, intermodal operators, ship and air lines) and a network of warehousing, customs clearance operations, and other supply-chain components to provide a complete, flexible, and tailored solution to customers across and around the world. In addition to transportation, the company has a division called Robinson Fresh that provides sourcing services in the perishable food industry buying, selling, and marketing fresh fruits, vegetables, and other perishable items and transporting them to market—120 million cases annually for 2,000 growers. The fresh produce division accounts for about 11 percent of revenues, while "Transportation" accounts for the other 89 percent (and about 78 percent of that comes from trucking services).

In 2015, C.H. Robinson handled approximately 16.9 million shipments and worked with over 110,000 active customers. The customer base is diverse—manufacturing, food and beverage, retail, chemical, and automotive are the largest customer segments. The company has 285 offices across North and South America, Europe, and Asia.

The company has invested heavily in technology; its Navisphere single global technology "ecosystem" connects 150,000 customers, carriers, and suppliers and covers the entire life cycle of a shipment from notification to scheduling to delivery. Customers can track their shipments down to a single item; about 70 percent of Robinson's customer contacts come through this platform. The 2015 acquisition of electronic freight broker Freightquote added significant revenues and customer convenience especially in the LTL ("less than truckload") shipping market for smaller customers.

Financial Highlights, Fiscal Year 2015

Increased volumes, the Freightquote acquisition (which brought connections to 80,000 customers), and greater efficiency and scale offset currency effects to bring a 13 percent increase in FY2015 net income and "net revenue" (after freight charges) on relatively flat reported total revenue. Significantly, operating margins improved from 6.0 to 6.9 percent. Net income is forecast to rise another 8 percent by 2017 again on relatively flat total revenues. The company stated a goal to return 90 percent of net income to shareholders annually, foreshadowing continued dividend increases and capturing the fact that the company has bought back about 20 percent of its shares since 2011.

Reasons to Buy

"Connecting the World—One Supply Chain at a Time" is Robinson's apt slogan. The main idea behind C.H. Robinson is to provide businesses, large and small, with a flexible and scalable (okay, we'll not overuse the buzz-words!) way to outsource their logistics operations, thus reducing poorly matched capacities and risks (Do you, as operator of a private trucking fleet, ever have the right number of trucks? Nope—always too few or too many!).

A 3PL firm can also achieve efficiencies by combining loads for different customers. The company's value proposition for customers, in fact, is to "drive costs down," "improve efficiency," "mitigate risk," and "manage change." In today's fast-moving business world, products and supply chains change quickly and companies have an increasing mandate to find ways to control costs and create supply-chain advantages. As top-line improvements are hard to come by, services such as those offered by C.H. Robinson seem to make sense for an ever-increasing customer base. And we like the way they do this with a minimal asset base—no trucks, ships, or trains of their own!

Traditionally, the company operated as a procurement, or forwarding, service for transportation services for its customers; today as much as anything else, it is a technology company deploying technology solutions to not only procure but manage and optimize the network. We like companies that deploy technology to create an advantage, particularly when it's an advantage for their customers. The strategy seems to be to become a fully integrated, technology-connected solution for firms shipping big stuff, just as FedEx and UPS have for firms shipping small stuff. The strong commitment to shareholder returns and the steady price related to the market (beta = 0.36) add to the list of attractions.

Reasons for Caution

Shipping and transportation services are always cyclical; in addition, large changes in fuel costs can be difficult to adjust to. Changes in transportation economics—like those caused by fuel prices, shortages of truck drivers, environmental regulations, and the like—can disrupt supply-chain networks and be costly to comply with. Competition in the industry is fierce, but C.H. Robinson has a pretty strong lead in integrating its suppliers and customers, and even the 68,000 transportation suppliers stand to gain from the Robinson intermediary even if it crimps their own margins. The company is a "win-win" in the transportation and logistics market.

SECTOR: **Transportation** ◻ BETA COEFFICIENT: **0.36** ◻ 10-YEAR COMPOUND EARNINGS
PER-SHARE GROWTH: **16.5%** ◻ 10-YEAR COMPOUND DIVIDENDS PER-SHARE GROWTH: **23.5%**

	2008	2009	2010	2011	2012	2013	2014	2015
Revenues (mil)	8,577	7,577	9,274	10,336	11,369	12,752	13,470	13,476
Net income (mil)	359	361	387	432	594	416	450	510
Earnings per share	2.08	2.13	2.33	2.82	3.67	2.65	3.05	3.51
Dividends per share	0.88	0.97	1.04	1.20	1.67	1.40	1.43	1.57
Cash flow per share	2.29	2.34	2.51	2.62	3.92	3.18	3.46	4.00
Price: high	67.4	61.7	81.0	82.8	71.8	67.9	77.5	76.2
low	36.5	37.4	51.2	62.3	50.8	53.7	50.2	59.7

Website: www.chrobinson.com

AGGRESSIVE GROWTH

Ross Stores, Inc.

Ticker symbol: ROST (NASDAQ) ◻ S&P rating: A- ◻ Value Line financial strength rating: A
◻ Current yield: 0.9% ◻ Dividend raises, past 10 years: 10

Company Profile

"It's All About the Bargains" is the motto of Ross Stores, the second-largest off-price retailer in the United States. Ross and its subsidiaries operate two chains of apparel and home accessories stores. As of 2015 the company operated a total of 1,446 stores, up from 1,362 in 2014 and 1,125 in 2011. Of that total, 1,274 were Ross Dress for Less locations in 34 states, D.C., and Guam and 172 were dd's DISCOUNTS stores in 15 states. Just under half the company's stores are located in three states—California, Florida, and Texas.

Both chains target value-conscious women and men between the ages of 18 and 54. Ross's target customers are primarily from middle-income households, while dd's DISCOUNTS target customers are typically from lower- to middle-income households. Merchandising, purchasing, pricing, and the locations of the stores are all aimed at these customer bases. Ross and dd's DISCOUNTS both offer first-quality, in-season, name-brand and designer apparel, accessories, and footwear for the family at savings typically in the 20–60 percent range off department store prices (at Ross) or 20–70 percent off (at dd's DISCOUNTS). The stores also offer discounted home fashions and housewares, educational toys and games, furniture and furniture accents, luggage, cookware, and at some stores jewelry.

Sales break down by category roughly as follows: 29 percent Ladies'; 25 percent Home Accents, Bed, and Bath; 13 percent each for Men's and for Accessories, Lingerie, Jewelry, and Fragrances; 12 percent for shoes; and 8 percent Children's. The shopping demographic is 75–80 percent female, shopping for herself or other family members; the core customer averages about three store visits a month. Their market research also suggests that the average customer "wants"—not "needs"—a bargain; there are a number of frugal but fairly well-heeled customers looking for a brand at a price.

Ross's strategy is to offer competitive values to target customers by offering a well-managed mix of inventory with a strong percentage of department store name brands and items of local and seasonal interest at attractive prices. The company plans to add 70 Ross stores and 20 dd's DISCOUNTS stores for 2016, and to grow to about 2,000 Ross and 500 dd's DISCOUNTS stores by the end of the decade.

Financial Highlights, Fiscal Year 2015

The Great Recession was nothing but good news for this company, bringing in newly cost-conscious customers by the busload. The question was—what would happen after that? Would people feel they were on more solid footing and abandon Ross in droves for more fully priced favorites? The answer, so far, continues in a large measure to be "no."

The main growth vector is store base expansions, which continue at a healthy clip; Ross added 84 new stores again in FY2015 onto a 1,362-store base. A 4 percent increase in same-store sales drove an 8 percent revenue increase, somewhat ahead of the 6.2 percent increase in the store base. Both pricing and average size of sale in turn drove the comp increase. Operating margins grew sequentially about 0.3 percent (significant for a retailer) mostly on supply-chain efficiency initiatives to 15.9 percent; net income rang up a nice 10.4 percent gain. A 3 percent share buyback rounded out the picture, helping per-share earnings to a 13.6 percent gain for the year. (Those of you who read last year's edition will recognize all of these numbers as nearly identical to gains registered last year.)

FY2016 forecasts call for a 5–6 percent revenue gain on 1–2 percent comp growth, with a moderation in efficiency measures leading to constant margins and a 4–5 percent net earnings increase. Wage increases and distribution costs will tug against margins, while a large surplus of winter wear coming back from retailers after a warm winter might help out. FY2017 projections look a bit stronger with a 7–8 percent earnings gain on a 5–6 percent growth in revenues. Cash flows are strong, and we do believe the company will step up the dividend more quickly and continue moderate share buybacks in the 1–3 percent range annually.

Reasons to Buy

We had become a little tired of this story, which really got a boost from the now-fading Great Recession years. We saw revenue growth being driven mainly by store expansion, and profit growth attenuating. Did we also see that, with more disposable income, consumers may wander away? Did we see signs of too many stores? All might be warning signs of future trouble, and gives us a bit of fright every year. But we've stayed on this horse year after year for one big reason: profitability. Net profit margins—after taxes and everything else—run in the 8–9 percent range. And they've been steadily improving over the years. Where else can you find that in the retail world? Answer: nowhere—at least on as sustained a business as Ross Stores. So, welcome back, Ross, to our 2017 *100 Best Stocks* shelf once again.

The recession apparently helped Ross gain mainstream appeal across a wider set of customers. While some of those customers defected back to full-price retail stores as things improved, a greater number have shown that they will continue to shop at the stores. At the same time, the company was successful with operational changes begun years ago to improve merchandising and inventory management, which led to better stocking of a more favorable mix of goods and better inventory turnover. The higher store count has increased operating leverage as well—more volume through the same infrastructure and cost base. Nothing is mentioned about international expansion, but we wonder if there too lies an opportunity.

Moderate expansion, operational excellence, sustained shareholder returns; it's an attractive formula and the results speak for themselves as well as pointing to good management. And one more thing: We like how they present all of this to shareholders; their Investor Relations materials are better than average.

Reasons for Caution

One concern is that the company is dependent on the actions of others—mainly first-line apparel retailers—for its success. Currently there is a glut of supply in the clothing business with last year's warm winter and as more "trendy" styles and colors hit department store shelves only to be changed out more frequently, presenting opportunity to Ross. This may or may not continue as tastes change or as department stores become fed up trying to chase these trends and changes. This inventory cycle may present some challenges for Ross. We also remain concerned that the company still depends to a degree on store expansion, which carries its own risks, and could make supply bubbles and constraints hurt even more.

SECTOR: Retail □ BETA COEFFICIENT: 0.78 □ 10-YEAR COMPOUND EARNINGS PER-SHARE GROWTH: 19.5% □ 10-YEAR COMPOUND DIVIDENDS PER-SHARE GROWTH: 26.5%

	2008	2009	2010	2011	2012	2013	2014	2015
Revenues (mil)	6,486	7,184	7,866	8,608	9,721	10,230	11,042	11,940
Net income (mil)	305	443	555	657	787	837	925	1,021
Earnings per share	0.58	0.89	1.16	1.43	1.77	1.94	2.21	2.51
Dividends per share	0.10	0.12	0.18	0.24	0.30	0.36	0.40	0.47
Cash flow per share	0.88	1.22	1.52	1.81	2.21	2.44	2.79	3.22
Price: high	10.4	12.6	16.8	24.6	35.4	41.0	48.1	56.7
low	5.3	7.0	10.6	15.0	23.5	26.5	30.9	43.5

Website: www.rossstores.com

AGGRESSIVE GROWTH

RPM International Inc.

Ticker symbol: RPM (NYSE) □ S&P rating: BBB- □ Value Line financial strength rating: B+ □ Current yield: 2.6% □ Dividend raises, past 10 years: 10

Company Profile

Have you ever finished a piece of furniture or a wood floor with Varathane? Stained it with Watco? Caulked a bathtub or leaky sink with DAP? Spray-painted a rusty gate with Rust-Oleum? Primed bathroom walls with Zinsser primers before painting it? Glued a model airplane together with Testors? We have—and it seems like every time we do those little weekend warrior tasks around the house, we're using one of these products.

So we wondered, who makes and markets this stuff? Where do these well-established brands that seem to show up in every hardware store and home improvement center we go into come from? How did they become household names, even category-defining names like Kleenex? After a little digging, we came up with a company we'd never heard of. Sometimes, that's a really good sign. A "house of brands," each with its own strength, image, and loyal following, can have more staying and growing power than a "branded house." Just ask anyone on the marketing team at Procter & Gamble.

Anyway, the company we found is in all likelihood one you've never heard of, based in Medina, OH—a town you've probably never heard of, either. The company is RPM International. RPM International makes and markets an assortment of specialty chemicals and coatings, targeted mostly to repair, maintenance, and replacement, for consumer and industrial markets.

Industrial markets? Indeed, only about a third (35 percent, actually) of RPM's sales come from the aforementioned "consumer" brands found in Home Depot and the like. The company also makes and markets a vast line of brands for industrial and construction use—sealants, chemicals, roofing systems, corrosion control coatings, marine paints and coatings, fluorescent pigments (you've probably heard of DayGlo, their line of fluorescent paints), powder coatings, fire coatings, and concrete waterproofing and repair products. There are 27 "Industrial" brands in all, and if you take a tour of their well-organized and informal website, which includes brands such as Increte Systems, a maker of textured stamped concrete systems, or USL bridge-care solutions, you'll get the idea. The Industrial segment makes many products aimed at the preservation and corrosion protection of existing structures, which makes the company a strong play in the infrastructure reinvestment market. About 85 percent of the company's business comes from repair and maintenance, and about 15 percent comes from new construction. The Industrial segment accounts for 53 percent of the business, and many of its brands are made and sold in foreign markets. In fact, about 50 percent of Industrial business is overseas, while 85 percent of the consumer business originates in North America. The "Specialty" segment produces DayGlo as well as other specialty coatings for specialty powder and marine coatings, edible coatings, insulation, and concrete repair, with 18 brands and about 15 percent of RPM's business.

Not to beat the brand thing to death, but Rust-Oleum, Varathane, DAP, and Zinsser on the consumer side own number one positions in their respective markets, while eight industrial and specialty brands, including DayGlo of course, own number one positions in their markets.

Financial Highlights, Fiscal Year 2015

We like the products and the brand strength, but we also continue to like the improving financials of this company. Competitive strength in most of its markets and lower input costs overcame a 6 percent currency headwind to give a 5 percent revenue gain (after currency) and a pleasant sheen of a 9 percent gain in net earnings. Revenue gains should continue in the 5–6 percent range through FY2017 with earnings gains in the 5–10 percent range each year. Steady dividend increases should continue; the company has increased its dividend for 42 consecutive years.

Reasons to Buy

We always like premier brands in relatively simple, well-managed businesses, and RPM International seems to fit the model. The company presents itself well—its website is one of the best and most informative we've encountered (maybe this goes hand in hand with a relatively straightforward business; anyway, kudos to management or to the web designer). These factors alone wouldn't be enough to land RPM on our *100 Best* list; however, we also take notice when financials improve, especially when they improve at an accelerating rate. We also take notice of a company that has raised its dividend 42 straight years, and we like the defensive nature of its repeat-purchase, mainly maintenance and repair, product lines. We think other investors—large and small—are beginning to refinish their portfolios with some RPM shares, too.

Reasons for Caution

While we were impressed with the breadth of the RPM brand universe and the depth and strength of a few of them, we wonder if the business is stretched a bit too thin and if consolidating some of those brands to make stronger brands might make sense. That said, the way these brands are presented on the website leads us to believe that a Berkshire Hathaway model is in effect here: Let the business leaders of those business units do things as they see fit without undue influence from headquarters. RPM would also be somewhat exposed to price recovery in petrochemical inputs.

RPM is also not on as solid a financial footing as other companies on our *100 Best* list, with a debt-to-total-capital ratio exceeding 50 percent. That explains why the company isn't doing buybacks and why it may increase share counts slightly over the next few years—to reduce debt and improve this ratio. We agree with this direction, particularly in light of the increasing cash dividends.

SECTOR: **Materials** ☐ BETA COEFFICIENT: **1.28** ☐ 10-YEAR COMPOUND EARNINGS PER-SHARE GROWTH: **6.0%** ☐ 10-YEAR COMPOUND DIVIDENDS PER-SHARE GROWTH: **5.5%**

		2008	2009	2010	2011	2012	2013	2014	2015
Revenues (mil)		3,644	3,368	3,413	3,382	3,777	4,081	4,376	4,595
Net income (mil)		233	135	188	189	215	241	292	323
Earnings per share		1.81	1.05	1.45	1.45	1.65	1.83	2.18	2.38
Dividends per share		0.75	0.79	0.82	0.84	0.86	0.89	0.95	1.02
Cash flow per share		2.60	1.71	2.10	2.01	2.20	2.45	2.86	3.17
Price:	high	25.2	21.0	22.9	26.0	29.6	41.6	52.0	51.4
	low	10.0	9.1	16.1	17.2	23.0	29.1	37.6	40.1

Website: www.rpminc.com

AGGRESSIVE GROWTH

Schlumberger Limited

Ticker symbol: SLB (NYSE) ☐ S&P rating: AA- ☐ Value Line financial strength rating: A++ ☐ Current yield: 2.9% ☐ Dividend raises, past 10 years: 9

Company Profile

Schlumberger Limited is the world's leading oil field services company. It provides technology, information solutions, and integrated project management services with the goal of optimizing reservoir performance for its customers in the oil and gas industry. Founded in 1926, today the company has a large international footprint, employing more than 95,000 people in 85 countries, with 72 percent of revenue generated outside of North America. The company currently operates in three primary business segments:

- The Reservoir Characterization Group (24 percent of FY2015 revenues, 34 percent of pretax income) is mostly a consulting service, applying many digital and other technologies toward finding, defining, and characterizing hydrocarbon deposits. Interestingly, the company compares the electronic characterization of a hydrocarbon-producing zone to the imaging of a human body, using an assortment of technologies (for example, a technology referred to as a "Saturn 3D radial fluid sampling probe") to identify what you can't see directly.

- Not surprisingly, the Drilling Group (37 percent of revenues, 35 percent of pretax income) does the actual drilling and creation of wells for production, both in onshore and offshore environments. Again, a number of new drilling, drill bit, and drilling fluid technologies are in play, and naturally, so-called "fracking" is an important new part of the product offering.

- The Reservoir Production Group (39 percent of revenues, 32 percent of pretax income) completes and services the well for production, maintaining and enhancing productivity through its life.

Throughout the petroleum production process, the company not only provides physical onsite services but also substantial consulting, modeling, information management, total cost, yield, and general project management around these activities. In short, SLB offers a fully outsourced supply chain for oil and gas field development and production.

Schlumberger manages its business through 28 GeoMarket regions, which are grouped into four geographic areas: North America (29 percent); Latin America (21 percent); Europe, Commonwealth of Independent States, and Africa (22 percent); and Middle East and Asia (28 percent). The company made the big-ticket acquisition of oil services giant Smith International, which was integrated into the operations and financials during FY2011. By 2017 SLB will have also completed the acquisition of equipment supplier Cameron International (which will become a fourth operating group) and illustrates how the company intends to acquire assets "on the cheap" during the slump.

You might have expected that such an oil field services company, dependent on the now-attenuated production plans of oil "E&P" producers worldwide, who are suffering from the 40 percent drop in oil prices in 2014 and 20 percent in 2015, might have been cut from our *100 Best* list. Obviously, we didn't drop it. The question, of course and as always, is whether the market changes represented a fundamental and irreversible negative shift in the business. In the end, we determined that the changed markets present a challenge to the company, but not an irreversible one. We also think the slump will both shake out weak competitors and lead to efficiency measures within the company, both of which bode well during an eventual recovery. Being the biggest and best in the business helps a lot in these situations.

Too, the company maintains, probably correctly, that U.S. producers will have to lower costs, and thus apply SLB technologies and know-how to producing shale oil and gas at a cost economical to a $50 or $60 oil price. In the company's view, the shakeout, the need to produce more cheaply, and a strong financial base to weather a downturn and the inevitable long-term growth in world oil consumption, will get them by and position them well for recovery, probably starting in late 2016 and strengthening beyond that year.

We continue to agree—but it's worth watching carefully.

Financial Highlights, Fiscal Year 2015

"Better decrementals than the competition" boasts one company slide presentation. We've never seen such a statement in a corporate pitch before. It's a good example of "thinking positive"—but as you look at SLB revenue and margin declines they aren't as bad as the competition, many of whom have slipped into the red. Not SLB. While revenues did drop about 25 percent for FY2015 and net earnings by more than that as a percentage, the company still managed earnings of $2.1 billion even with significant asset write-downs. Strong cash flows led to both a dividend increase and an aggressive share buyback plan, mostly to replace the shares used to buy Cameron. A lot of this relative strength in earnings and cash flow (beyond what one might have expected for the industry) was from "rightsizing" operations and rapid response to changing business conditions.

Not surprisingly, the financial picture is mixed, especially going forward into 2016 and 2017 as customers reduce rig counts. The company sees this downturn as more severe and longer than the preceding five energy down cycles. As SLB put it, "near-term visibility remains poor."

Even with poor visibility, the company projects a continued 15 percent drop in FY2016 revenues to about $30 billion, although earnings should rise about that much as write-downs fade into the past. Share buybacks will take a pause, although dividend increases in the low double digits beyond 2016 still look possible. The company projects a return to full health—and likely beyond as weaker hands in the industry decline—in the 2018–2020 timeframe.

Reasons to Buy

"Transformation as a Pathway to Growth" is Schlumberger's new annual report headline (the old one was "The Age of Easy Oil is Over.") Such is the dynamic shift occurring in the oil service business. SLB brings the largest, most complete, and most technically advanced offering to the oil patch, and as the supply geography shifts first toward OPEC, then back to the *most efficient* producers in the U.S., it isn't lost on us—nor on SLB—that major producers *still* have to replace depleted reserves, and that world oil demand will continue to grow, albeit slowly, in the longer term. All that international oil causing the glut still needs to be produced somehow. SLB is well positioned, with its size, present geography, and expertise, to move with these shifts. The company appears to be embracing these crosscurrents and is applying its competitive advantages in technology and size strategically. Too, SLB appears committed to keeping shareholder returns moving forward despite the short-term weakness.

In the long term, we agree that SLB could come out of this shift stronger than ever as the oil service industry and the U.S. producer landscape both consolidate.

Reasons for Caution

The shifts and uncertainties caused by the oil market disruption could get larger, and that plus cutthroat competition could put a bigger dent in the oil service industry. The fortunes of SLB are inevitably tied to the price of oil, and nobody is predicting with any great certainty where that price will end up by 2017—although most agree that it will be north of the low-$30s low experienced in January 2016. The company will always face the traditional risks of oil drilling—particularly offshore drilling—that culminated in the BP disaster of 2010.

SECTOR: Energy ◻ BETA COEFFICIENT: **1.50** ◻ 10-YEAR COMPOUND EARNINGS PER-SHARE GROWTH: **18.5%** ◻ 10-YEAR COMPOUND DIVIDENDS PER-SHARE GROWTH: **13.5%**

	2008	2009	2010	2011	2012	2013	2014	2015
Revenues (mil)	27,163	22,702	27,447	39,540	42,14	45,266	48,580	35,475
Net income (mil)	5,397	3,142	3,408	3,954	5,439	6,210	5,643	2,072
Earnings per share	4.42	2.61	2.70	3.51	4.06	4.70	4.32	1.63
Dividends per share	0.81	0.84	0.84	0.96	1.06	1.25	1.60	1.90
Cash flow per share	6.42	4.70	4.55	6.05	6.73	7.55	7.64	4.80
Price: high	112.0	71.1	84.1	95.6	80.8	94.9	118.8	92.1
low	37.1	35.1	54.7	54.8	59.1	69.1	78.5	66.6

Website: www.slb.com

AGGRESSIVE GROWTH

Schnitzer Steel Industries, Inc.

Ticker symbol: SCHN (NASDAQ) □ S&P rating: NR □ Value Line financial strength rating: B □ Current yield: 4.7% □ Dividend raises, past 10 years: 3

Company Profile

Schnitzer Steel provides yet another example (and we've had several this year) of good companies having bad years largely caused by the commodity bust and related supply-chain disruptions. While we normally strive for peace of mind and safety with our picks, we also recognize that opportunity, too, is part of the value equation. We also like companies that are innovative, that are good citizens, and that think shareholders are important and return lots of cash to them. We see a significant chance for a rebound and a payoff here as markets normalize, and as the efficiency measures Schnitzer has enacted take hold. Finally, we wanted to offer another "small-cap" stock for those who might like to feel as if they own a bigger part of a smaller but successful and dynamic business. So we're keeping Schnitzer on the *100 Best* list for 2017.

Founded in 1946, Schnitzer Steel is mainly a collector and recycler of ferrous and non-ferrous scrap, with smaller operations that collect, dismantle, and market auto and truck parts and a steel mill "mini mill" finished steel product business. Segments were reorganized from three business segments to two: the Auto and Metals Recycling business and the Steel Manufacturing Business.

The "AMR" business, which accounts for about 90 percent of Schnitzer's revenues, includes the Metals Recycling business (about 80 percent of AMR) which collects, recycles, processes, and brokers scrap steel and nonferrous metals to domestic and foreign markets—3.7 million tons of ferrous scrap metal and 585 million pounds of nonferrous metal in all. Larger scrap mills are located in Oregon; Washington; Oakland, CA; and Massachusetts, with smaller mills in Rhode Island, Puerto Rico, Hawaii, and Alaska, all with adjacent deep-water ports, correctly suggesting an orientation toward international export of scrap metal for foreign mills. Indeed, that is true—some 50 percent of ferrous shipments go to Asia, 25 percent to Europe/Africa/Middle East, and 25 percent to U.S. steel mills (this means that it doesn't matter who wins the current trade wars in steel). The company operates 60 metals recycling facilities ("scrapyards," in popular vernacular) in 23 states, mostly on the coasts and in the south, seven in

Canada, and five in Puerto Rico. The operation adds value in part by sorting and shredding input scrap into homogenous materials well suited to the needs of downstream customers.

The Auto Parts business portion of the AMR segment operates 55 self-serve locations and remarketing centers, some co-located with Metals Recycling facilities, in 16 states with a concentration in California under the "Pick-n-Pull" name. This operation processes about 350,000 cars per year. Inventories of scrapped autos and common parts from those autos are posted online and updated as new inventory is received.

The Steel Manufacturing business (10 percent of revenues) operates an electric arc furnace mini mill in McMinnville, OR, producing rebar, wire rod, merchant bar, and other specialty products, of course from scrap steel available from the company's own Metals Recycling facilities.

Appropriately, "Recycling for Value" is the company's slogan, and the synergies among the three businesses are obvious; the company is also thought to have some of the better locations and especially port facilities in the industry.

Schnitzer's strong and respected management team is exemplified by its selection by the Ethisphere Institute as a 2015 World's Most Ethical Company, recognizing its "culture of ethics and transparency at every level of the company"—a nice honor for a steel company. President and CEO Tamara Lundgren has also served as board chairman and is currently chair of the executive committee for the United States Chamber of Commerce.

Financial Highlights, Fiscal Year 2015

The late-2014 commodity price and oil price collapse, shrinking China end-user demand, soft Europe, continued production and a supply glut of iron ore and certain other metals, and the strong dollar were negatives that continued to plague the business through the year. Bright spots were firming domestic finished steel demand and the realization of productivity improvements started earlier—but both the volume and price environment were very difficult and frankly, probably not sustainable for Schnitzer. Iron ore prices continued soft—as much as 60 percent off of 2014 levels—although they started to recover as certain miners curtailed production and China talked of stimulating its economy; iron ore prices rose 40 percent in early 2016. The company's "average inventory cost" accounting policy means that costs declines lag sales and selling price declines which hurt revenues and profits further. Altogether, FY2015 was a very forgettable year—you can look at the numbers that follow if you'd like. Forecasts call for a recovery to $1.6 billion in sales and 40 cents in per-share earnings for FY2017, with cash flows well north of $3.00 per share, which should keep the dividend safe as the company indicates it would like to do.

Reasons to Buy

Clearly we're betting on a turnaround in steel and especially steel scrap prices as demand improves and competing iron ore supplies dwindle. Scrap as a source of supply is much more flexible and environmentally sound and should lead the way in a metals-industry recovery. We don't believe the fundamental recycling-based business model is by any means broken. Too, and perhaps most importantly, today's modern electric-arc furnace mills such as those operated by Nucor are more cost-effective and flexible than traditional blast furnaces and tend to use scrap as the main input resource. Scrap is easier to source, more flexible, and more local than traditional iron ore inputs for these modern mills.

There are a lot of mom-and-pop scrap dealers around the world, but few have the size, operating leverage, and remarketing abilities of Schnitzer. The company is a strong and recognized brand in a fragmented and unbranded industry, offering advantages both on the sales and operational side. When prices and markets are soft, the company loses, but as we saw particularly in 2008, when markets are strong, the company does really, really well. And, whether steel is made domestically or imported, Schnitzer wins as a universal supplier. Schnitzer is well managed, adds a lot of value in a relatively non-value-add industry, and keeps its shareholders in mind. Much better numbers are expected in 2018 and going forward; we feel these will be reflected in the depressed stock price much sooner. The risk/reward profile still seems favorable.

Reasons for Caution

There is risk here—more than we embrace with most other *100 Best* stocks. Schnitzer is very sensitive to global steel and nonferrous metals markets and the ups and downs of pricing. While its size and marketing advantages serve it well in tough times, inventory is inventory, and the company can get caught with a lot of it purchased at higher prices if the markets don't move to its advantage. It does okay in bad economic climates, but the company is really a bet on recycling value add and on good times in global manufacturing. If you buy in, you'll want to watch global steel and other metals prices. Too, while the company has a good track record, there are always some environmental risks and costs in this sort of business. The high beta of 1.79 reflects some of this risk and the volatility inherent in the relatively low share count.

SECTOR: **Industrials** ❑ BETA COEFFICIENT: **1.79** ❑ 10-YEAR COMPOUND EARNINGS PER-SHARE GROWTH: **NM** ❑ 10-YEAR COMPOUND DIVIDENDS PER-SHARE GROWTH: **27.0%**

	2008	2009	2010	2011	2012	2013	2014	2015
Revenues (mil)	3,641	1,900	2,301	3,459	3,341	2,621	2,544	1,915
Net income (mil)	249	(32.2)	67	119	30	(2.0)	5.1	(58.8)
Earnings per share	8.61	(1.14)	2.86	4.24	1.10	(0.07)	0.19	(1.90)
Dividends per share	0.10	0.20	0.20	0.20	0.41	0.75	0.75	0.75
Cash flow per share	10.74	1.03	4.75	7.08	4.28	3.05	3.19	0.34
Price: high	118.5	64.0	66.9	69.4	47.4	33.0	33.3	22.8
low	16.5	23.3	37.0	32.8	22.8	23.1	21.4	12.6

Website: www.schnitzersteel.com

GROWTH AND INCOME

The Scotts Miracle-Gro Company

Ticker symbol: SMG (NYSE) ❑ S&P rating: BB+ ❑ Value Line financial strength rating: B++ ❑ Current yield: 2.7% ❑ Dividend raises, past 10 years: 7

Company Profile

Scotts Miracle-Gro, formerly Scotts Co., formerly O.M. Scott & Sons, is a 148-year-old provider of mostly packaged lawn- and garden-care products for consumer markets. Originally a seed company, today its lawn-care products include packaged, pre-mixed fertilizers and combination fertilizer and weed/pest-control products marketed mainly under the Scotts and Turf Builder brand names. The company also markets packaged grass seed and a line of individually packaged pest/disease-control products mainly under the Ortho brand, acquired in 1997, and a line of specialty garden fertilizers and pest-control products under the Miracle-Gro name, acquired in 1995. The company also markets a line of home protection pest-control products, and acts as the exclusive worldwide distributor for the consumer Roundup brand (from Monsanto, another *100 Best* stock). Through a series of small acquisitions, the company has entered the lawn service business, which now operates out of 88 company-operated and 94 franchised locations. Consumer businesses account for about 90 percent of revenues, Lawn Service another 9 percent.

Scotts is a study in branding in an otherwise highly fragmented market. The attractive core brands of Scotts, Turf Builder, Miracle-Gro, and Ortho are being leveraged into other businesses, such as lawn service under the Scotts LawnService brand and home pest control under the Ortho brand. The company acquired Action Pest Control in FY2014 to add to this line.

The vision is interesting: "To help people of all ages express themselves on their own piece of the earth." While this sounds pretty groovy, it also connotes the possibilities to expand markets. Further trendy elements in this business include an ongoing demographic shift—more returning to cities—different styles of gardening, more specialty products—a shift that may prove positive but will take some work. To that end, in 2015 the company completed the purchase of two leading producers of equipment and consumables for hydroponic gardening. People are also seeking organic gardening products in consumer packages; Scotts is testing a new line of organic Miracle-Gro products to address this trend. Innovations also include new packaging to simplify the measurement and application and improve the safety of key products. Recently the company has embarked on some internal restructuring to simplify the organization structure and to become more nimble going forward.

Financial Highlights, Fiscal Year 2015

All things considered, things could have been worse for Scotts in FY2015. Several large acquisitions put pressure on earnings, even as sales increased 7 percent. Looking forward, FY2016 should provide a nice rebound in reported profits. As with other of our selections with international exposure, currency headwinds had a strong negative effect on earnings, as did drought conditions in geographies where seed providers are located. Both company business segments showed strong growth in sales (5.8 percent to Global Consumer and 9.7 percent to Lawn Service). In short, the signs are good going forward, with the recent acquisitions already providing strong positive impact on both reported sales and earnings through 2016 second quarter. The company recently offered an additional dose of confidence to investors, revising projected EPS numbers upward to $3.95. A reported gross margin increase of 2.2 percent was attributed to improved operating efficiencies, one of our favorite signs of greener grass to come.

Reasons to Buy

Scotts Miracle-Gro is increasingly leveraging its brand strength both in the U.S. and abroad. Beyond focus and increased prominence of core brands, there continue to be several tailwinds that should help the company. First on the list is the economy and renewed strength in the housing market; new homes come with new lawns and gardens, and an increase in home value should mean people will be spending more on their homes. We see more emphasis on quality landscapes over quantity and size of lawn, which should help Scotts. Too, we see help coming from changing demographics and aging clientele with disposable income and physical limitations who want easier, more complete solutions like Scotts LawnService and similar services we think will take root. Finally, recent demographic data shows a decline in the growth rate of urban populations (after a decade of accelerated growth there) and an increase in the growth rate of suburban and rural locales. It's not clear if this data is corrected for Detroit, where recently people find that they can move from urban to rural without actually moving (sorry Detroit, we love you). In any case, the upshot is a renewed interest in home gardens and their attendant enabling products.

The company has seen some recent market-share gains in its core products and is a mainstay at key channel partners like Home Depot, Lowe's, and Wal-Mart. The set of brands remain strong and trusted, and we expect to see it in more places and connected to higher-margined services; Ortho pest-control services is but one example.

The company recently announced a joint venture agreement with TruGreen, a privately held lawn-service provider. Scotts' and TruGreen's lawn-care operations would merge in the joint venture, creating the largest business in the industry. Last year we mentioned potential opportunities in the international sector for Scotts. This year the company announced it is looking into a joint venture for its European operations, similar in nature to the TruGreen model. We like both of these moves, as volume agreements with suppliers are a significant driver of profits here.

Finally, the company has announced a new share repurchase program in the range of 10 percent of its outstanding shares through FY2020.

Reasons for Caution

Scotts isn't the only brand in town, and the company does face some competition from less expensive house brands such as those sold at Ace Hardware, Home Depot, Lowe's, and elsewhere. Scotts' aggressive marketing, while clever ("Feed your lawn. Feed it!") and apparently effective, is not cheap. Lawn and garden spend is naturally sensitive to sluggish economies, but we do think that there is a baseline level people will drop to and remain at; they want to maintain their lawns and provide pleasant stay-at-home environments if they can't do much else. Finally, the past decade of demographic shifts away from the suburbs, including downsizing and increases in renting versus owning will continue to put pressure on the traditional bagged fertilizer and lawn goods business; Scotts' new products and services in new niches will come into play here.

SECTOR: **Materials** ▫ BETA COEFFICIENT: **0.90** ▫ 10-YEAR COMPOUND EARNINGS PER-SHARE GROWTH: **5.5%** ▫ 10-YEAR COMPOUND DIVIDENDS PER-SHARE GROWTH: **25.0%**

		2008	2009	2010	2011	2012	2013	2014	2015
Revenues (mil)		2,983	3,141	3,139	2,835	2,826	2,819	2,841	3,017
Net income (mil)		(10.9)	153.3	212.4	121.9	113.2	161.2	165.4	158.7
Earnings per share		(0.17)	2.32	3.14	1.84	1.62	2.58	2.64	2.57
Dividends per share		0.50	0.50	0.63	1.05	1.23	1.41	1.76	1.82
Cash flow per share		0.91	3.23	4.07	3.00	2.86	3.67	3.74	3.64
Price:	high	40.7	44.3	55.0	60.8	55.9	62.6	64.0	72.3
	low	16.1	24.9	37.5	40.0	35.5	42.0	52.4	58.1

Website: www.scotts.com

GROWTH AND INCOME

The J.M. Smucker Company

Ticker symbol: SJM (NYSE) ▫ S&P rating: NR ▫ Value Line financial strength rating: A++ ▫ Current yield: 2.1% ▫ Dividend raises, past 10 years: 10

Company Profile

"With a name like Smucker's, it has to be good!" This ad copy says it all about this eastern Ohio–based firm, a leading manufacturer of jams, jellies, and other processed foods for years. Thanks in part to divestitures from the Procter & Gamble food division and other companies, it has grown itself into a premier player in the packaged food industry. The 2015 acquisition of Big Heart Pet Brands, a premier player in the pet food industry, signals further expansion into adjacent markets.

Smucker manufactures and markets products under its own name, as well as under a number of other household names such as Crisco, Folgers, Millstone, Knudsen, Hungry Jack, Eagle, Carnation, Pillsbury, Jif (why not sell the peanut butter if they sell the jelly?), and naturally, Goober (a combination of peanut butter and jelly in a single jar), and Uncrustables (why not just sell the whole sandwich?). The company also produces and distributes Dunkin' Donuts coffee and produces an assortment of cooking oils, toppings, juices, and baking ingredients. The company has revitalized such brands as Folgers and Jif through improved marketing, channel relationships, and better focus on the packaging and delivery of these brands to the customer. In the coffee business, for example, for custom blends, K-cup offerings, etc. "Coffee Served Your Way" is their motto, and there are new convenience packages for peanut butter, jelly, and other spreads as well. Organic brands, most of which have been around for a while, include Santa Cruz Organic, Smucker's Natural, Laura Scudder's, and a handful of others; they also produce a line of sugar-free, reduced sugar, and sugar alternative products. The Big Heart acquisition brought some top brands in the pet food business, including Meow Mix, 9Lives, Milk Bone, and others, and grew the total business by about a third. Overall, the company aims to sell the number one brand in the various markets it serves.

The company is currently organized into four reporting segments with the Big Heart acquisition: Retail Coffee (27 percent of revenues), Retail Consumer Foods (27 percent), Retail Pet Foods (30 percent), and International, Foodservice, and Natural Foods (17 percent). The pet food segment had not seen a whole year's integration at the time of this narrative, so the previous figures are estimates. Operations are centered in the United States, Canada, and Europe, with about 10 percent of sales coming from overseas.

Smucker's, like most other food companies these days, is emphasizing innovation, which includes not only new food products in new arenas like organic, but also new convenience packages to fit modern lifestyles. Examples of the latter include Smucker's Fruit Fulls blended fruit pouches and Jif To Go Dippers packaged peanut butter snacks. Some 7 percent of products (and packages) were not offered three years ago—a significant amount for a food company.

Even as a nearly $8 billion-a-year enterprise (in 2016), the company still retains the feel of a family business, with brothers Tim and Richard Smucker sharing the CEO responsibilities as chairman and president respectively. Their annual report is the only one we've come across that has recipes in it. Last but not least, the Company Store and Café located just outside of Orrville, Ohio, is a national treasure and a classic case study in branding and brand image.

Financial Highlights, Fiscal Year 2015

Headwinds in the form of high coffee prices and intense competition in that market, and to a degree, competition everywhere led to a relatively lackluster performance again in FY2015, with revenues (without Pet Food) down about 3 percent again and net earnings down a slightly heftier 4 percent. Against a backdrop of changing consumer tastes and competition that isn't going away anytime soon, these figures would have caused considerable concern. But brand strength is brand strength, and execution is execution: The large acquisition adds more to what is already shaping up as a turn-around year in FY2016. The acquisition plus modest core growth should bump revenues up about 37 percent for 2016 with a more modest "organic" gain of 3 percent into 2017. Net earnings should also step up about the same amount, with a stronger 5–7 percent gain into 2017 as acquisition synergies take hold, as coffee prices moderate, and as new, more profitable products hit the market. The company issued nearly 20 million shares to finance the acquisition; the shares will likely be bought back gradually through the decade. Dividend growth should continue in the mid-single-digit range.

Reasons to Buy

This is a very well-managed company with an excellent and lasting reputation in its markets. In recent years, it has a proven track record in buying and revitalizing key brands, the most prominent being former Procter & Gamble food brands, Sara Lee food-service coffee and beverage brands, and a few International Multifoods brands. We expect this trend to continue. The company's aggressive moves into coffee and other beverages were well timed and have provided a boost to the bottom line; that story appears to be repeated with the Big Heart acquisition, which should bring a measure of stability, profitability, and growth to the table.

Overall growth and profitability figures are both among the best for the relatively staid food industry; the base for steady growth in cash flows and investor returns is well established over the long term. Steady and safe: Smucker is the ever-improving peanut butter and jelly sandwich of the investing landscape.

Reasons for Caution

The prepared-food business is very sensitive in the short term to commodity and energy costs. As the company relies heavily on coffee products for earnings growth, it will find itself exposed to instability in the cost of raw materials and transportation and to changes in consumer tastes; both have provided headwinds in the near term. Yes, these are costs that also affect all of their competitors, but Smucker is in competition with a number of low-margin brands and has customers (such as Walmart) that have enormous buying power. One of the stated acquisition strategies was to "bulk up" to become the tenth-largest U.S. food supplier to put some strength on their side of the table.

Smucker's will need to rely on brand strength and breadth should the economy slow again. And we do respect changing consumer tastes and the emergence of the Millennial generation, and hope the company can extend its healthy and wholesome image into this group, too.

We do wonder if the company has strayed just a bit outside of its traditional feel-good, relatively healthy or at least wholesome, peanut-butter-and-jelly base. While you can't grow a business much on peanut butter and jelly alone, ventures into donut-shop coffee, and now, pet food especially may not be such a good fit with what has made Smucker's taste so good up to now.

SECTOR: Consumer Staples ▫ **BETA COEFFICIENT: 0.52** ▫ 10-YEAR COMPOUND EARNINGS PER-SHARE GROWTH: **8.5%** ▫ 10-YEAR COMPOUND DIVIDENDS PER-SHARE GROWTH: **9.5%**

	2008	2009	2010	2011	2012	2013	2014	2015
Revenues (mil)	3,758	4,605	4,826	5,526	5,897	5,611	5,450	7,775
Net income (mil)	321.4	520.3	566.5	535.6	584	588	540	705
Earnings per share	3.77	4.15	4.79	4.73	5.37	5.64	5.30	5.90
Dividends per share	1.31	1.40	1.68	1.88	2.06	2.32	2.56	2.65
Cash flow per share	3.73	5.60	7.06	6.75	7.85	8.30	6.87	9.65
Price: high	56.7	62.7	66.3	80.3	89.4	114.7	107.1	125.3
low	37.2	34.1	53.3	61.2	70.5	86.5	87.1	97.3

Website: www.smuckers.com

AGGRESSIVE GROWTH

Southwest Airlines Co.

Ticker symbol: LUV (NYSE) ▫ S&P rating: BBB ▫ Value Line financial strength rating: B+ ▫ Current yield: 0.7% ▫ Dividend raises, past 10 years: 4

Company Profile

Here we have it—finally: a stock that has wholly benefitted from the recent tumble in oil prices, and one that has added marketing excellence, operational excellence, and fine-tuning from the previous downturn to boot. For a number of reasons, Southwest has reached cruising altitude—but we think it may have farther to go.

Loyal *100 Best Stocks* readers will recall that for years we were critical of the airline industry for its inability to control prices because of intense competition and costs that largely are comprised of fuel, airport, and unionized labor. Lack of profitability and inability to control these factors made airlines into poster children for the kinds of stocks we tend to avoid. That's hardly the case anymore. Fuel costs have gone down and look to stay there for a while. Most airlines have, by design or by default, rationalized their route structures and capacity, necessitated by once-high fuel costs, airport constraints, and the Great Recession. With this rationalized capacity, they are better able to control both prices and costs, and their outlooks are much brighter.

That said, we're still not sold on the idea that all airlines are well managed. But we'll stick with our favorite; one is far better managed than most and in fact has scored us a quintupling in price since we added it to the *100 Best* list for 2012. That fave: Southwest Airlines.

Southwest Airlines provides passenger air transport mainly in the United States, all within North America. In early 2016, the company served 97 cities in 41 states, and with the acquisition of AirTran it also serves Mexico, Central America, and the Caribbean with point-to-point, rather than hub-and-spoke, service. The company serves these markets almost exclusively with 704 Boeing 737 aircraft. Southwest continues to be the largest domestic air carrier in the United States, as measured by the number of domestic originating passengers boarded. At 3,900 peak-season departures per day, the airline also originates the most flights. This should give an idea of their business model—low cost, shorter flights, and maximum passenger loads.

The business model is one of simplicity—no-frills aircraft, no first-class passenger cabin, limited interchange with other carriers, no onboard meals, simple boarding and seat assignment practices, direct sales over the Internet (over 80 percent of sales processed online), no baggage fees—all designed to provide steady and reliable transportation, with one of the best on-time performances in the industry, and to maximize asset utilization with minimal downtime, crew disruptions, and other upward influences on operating costs. The company has long used secondary airports—such as Providence, RI, and Manchester, NH, to serve Boston and the New England area; Allentown, PA, and East Islip, NY, to serve the New York/New Jersey area (though it now serves LaGuardia, too, if you want that choice); and Chicago Midway to reduce delays and costs. This strategy has worked well.

Southwest has successfully implemented a few initiatives to squeeze out some extra revenue without alienating the core passenger group, mostly business travelers. One such initiative is Business Select, which offers priority boarding, priority security, bonus frequent flyer credit, and a free beverage for an upgrade fee. The company also sells early boarding for a small fee. They're also tinkering with baggage fees, raising fees for overweight or excess bags, though leaving the basic two-bag limit free for now (we continue to applaud that move). Southwest also produces more than $600 million in revenue annually from its Rapid Rewards loyalty point program through partnerships and sales of points. The program routinely wins "best of" rewards in the industry.

New initiatives include a transition to newer Boeing 737 aircraft, including more 143-seat 747-700s and 175-seat 737-800s (typical older 737 models range from 117 to 132 seats) and a new branding, "heart" logo, and paint scheme for its aircraft.

Financial Highlights, Fiscal Year 2015

Southwest had already been taxiing into position with operational improvements, capacity rationalization, the AirTran acquisition, and other market and efficiency gains. The 70 percent drop in oil prices cleared Southwest for takeoff, and take off it did.

FY2015 revenues advanced 6.5 percent, good but not the heart of the story. Earnings jumped a full 92 percent—and as the following numbers show, this is no cyclic recovery but a real gain! Not only did fuel prices help, but so did strong gains in revenue seat miles. The load factor hit a record 83.5 (percentage of seats paid for and occupied—*that's* why their planes have been so crowded lately!), and that combined with more available seat miles, higher fares, and longer average trips really helped the top line; the aforementioned fuel cost declines and efficiencies owing to a gradual fleet replacement with more efficient versions of its Boeing 737 aircraft all contributed to solid results.

If the story stopped there, we might be inclined to land and get off, but the company is projecting another 14–15 percent gain in earnings on a 6 percent revenue rise in FY2016, finally leveling off a bit in FY2017—but at that altitude, we're still strapped comfortably in our seats (the P/E ratio, not always our favorite measure, would be somewhere around 10). Annual share buybacks in the 2–4 percent range add to the story, as does (finally) a modernization of the dividend policy; while the yield is still very modest, it's getting better.

Reasons to Buy

Southwest continues to be the best player in an industry whose fundamentals have dramatically improved. The company continues to be the "envy" value proposition of the industry, and we continue to be surprised that no one else has been able to emulate it successfully—but at this point, even if they do, Southwest has a decades-long first mover advantage.

The airline "gets it" that what customers want is no-hassle transportation at best-possible prices—and yes, no bag fees—and has been able to do that better than anyone else for years, and is now extending its value proposition further for business travelers, who increasingly book their own fares and respond well to $15 priority boarding upgrades and other offers. Good management, efficient operation, and excellent marketing make it all possible. With merit, the company refers to its customers as "fans." Financially, the company has earned a profit for 43 consecutive years—in the volatile airline industry we know no greater testimonial to good marketing and good management.

Reasons for Caution

Fuel prices are a big part of the recent success but are still—and will always be—a wild card. The company has shown in the past that it can use hedges to manage fuel price shocks, and we're guessing they're putting their hedges in place now.

We hope the company doesn't become complacent with its recent success, assume low fuel prices will last forever, and start flying 747s to London or some such nonsense. The recession forced all airlines, even Southwest, to "fly smart," and we hope this continues.

Generally we fear anything that would move Southwest away from its core competencies—complacency in the short run, acquisitions in the longer term. The AirTran acquisition story appears to have a happy ending but was also a challenge—different practices, processes, and cultures. The longer Southwest can stay Southwest, and avoid looking like other airlines, the better.

Finally, much of the good news may have already been priced into the stock's steep ascent; it may be time to level off just a bit.

SECTOR: Transportation ◻ BETA COEFFICIENT: **1.00** ◻ 10-YEAR COMPOUND EARNINGS PER-SHARE GROWTH: **16.5%** ◻ 10-YEAR COMPOUND DIVIDENDS PER-SHARE GROWTH: **28.5%**

	2008	2009	2010	2011	2012	2013	2014	2015
Revenues (mil)	11,023	10,350	12,104	15,658	17,088	17,699	18,605	19,820
Net income (mil)	294	140	550	330	421	754	1,136	2,161
Earnings per share	0.40	0.19	0.73	0.42	0.58	1.05	1.64	3.27
Dividends per share	0.02	0.02	0.02	0.03	0.04	0.10	0.22	0.29
Cash flow per share	1.41	1.21	1.02	1.35	1.73	2.35	3.07	4.94
Price: high	16.8	11.8	14.3	13.9	10.6	19.0	43.2	51.3
low	7.1	4.0	10.4	7.1	7.8	10.4	18.8	31.4

Website: www.southwest.com

AGGRESSIVE GROWTH

St. Jude Medical, Inc.

Ticker symbol: STJ (NYSE) ◻ S&P rating: A ◻ Value Line financial strength rating: A ◻ Current yield: 2.3% ◻ Dividend raises, past 10 years: 5

Company Profile

Some would recommend we perform a "transplant" on St. Jude Medical. St. Jude's 2015 results were worse than expected in the wake not only of the usual currency woes, but also what would seem to be an avoidable product strategy error in not making their major cardiac rhythm–monitoring products MRI-compatible. They lost a big step with their competition and scuttled the results for the year. But will they come back beating strong, or is this a sign of continued weakness in their products and markets? Always difficult to tell, but at this juncture it looks like STJ will avoid a flatline and resume in 2016 with a corrected product line. We hope this to become another example of where patient (pardon the pun) investing pays off.

St. Jude Medical, Inc. designs, manufactures, and distributes cardiovascular medical devices for cardiology and cardiovascular surgery, including pacemakers, implantable cardioverter defibrillators (ICDs), vascular closure devices, catheters, neuromodulation devices, and heart valves. The company has four main business segments:

- The Cardiac Rhythm Management (CRM) portfolio (responsible for about 47 percent of 2015 sales) includes products for treating heart rhythm disorders as well as heart failure. Its products include ICDs, pacemaker systems, and a variety of diagnostic and therapeutic electro-physiology catheters. The company also develops catheter technologies for the Cardiology/Vascular Access therapy area. Those products include hemostasis introducers, catheters, and a market-leading vascular closure device. Many products in this portfolio use RF (radio frequency) and other leading technologies for rhythm management, ablation, and other advanced cardiovascular problems.

- The Cardiovascular segment (24 percent) has been the leader in structural heart and mechanical heart valve technology for more than 25 years. St. Jude Medical also develops a line of tissue valves, intravascular imaging systems, vascular closures, and valve-repair products for various cardiac surgery procedures.

- The company's Neuromodulation segment (9 percent) produces implantable stimulation devices and drug-delivery systems for use primarily in chronic pain management and in treatment for certain symptoms of Parkinson's disease and epilepsy.

- The Atrial Fibrillation business (20 percent) markets a series of products designed to map and treat atrial fibrillation and other heart rhythm problems.

St. Jude Medical products are sold in a highly targeted niche market in more than 100 countries. International sales account for about 53 percent of the total; R&D investment is also substantial at more than 12 percent of sales. The company just introduced a new treatment system known as "CardioMEMS" designed to wirelessly measure and monitor pulmonary artery pressure, thus reducing readmission rates for patients with heart failure. In today's environment of increased scrutiny of readmissions and capitated care payments for various conditions, such a product has good business prospects going forward and exemplifies the kinds of technology applications and niche markets St. Jude is involved with—but the product has taken off more slowly than expected.

Financial Highlights, Fiscal Year 2015

The cardiac care business is by nature really two businesses. The cardiac surgery business is critical and almost completely immune to economic cycles; when you need it, you need it. The largest segment, Cardiac Rhythm Management, which essentially makes pacemakers and related products, is a bit more discretionary and vulnerable to expense cuts on the part of patients and care providers and contractions in the inventory pipeline.

With the aforementioned product hiccup, FY2015 was bad and worse than the "flatline" figures that follow would indicate. The company acquired mechanical circulatory systems provider Thoratec during the year, which should have increased sales about 3–5 percent. So STJ lost significant ground. Setting that year aside and assuming the successful introduction of MRI-compatible devices in 2016, and adding a full year of Thoratec results (roughly $500M sales, $70M earnings) we get to an 8 percent revenue gain for FY2016 and a further 4–5 percent gain in FY2017 with slightly increased margins, and a 10 percent "catch-up" earnings gain FY2017 over FY2016. We would expect 5 percent top-line and bottom-line advances going forward with regular 6–7 percent dividend increases.

Reasons to Buy

We expect problems to be solved—keeping a solid device-making play in the critical healthcare field is a main reason to hold on to St. Jude. St. Jude continues to be a market leader in the heart rhythm and vascular surgery niche, a solid position in the healthcare industry. Both the Neuromodulation and Atrial Fibrillation segments have grown rapidly and seem well positioned for growth. The techniques employed in neuromodulation are growing quickly in the field as a preferred treatment for long-term pain management. St. Jude (and others) see this as a disruptive technology, potentially replacing drug and physical therapy regimens and offering improved lifestyle at a reduced cost. These two businesses, while small, serve as solid growth kickers, complementing the flatter CRM and Cardiovascular segments.

Reasons for Caution

We almost jumped off the bandwagon in 2014 due to flat performance and cost moderation trends in the industry, but STJ is one of the steadier hands in a solid industry with a good innovation track record. Now we're almost off again because of what seems a rather obvious product stumble. Such a misstep makes us scratch our heads about how effective their internal decision making really is. But once again, we couldn't find anything better to buy; St. Jude has a key position in a key industry. We'll hang on for another year as the company heals; we think patient investors may be well rewarded. One more slip-up, though, and it's off to the morgue.

SECTOR: **Healthcare** □ BETA COEFFICIENT: **1.39** □ 10-YEAR COMPOUND EARNINGS PER-SHARE
GROWTH: **15.0%** □ 10-YEAR COMPOUND DIVIDENDS PER-SHARE GROWTH: **NM**

	2008	2009	2010	2011	2012	2013	2014	2015
Revenues (mil)	4,363	4,681	5,165	5,612	5,503	5,501	5,622	5,541
Net income (mil)	807	838	995	1,074	1,095	1,094	1,153	1,128
Earnings per share	2.31	2.43	3.01	3.28	3.48	3.76	3.98	3.94
Dividends per share	—	—	—	0.84	0.92	1.00	1.08	1.16
Cash flow per share	2.92	3.24	3.70	4.35	4.50	4.79	4.79	4.85
Price: high	48.5	42.0	43.0	54.2	44.8	63.2	71.9	80.8
low	25.0	28.9	34.0	32.1	30.3	36.1	54.8	59.9

Website: www.sjm.com

AGGRESSIVE GROWTH

Starbucks Corporation

Ticker symbol: SBUX (NASDAQ) □ S&P rating: A- □ Value Line financial strength rating: A++
□ Current yield: 1.3% □ Dividend raises, past 10 years: 6

Company Profile

Starbucks Corporation, formed in 1985, is the leading retailer, roaster, and brand of specialty coffee in the world. The company sells whole-bean coffees through its retailers, its specialty sales group, and supermarkets. The company footprint continues to expand, with 8,752 company-owned stores in the Americas (8,462 at the end of 2014) and 3,614 in international markets (3,391 at the end of 2014), in addition to 11,205 licensed stores worldwide (10,025 at the end of 2014). Retail coffee shop sales constitute about 89 percent of its revenue, unchanged from last year and up from 86 percent in 2012. About 79 percent of revenue originates in company-operated stores. Unlike many in the restaurant sector, the company does not franchise its stores—all are either company owned or operated by licensees in special venues such as airports, college campuses, and other places where access is restricted, and in foreign markets where it is necessary or advantageous.

The company continues to expand overseas, usually at first through partnerships and joint ventures; sometimes it buys out the partner as it did in China in 2011. The FY2015 sales breakdown: 74 percent Americas, 8 percent Europe/Middle East/Africa, 7 percent China/Asia-Pacific, and 11 percent other segments and "channel development," which is largely made up of branded product sales through non-Starbucks retailers. The company now operates in 62 countries in total; India is one of the fastest growing countries, followed by Vietnam.

The company is gradually expanding beyond its traditional coffee base, opening a new Teavana Fine Teas Bar in New York and adding Teavana tea-related items into its traditional store offering. Evolution Fresh juices are now widely available, and the company has done well with its food menu, including its "La Boulange" line of pastries. Specialty packaging, including "Via" and Keurig-compatible single-serve packages have done well also. Finally, Starbucks has joint ventures with PepsiCo and Dreyer's to develop bottled coffee drinks and coffee-flavored ice creams.

In 2015, the sum total revenue mix was 58 percent beverages, 16 percent food, 14 percent packaged and single-serve coffees and teas, and 12 percent "other" including the aforementioned joint venture–produced drinks and ice creams.

Starbucks continues to invest and expand its leadership in the deployment of technology. Always a leader in providing wi-fi connectivity to users in its stores, the company's "Mobile Order and Pay" app and platform, where users can order and pay for their drinks using smartphones, then subsequently arrive at locations to pick up their drinks, is doing quite well. Not only is this convenient for the customer, it effectively increases capacity and reduces wait time in the stores, and provides a platform to offer more items for sale.

The company's retail goal continues to be the unique Starbucks experience, which the company defines as a third place beyond home and work. The "experience" is built upon superior customer service and a clean, well-maintained retail store that reflects the personality of the community in which it operates—all aimed at building loyalty and frequent repeat visits.

The company also gets high marks for citizenship, continuing to offer health coverage, equity participation, and even college assistance for its 238,000 employees ("partners"). It has made a recent commitment to hire 10,000 veterans and military spouses over the next five years, among a list of other commitments to community service and social issues of the day.

Financial Highlights, Fiscal Year 2015

Technology, brand, optimized store locations, expansion, and favorable coffee prices all helped the business along in FY2015. Same-store sales grew 7 percent across the board on the back of a 3 percent rise in transactions and a 4 percent rise in the average "ticket"—all good signs. Figures in the Americas mapped those totals; those in EMEA and Asia were strong on the volume growth but weaker on the average ticket—suggesting an opportunity there. These comps and store expansion drove a "perky" (sorry about that) 17 percent growth in revenues for the year with a comparable 16 percent growth in net income and per-share earnings.

Estimates call for a 7–13 percent revenue growth each year through 2017 with earnings growth in the mid to high teens as margins improve. Pretty good for a maturing company thought to have maxed out its potential years ago. "Room for cream" comes in the form of dividend increases in the low double digits with a moderate amount of share buyback activity added in for good measure.

Reasons to Buy

Starbucks is still a great story. The company's stores continue to be more than coffee shops and are really that "third place" where professionals, students, moms, and other prosperous folks will meet and dole out a few bucks for quality drinks. The "third place" aura creates a lot of the brand strength and, in our view, represents the company's *true* strength—well beyond the quality of the coffee itself and related products. The company has a steadily (and profitably) growing presence on the world stage and has learned how not to overbuild and cannibalize its business in the U.S. New packaging and food products are broadening appeal to larger customer segments and the single-cup market is going strong. And we believe the technology improvements will be big both for customers and operations.

The company is well managed, has an extremely strong brand, has solid financials, and, once again, a steady growth track record, and it is carving out an ever-stronger international footprint. Cash returns to investors are on the rise, and safety (as proxied by beta) has improved sharply from years ago. Starbucks offers both growth and, increasingly, cash and safety—a very nice brew for investors indeed.

Reasons for Caution

The biggest risk used to be overexpansion and competition—both of which they've encountered and dealt with well in recent years but could reemerge as trouble spots down the road. Perhaps our biggest fear now remains the temptation to expand the foodservice business, which could reduce margins, dilute the experience, and make the stores smell like a sandwich shop, far less appealing for most than the aroma of coffee. Too, it brings operational complexities. So we score the experience with food so far as mostly a success but continue to keep our eyes (and noses) open for signs of stress.

Coffee prices are volatile, but as experienced before, they don't really affect this story much since coffee is a small part of the company's total cost picture. Historically, coffee price surges have presented good buying opportunities—but right now coffee prices are weak; that and other factors have brewed up quite a strong stock price lately. Be careful not to burn yourself.

SECTOR: **Restaurant** ◻ BETA COEFFICIENT: **0.76** ◻ 10-YEAR COMPOUND EARNINGS PER-SHARE GROWTH: **19.0%** ◻ 10-YEAR COMPOUND DIVIDENDS PER-SHARE GROWTH: **NM**

		2008	2009	2010	2011	2012	2013	2014	2015
Revenues (mil)		10,383	9,774	10,707	11,701	13,299	14,892	16,448	19,163
Net income (mil)		525	598	982	1,174	1,385	1,721	2,068	2,394
Earnings per share		0.36	0.40	0.64	0.76	0.90	1.13	1.36	1.58
Dividends per share		—	—	0.12	0.26	0.34	0.42	0.52	0.64
Cash flow per share		0.73	0.76	1.01	1.14	1.29	1.58	1.85	2.21
Price:	high	10.5	12.0	16.6	23.3	31.0	41.3	42.1	64.0
	low	3.5	4.1	10.6	15.4	21.5	26.3	34.0	29.3

Website: www.starbucks.com

CONSERVATIVE GROWTH

State Street Corporation

Ticker symbol: STT (NYSE) ◻ S&P rating: A+ ◻ Value Line financial strength rating: B++ ◻ Current yield: 2.5% ◻ Dividend raises, past 10 years: 8

Company Profile

Are you afraid of SPDRs? Not the eight-legged kind, but the original and one of three leading brands of exchange-traded funds (ETFs) out there rapidly gaining ground on the "traditional" fund industry? If you aren't afraid of SPDRs, and you aren't too afraid of financial stocks in general. In the midst of the recent downturn that has dragged everybody down, State Street continues to be, in our opinion, more than most, a safe and sane way to play the Financials sector, which we continue to hold generally out of favor.

Like many financial powerhouses, State Street has a number of businesses under its umbrella. But unlike many, its core products are concentrated on offering services to other financial services firms and on offering the relatively new and growing ETF investment package to individual and institutional investors. It is often analyzed as a bank, but it acts more like a company providing services to other financial institutions and the public, receiving a steady and growing stream of fees for those services. The recent downturn hurt the value of the assets they hold, and thus fees, and also hurt other revenue streams from investment banks. But we think the work they do must still be done, and that they will emerge more efficient and stronger than ever.

The company operates with two main lines of business: Investment Servicing and Investment Management:

■ Investment Servicing (66 percent of revenues) provides fee-based administrative, custodial, analytic, and other value-add functions to investment companies—mainly mutual funds, hedge funds, and pension funds, including settlement and payment services, transaction management, foreign exchange trading and brokerage, and setting the NAV (net asset value, or price) of about 40 percent of U.S.-based mutual funds on a daily basis.

■ Investment Management (about 12 percent of revenues) provides investment vehicles and products through its State Street Global Advisors, or SSGA, subsidiary, including the well-known SPDR ETFs and some of the analytic tools and indexes supporting these products.

With these two fee-based business units accounting for 78 percent of total revenues, you might wonder where the rest of its $10.3 billion in revenues come from. The answer lies in interest and related income—some 22 percent of revenues are derived from the net interest generated on asset holdings.

State Street has operations in 29 countries, and about 64 percent of revenues come from assets managed in the U.S., 23 percent from the EMEA region, and 13 percent from Asia-Pacific.

Financial Highlights, Fiscal Year 2015

Currency effects, market downturns that affected asset valuations and management fees, and general malaise in the investment banking sector resulted in flat revenues in FY2015 and a forecast of continued weakness in FY2016. Despite the recent Fed move, interest income continues to be soft. Total assets under management declined 8 percent, again reflecting recent market declines. Investments in the new "Beacon" IT infrastructure impaired earnings somewhat as well; net profits declined about 2 percent in FY2015 and look to do about the same in FY2016. Due to rather aggressive 4 percent share buybacks, however, per-share earnings will stay fairly constant through FY2016. Payoff from the IT investment, and dollar and market stabilization bode well for FY2017, but we don't yet have a forecast. By 2016, the company will have bought back about 25 percent of its float, most of which was issued to bolster finances during the Great Recession.

Reasons to Buy

When there's a gold rush, the people who sell picks, shovels, and maps usually win. That's sort of the case with State Street. It makes a lot of steady money selling services to other financial services firms. It's a steadier income stream absent some (but not all) of the risks facing its other financial brethren. We think that State Street has a steady business with an innovative growth path in the ETF business, and we like the SPDR brand. We also like the fact that, unlike most financial firms, the company's income is more heavily based on fees and services than on interest margins and investment gains—more than 75 percent of revenues arise from fees and services. That said, the prospect for increased interest rates would bode well for interest income. The company continues to focus on financial strength, with a Tier One capital ratio exceeding 16.0 percent (anything over 10 percent is considered good; 8 percent is required under the new rules) and operational efficiency through the Beacon program, and should be well positioned to respond to a more favorable economic environment. State Street also continues to focus on investor returns, aggressively retiring shares and raising the dividend regularly.

Reasons for Caution

Despite the fact that State Street sells picks and shovels to other investment funds, many of its fees are based on asset valuations—which are in turn vulnerable to market downturns. The company estimates that every 10 percent drop in the markets reduces total equity-based revenues about 2 percent and total fixed income revenues about 1 percent. That's what has occurred recently.

Like other financial firms, State Street is enormously complex and hard to understand—we almost gave up when we introduced this issue for 2014. If you insist on fully understanding how a business works, what it sells, how it delivers, and so forth, this one might not be for you. Although the business is different than most financials, it could be swept up in another financial crisis. Likewise, a major market pullback and a decline in public interest in investing could hurt. We have to admit, we're being a bit patient with this one waiting for better times.

SECTOR: **Financials** ▫ BETA COEFFICIENT: **1.48** ▫ 10-YEAR COMPOUND EARNINGS PER-SHARE GROWTH: **6.5%** ▫ 10-YEAR COMPOUND DIVIDENDS PER-SHARE GROWTH: **6.5%**

	2008	2009	2010	2011	2012	2013	2014	2015
Assets (bil)	173.6	157.9	160.5	216.8	222.6	243.3	274.9	245.2
Revenues (mil)	10,693	8,640	8,953	9,594	9,649	9,881	10,235	10,350
Net income (mil)	1,811	1,803	1,559	1,920	2,061	2,136	2,037	1,980
Earnings per share	4.30	3.46	3.09	3.79	4.20	4.62	4.57	4.47
Dividends per share	0.95	0.04	0.04	0.72	0.96	1.04	1.16	1.32
Price: high	86.6	55.9	48.8	50.3	47.3	73.6	80.9	81.3
low	28.1	14.4	32.5	29.9	38.2	47.7	62.7	64.0

Website: www.statestreet.com

AGGRESSIVE GROWTH

Steelcase, Inc.

Ticker symbol: SCS (NYSE) ▫ S&P rating: BBB ▫ Value Line financial strength rating: B+ ▫ Current yield: 3.3% ▫ Dividend raises, past 10 years: 6

Company Profile

Steelcase is the world's leading producer of office furniture, and more importantly, office systems. The company makes several lines of more traditional modular walls, chairs, desks, files, and other kinds of cabinets, etc. But in addition, in part through emerging subbrands such as Coalesse, Nurture, Workspring, and Turnstone, Steelcase is bringing to market new ideas and office concepts that we'd probably all like to see and work in. Call it office *architecture* if you will.

Imagine arriving at the office, heading to a small visible conference area with two glass walls, a floor-to-ceiling whiteboard, and devices that connect immediately and wirelessly to your mobile device to display your work or your multimedia presentation. Imagine sitting (or standing) in small, comfortable work areas, again with a display, possibly built into the table in front of you, to work alone or with others. Impersonal, boring, paper-ridden, PC-based, space-consuming cubicle—be gone! And most cubicles in today's offices are empty anyway—so they might as well be gone. Steelcase continues to really be a bet on the demise of today's traditional office space. Why is that space going away? Several factors. One, today's new mobile worker, who doesn't spend so much time in the office. When she or he does, it's to get together, to collaborate, often on a ceramic or glass whiteboard, with other workers and to demonstrate their work. Most don't have traditional PCs. Less paper moves around, so workers don't need as much storage. What they need is a workbench, places to stash their backpacks, meet, ways to connect and display what they're working on and work together, places to rest and contemplate in ergonomic comfort, possibly with an adjustable standup desk, all the while connected to the business and to each other. "Work has been freed" is the slogan on the company's subbrand "Coalesse" website (www.coalesse.com).

Another factor in the death of the cube is the desire to reduce office space—and cost. Cubes, especially empty ones, take a lot of space. Just as the traditional four-walled, sometimes-windowed office went out in favor of the cubicle and cube farm when PCs took over and nobody needed a secretary pool any more, we think the office is ready for another transition. Steelcase has been studying and innovating in that space for quite some time, and it appears in our view to be ready to bring it to market, as a market leader. We think it could be big.

Steelcase doesn't just produce broad lines of office furnishings. It has conducted deep, customer-based studies of workplace activity, especially innovation, teamwork, leadership, and worker disengagement and it has studied and marketed to key vertical markets like healthcare, education, and hotels and hospitality—a case study for market-driven innovation. About 29 percent of sales come from overseas.

Financial Highlights, Fiscal Year 2015

A persistent slowdown in capital spending both in the U.S. and abroad has pushed out the demand acceleration we had expected to materialize; currency translation hurt too. FY2015 ended on a weak note, and sales were flat for the entire year while net earnings advanced a healthy 17 percent on an improved product mix and improved margins. We still expect demand to pick up especially by FY2017, with 3–5 percent revenue gains likely, persistent margin improvement, and earnings gains in the 10–15 percent range.

Reasons to Buy

We still think we are in the early stages of an accelerating trend—a couple of trends, really. First, traditional organizations are looking for new ways to meet the needs and reduce the stress of today's mobile worker. They are also looking to optimize floor space, which the new designs tend to use less of. Second, new companies (and there are a lot of them) cater to the new Millennial worker and aspire to create the perfect workspace for mobile collaboration and innovation. This trend is spreading around the world; currently, only 29 percent of sales are overseas, but the company's concepts are picking up particularly in the space-constrained Asia-Pacific region. In short, we think the update of today's traditional cube farm, born in the 1980s, is well underway. Steelcase gets this and has been investing in it for years. We like the designs and its approach to key vertical markets like healthcare, hospitality, and education, which have their own special needs. As these trends accelerate, we expect stronger sales, an improved sales mix, higher profitability, and more brand recognition moving forward. The decent dividend yield gives you something to count on while you wait.

Reasons for Caution

Quite simply, the evolution we've been anticipating has taken longer than we thought to materialize. The office furniture business is subject to wide swings, and renovations can be one of the first things cancelled or delayed when business conditions shift. We are also concerned that a glut of office space may be forming (which, ironically, could result from the adoption of Steelcase's more space-efficient designs!). Too, while margins are improving, 8–12 percent operating margins and 3–5 percent net profit margins are nothing to write home about.

SECTOR: **Industrials** ❑ BETA COEFFICIENT: **1.35** ❑ 10-YEAR COMPOUND EARNINGS PER-SHARE GROWTH: **6.0%** ❑ 10-YEAR COMPOUND DIVIDENDS PER-SHARE GROWTH: **4.5%**

	2008	2009	2010	2011	2012	2013	2014	2015
Revenues (mil)	3,184	2,292	2,437	2,749	2,669	2,990	3,060	3,050
Net income (mil)	91	(12.2)	51	76	101	106	112	130
Earnings per share	0.68	(0.09)	0.38	0.58	0.79	0.84	0.89	1.03
Dividends per share	0.60	0.24	0.16	0.24	0.36	0.36	0.42	0.44
Cash flow per share	1.34	0.47	0.87	1.05	1.27	1.36	1.42	1.60
Price: high	16.7	7.7	10.9	12.1	13.3	17.0	18.8	20.5
low	5.0	3.0	6.2	5.4	7.3	12.2	13.6	14.1

Website: www.steelcase.com

Stryker Corporation

Ticker symbol: SYK (NYSE) ❑ S&P rating: A+ ❑ Value Line financial strength rating: A++
❑ Current yield: 1.5% ❑ Dividend raises, past 10 years: 9

Company Profile

Stryker Corporation was founded as the Orthopedic Frame Company in
1941 by Dr. Homer H. Stryker, a leading orthopedic surgeon and the inven-
tor of several orthopedic products. The company now ranks as a dominant
player in the global orthopedics industry with more than 59,000 products
in its catalog and a strong innovation track record, with more than 6 percent
of sales invested in R&D.

The Orthopaedics segment (that's how the company spells it) accounts
for about 43 percent of 2015 sales and has a significant market share in such
"spare parts" as artificial hips, prosthetic knees, implant products for other
extremities, and trauma and recovery products. Within that group, knees are
33 percent, hips are 30 percent, and "Trauma & Extremities" are another
31 percent of sales.

The MedSurg unit, about 39 percent of sales, develops, manufactures,
and markets worldwide powered and computer-assisted and robotic surgical
instruments, endoscopic surgical systems, hospital beds, and other patient
care and handling equipment. Instruments (38 percent of this group),
endoscopy (36 percent), and medical devices, including emergency devices
(21 percent), are the largest contributors.

The Neurotechnology & Spine segment, a large part of which was
acquired from Boston Scientific in 2010, accounts for 19 percent of sales
and sells spinal reconstructive and surgical equipment, neurovascular
surgery equipment, and craniomaxillofacial products. This is the smallest
but fastest-growing segment in the company.

Stryker's revenue is split roughly 72/28 percent domestic and
international. The company scored a nineteenth position on the annual
"*Fortune* 100 Best Companies to Work For" list for 2015, up a full 23 places
from 2014 and is recognized as one of the top players in the healthcare
industry and one of the leading big companies as well.

Stryker has been active on the acquisition front. The early 2016 medium-
sized complementary acquisition of Sage Products, a provider of disposable
products mainly in the MedSurg segment, will add $400 to $500 million in
mostly recurring revenues by FY2017. Another acquisition brings portable

defibrillators and monitors into the Emergency Medical Services business, part of the MedSurg group. Still another brings Synergetics USA into the Neuro group. These all-cash transactions are made from cash reserves and will not increase share counts.

Financial Highlights, Fiscal Year 2015

Currency effects continued to bring some sore joints for Stryker; net sales were up about 3 percent anyhow (6.1 percent in constant currency); net earnings on an apples-to-apples basis (there were some product recalls in 2014) were up a bit over 12 percent. Going forward, Stryker projects (with some effects from acquisitions) a 5–6 percent gain and possibly more in the top line for FY2016, and a 6–7 percent gain in FY2017. A moderate margin growth and operating leverage should bring earnings forward about 7 percent in FY2016 and as much as 10–12 percent in FY2017, depending on acquisition costs. Share buybacks will stop for now due to acquisitions, but dividends should rise in the 8–10 percent range over the next few years.

Reasons to Buy

We continue to see Stryker as an innovative healthcare products company with relatively less-entrenched competition than many others and a strong presence in the orthopedic market. This should allow it to capitalize on aging and the availability of health insurance to greater numbers under the Affordable Care Act. Emerging markets, particularly China, present a good opportunity, and recent acquisitions should strengthen the portfolio and brand worldwide. We also see ample dividend growth.

Reasons for Caution

Ongoing scrutiny of healthcare costs and a continuation of small acquisitions bring some risks to the company, but we don't think they are excessive. The company makes fairly high-tech medical products and as such is exposed to legal, regulatory, and manufacturing risks, and the recent product recall did hurt. Ongoing efforts to contain medical costs could hurt the more elective orthopedic procedures, but that should be offset by the wider availability of covered care to more people. While the dividend is increasing at a good pace, the yield could still be higher given the company's strong cash flow—obviously they think they can invest your cash (in acquisitions) better than you can—and they may be right for now given projected earnings increases.

SECTOR: **Healthcare** ▫ BETA COEFFICIENT: **0.83** ▫ 10-YEAR COMPOUND EARNINGS PER-SHARE GROWTH: **9.5%** ▫ 10-YEAR COMPOUND DIVIDENDS PER-SHARE GROWTH: **31.0%**

	2008	2009	2010	2011	2012	2013	2014	2015
Revenues (mil)	6,718	6,723	7,320	8,307	8,656	9,021	9,675	9,946
Net income (mil)	1,148	1,107	1,330	1,448	1,298	1,006	1,460	1,639
Earnings per share	2.78	2.77	3.30	3.72	3.39	2.63	3.85	4.31
Dividends per share	0.33	0.50	0.63	0.72	0.85	1.10	1.22	1.38
Cash flow per share	3.87	3.75	4.40	5.08	4.69	4.01	5.45	5.90
Price: high	74.9	52.7	59.7	65.2	64.1	75.8	96.2	108.3
low	35.4	30.8	42.7	43.7	49.4	55.2	74.0	89.8

Website: www.stryker.com

CONSERVATIVE GROWTH

Sysco Corporation

Ticker symbol: SYY (NYSE) ▫ S&P rating: A ▫ Value Line financial strength rating: A+ ▫ Current yield: 2.7% ▫ Dividend raises, past 10 years: 10

Company Profile

Sysco is the leading marketer and distributor of food, food products, and related equipment and supplies to the U.S. foodservice industry. The company distributes fresh and frozen meats, prepared entrées, vegetables, canned and dried foods, dairy products, beverages, and produce, as well as paper products, restaurant equipment and supplies, and cleaning supplies. The company might be familiar for its "institutional" number-ten-sized cans of food found in many high-volume kitchens, but the product line and customer base is much larger, including many specialty and chain restaurants, lodges, hotels, hospitals, schools, and other distribution centers across the country. Restaurants account for about 64 percent of the 2015 business; healthcare (mainly hospitals and nursing homes) 9 percent, education (schools and colleges) about 8 percent, travel and leisure (hotels and motels) also about 8 percent, and "other" categories make up the rest—about 11 percent. You see their lift-gated "bobtail" delivery trucks continuously, but you may not notice them delivering and unloading a pallet or two of goods at a time for a broad assortment of foodservice venues in your area. If you eat out at all, you've most likely consumed Sysco-distributed products. Sysco was founded in 1969 with the goal of becoming a national foodservice network. By 1977, the company had become the largest foodservice supplier to the $255 billion restaurant market in North America, a position it has retained for more than 30 years. It has over 425,000 customers and distributes over 400,000 products, including 41,000 under its own label. Sysco operates 197 distribution facilities and conducts business in more than 90 countries through company-owned facilities and joint ventures. From these centers, Sysco distributes 1.4 billion cases of food annually. The facilities include its 95 Broadline facilities, which supply independent and chain restaurants and other food-preparation facilities with a wide variety of food and nonfood products. It has 11 hotel supply locations, 25 specialty produce facilities, 17 SYGMA distribution centers (specialized, high-volume centers supplying to chain restaurants), 27 custom-cutting meat locations, and two distributors specializing in the niche Asian foodservice market. The company has recently been adding healthier, non-GMO, sustainably sourced and other such items into its menu, which should play well with foodservice customers expanding their menus in this direction.

The company also supplies the hotel industry with guest amenities, equipment, housekeeping supplies, room accessories, and textiles. By product type, the top five products are: 21 percent meat and frozen meals, 16 percent canned/dry, 13 percent frozen, 11 percent dairy, and 11 percent poultry, with produce, paper goods, seafood, beverages, janitorial products, and others making up the rest.

Sysco is by far the largest company in the domestic foodservice distribution industry. Up until recently, it grew via small "bolt-on" acquisitions in specialty food companies (such as seafood) or new geographies, but for the most part avoided the "blockbuster" acquisition. In late 2013 it tried to acquire rival and number two market player U.S. Foods but ran into so much legal and customer opposition that it dropped the merger in 2015. It then shifted its sights overseas and acquired U.K.-based Brakes Group in 2016 to become a leading foodservice provider in England, France, and Sweden. This move will add about 10 percent to the top line and establish a solid beachhead for growth in Europe.

Financial Highlights, Fiscal Year 2015

After a few relatively flat years due to more people "eating in" after the recession and commodity inflation, FY2015 perked up on the back of stronger consumer trends, commodity price reductions (which helped both food and fuel, major ingredients to the Sysco business), and a series of productivity improvements. Taken together, sales rose almost 5 percent and net income rose a very respectable 18 percent. Net profit margins increased from 2.0 to

2.3 percent—a big deal in this business. Not including the Brakes Group acquisitions, revenues should rise in the 3–6 percent range over the next two years, with net earnings up a similar amount. A $1.5 billion annual share buyback will retire 3–5 percent of outstanding shares each year through 2017 and lead to per-share earnings gains in the 8–10 percent range. Dividend raises should continue at a steady pace.

Reasons to Buy

Sysco continues to be a dominant player in a niche that won't go away anytime soon. The current foodservice environment is improving, and the company still has plenty to work on in the form of operational efficiencies, and now international expansion is added to the mix as a growth driver.

Sysco's recent investments in technology continue to bear fruit, and we like to see innovation in an industry not known for it. New analytics, routing optimization, and recycling initiatives are being applied to realize savings in people, fuel, and other costs; the effects are manifest in the profit margin improvement noted previously and should continue. New supply-chain tools—even a "My Sysco Truck" app—allow customers to view the location and status of the deliveries and more generally will expand efficiencies and extend the customer relationship. In sum, this is a steady and safe company with a pretty good track record for steady business, decent cash flow, and decent shareholder payouts.

Reasons for Caution

Although the trend is slowly reversing, the recession got many folks away from the habit of eating out, and many restaurants disappeared altogether during this period. Volatility in food and ingredient prices, and fuel costs too, can pressure margins; this is always a cause for concern. We also now worry that new dining trends and tastes of the Millennials and others will require more specialization in the restaurant market, something Sysco will need to adapt to at least to a degree (and has begun to).

As described previously, this is a low-margin business with not a lot of room for error. Sysco, more than most, is a "sleep at night" kind of investment.

SECTOR: **Consumer Staples** □ BETA COEFFICIENT: **0.60** □ 10-YEAR COMPOUND EARNINGS PER-SHARE GROWTH: **2.5%** □ 10-YEAR COMPOUND DIVIDENDS PER-SHARE GROWTH: **9.0%**

	2008	2009	2010	2011	2012	2013	2014	2015
Revenues (mil)	37,522	36,853	37,243	39,323	42,381	44,411	46,517	48,681
Net income (mil)	1,106	1,056	1,181	1,153	1,122	992	931	1,100
Earnings per share	1.81	1.77	1.99	1.96	1.90	1.67	1.58	1.84
Dividends per share	0.82	0.93	0.99	1.03	1.07	1.11	1.16	1.19
Cash flow per share	2.46	2.44	2.67	2.62	2.63	2.57	2.54	2.78
Price: high	35.0	29.5	32.6	32.6	32.4	43.4	41.2	42.0
low	20.7	19.4	27.0	25.1	27.0	30.5	34.1	35.4

Website: www.sysco.com

AGGRESSIVE GROWTH

Target Corporation

Ticker symbol: TGT (NYSE) □ S&P rating: A □ Value Line financial strength rating: A □ Current yield: 2.8% □ Dividend raises, past 10 years: 10

Company Profile

As you know by now, we take a long-term view when we include a company on our *100 Best* list. A good company with a good and long-standing business model will stay on our list despite a stumble; in fact, many a stumble can give a company strength, as we've seen over the years with the likes of Starbucks, Johnson & Johnson, and Procter & Gamble. Target, as most who follow the company know, is just such a story. A well-publicized data breach and a less well-publicized failed venture in Canada were just the sort of financial and PR stumbles that could take the company off the shopping lists of a less patient investor—and they did. But the company's core strengths remained intact; it survived and has thrived since. The lesson, once again: Patience and the recognition of a company's core strengths are true virtues of the successful investor. Target is the nation's second-largest general merchandise retailer and specializes in general merchandise at a discount in a large-store format. The company now operates 1,792 stores in 49 states (Vermont is the only state not represented), including 250 Super Targets, which also carry a broad line of groceries. The greatest concentration of Target stores is in California (15 percent), Texas (8 percent), and Florida (7 percent), with a combined total of about 30 percent of the stores. There is another concentration in the upper Midwest. Target positions itself against its main competitor, Walmart, as a more upscale and trend-conscious "cheap chic" alternative. The typical Target customer has a higher level of disposable income than that of Walmart, which the company courts by offering brand-name merchandise in addition to a series of largely successful house brands such as Michael Graves, Market Pantry, Smith & Hawken, Fieldcrest, and Archer Farms. These and about 25 other brands generate about a third of Target's sales. The company's revenues come from retail exclusively; it sold its credit card operations to TD Bank in late 2012. Digital sales, while accounting for only 3.4 percent of total sales, grew at 30 percent last year and are considered a strategic priority not only for the sales themselves but also for brand recognition and for driving traffic to the stores.

The company is also investing domestically in its food lines, which now account for 21 percent of total 2015 sales. Food is sold in about 70 percent of stores. The total sales breakdown—largely unchanged from last year—is: 26 percent household essentials, 21 percent food and pet supplies, 19 percent apparel and accessories, 17 percent hardlines, and 17 percent home furnishings and décor. These percentages are largely unchanged from last year.

Target is still executing on a new "roadmap to transform business" shared by Target management in early 2015. Highlights include an emphasis on what other retailers call "omnichannel" development—combining web, mobile, and in-store experiences (and supply chains) to offer a better customer experience. The company estimates that "guests" who shop online generate three times the sales of guests who shop in stores only. We applaud this effort to differentiate customers by value and tailor experiences; far too few companies do this in our opinion. Target will prioritize Style, Baby, Kids, and Wellness categories in addition to Groceries as "targets" to improve merchandising and overall experience. The company has also admitted that its traditional store format is saturated. It's hard to find more locations (another "admission" we admire, since most retail managers have a hard time admitting this). To address this issue and to spruce up its merchandising, Target is embarking on a "local relevance and flexible formats" campaign, extending experiments with smaller TargetExpress and CityTarget formats and tailoring merchandise assortments to specific markets with richer presentation of certain product lines. Finally, supply-chain and operational improvements will cut $2 billion in costs over the first two years of this plan.

Finally, Target made a big move in late 2015 with the announcement of the sale of its in-store pharmaceutical business to CVS Health (another *100 Best* stock). The $1.9 billion deal gets Target out of the relatively low-margin, high-maintenance drug business while still preserving—really, increasing—store traffic as CVS customers can come to Target stores to pick up their meds. The deal will fund some capital improvements but also provided funds for major share repurchases—over 8 percent of the float will be retired in the two years 2015–2016.

Financial Highlights, Fiscal Year 2015

Same-store sales rose a healthy 2.1 percent in FY2015, a nice increase from 2014's 1.3 percent and far better than the 0.4 percent *decrease* in 2013, the year of the data breach. Total revenues advanced 1.6 percent, the difference being $550 million taken out of the top line by the prescription counter divestiture. Gross, operating, and net profit margins all ticked upward, leading to a 9 percent net income gain; share buybacks led to a 10 percent gain in earnings per share. FY2016 revenues will drop about 3 percent due to the pharma divestiture (which accounted for about 5 percent of sales) but net profit is expected to rise 6 percent as the mix improves and cost cuts take hold. FY2017 should see earnings gains in the 5–6 percent range (8–10 percent on a per-share earnings basis) on revenues advancing in the 2–3 percent range. Dividend increases look to continue in the high single digits after stronger bumps recently in part due to the divestiture; share counts will continue to drop by about 2 percent each year. The overall picture is one of a return to stability with a stable growth component.

Reasons to Buy

We thought the long-term consequences of FY2013's problems would fade rather quickly, and we were right. The company handled Canada and particularly the data breach quite effectively; in the long term it not only assuaged customer concerns but also gained their confidence and attracted new customers. The company is simply too strong in its brand and position to lose in the long term over such an incident.

Target remains a classic positioning success story. Customers understand and appreciate Target, and it has some of the highest customer satisfaction numbers in the industry. The company continues to take shares away from specialty retailers in home lines, clothing, children's items, and other areas. People like the Target brand and associate it with well-managed stores and quality and good taste at a reasonable price with good locations. More recently they appear to be making more regular and frequent visits to the store because of the grocery department.

Better economic conditions and more spending on home and domestic goods should improve Target's market share. Share counts have dropped from

911 million in 2003 to about 600 million recently. We like the "roadmap," and feel the overall story remains solid.

Reasons for Caution

Target is up against some very tough competitors: Walmart, Costco, and others. And one cannot ignore the Internet's destructive effects on "bricks and mortar" these days—even if the company operates one of the best online sites (target.com) out there. It looks like international expansion is off the table, at least for now. We still see some risk in the grocery business, as groceries are very low margin, and the company hasn't really figured out how to make the grocery offering complete with meats and fresh produce. From our personal observations, the grocery department seems pretty empty by comparison to other grocery stores and other parts of Target stores. Gross and operating margins may see some pressure from this business, depending on how valuable the generation of more frequent store visits turns out to be. And while we're thrilled at the recovery in the stock price from 2014, it does present some challenges to finding the right "target" price to make a new investment.

SECTOR: **Retail** ❑ BETA COEFFICIENT: **0.59** ❑ 10-YEAR COMPOUND EARNINGS PER-SHARE
GROWTH: **7.0%** ❑ 10-YEAR COMPOUND DIVIDENDS PER-SHARE GROWTH: **19.5%**

	2008	2009	2010	2011	2012	2013	2014	2015
Revenues (mil)	64,948	63,435	67,390	69,865	73,301	72,596	72,618	73,785
Net income (mil)	2,214	2,488	2,830	2,829	2,925	2,060	2,734	2,978
Earnings per share	2.86	3.30	3.88	4.28	4.38	3.21	4.27	4.69
Dividends per share	0.60	0.66	0.84	1.10	1.32	1.58	1.90	2.16
Cash flow per share	5.37	5.90	6.98	7.46	7.82	6.77	7.60	8.62
Price: high	59.6	51.8	60.7	61.0	65.5	73.5	76.6	85.8
low	25.6	25.0	46.2	45.3	47.3	55.0	54.7	68.1

Website: www.target.com

CONSERVATIVE GROWTH

Time Warner Inc.

Ticker symbol: TWX (NYSE) ❑ S&P rating: BBB ❑ Value Line financial strength rating: A ❑ Current yield: 2.3% ❑ Dividend raises, past 10 years: 9

Company Profile

Time Warner is a $28 billion media and entertainment company aimed squarely at producing and distributing media in both traditional and innovative ways. Seven years ago, the company undertook a well-publicized—and necessary—downsize, untying itself from America Online (AOL) and separating from its Time Warner Cable business too, and went back to working in the areas it knows best—content—and working on new ways to make more money producing and delivering that content. In 2014 it spun off its print media—translation, "magazine"—unit into a separate company, Time Inc., to focus on its core film, television, and digital businesses. We continue to like this movie.

With the disposal of much of the publishing operation, and an expansion in digital and content services, the company reorganized itself into three reporting business segments:

■ *Turner* (38 percent of 2015 revenues), which brands itself "The Best in Entertainment, Sports, Kids, and News," includes industry-leading properties formerly part of the Turner Broadcasting System, including CNN, TBS, TNT, and Turner Classic, as well as other standards such as Cartoon Network, Adult Swim, Boomerang, TMZ, and a series of digital sports networks including NBA.com, PGA.com, and others. The unit is investing heavily in on-demand viewing and live streaming of content, which it now estimates to be available to 82 million U.S. households. The unit, in all, has 165 channels broadcast in 36 languages in 200 countries worldwide. The unit claims to be the most watched provider on basic cable. TBS, TNT, and Adult Swim had three of the top ten prime time ad-supported viewing slots for adults 18–49 in 2015. The unit brings in almost half of TWX's operating profits.

■ *HBO* (18 percent of revenues), which brands itself as "The World's Most Successful Premium Television Company," delivers premium pay-TV services in the U.S. with an estimated 43 million subscribers, and premium and basic pay services internationally (direct in 60 countries, licensed in 150) with about 122 million subscribers. The unit has had increasing success in producing its own shows—its *Game of Thrones*, *The Sopranos*, and *True Detective* are long-standing favorites with several successful new series coming online recently, including *Citizenfour*, *The Leftovers*, and *Silicon Valley*.

■ **Warner Bros.** (44 percent) brands itself "The Global Leader in Entertainment," and includes Warner Bros. Pictures and New Line Cinema. Warner Bros. produces more than 70 TV shows (including *The Big Bang Theory* and *Gotham*) and about 18–22 feature films a year and distributes hundreds of others. (There are 7,400 feature films in its library. *Batman v Superman: Dawn of Justice* was a big 2016 title.) The unit also produces and licenses content for video games (*The LEGO Movie Videogame* is an example) and other delivery modes, and distributes its content in more than 125 countries, many in local languages.

The details of these businesses and sub-businesses expand far beyond what is described here; suffice it to say TWX has a huge presence in the creation and distribution of many forms of media. The company has two major strategic directions. The first is to expand global reach, and the company now tallies 32 percent of its revenues from outside the U.S. The second, and perhaps most important, is to get more content to more people in more places at more times than ever before—mostly digitally ("Content Everywhere," as they refer to it). The company is leading the way in live streaming of all of its TV content to valid subscribers through a "TV Everywhere" initiative to a variety of devices, including mobile. "HBO NOW" is one branding of this service, and it plays well to keep TWX products in front of so-called cable "cord cutters." A new "UltraViolet" cloud content service now makes 110 movies and TV shows available to 21 million users worldwide; there are many more innovations in the digital space.

Financial Highlights, Fiscal Year 2015

Now firmly set in the post-Time era, revenues are growing in the 3–5 percent range, although FY2015 finished a bit weak due to disappointing results with a pair of feature films. Earnings were flat in FY2015 but are projected to gain momentum through FY2016 as the company gains leverage by selling the same content into more platforms; guidance now calls for a $5.35–$5.40 per-share earnings performance—a 15 percent gain over FY2015. Share buybacks and dividend increases are coming at a steady rate.

Reasons to Buy

By splitting from AOL, then selling the cable business and now the magazine business, we think Time Warner has gotten to where it wants to be, particularly as it makes headway in the digital space. Especially considering the "everywhere" digital expansion, we think the demand for content will only go up, and TWX has some of the great properties and brands, such as CNN, HBO, and TBS, to leverage as platforms to develop and deliver this content in traditional and new, multichannel formats. The content appears to play well with the younger Millennial generation and their slightly older brethren, and the digital "when you want it, where you want it, how you want it" delivery should only make this better. There have been some takeover rumors concerning possible content-hungry suitors such as Apple and 21st Century Fox, which already made an unsuccessful play in 2014. Finally this is a cash-generating business, and the cash returns to investors, especially the buybacks, which have dropped share counts 47 percent since 2005, should receive an Academy Award.

Reasons for Caution

The entertainment business is complex, fickle, and ever changing, which in part explains why we had no such companies on our *100 Best* list until 2013—and why we have only one today. It's a struggle to keep up with what's new and what's changing, and in particular, what's working, but we've admired this company's ability to build good brands, put good products on the market, and achieve lasting revenue streams from all of it.

SECTOR: **Entertainment** ❑ BETA COEFFICIENT: **1.28** ❑ 10-YEAR COMPOUND EARNINGS PER-SHARE GROWTH: **9.0%** ❑ 10-YEAR COMPOUND DIVIDENDS PER-SHARE GROWTH: **17.0%**

	2008	2009	2010	2011	2012	2013	2014	2015
Revenues (mil)	46,894	25,785	26,888	28,944	29,729	29,795	27,359	28,615
Net income (mil)	3,574	2,079	2,578	2,886	3,019	3,554	3,894	3,800
Earnings per share	2.88	1.74	2.25	2.71	3.09	3.77	4.41	4.70
Dividends per share	0.75	0.75	0.85	0.94	1.04	1.15	1.27	1.40
Cash flow per share	6.83	2.66	3.20	3.91	4.20	4.96	5.56	5.75
Price: high	50.7	33.5	34.1	38.6	48.5	70.8	88.1	91.3
low	21.0	17.8	26.4	27.6	33.5	48.6	60.7	62.9

Website: www.timewarner.com

The Timken Company

Ticker symbol: TKR (NYSE) ❑ S&P rating: BBB- ❑ Value Line financial strength rating: B++
❑ Current yield: 3.1% ❑ Dividend raises, past 10 years: 8

Company Profile

When you operate a 140-ton loaded railroad car, a giant windmill, or a rolling mill in a steel-fabricating plant, you have tremendous frictional forces to overcome, often in harsh environments, for long periods of operating time and with 100 percent reliability required. Without a dependable and efficient friction solution to these moving parts, they can overheat, fail, get out of alignment, and otherwise wreak havoc on your mobile system or stationary machine—not to mention make it cost more to operate. That's where premium-engineered, replaceable bearing assemblies come into play.

On rail cars, for instance, roller bearings—small, tapered, hardened steel bearings "rolling" between the rotating axle and the wheel housing—solved years of headaches (and fires and accidents) caused by oiled brass bearings. Years ago roller bearings became mandatory for U.S. railroad operation. Similar gains in performance, reliability, reduced friction, and cost came to other businesses. These specialized, high-value-add bearings—and now application-specific bearing assemblies and housings that hold them—are a critical manufactured and serviced component of most of today's mobile and many of today's stationary systems.

"Stronger, by Design" is the apt slogan for Timken, the world's oldest, most established and focused, and largest producer of bearings and bearing products. Over time, they have evolved the product line from relatively simple tapered and ball bearings to a greater number of protected bearing assemblies, or "housed units" which enable solutions in harsher operating environments and create maintenance cost savings for the customer.

The company, after spinning off its steelmaking business in 2014, is made up of two business segments:

- *Mobile Industries* (53 percent of 2015 sales) offers bearings, bearing systems, seals, lubrication devices, and power transmission systems mainly to OEMs and operators of trucks, automobiles, rail cars and locomotives, rotor and fixed-wing aircraft, construction and mining machinery, and certain military items. There had been a separate Aerospace segment; it is now part of Mobile.

- *Process Industries* (47 percent of sales) supplies industrial bearings, bearing systems and assemblies, and power transmission components to OEMs and operators in metals, mining, cement, aggregates production, food processing, wind energy, turbine and oil drilling equipment, material handling equipment, and certain marine applications among many applications. These are stationary machines without wheels, whereas Mobile mainly supports things *with* wheels (or rotors or wings).

The company is still adding to its portfolio of adjacent machinery and mechanical power transmission parts, including chains, belts, gear drives, couplings, brakes, sprockets, and clutches, including sales but also service and reconditioning businesses. Like bearings, these are relatively mission-critical, high-value–add components with serviceable lives requiring replacement, and Timken would like to expand its position as a single-source, branded, full-service vendor for such components. The top five end-user markets are Industrial Machinery (20 percent), Automotive (14 percent), Rail (11 percent), Energy (10 percent), and Heavy Truck (8 percent). About 56 percent of Timken's business originates in North America; EMEA (16 percent), Asia (23 percent), and Latin America (6 percent) make up the rest. The company projects that 26 percent of revenues come from developing markets.

Financial Highlights, Fiscal Year 2015

Currency, general malaise in the U.S. and China industrial sectors, and segment-specific slowdowns in energy, rail, and other transportation businesses led to a just under 7 percent drop in revenues (2 percent without currency) for FY2015. Despite lower material costs, lower production volumes led to a 28 percent decrease in net earnings; however, a 6 percent share buyback attenuated the per-share earnings drop to only 13 percent. The company expects continued currency, China, and energy headwinds through FY2016, with relatively flat earnings on a 5 percent (3 percent without currency) revenue decline. FY2017 looks to be better, with a 12 percent earnings advance on 5 percent revenue increase. Cash flow, buybacks, and dividends are a big part of the Timken story. A 2016 authorization calls for a repurchase of 5 million common shares—another 6 percent of its float. The company has been paying dividends since its IPO in 1922 and has been raising dividends albeit more moderately lately.

Reasons to Buy

We like companies with strong brands and legacies that also happen to supply very key high-value-add components to a value chain. Timken offers such key components in several important value chains, and these components wear out and must be replaced periodically—they aren't just depending on new capital investment for business. Timken's presentations drive this home—one highlights the rail car example (although the rail business has slowed recently), where a given rail car has a 35-year life and requires bearing replacement every five years—bringing $800,000 in lifetime revenue to Timken for a 100-car train (or $8,000 per rail car for life for the million-and-a-half-plus of them out there if you'd prefer to look at it that way). Lifetime value calculations like this, spread across many industries, really bring Timken's value proposition home. The net profit margin of roughly 6 percent indicates a differentiated industry (not a commodity) and a strong market position.

Reasons for Caution

Economic cycles, of course, will affect Timken's fortunes, as will competition from foreign manufacturers mainly in China and other parts of Asia. Despite the recognized brand and market leadership position, the company still has only 5 percent of the overall bearing and 30 percent of the tapered bearing market; competitors are out there. Some of the company's products go into the depressed energy extraction and mining industries—maintenance and replacement volume from these industries will probably stay soft at least through 2016, and now rail volumes are declining too.

SECTOR: **Industrials** ❑ BETA COEFFICIENT: **1.72** ❑ 10-YEAR COMPOUND EARNINGS PER-SHARE GROWTH: **13.0%** ❑ 10-YEAR COMPOUND DIVIDENDS PER-SHARE GROWTH: **6.0%**

		2008	2009	2010	2011	2012	2013	2014	2015
Revenues (mil)		5,664	3,142	4,056	5,170	4,987	4,341	3,076	2,872
Net income (mil)		313	51	289	457	456	263	234	189
Earnings per share		3.26	0.53	2.95	4.59	4.66	2.74	2.55	2.21
Dividends per share		0.70	0.45	0.53	0.78	0.92	0.92	1.00	1.03
Cash flow per share		5.64	2.61	4.89	6.65	6.81	4.93	4.19	3.85
Price:	high	38.7	26.1	49.3	57.8	57.9	64.4	69.5	43.6
	low	11.0	9.9	22.0	30.2	32.6	47.7	37.6	26.4

Website: www.timken.com

GROWTH AND INCOME

Total S.A. (ADR)

Ticker symbol: TOT (NYSE) ❑ S&P rating: AA- ❑ Value Line financial strength rating: A++ ❑ Current yield: 5.7% ❑ Dividend raises, past 10 years: 7

Company Profile

Total S.A. (S.A. is short for Société Anonyme, which is the French equivalent of "incorporated") is the fourth-largest publicly traded oil and gas company in the world. Headquartered in France and primarily traded on the French CAC stock exchange, the company has operations in more than 130 countries. Total is vertically integrated with upstream operations engaged in oil and gas exploration and downstream operations engaged in refining and distribution of petroleum products; the company also has a chemicals and a solar subsidiary.

Upstream activities are geographically well diversified, with exploration occurring in 50 countries and production happening in 30 of them. Many of the E&P projects are done through partnerships to spread risk. The largest production regions are (in production-volume sequence) in the North Sea, North Africa, West Africa, and the Middle East, with smaller operations in Southeast Asia and North and South America. Liquids (oil) account for about 61 percent of production, while natural gas is 39 percent. The company is a leader in the emerging liquefied natural gas (LNG) market for export, and recently strengthened an agreement to supply LNG to the China National Offshore Oil Corporation (CNOOC).

Downstream operations are also worldwide and centered in Europe. Operations include interests in 21 refineries worldwide, with 11 refineries and 85 percent of total refining capacity in Europe. There are also 20 petrochemical plants. Total also operates 15,500 service stations in 65 countries, mainly under the Total, Elf, and Elan names, again weighted toward Europe and North Africa. The downstream presence is also growing in Asia-Pacific (including China), Latin America, and the Caribbean. The company now has a leading market presence in those regions.

Total also has ventures in alternative energy, notably solar. It owns a 65 percent interest in global solar leader Sunpower, making it the number two solar operator in the world. With two major partners it brought online in 2013, it also has an interest in what is thought to be the world's largest concentrated solar power plant at 100 megawatts in Abu Dhabi. The company started an initiative known as Awango to sell solar-powered lamps in remote regions of Indonesia and Africa along with traditional energy products.

Financial Highlights, Fiscal Year 2015

World energy price declines and slack emerging market demand led to a very challenging year in FY2015. Revenues dropped a full 26 percent—a figure not as bad as some in the industry—and earnings dropped 60 percent with asset write-downs. The strategy, again like many, is to improve operational efficiencies, reduce capital expenditures, sell assets, and fine-tune the relatively more prosperous downstream operations. With these in mind and a modest forecasted oil price increase by 2017, the company predicts flat revenues in 2016 with a partial earnings recovery, then a more substantial 15–20 percent revenue and a strong 40–45 percent earnings gain for FY2017 as margins improve. Dividends should continue to flow adequately.

Reasons to Buy

We think that good management and geographic positioning will help this giant lead the way in an eventual recovery, which should pick up steam in 2017. As oil prices rebound (and we think they will gradually), efficiencies gained through this "crisis" will bear more fruit in the future. We like their branding and dominance in the key worldwide markets they serve. Total has done better than most "big oils" in reserve replacement. The down cycle in the oil business offers a good buying opportunity for those who can stomach the ups and downs; we think long-term prospects are bright for a solid recovery, persistent and growing cash returns, and growth beyond that.

Reasons for Caution

This year's review—and downsides—are pretty much the same. Clearly, the current situation is a test of our patience and appetites for risk, and it appears likely to continue into FY2017, although we do view the year as a recovery year. Generally, the level of risk is higher with (1) oil prices, (2) dollar versus euro fluctuations, and (3) international tensions. More aggression on Russia's part, both militarily and economically, would add risk to a situation already destabilized by the usual Middle East tensions, European economic softness, and European Central Bank adventures. Finally, the company appears to be taking on more long-term debt to get it through the bump.

More generally, we remain cautious on investing in foreign companies because of differences in management style and accounting rules; they aren't necessarily bad but are difficult to understand and follow. Antiquated

European pension rules and other labor practices could also be a disadvantage. All of these risks and downsides appear to be priced into the stock as of early 2016, but Total would not qualify as one of our "sleep at night" stocks. However, we still think the rewards outweigh the risks for now.

SECTOR: **Energy** ❑ BETA COEFFICIENT: **1.20** ❑ 10-YEAR COMPOUND EARNINGS PER-SHARE
GROWTH: **7.0%** ❑ 10-YEAR COMPOUND DIVIDENDS PER-SHARE GROWTH: **8.0%**

	2008	2009	2010	2011	2012	2013	2014	2015
Revenues (bil)	236	157	186	216	234	228	212	143
Net income (bil)	18.2	11.6	14.0	15.9	15.9	14.2	12.8	5.1
Earnings per share	8.55	5.31	6.24	7.05	7.01	6.28	5.63	2.19
Dividends per share	3.10	3.28	2.93	3.12	2.98	3.10	3.21	2.73
Cash flow per share	12.42	9.49	11.25	11.37	12.46	11.57	10.90	9.76
Price: high	91.3	66.0	67.5	64.4	57.1	62.4	74.2	55.9
low	42.6	42.9	43.1	40.0	41.8	45.9	48.4	40.9

Website: www.total.com

CONSERVATIVE GROWTH

Union Pacific Corporation

Ticker symbol: UNP (NYSE) ❑ S&P rating: A ❑ Value Line financial strength rating: A++ ❑ Current yield: 2.8% ❑ Dividend raises, past 10 years: 10

Company Profile

Welcome to yet another stock that has been dinged by the commodity bust. Welcome to another excellent business that we think will prosper—perhaps better than before—for investors with patience. Climb on board . . .

Union Pacific has been a familiar name and logo in the railroad business since its inception during the Civil War. With about 32,000 miles of track covering 23 states in the western two-thirds of the United States, today's Union Pacific Railroad, the primary subsidiary of the Union Pacific Corporation, describes itself as "America's Premier Railroad Franchise." The route system is anchored by Gulf Coast and West Coast ports and areas in between and has coordinated schedules and gateways with other lines in the eastern U.S., Canada, and Mexico.

With 10,000 customers, a large number in today's era of trainload-sized shipments, UNP has a more diversified customer and revenue mix than the other rail companies, including the other three of the "big four" railroads: Burlington Northern Santa Fe, Norfolk Southern, and CSX. Energy (mainly Powder River Basin and Colorado) accounts for 16 percent of revenues (down from 18 percent, more in a moment); Intermodal (trucks or containers on flatcars), 20 percent; Agricultural, 17 percent; Industrial, 19 percent; Chemicals, 16 percent; and Automotive, 11 percent of FY2015 revenues. These figures represent a continued shift away from coal and autos and toward agriculture and industrial, following industry trends and reflecting an even more diversified traffic base and a probable gain in market share versus trucking.

The company has long been an innovator in railroad technology, including motive power, communications and technology automation, physical plant, community relations, and marketing. The company functions with the lowest operating ratio in the industry, 63.2 percent, meaning that operating costs account for 63.2 percent of revenue (63.5 percent in FY2014, 65.0 percent in FY2013, 67.8 percent in FY2012, 70.6 percent in FY2011—you can see the trend). This allows a solid contribution to the substantial fixed costs of owning and running a railroad. This success has translated to continued strong operating margins, which of course have helped earnings and cash flows and in turn have funded physical plant improvements and shareholder returns over time.

The company also invests a lot in marketing and community relations. One example is the steam-powered "Heritage Fleet" excursion train program, through which the company operates excursions with vintage equipment on selected lines. Literally thousands of people (and current and prospective customers) gather trackside in every town along the way as these beautiful trains roll through. The company recently began a five-year program to restore a "Big Boy" steam locomotive, the largest ever used in regular service (of course, for the UP originally), for a Golden Spike sesquicentennial rollout in 2019. Such public relations efforts show an extraordinary measure of pride, and an appreciation for heritage and community. We continue to applaud this effort.

Railroads have quietly been learning to use technology to improve operations and deliver better customer service. New tools can track shipments door-to-door using GPS-based technology, and the railroad will accept shipments and manage them door-to-door, even over other railroads or with other kinds of carriers. Customers can check rates and routes and track shipments online. These services have led to a continuing migration from trucks back to rail and intermodal rail services.

Financial Highlights, Fiscal Year 2015

The company was already dealing pretty well with the shift away from coal. But one major coal replacement was oil, and that has now fallen on hard times, too. The strong dollar and high supply-chain inventory levels are now eating away at intermodal shipments while lower emerging market demand has hurt agricultural and chemical shipments. Translation—all commodity groups are lagging, which is bad if you're in the railroad business—only automotive has been stronger due in part to expanded production in Mexico.

All of this led to a 9 percent drop in FY2015 revenues and a similar drop in earnings.

In this time of significant headwinds, the good news really lies in the payoff from previous investments in physical plant and equipment, which continue to deliver operating efficiencies. The drop in operating ratio in five years from 70.6 percent to 63.2 percent is remarkable and probably an industry first—and most of this efficiency drops straight to the bottom line. Forecasts call for continued weakness both on the revenue and profit front for FY2016 with 4–5 percent declines expected, with a rebound beginning in FY2017. Earnings should recover to near pre-downturn levels. Cash flows remain strong and should support persistent buybacks; the company has retired 20 percent of its shares since 2009, but whether it keeps its strong dividend increase record intact remains to be seen.

Reasons to Buy

Put simply—whether or not you enjoy watching trains, this company had been as exciting as any tech stock, and it has also returned plenty of cash to shareholders. Now it hits a soft spot—but will it emerge stronger than ever? We think so.

UNP is an extraordinarily well-managed company and has become more efficient and at the same time more user friendly to its customers and to the general public. The company continues to make gains at the expense of the trucking industry, and new short- and long-distance intermodal services move higher-valued goods more quickly and cost-effectively; we see a steady shift toward this business. The company has a solid and diverse traffic base and continues to have a good brand and reputation in the industry. The company got an early start expanding and modernizing its physical plant and technology base; that has paid off well and will continue to do so.

Reasons for Caution

No doubt, the breadth and depth of the downturn is strong. Railroads are chiefly a commodity-hauling business, and when commodities are down, they suffer. Coal shipment volumes were off as much as 26 percent during 2015. Worse, some of the higher-value traffic, like China imports, is soft too. The company is getting hit on almost all fronts right now, and depending on previous efficiencies and sound management to get them through. We think they will succeed in the long run, but when does the "long run" finally come to prevail?

Railroads are and will always be economically sensitive because of commodity revenue and their high fixed-cost structure. They also have significant headline risk—a single event like a derailment or spill can put them in a bad public eye or worse, tangle them up in regulation, lawsuits, and unplanned costs. Regulation and mandates for Positive Train Control and other safety features can be expensive. Another longer-term factor may be the widening of the Panama Canal, which may shift some Asian import/ export traffic to southern and eastern ports and away from the West Coast.

Railroads will always struggle to put the right amount of capacity on the ground—too little causes service problems and delays; too much eats into profits. Right now, UNP is dealing with "too much," but, while budgets are trimmed, capital improvements are still going in for the long term.

SECTOR: **Transportation** ▫ BETA COEFFICIENT: **1.02** ▫ 10-YEAR COMPOUND EARNINGS PER-SHARE GROWTH: **20.0%** ▫ 10-YEAR COMPOUND DIVIDENDS PER-SHARE GROWTH: **21.0%**

	2008	2009	2010	2011	2012	2013	2014	2015
Revenues (mil)	17,970	14,143	16,965	19,557	20,926	21,953	23,988	21,813
Net income (mil)	2,338	1,826	2,780	3,292	3,943	4,388	5,180	4,702
Earnings per share	2.27	1.81	2.77	3.36	4.14	4.71	5.75	5.41
Dividends per share	0.47	0.54	0.66	0.97	1.25	1.48	1.91	2.20
Cash flow per share	3.70	3.24	4.34	5.11	6.07	6.76	8.02	7.91
Price: high	42.9	33.4	47.9	53.9	64.6	84.1	123.6	124.5
low	20.9	16.6	30.2	38.9	52.0	63.7	82.5	74.8

Website: www.up.com

CONSERVATIVE GROWTH

United Parcel Service, Inc.

Ticker symbol: UPS (NYSE) □ S&P rating: A+ □ Value Line financial strength rating: A □ Current yield: 3.0% □ Dividend raises, past 10 years: 10

Company Profile

UPS is the world's largest integrated ground and air package delivery carrier. UPS and rival FedEx have converged on the same business from different directions—FedEx being an air company getting ever more into the ground business; UPS being a ground business taking to the air. That convergence is now nearly complete. Both companies continue to build international capabilities, invest in technology to track shipments, and provide logistics services beyond basic assortments of transportation services. UPS derives just over 62 percent of revenues from U.S. package operations, 22 percent from international, and 16 percent from Supply Chain & Freight, an assortment of bundled logistics and supply-chain services and solutions. The company operates 649 aircraft and 106,000 ground vehicles ("package cars"), most of the familiar brown variety. They serve more than 220 countries with an assortment of priority to deferred services, with 154,000 domestic and international entry points including 39,000 drop boxes, 1,600 customer service centers, and 4,800 independently owned "UPS Store" (formerly "Mailboxes Etc.") storefronts.

Once thought to be old-fashioned and averse to innovation, the company has invested in sophisticated package-tracking systems and links for customers to tie into them. An example is My Choice, which allows a customer to control the timing of deliveries mid-service—by smartphone if they choose—so no more waiting half a day at home for a delivery that might come anytime (hallelujah!), a nice perk for a consumer waiting for an e-commerce shipment as well as a savings for the company, avoiding multiple delivery attempts and possible door-front theft. The company is also creating specialized logistics services for vertical markets, such as the auto industry "Autogistics" and the healthcare industry, retail, high tech, and more.

The company has embarked on numerous revenue and cost-optimization campaigns, among them a detailed analysis of the cost drivers for their businesses. As an example, they report that one mile saved in their Small Package Pickup & Delivery business across all delivery routes would save $50 million per year; one minute saved would save $14.6 million per year, and one minute of idle time reduced would save $515K. From this point, the company is working to improve these metrics one step at a time through technologies and analytics designed to predict and optimize route selection and other aspects of the delivery network. One such project, called "Orion," is dubbed as the "world's largest operations research project."

Financial Highlights, Fiscal Year 2015

Economic recovery, stronger e-commerce business, price hikes, a shift to air volume, and a decent holiday season after operational and capacity fumbles in the previous two years were offset by weaker industrial shipments to lead to a virtually flat revenue year for FY2015. Lower fuel costs, a favorable shipment mix, and operational improvements produced a healthy 12 percent gain in net income. Although economic uncertainties may ding the forecast, current projections call for revenue gains in the 3–7 percent range with similar earnings gains through FY2017. The continued shift to e-commerce and especially air-oriented services such as Amazon Prime are key drivers of these gains. Attaining critical mass in this dispersed "B2C" business is probably at hand—which will boost margins and earnings. Gradual share buybacks should also help.

Reasons to Buy

The "fastest ship in the shipping business" continues to also be one of the most stable; UPS continues to position itself as the standard logistics provider of the world. The mainstay businesses are cyclical but sound; the emerging e-commerce business is gaining critical mass (volumes rising to the point of optimal efficiency) and will lead to better capacity utilization overall. E-commerce will become a bread-and-butter business as more Millennials take to the Internet as a first choice in shopping. UPS is well positioned to be a key "picks and shovels" provider for this trend—no matter who in the e-commerce business strikes gold, UPS will sell the freight service.

In general, we applaud the use of technology to get "details" right on the operational front.

We are also fans of its logistics and supply-chain management businesses and the many innovations in that space, as the push for many customers to optimize this part of their business will lead them to UPS's front door.

Reasons for Caution

Competition in this industry is fierce. The Postal Service is getting more aggressive in marketing its small-package and logistics services as it sees the writing on the wall for traditional mail services, and rival FedEx has made gains on UPS's traditional turf. Also of note is Amazon's saber rattling to get into the freight business itself—apparently they have started acquiring aircraft and assets in the ocean freight business. We think they would have a long way to go to displace the well-established supply-chain network of a UPS or a FedEx, but their actions (or threat) could force price concessions, and Amazon has been known to be surprisingly successful when attacking adjacent markets (like cloud computing). Labor relations and pension funding both bear watching. Of course, fuel prices are a wild card, and can turn back upward at any time.

SECTOR: Transportation ◻ BETA COEFFICIENT: 0.89 ◻ 10-YEAR COMPOUND EARNINGS PER-SHARE GROWTH: 6.5% ◻ 10-YEAR COMPOUND DIVIDENDS PER-SHARE GROWTH: 10.5%

	2008	2009	2010	2011	2012	2013	2014	2015
Revenues (mil)	51,466	45,297	49,545	53,105	54,127	55,438	58,232	58,363
Net income (mil)	3,581	2,318	3,570	4,213	4,389	4,372	4,389	4,923
Earnings per share	3.50	2.31	3.56	4.25	4.53	4.61	4.75	5.43
Dividends per share	1.77	1.80	1.88	2.08	2.28	2.48	2.68	2.92
Cash flow per share	5.42	4.09	5.43	6.60	6.90	6.75	6.97	7.87
Price: high	75.1	59.5	73.9	77.0	84.9	105.4	113.1	114.4
low	43.3	38.0	55.6	60.7	75.0	75.0	93.2	93.6

Website: www.ups.com

CONSERVATIVE GROWTH

United Technologies Corporation

Ticker symbol: UTX (NYSE) ◻ S&P rating: A ◻ Value Line financial strength rating: A++ ◻ Current yield: 2.4% ◻ Dividend raises, past 10 years: 10

Company Profile

United Technologies is a large and diversified provider of mostly high-technology products to the aerospace and building systems industries throughout the world, selling to an assortment of mostly commercial and public sector customers. To many, it is an aerospace company, to others it is a producer of key pieces, parts, and systems for the building industry; to most investors it is a broadly diversified industrial conglomerate.

In 2015, the organizational sands continued to shift at UTX, with a management shakeup and the long-awaited sale of the Sikorsky helicopter unit. That turned out to be a good move as helicopter demand has crash-landed with the decline in offshore drilling and the necessary logistical support in the oil industry. Additionally, a regime change that started in 2014 has led to a fairly vast restructuring, reorganizing, and streamlining of existing assets, which is still in progress. Then, if that wasn't enough, in 2015 and again in early 2016 Honeywell (another *100 Best* stock) made a $90 billion merger offer for the company, which was turned down mostly citing "regulatory concerns." This offer underscored the underlying value of the company and likely has stimulated management to continue its streamlining; we would expect more of the same and probably more restructuring, including asset sales and/or acquisitions, to occur into the 2017 time frame. That sets the stage; we'll return to describing the company and its now four current business units:

- UTC Propulsion & Aerospace (25 percent of FY2015 revenues) produces aircraft electrical power generation and distribution systems; engine and flight controls; propulsion systems; environmental controls for aircraft, spacecraft, and submarines; auxiliary power units; space life-support systems; and industrial products including mechanical power transmissions, compressors, metering devices, and fluid handling equipment. It also provides product support and maintenance and offers repair services.

- Pratt & Whitney (25 percent) produces large and small commercial and military jet engines, spare parts, rocket engines and space propulsion systems, and industrial gas turbines, and it performs product support, specialized engine maintenance and overhaul, and repair services for airlines, air forces, and corporate fleets.

- UTC Climate, Controls & Security (formerly Building & Industrial Systems—30 percent) produces heating, ventilating, and air conditioning (HVAC) equipment for commercial, industrial, and residential buildings; HVAC replacement parts and services; building controls; and commercial, industrial, and transport refrigeration equipment, much of it under the "Carrier" brand name. The group also includes the old UTC Fire and Security business, which provides security and fire protection systems; integration, installation, and servicing of intruder alarms, access control, and video surveillance and monitoring; response and security personnel services; and installation and servicing of fire detection and suppression systems.

- Otis (21 percent) is one of UTX's most recognizable brands. It designs and manufactures elevators, escalators, moving walkways, and shuttle systems, and performs related installation, maintenance, and repair services; it also provides modernization products and service for elevators and escalators.

The company continues to provide another useful breakdown to help understand its businesses with the Sikorsky disposition and other changes:

- Commercial & Industrial: 52 percent (was 45 percent)
- Commercial Aerospace: 36 percent (was 35 percent)
- Military Aerospace & Space: 12 percent (was 25 percent)

These figures reflect the sale of Sikorsky and other changes, and reveal that UTX is not as tied to military and government contracts as many think. About 62 percent of sales are outside the U.S.

Financial Highlights, Fiscal Year 2015
Restructuring, the Sikorsky sale, currency effects, and emerging market softness led to a mixed FY2015 performance difficult to compare to previous years. If you add back the Sikorsky business (about 10 percent of FY2014 sales) you arrive at a 3.8 percent top-line decrease FY2015 versus FY2014. The bottom line did not decrease as much as the top line as a percentage, reflecting greater profitability in the remaining mix. With all the changes on the table, it's more useful to look at forward projections, which call for a 3 percent per-share earnings gain on largely flat revenue performance in 2016 and a heftier 7–8 percent per-share gain on a 3–5 percent revenue increase in 2017. Gross and net margins will grow through the period as efficiency measures take hold. Cash returns to shareholders will be led by high single-digit dividend increases over the period; as the company consolidates over the next two years buybacks will diminish but should return to the table in 2017 and thereafter.

Reasons to Buy
UTX has been a question mark for the last couple of years (especially with peers Honeywell and GE already on our *100 Best* list) and with the relatively tumultuous management and business structure and soft earnings performance. Once again, based on how the business mix is evolving and, frankly, the fact that Honeywell and others have seen value in this business for years, we'll keep UTX on the table for at least one more year.

UTX is a classic conglomerate play and is becoming more focused on good commercial (and non-military) businesses. The recent surge in the airline industry will help the business going forward. The company's brands, particularly Otis, are well-known and very well supported worldwide, and a return of strength in global construction should help its two largest businesses.

We think the company has seen the worst of its recent instability and will hunker down to get the most out of its businesses with or without the influence of a potential acquisition. Like many similar businesses, the prospect of acquisition speeds up necessary transformations—and the company was already well on its way to a more efficient form, a pattern commenced in the dark days of the Great Recession. Cash flow is solid and cash returns are growing.

Reasons for Caution

Instability is good because it fosters necessary change, and it is bad because it distracts management from what it really should be doing. There's a little of both going on here. The company is still sensitive to construction, and construction may not be out of the woods yet and there is plenty of competition in most of its construction businesses. If the recent airline boom falters, that too could bring UTX back to earth. While Goodrich (acquired in 2012) was a good fit, we would hope the company doesn't get too intoxicated with acquisitions, and we would especially hope it doesn't pursue a *large* acquisition for the sake of making itself harder to acquire. Like all conglomerates, UTX is a very complex business to manage. It can also be vulnerable to headline risk, such as aviation accidents resulting from failure of its jet engines.

SECTOR: **Industrials** ❑ BETA COEFFICIENT: **1.11** ❑ 10-YEAR COMPOUND EARNINGS PER-SHARE GROWTH: **9.0%** ❑ 10-YEAR COMPOUND DIVIDENDS PER-SHARE GROWTH: **12.5%**

	2008	2009	2010	2011	2012	2013	2014	2015
Revenues (mil)	58,681	52,920	54,326	58,190	57,708	62,626	65,100	56,098
Net income (mil)	4,689	3,829	4,373	4,979	4,840	5,685	6,220	5,563
Earnings per share	4.90	4.12	4.74	5.49	5.34	6.21	6.82	6.29
Dividends per share	1.55	1.54	1.70	1.87	2.03	2.20	2.36	2.56
Cash flow per share	6.38	5.43	6.22	6.97	6.93	8.19	8.94	8.86
Price: high	77.1	70.9	79.7	91.8	87.5	113.9	120.7	124.4
low	41.8	37.4	62.9	66.9	70.7	92.1	97.2	85.5

Website: www.utc.com

AGGRESSIVE GROWTH

UnitedHealth Group, Inc.

Ticker symbol: UNH (NYSE) ❑ S&P rating: A- ❑ Value Line financial strength rating: A++ ❑ Current yield: 1.6% ❑ Dividend raises, past 10 years: 6

Company Profile

UnitedHealth Group is the parent company of a number of health insurers and service organizations. It is the largest publicly traded health insurance company in the United States, with more than $155 billion in revenue reported in 2015 and a Number 14 ranking on the *Fortune* 500 list.

The company has reorganized and rebranded part of its business and now operates in two major business segments: UnitedHealthcare (health insurance and benefits) and Optum (health services), which, combined, touch about 78 million people worldwide in 50 U.S. states and 125 countries globally.

UnitedHealthcare provides traditional and Medicare-based health benefit and insurance plans for individuals and employers, covering approximately 30 million individuals, with about 400 national employer accounts and 190,000 other smaller employer accounts. The company estimates that it serves more than half of the *Fortune* 100 companies list. The company, mainly through this unit, has been an active acquirer of other familiar healthcare and insurance brands, including Oxford Health in 2004, PacifiCare in 2005, Sierra Health Plans and Unison Health Plans in 2008, AIM Healthcare Services in 2009, and more recently an assortment of small, mostly Medicare-related providers. The UnitedHealthcare insurance business in total accounts for 66 percent of FY2015 revenues and 61 percent of profits.

The UnitedHealthcare business unit actively markets traditional individual and employee health plans, and is also very active in the senior and military market, with a growing assortment of Medicare Advantage, Medicare Part D, and Medicare supplement plans. Revenues in this subsegment accounted for 37 percent of UNH's total business. The recently added TRICARE insurance program for active and retired military is another large subsegment. It is a $3 billion business at present and will grow as a five-year transition plan moves forward.

The "other side" of the business is its health services businesses, which it markets under the Optum brand umbrella. This segment, which touches some 78 million customers, is far and away big enough to be a separate company and is an increasingly important part of the overall UNH business offering. Optum delivers service through three separate businesses. OptumHealth is an "information and technology"–based health population management solution, deploying mostly remote telesupport for well care, mental health, ongoing disease management, and substance abuse programs. The OptumRx business is a pharmacy benefits provider serving 60 million customers and a network of 67,000 pharmacies and other outlets with about 600 million prescriptions annually, while OptumInsight is a management information, analytics, and process-improvement arm providing an assortment of services for health plans, physicians, hospitals, and life science research, formerly marketed under the Ingenix brand. Of the total Optum-branded business of $67 billion (41 percent ahead of FY2014), Rx accounts for the lion's share at $48 billion, while OptumHealth, which grew 26 percent in FY2015, weighs in at $14 billion and OptumInsight at $6.2 billion with 18 percent annual growth. Although these numbers may seem small in the context of UNH's total $157 billion annual revenue footprint, they are sizeable businesses when looked at individually; all would be sizeable and significant standalone businesses. The Optum umbrella brand is gaining in prominence, and even has its own unique web presence at www.optum.com.

UnitedHealth Group has been a leader in process, delivery, and cost improvement and a recognized innovator in the industry. Currently, while not participating in all Affordable Care Act exchanges—and threatening to reduce its participation—the company is learning to adapt to the new environment and has moved aggressively to offer tools to manage and contain costs in the healthcare system, mostly through the Optum business. The company sits on top of a mountain of healthcare data and is putting it to good use, and has emerged as a leader in developing remote and preventative care models.

Financial Highlights, Fiscal Year 2015

Increasingly favorable performance from the Optum units, each of which grew by 19 percent or more, and due to a better revenue and cost environment for traditional insurance (ACA excepted) and the acquisition of Catamaran on the Optum Rx (pharmacy benefits) side, drove a 20 percent year-over-year revenue gain for FY2015 but only a 6 percent earnings increase due in part to the ACA business. Revenues are forecast ahead another 15 percent in FY2016 and 7–9 percent in FY2017, with earnings gains in the 20–25 percent range in FY2016 and the 10–15 percent range in FY2017 as margins improve and volumes expand across all business fronts.

Dividend growth prospects are equally healthy, and share repurchase, while attenuated somewhat from 2014, should chip in as well.

Reasons to Buy

This bellwether company is one of the most solid, diverse, and innovative enterprises in the health insurance industry. Health insurers such as Aetna, included on our *100 Best* list, seem to be getting past many of the fears of reform and other contrary public opinion; these companies by design simply pass costs through but are doing more to control and reduce costs through utilization management and other initiatives, and these efforts are paying off. Too, the scale of UNH's operation gives it tremendous leverage when negotiating for the services of healthcare providers.

Meanwhile, like Aetna, UNH brings a fair amount of innovation to the marketplace, primarily through its Optum offerings. We like its initiatives to make use of its own "big data" with analytics; the size of its database and the tools it possesses can deliver efficiency improvements, and even slight efficiency improvements can help the bottom line substantially. If price competition eventually dictates lower premiums, UNH will be in good position with cost-side improvements.

Reasons for Caution

The outcomes of the Affordable Care Act—and even UNH's participation in it—are still not certain on both the cost and the revenue side; like others, the company is stepping through these changes at a deliberate pace while the final impact on the business is far from clear. The company is vulnerable to shifts in public opinion and to new regulation, as well as economic downturns, which can hurt employer participation. The company also has demonstrated a fairly aggressive acquisition strategy in the past. If current merger plans in front of Aetna (Humana) and Anthem (Cigna) come to be, UNH will face larger competitors as a member of a new "big three"; whether this results in more competition—or less—remains to be seen. A "less" answer could bring intense public and regulatory scrutiny.

SECTOR: **Healthcare** ❑ BETA COEFFICIENT: **0.58** ❑ 10-YEAR COMPOUND EARNINGS PER-SHARE GROWTH: **14.0%** ❑ 10-YEAR COMPOUND DIVIDENDS PER-SHARE GROWTH: **58.5%**

	2008	2009	2010	2011	2012	2013	2014	2015
Revenues (bil)	87.1	87.1	94.1	101.9	110.6	122.5	130.5	157.1
Net income (mil)	3,660	3,822	4,633	5,142	5,526	5,625	5,619	5,947
Earnings per share	2.95	3.24	4.10	4.73	5.28	5.50	5.70	6.15
Dividends per share	0.03	0.03	0.41	0.61	0.80	1.05	1.41	1.88
Cash flow per share	3.86	4.20	5.25	5.86	6.67	7.09	7.44	8.02
Price: high	57.9	33.3	38.1	53.5	60.8	75.9	104.0	126.2
low	14.5	16.2	27.1	36.4	49.8	51.4	69.6	95.0

Website: www.unitedhealthgroup.com

AGGRESSIVE GROWTH

Valero Energy Corporation

Ticker symbol: VLO (NYSE) ❑ S&P rating: BBB ❑ Value Line financial strength rating: A+ ❑ Current yield: 3.8% ❑ Dividend raises, past 10 years: 9

Company Profile

Valero Energy is the largest independent oil refiner in the United States. The company owns 15 refineries and distributes primarily through a network of 7,400 retail combined gasoline stations and convenience stores throughout the United States, the U.K. and Ireland, and Canada, most of it under the Valero, Ultramar, Shamrock, Diamond Shamrock, and Texaco brands. In 2013 the company spun off the Valero-branded retail operations, mostly U.S. based, to shareholders in the form of an independent public company called CST Brands but still maintains distribution to most of these outlets, which total 1,900 in number. Aside from unlocking capital and increasing focus on refining, the separation of these businesses allows more refining sales to other channels, and allows the retailers to source from their lowest-cost supplier—improving the performance of both.

Most of the 15 Valero refineries are located in the United States, centered in the South and on the Texas Gulf Coast with others in Memphis, Oklahoma, and on the West Coast. Others are located in Quebec and Wales in the U.K. The refinery network was mostly assembled through a series of acquisitions from Diamond Shamrock in 2001; El Paso Corporation in the early 2000s; and, more recently, the Pembroke (Wales) refinery from Chevron in 2011. The refining operations produce the full gamut of hydrocarbon products: gasoline, jet fuel, diesel, asphalt, propane, base oils, solvents, aromatics, natural gas liquids, sulfur, hydrogen, middle distillates, and special fuel blends to meet California Air Resources Board requirements. The company markets these products where the refineries are located, plus in the Caribbean and in Ireland.

Valero is strictly focused on downstream operations—now just the refining portion, not retail—and owns no oil wells or production facilities. Instead, they purchase a variety of feedstocks on the open market and can adjust those purchases to market conditions while using contracts and hedging tools to manage input prices to a degree—and rail transport to get it to the refinery. About half of feedstocks are purchased under contracts, with the other half on the spot market. Most of these refineries are legacy operations and have been in place for many years, as far back as 1908. The company has invested heavily in upgrading these refineries to improve capacity, efficiency, and environmental compliance and in recent years has grown its utilization rates to a strong 87 percent. The company has also added capacity in two plants to produce high-quality distillates from low-quality feedstocks and natural gas.

The company is increasing its activities in transportation and logistics, where it already owns key pipelines—by adding approximately 4,100 rail cars to its fleet as part of a 5,300-car expansion, all using the new accident-resistant designs. While oversupply, relatively higher-cost "fracked" crude, and a lifting of a 40-year-old U.S. export ban have disrupted logistics patterns recently, this logistics flexibility represents a key strategy toward optimizing input costs. The company now imports about half the amount of crude that it did back in 2006.

Bulk sales to other retail outlets, commercial distributors, and large-end customers like airlines and railroads are also important. The company also owns and operates 11 ethanol plants in the U.S. Midwest, producing and shipping 1.3 billion gallons per year, and a 50 percent interest in a 10,500 barrels-per-day renewable diesel plant.

Financial Highlights, Fiscal Year 2015

Lower fuel prices reduced FY2015 revenue by about a third, but what's really important in this type of business is profits—the difference between revenue and costs. Lower oil prices led to another dramatic increase in net margins (from 2.8 percent to 4.5 percent)—small numbers but huge impact, especially considering the 1.5–1.7 percent "run rate" for several years before that. As such, net income rose a healthy 9 percent, and with a substantial 7 percent share buyback, per-share earnings rose 17 percent. Revenues stand to lag again in FY2016 and FY2017 as energy prices continue to languish. Earnings may also stagnate a bit as captive stored domestic supply can now be exported and as oil prices gently recover amidst a current glut of gasoline and refined products. Estimates vary, but a 10 percent drop in FY2016 earnings is possible followed by some recovery in FY2017.

Overall the company continues to benefit from lower oil prices and strategic domestic and international sourcing ("strategic" because rail car shipments bind the company less to fixed sources); this looks to continue particularly as worldwide and domestic oil inventories rise. While earnings and revenues fluctuate considerably, cash flows remain exceptionally strong. Valero raised the dividend some 45 percent in early FY2015, a strong nod to projected continued success, and appears ready to raise it another 40 percent in FY2016.

Reasons to Buy

The profitability of this business, like other refining businesses, depends on the supply and cost of feedstocks and the wholesale and retail prices of finished products. In addition, the availability of refining capacity is also a factor; when markets get tight, it is extremely difficult to put another refinery on the ground to handle demand. These two factors together work very favorably for Valero—lower input costs, no new competition—it's an oligopolistic dream and should bode well for profits for years to come, especially in today's new world of crude oil (over)abundance.

Flexibility is the key, and is a key part of Valero's strategy. Rail transport provides excellent flexibility, and some say flexible methods, not fixed pipelines, are the optimal way to distribute crude from multiple sources in the future. Valero's investments in rail cars will help to capitalize on this trend.

We like Valero's leading position in the refining business, and having 15 well-distributed, efficient, and largely successful operating refineries on the ground already is a good thing. We also like the branding, abundance, look, and feel of the retail presence—even though the company no longer owns the stations outright.

Reasons for Caution

The refining business in particular is inherently volatile and complex, and what may appear today as an advantageous input and output pricing profile might disappear in a minute. Indeed, refined products are in a glut too, making future prices uncertain, and the recent allowance of crude exports makes less oil available in Valero's own back yard.

Gross, operating, and net margins can be very thin, typically in the 1–2 percent range—although much of Valero's recent success is due to breaking out of that range. Refiners also endure the headline risk of refinery mishaps, a few of which have already come Valero's way in recent years. And now we incur more risks in rail transport of crude and saw what can happen in recent mishaps (neither of which affected Valero directly). We doubt if rail shipment of crude will be shut down, but it could become more expensive as mandates for safer cars, slower speeds, track improvements, etc., come into play.

SECTOR: Energy ❑ **BETA COEFFICIENT: 2.00** ❑ **10-YEAR COMPOUND EARNINGS PER-SHARE GROWTH: 12.0%** ❑ **10-YEAR COMPOUND DIVIDENDS PER-SHARE GROWTH: 22.0%**

		2008	2009	2010	2011	2012	2013	2014	2015
Revenues (bil)		118.3	87.3	81.3	125.1	138.3	138.1	130.8	87.8
Net income (mil)		(1,131)	(352)	923	2,097	2,083	2,395	3,630	3,990
Earnings per share		(2.16)	(0.65)	1.62	3.69	3.75	4.37	6.85	7.99
Dividends per share		0.57	0.60	0.20	0.30	0.65	0.85	1.05	1.70
Cash flow per share		0.67	1.91	4.10	6.52	6.60	7.65	10.47	12.25
Price:	high	71.1	26.2	23.7	31.1	34.5	50.5	59.7	73.9
	low	13.9	16.3	15.5	16.4	16.1	33.0	42.5	43.4

Website: www.valero.com

AGGRESSIVE GROWTH

Valmont Industries, Inc.

Ticker symbol: VMI (NYSE) ❑ S&P rating: BBB ❑ Value Line financial strength rating: A+ ❑ Current yield: 1.3% ❑ Dividend raises, past 10 years: 10

Company Profile

Those of you who read our work annually probably recall that engineered infrastructure and specialty products Valmont Industries was called on the carpet last year as a cyclical perfect storm performance ding to our 2015 *100 Best Stocks* portfolio. When a company gets called on the carpet we review carefully to try to separate cyclical downside perfect storms—particularly when they follow upside perfect storms—to see whether the fundamental business, and its future prospects, have changed.

The answer was "no" last year. And now you see the company on our *100 Best* list again, despite another very lackluster—no, pretty darned negative—year. Once again we ask the questions: Has the business changed? Has the business model been disrupted? Has the company lost a key position in its marketplace? Have its products been commoditized? Has it restructured itself or acquired its way into mediocrity or excess complexity?

The short answers again: "No, no, no, no, and no." We continue to like Valmont's market leadership and niche strength in what we see as important end markets, and we're still calling on that strength to pull Valmont through to higher ground starting in 2017 and possibly sooner—especially as the company like many in such straits has taken measures to become more efficient in the interim.

Valmont Industries was founded in 1946 as a supplier of irrigation products and became one of the classic postwar industrial success stories, growing along with the need for increased farm output. It was an early pioneer of the center-pivot irrigation system, which enabled much of that growth and now dominates the high-yield agricultural business. These machines remain a mainstay of this most profitable product line. But the company has expanded on that core expertise in galvanized metal to make such familiar infrastructure items as light poles, cell phone towers, and those familiar high-tension electric towers that crisscross the landscape, and to provide such galvanizing services to other product manufacturers.

Valmont separated its energy and mining infrastructure products business away from its Engineered Infrastructure Products unit and now operates in five instead of four segments. Products and product lines now include:

- Engineered Support Structure products (28 percent of FY2015 revenues, 24 percent of operating incomes)—Lighting poles, including decorative lighting poles, guard rails, towers, and other metal structures used in lighting, communications, traffic management, wireless phone carriers, and other applications. Products are available as standard designs and engineered for custom applications as needed for industrial, commercial, and residential applications. If you've ever sat at a stoplight and wondered how a single cantilevered arm could support four 400-pound traffic signals, these are the folks to ask.
- Utility Support Structures (26 percent, 21 percent)—This segment produces the very large concrete and steel substations and electric transmission support towers used by electric utilities. We like this unit's prospects

as utility infrastructure is replaced and modernized in the interest of grid efficiency, and now, aesthetic and environmental sensibility.

- Irrigation (23 percent, 33 percent)—Under the Valley brand name, Valmont produces a wide range of equipment, including gravity and drip products, as well as its center-pivot designs, which can service up to 500 acres from a single machine. Valmont also sells its irrigation controllers to other manufacturers.

- Energy and Mining (13 percent, 5 percent)—Produces a series of products once mostly found in the Engineered Infrastructure Products segment but includes tubing and piping products, conveyance systems, grinding products, grates and screens for separation, windmill towers, and parts and products for human access like walkways and stair structures.

- Coatings (10 percent, 18 percent)—Developed as an adjunct to its other metal products businesses, the coatings business now provides services such as galvanizing, electroplating, powder coating, and anodizing to industrial customers throughout the company's operating areas.

The company is a market leader in a number of segments including irrigation, power transmission poles, highway infrastructure, and certain coated products.

Financial Highlights, Fiscal Year 2015

Cyclical slowdowns in manufacturing activity, utility replacement, agriculture, emerging market economies, and energy and mining in particular dogged 2015 results, along with the usual currency effects. Revenues dropped another 16 percent after a 5 percent dip in FY2014, and with decreased volumes, earnings suffered a far greater 78 percent decline.

This is a deep cycle and follows a "perfect storm" to the upside, where all business units were clicking in 2012 and 2013. Although the company has been conservative with its forecasts, there are initiatives to improve business in all segments, cut costs, and generally leverage number one positions to deliver more strength in a recovery. That said the company isn't looking for 2013-sized results in the next few years. Revenues are expected to start modestly to the upside in 2017 with a stronger recovery in earnings to 2014 levels by 2018. The real upside comes beyond that year as the cycles recover and volumes, prices, and margins improve. Dividend and buyback activity will probably be steady state until the recovery takes hold.

Reasons to Buy

Admittedly you might need the strength of one of those traffic signal arms to stay with this issue, but once again, we think long term when we make (and keep) *100 Best* picks. We remain attracted to the fundamental strengths of Valmont and its core businesses, and in particular their strategic importance to the interests of agriculture, water conservation, and infrastructure.

As much as anything we continue to view Valmont as a key infrastructure play. America's infrastructure needs to be replaced, as does infrastructure in much of the developed world. As for the less-developed world, that infrastructure needs to be built in the first place. We think, long term, that Valmont is in the right place to capture a decent share of this replacement business, including electric utility infrastructure—which in particular may be moving away from the traditional wooden telephone pole (as it has in most of the rest of the world) and as more aesthetic high tension power poles come into favor. The original irrigation business should also do well in the long term as global food consumption increases and as agriculture, farmland, and farm commodity prices eventually strengthen—and as droughts in key "ag" markets like California persist. The company's continued emphasis on growth into new geographies should pay dividends as India and China begin to build infrastructure and adopt more modern agricultural methods. We also like the relatively simple, straightforward nature of this business and the way the company presents itself online and in shareholder documents.

Reasons for Caution

Of course, we could be wrong about the cyclical perfect storm call and the long-term fundamentals of Valmont's businesses. The relatively small size and deep, large-scale manufacturing infrastructure of a company like Valmont makes it more vulnerable to cyclical weakness—although steadier public sector demand mitigates that somewhat. Valmont presents plenty of long-term opportunity in our view, but that doesn't come without some risk.

SECTOR: **Industrials** ❑ BETA COEFFICIENT: **1.10** ❑ 10-YEAR COMPOUND EARNINGS PER-SHARE GROWTH: **17.5%** ❑ 10-YEAR COMPOUND DIVIDENDS PER-SHARE GROWTH: **15.0%**

	2008	2009	2010	2011	2012	2013	2014	2015
Revenues (mil)	1,907	1,787	1,975	2,661	3,029	3,304	3,123	2,619
Net income (mil)	132.4	155.0	109.7	158.0	234.1	278.5	184.0	40.0
Earnings per share	5.04	5.70	4.15	5.97	8.75	10.35	7.09	1.71
Cash flow per share	6.57	7.43	6.46	8.80	11.40	13.27	11.39	5.74
Dividends per share	0.50	0.58	0.65	0.72	0.88	0.98	1.38	1.50
Price: high	120.5	89.3	90.3	116.0	141.2	164.9	163.2	129.1
low	37.5	37.5	65.3	73.0	90.2	129.0	116.7	92.3

Website: www.valmont.com

GROWTH AND INCOME

Verizon Communications Inc.

Ticker symbol: VZ (NYSE) ❑ S&P rating: BBB+ ❑ Value Line financial strength rating: A++ ❑ Current yield: 4.5% ❑ Dividend raises, past 10 years: 9

Company Profile

Verizon operates two telecommunications businesses: Domestic Wireless, which provides wireless voice and data services, and Wireline, which provides voice, broadband data and video, Internet access, long-distance, and other services, and which owns and operates a large global Internet protocol network. The wireless business represents about 67 percent of total revenues; Wireline about 33 percent. As we'll get to shortly, the company's data and cloud computing business is one of its more exciting prospects.

In the consumer space, the Wireline segment also supplies Verizon's fiber-to-the-home (FiOS) broadband data infrastructure. One of Verizon's largest investments, FiOS provides a very high bandwidth link to the Internet, easily surpassing DSL and even cable. Over this network, Verizon can provide hundreds of HD video streams, high-speed data, and voice all simultaneously. This service competes head-to-head with AT&T's (a *100 Best* stock) U-verse and Comcast's (another *100 Best* stock) Xfinity services among others.

The Domestic Wireless segment is served by the now wholly owned Verizon Wireless, the largest wireless carrier in the United States (approximately 300 million in population coverage and 110 million customers in service), and international coverage in 19 countries. The wireless side of the business has been rolling out its new LTE mobile broadband network, a leading-edge 4G network designed to be ten times faster than the standard 3G network, and now available in some 500 U.S. markets to more than 97 percent of the U.S. population.

As the company has grown its investment in fiber and other leading-edge technologies, it has been actively shedding pieces of its legacy plant—mainly the copper-based wireline services inherited in earlier acquisitions. In early 2015 the company moved to sell local wireline services in California, Florida, and Texas and to sell a big chunk of cell phone tower rights and some complete towers to American Tower. These transactions alone amount to some $15 billion and will be used for other acquisitions and to accelerate share buybacks.

Financial Highlights, Fiscal Year 2015

FY2015 for Verizon was a year much like FY2014, with steady revenue growth and much improved earnings growth, accompanied by several acquisitions and continued divestiture of non-strategic assets. And once again, top- and bottom-line figures have been a difficult read, but it's clear that VZ has things moving in the right direction with a 20 percent year-over-year jump in net profits. The disposal of some non-productive, cost-laden assets, as well as a moderate bump in subscriber numbers are two of the main drivers of this year's improved financials.

Once again, growth in 4G device installed base was particularly strong, up 23 percent to a total of 85 million. And customers are sticking around—the churn rate is the best in the industry at less than 1 percent. The FiOS business expansion continues, adding 8.6 percent in revenues.

We expected 10 percent net margins for the year, but actuals came in at 12.2 percent. Per-share earnings came in at the very top of predictions at $4.00, which is nearly a 20 percent jump from the prior year. The dividend increased a moderate 3 percent, but share buyback was a healthy 2 percent and should increase over the next few years.

Reasons to Buy

We continue to like what Verizon offers investors: a good combination of stability, financial strength, and income with a play in the growth of the "new economy" and supporting technology. After a few years of lean profit growth as the company invested in infrastructure and iPhones, earnings growth for the past two years is well ahead of top-line growth. Having built out the most robust wireless network in the business, VZ is beginning to generate additional revenue streams via this infrastructure over and above voice and data plans. We especially like the new cloud and wireless data services for the commercial market, which offer good promise and significant leverage of existing investments, and the promise of emerging services in the consumer space such as video-on-demand.

In a move that had a lot of people scratching their heads, Verizon completed the purchase of what was left of AOL. Some were surprised simply by the fact that AOL was still around, but most of us just wondered "why"? As we see it, this is a forward-looking move in the face of the coming market saturation for their existing communications business. Earnings growth in simple network provision may be peaking soon, so Verizon plans to offer something for sale on their networks. AOL brings two things to the table: content and a strong video advertising platform. Both of these are necessary components of an Internet media business, and Verizon is working to create businesses that monetize the space above the network. This is a long-term play, but we think Verizon is on the right path here.

Competing in telecommunications at this level requires large capital investments, and managing this part of the business (for better or worse) can have a large impact on the bottom line. Verizon has done this better than most as of late, especially with regard to the sale of their landline operations to Frontier Communications. Verizon's total capital investment has remained steady at roughly $90 billion for the past seven years, while their return on that capital has grown 60 percent over the same period.

The company has shown strong commitment to a much higher than average dividend compared to its competitors and most in the overall market. That dividend is very well supported out of $11.2 billion in free cash flow (FY2016), even leaving some room for growth.

Reasons for Caution

The telecommunications business is always capital intensive, and Verizon, like others, must spend heavily just to keep up with technology and competition. The business environment is extremely competitive, and Verizon's sheer size means the ship's course is not quickly changed—strategic technology investments in this business tend to be binding and long-term. Verizon's recent growth-by-acquisition strategy, essentially swapping cash for time, makes sense in their current position, but needs to be monitored lest it become an expensive habit.

Finally, the Fed seems to have sent a clear message with their rejection of not one but two attempts to buy T-Mobile that the days of large consolidation among nationwide operators are over for now. If Verizon wants new customers or expanded coverage, they'll likely have to bid and compete for them.

SECTOR: **Telecommunications Services** ◻ BETA COEFFICIENT: **0.75** ◻ 10-YEAR COMPOUND EARNINGS PER-SHARE GROWTH: **1.5%** ◻ 10-YEAR COMPOUND DIVIDENDS PER-SHARE GROWTH: **3.0%**

	2008	2009	2010	2011	2012	2013	2014	2015
Revenues (bil)	97.4	107.9	106.6	110.9	115.8	120.6	127.1	131.6
Net income (mil)	7,235	6,805	6,256	6,087	5,970	11,497	13,337	16,040
Earnings per share	2.54	2.40	2.21	2.15	2.32	4.00	3.35	3.99
Dividends per share	1.78	1.87	1.93	1.96	2.02	2.08	2.16	2.23
Cash flow per share	7.65	7.70	7.60	7.96	7.85	6.79	7.19	5.85
Price: high	44.3	34.8	36.0	40.3	48.8	54.3	53.7	50.9
low	23.1	26.1	26.0	32.3	36.8	41.5	45.1	38.1

Website: www.verizon.com

AGGRESSIVE GROWTH

Visa Inc.

Ticker symbol: V (NYSE) ◻ S&P rating: A+ ◻ Value Line financial strength rating: A++ ◻ Current yield: 0.8% ◻ Dividend raises, past 10 years: 7

Company Profile

If we wrote about a company with a 40 percent *net* profit margin—and *growing rapidly*—and a global brand that was in the business of collecting small fees on every one of the billions of transactions worldwide; a company that required almost no capital expenditures, plant, equipment, or inventory; a company that brought in almost 1.6 million dollars per employee in revenue (up from $1.3 million in 2014) and almost $750,000 per employee in net profit (the company refers to this as "people light and technology heavy"); a company growing earnings 10–30 percent a year; a company with a time-tested business model and absolutely zero long-term debt until recently (to fund an acquisition)—would you believe that it existed? Not to mention a company with a share price that rose steadily and annually from a four-for-one split adjusted to $18 in 2011 to $75 recently?

It's all true. And the company, formed in a 2007 reorganization and taken public in 2008, is Visa. Yes, the same Visa whose emblem has traditionally appeared on a majority of the world's credit cards—and now debit cards. In fact, there are about 2.5 *billion* such cards dispersed through 200 countries worldwide. The company operates the world's largest retail electronic payment network, providing processing services; payment platforms; and fraud-detection services for credit, debit, and commercial payments. The company also operates one of the largest global ATM networks with its PLUS and Interlink brands. In total, the company processes 109 billion transactions per year (which works out to about 3,500 transactions *per second*) and estimates that it can process about 15 times that amount in a peak scenario—while being operational 99.999999 percent of the time!

For years, Visa has been synonymous with credit and credit cards, but in recent years it has become more of a digital currency company, stitching together consumers, retailers, banks, and other businesses in a giant global network. Really, Visa is a global payments technology business that not only develops and supplies the technology but also collects fees upon its use.

The shift from traditional cash and check forms of payment to debit cards and other digital forms is growing at about a 12 percent annual rate, driven by the security and convenience of these transactions as well as a shift away from consumer debt to more "paid for today" debit transactions. Debit transactions now account for more than half the company's overall business volume, albeit at a small penalty, as average transaction sizes are smaller.

The company is an active innovator, with several initiatives in what it calls an "evolving payments ecosystem" and in network security. Mobile payment and mobile wallet innovations include "V.me" and "payWave" licensed products. Not surprisingly in light of recent news events, the company is also working on new payment and card security initiatives. A new platform called Visa Checkout makes it easier for merchants to integrate Visa payment into websites and mobile platforms, and the company has partnered with Apple to create new connections with Apple Pay, which should prove to be quite important going forward. A new mobile app allowing swipe-free payment at gas stations is but one example. The company is also very active in fraud prevention and into mining data to help merchants grow their businesses. All of these initiatives show how Visa thinks of itself as a data and IT company, not merely a financial firm.

The business continues to grow rapidly overseas; Visa has consolidated Visa Europe Limited into the fold via acquisition, which will close in 2016. Almost half its revenue comes from outside the U.S., far more than its rivals.

Financial Highlights, Fiscal Year 2015

Despite some international and currency headwinds, growth continued on track in FY2015. Revenues rose a healthy 9.3 percent, and net earnings rose a healthier 16 percent even with a one-time legal expense related to a 2014 payment fees dispute. Current projections call for revenue growth in the 10–15 percent range through FY2017 with commensurate gains in net earnings. The company authorized another $5.8 billion to repurchase shares—enough to retire 3–4 percent of the float—and has already retired 20 percent of its float since going public in 2008.

Reasons to Buy

"The Power of Digital Currency" continues as Visa's apt corporate mantra. Simply, it's hard to come up with a better business model—a company that develops and sells the network and collects fees every time it's used. It would be like Microsoft collecting fees every time a file is created and saved, or an e-mail platform that charges fees for every message. Visa is in a great position not only to capitalize on overall world economic growth, as most companies should be, but also to capitalize on a shift in this growth toward electronic and mobile payments. Even as debt-conscious consumers pull back on using credit cards, debit card usage continues to advance. This reinforces one of Visa's big strengths—unlike most other financial services businesses, Visa is relatively immune to downturns, as it makes its money by processing payments, not by extending credit. On the growth side, the company is expanding its footprint in emerging markets, and there is plenty of innovation opportunity in this business. Overall, while Visa has competitors (MasterCard, American Express, and Discover), it continues to have the strongest franchise, technology leadership, and pricing power at its back.

Reasons for Caution

The company has pricing power, but as with many companies that do, that power has come under government, merchant, and public scrutiny; the company must tread lightly or face possible consequences. Recent litigation and regulatory actions have presented some headline and profit risk and may be construed as a threat to the franchise—perhaps if it sounds too good to be true, it may be. But even after some legal and regulatory bumps, Visa has emerged rock solid. In fact, it's good to confront these issues and get past them even if they do cause some short-term stomach pain for investors—as they have recently with the fee settlement. Visa just took on its first long-term debt to finance the Visa Europe acquisition, but the balance sheet remains stellar. With the steady success, entry points have been hard to find.

SECTOR: Financials ❑ BETA COEFFICIENT: **0.84** ❑ 10-YEAR COMPOUND EARNINGS PER-SHARE GROWTH: **NM** ❑ 10-YEAR COMPOUND DIVIDENDS PER-SHARE GROWTH: **NM**

	2008	**2009**	**2010**	**2011**	**2012**	**2013**	**2014**	**2015**
Revenues (mil)	6,263	6,911	8,065	9,188	10,421	11,776	12,702	13,880
Net income (mil)	1,700	2,213	2,966	3,650	4,203	4,980	5,438	6,238
Earnings per share	0.56	0.73	0.98	1.25	1.55	1.90	2.27	2.62
Dividends per share	0.03	0.11	0.13	0.15	0.22	0.33	0.42	0.50
Cash flow per share	0.63	0.80	1.09	1.39	1.67	2.05	2.44	2.82
Price: high	22.5	22.4	24.3	25.9	38.1	55.7	67.3	81.0
low	10.9	10.4	16.2	16.9	24.6	38.5	48.7	60.0

Website: www.corporate.visa.com

GROWTH AND INCOME

Waste Management, Inc.

Ticker symbol: WM (NYSE) ❑ S&P rating: A- ❑ Value Line financial strength rating: A ❑ Current yield: 2.9% ❑ Dividend raises, past 10 years: 10

Company Profile

You may refer to it as a "garbage company" if you want—we won't take offense. Waste Management is the largest and steadiest hand in the North American solid waste disposal industry. Like most large waste firms, WM has grown over time by assembling smaller, more local companies into a nationally branded and highly scaled operation with a notable amount of innovation on several fronts in the core business and especially in material recovery—translation, recycling.

The business is divided into three segments:

- Collection, which accounts for 52 percent of the business, includes the standard dumpster and garbage truck operations. The company has about 600 collection operations, many of which have long-term contracts with municipalities and businesses. About 40 percent of the collection business is commercial, 30 percent residential, and 26 percent industrial. For the industry, WM is considered an innovator even in its traditional collection operations; examples include the Bagster small-scale disposal units now sold through retail home-improvement outlets and 3,700 collection trucks converted to natural gas (some of which the company produces from waste). The company perceives itself as a world-class logistics company (and why not?) and has equipped its trucks with the latest in onboard computers, centralized dispatching, and routing processes, reducing collection costs an additional 1 percent during FY2015.

- Landfill (17 percent of revenues). The company operates 265 landfills across North America, servicing its own collection operations and other collection service providers. Among these sites, there are 137 landfill-gas-to-energy conversion projects producing fuel for electricity generation. There are also five active hazardous waste landfills and one underground hazardous waste facility.
- Transfer, Recycling, and Other (31 percent). These operations perform specialized material recovery and processing into useful commodities. There are 300 transfer stations set up for the collection of various forms of waste, including medical, recyclables, compact fluorescent (CFL), and e-waste. The company has also pioneered single-stream recycling, where physical and optical sorting technologies sort out unseparated recyclable materials. Single-streaming has greatly increased recycling rates in municipalities where it is used and provides a steady revenue stream in recovered paper, glass, metals, etc., for the company. WM also further refines these materials into industrial inputs, e.g., glass or plastic feedstocks in certain colors. In total there are 76 traditional and 50 "single-stream" operations, recycling some 15 million tons of commodities annually today, a figure expected to grow to 20 million by 2020. "Capture Value from Waste" is a popular company slogan.

In 2014, the company sold its Wheelabrator Technologies subsidiary, which operated a network of waste-to-energy gasification plants at landfills. The sale affects the numbers presented. Recycling operations in general produce 17 percent of revenues and are not big profit producers with today's soft commodity prices and diminished China demand, but the company remains strategically committed to these operations for the long term.

In the waste business, environmental compliance and beyond to true "sustainability" are important both economically and as a public relations gesture. In response, the company has put together a platform of work and information on its "green" initiatives. It estimates that its "green" services outweighed its "traditional" services 57 percent to 43 percent in 2014. A more detailed breakdown:

- Traditional collection—38 percent
- Traditional landfill—5 percent
- Green collection—24 percent
- Recycling—17 percent
- Green energy—13 percent
- Innovation service lines (mainly consulting services)—3 percent

We like their approach to this issue, as well as their investments. More on WM's sustainability efforts can be found at www.thinkgreen.com.

Financial Highlights, Fiscal Year 2015

While the Wheelabrator sale and softness in the recycling business provided a headwind for FY2015, operational improvements and a 2 percent price increase led to some modest "organic" gains through the year. FY2016 and FY2017 provide more of an "apples-to-apples" comparison, with revenues forecast up 3–5 percent each year (which may include some small acquisitions) and earnings up 5–8 percent in each of those years on the back of higher margins, contribution from recent acquisitions, and possible further price hikes (it helps to be the biggest in the business). A "miss" would likely be on the upside if recycled commodity prices improve. Dividends look to rise steadily, and share buybacks (about 2 percent annually) will continue to come down the conveyor belt.

Reasons to Buy

WM is the strongest and most entrenched player in a business that isn't going away anytime soon. "Strategic" waste collection, particularly with the high-value-add material recovery operations that have become core to WM's business, is not only here to stay but also will only become more important to residential, industrial, and municipal customers as time goes on. Despite today's low energy and material prices, we feel the "sweet spot" in this trend is yet to come.

WM exhibits a lot of innovation in an industry not particularly known for it. We feel that WM's performance is solid, and could break out of the doldrums as operational improvements take effect, lower fuel costs weigh in, and as material recovery becomes an even more strategic and profitable enterprise. WM is a slow, steady, safe, well-managed investment with decent cash returns to shareholders.

Reasons for Caution

WM does rely on acquisitions for a lot of its growth. In this business, that might not be so bad, for existing companies have captive markets and disposal facilities and can likely benefit from proven management processes and reduced overhead costs. The recycling operations, while cool and sexy, aren't always profitable as we've seen, especially when competing material prices, like natural gas these days, are soft. The right combination of factors to drive improved recycling profitability may be close at hand or a ways off—you can have a clear environmental conscience (and collect your dividends) while you wait for better times. Additionally, any waste company runs the risk of going afoul of environmental regulations; WM has largely steered clear of trouble thus far (and has indeed been voted in as a "world's most ethical company" for the past eight years by the Ethisphere Institute—the only entry in the "environmental services" category), but there are no guarantees. More stringent regulations could also pose problems.

SECTOR: Business Services ❑ BETA COEFFICIENT: 0.59 ❑ 10-YEAR COMPOUND EARNINGS PER-SHARE GROWTH: 5.5% ❑ 10-YEAR COMPOUND DIVIDENDS PER-SHARE GROWTH: 6.0%

	2008	2009	2010	2011	2012	2013	2014	2015
Revenues (mil)	13,388	11,791	12,515	13,375	13,649	13,983	13,996	12,961
Net income (mil)	1,087	988	1,011	1,007	968	1,008	1,155	1,153
Earnings per share	2.19	2.00	2.10	2.14	2.08	2.15	2.48	2.53
Dividends per share	1.08	1.16	1.28	1.36	1.42	1.46	1.50	1.54
Cash flow per share	4.74	4.43	4.64	4.85	4.88	5.04	5.34	5.40
Price: high	39.3	34.2	37.3	36.7	36.3	46.4	51.9	55.9
low	24.5	22.1	31.1	27.8	30.8	33.7	40.3	45.9

Website: www.wm.com

AGGRESSIVE GROWTH

WD-40 Company

Ticker symbol: WDFC (NASDAQ) ❏ S&P rating: NR ❏ Value Line financial strength rating: A
❏ Current yield: 1.7% ❏ Dividend raises, past 10 years: 7

Company Profile

Want to keep squirrels from climbing the poles to your bird feeders? We
did, and we always have. And we found the solution through WD-40's website—spray the pole with WD-40.

Turns out, people have been spraying WD-40 on plenty of other things
over the years to get them to work right, stop squeaking, dry out properly, or
to be just plain in good repair. In fact, they've been spraying WD-40 for 61
years—only a few years after the Rocket Chemical Company first invented
the stuff for the aerospace industry in 1953 to protect the outer skin of the
SM-65 Atlas missile. And what is "WD-40"? It was the fortieth attempt to
develop a good Water Displacement formula. It was so good, and had so
many uses in unsticking stuck things, that employees started sneaking it
out of the factory in lunch buckets. Shortly thereafter, in 1958, the product
made its first appearance on store shelves as a spray.

Fast-forward to now: the professional and now-consumerized WD-
40 remains a product of a thousand uses—2,000 in fact, according to the
company's website—and a lesson in building a very effective brand around
a fairly plain consumer product for distribution into what the company
estimates to be four out of five U.S. households and into 188 countries
worldwide.

The base WD-40 product, in its familiar blue and yellow spray can
of various sizes, is still the brand cornerstone, even though the company
doesn't make a drop of it. They do the research and lab work but outsource
production to other specialty chemical companies. In fact, the company
in total has only 477 employees, probably the fewest on our *100 Best
Stocks* list. In the late 1990s, they sought to extend their presence in
the maintenance and repair market by acquiring canned light oil maker
3-IN-ONE, then went further into this market to acquire the maker and
distributor of Lava soap and Solvol heavy-duty hand cleaner. After initial
successes with these acquisitions, and as their products were adopted in
greater quantities as consumer products for use in the home, not just
the repair shop, they started adding cleaning products, including "X-14"

stain removers and "2000 Flushes" bath cleaners, Carpet Fresh and Spot Shot carpet cleaners, and a handful of other products, some with only international distribution.

In 2003 they added a "3-IN-ONE Professional" line, and in 2011 they sought to extend the WD-40 name itself beyond the namesake light oil spray with the addition of a "WD-40 Specialist" line for especially challenging jobs in maintenance and repair operations for the trade professional and the "doer enthusiast" like rust removal, engine degreasing, corrosion prevention, and electrical contact cleaning. They also introduced specialty lines for motorcycle maintenance, home maintenance, and a "WD-40 Bike" line specifically produced and packaged for bicycle maintenance. New packages, spray tubes, and injectors help users get the product into difficult spaces. The "Multipurpose Maintenance Products" line, which includes the broad family of lubricants, now accounts for 85 percent of the revenue.

In short, WD-40 is a classic case study in *brand extension*, with new ways to package and position its core WD-40 and 3-IN-ONE lubricants for new and existing markets, and *business model extension*, where they leverage their operating and marketing model into other useful product lines as exemplified by their cleaning products. That said, the company is considering a sale of some of the homecare brands to focus more on the niche it dominates—multipurpose maintenance products.

Financial Highlights, Fiscal Year 2015

Revenues for FY2015 fell 1 percent, due in large part to currency fluctuations in the EMEA region (EMEA accounts for 36 percent of consolidated net sales). Revenues from the Americas and APAC were up 4 and 6 percent, respectively. Backing out the effects of currency fluctuations results in a 2 percent increase in net sales. Long story short, 2015 was basically flat. Still, earnings were up 2 percent (6 percent when adjusted for currency). Revenues declined 1 percent in both the Maintenance and Homecare segments. As in 2014, the numbers reflect steady and gradually accelerating business success (though Homecare was off 2 percent). The $378 million in sales were split roughly evenly between the Americas and EMEA/APAC, with EMEA/APAC split 70/30. The company is gaining traction in APAC and expects China revenues to grow despite a slowing economy. The company added $75 million to its share repurchase plan, which represents about 5 percent of the base.

Reasons to Buy

We were somewhat late to the WD-40 party, adding it to our *100 Best* list just last year. Nonetheless, we thought the stock still had room to run, and the company rewarded us with 19 percent growth in share price over the year. There has been a recent pullback in share price due to stiff currency headwinds, but domestic sales growth in the first half of the year has been good and we like the company's focus on its Maintenance line (the company does not release unit sales numbers).

The company has a dominant market position in the U.S., so expanding geographic reach is a priority. Fortunately (and ironically) the company's product is "sticky." Few things work as well for the intended purpose, and lower-cost competitors are few, so market acceptance is high. We like the branding leverage and niche dominance of any business we see like this. Moreover, we like the way this company is run. A visit to their website and their "About Us" page will uncover their view of the world and clearly stated values: This is a leaner and better culture—or "tribe" as they refer to it—than we've seen in most consumer brand companies. Too, a trip through their investor presentations will shed an unusual amount of positive light on their concise management style. Management respects its employees . . . and respects its shareholders too. Finally—we can't ignore this—it has all the hallmarks of a Buffett acquisition: a simple business model, strong brand, and good management in place.

Reasons for Caution

The company has stated that the current lineup in the Homecare and Cleaning Products group are "harvest brands" (meaning there will be no further investment here and the brands will likely be sold off when they no longer meet the company's financial goals). There does not appear to be a replacement strategy for this segment, so revenue growth at WD-40 will have to come from increasing the breadth and/or market penetration/share of the Maintenance products line. Acceptance of the Specialist line has been good, but the sales decline in Homecare may accelerate as distributors re-balance to more heavily promoted brands.

The company's financial performance has not gone unnoticed over the past few years, and as a result the P/E ratio has risen steadily over the years to where it sits today at approximately 31. We feel this valuation is sustainable, given the company's growth projections, but it bears consideration when choosing a buy-in point.

SECTOR: **Industrials** ❑ BETA COEFFICIENT: **0.80** ❑ 10-YEAR COMPOUND EARNINGS PER-SHARE
GROWTH: **5.5%** ❑ 10-YEAR COMPOUND DIVIDENDS PER-SHARE GROWTH: **5.0%**

	2008	2009	2010	2011	2012	2013	2014	2015
Revenues (mil)	317	292	322	336	343	369	383	378
Net income (mil)	28.5	26.3	36.1	36.4	35.5	39.8	43.7	44.8
Earnings per share	1.69	1.56	2.15	2.14	2.20	2.54	2.87	3.04
Dividends per share	1.00	1.00	1.00	1.06	1.14	1.22	1.33	1.48
Cash flow per share	1.96	1.82	2.42	2.49	2.57	2.96	3.36	3.55
Price: high	40.0	34.6	41.8	48.0	54.4	79.3	87.1	105.0
low	23.1	21.6	29.3	35.4	39.4	47.0	65.2	80.0

Website: www.wd40.com

GROWTH AND INCOME

Wells Fargo & Company

Ticker symbol: WFC (NYSE) ❑ S&P rating: A+ ❑ Value Line financial strength rating: A ❑ Current
yield: 3.2% ❑ Dividend raises, past 10 years: 8

Company Profile

Wells Fargo & Company is a diversified financial services company, providing banking, insurance, investments, mortgages, and consumer finance from more than 8,700 offices (more than any other bank but down from 9,000 last year due to some efficiency measures) and other distribution channels, including mortgage, investment management, commercial banking, and consumer finance branches across all 50 states and 36 countries including locations in Canada, the Caribbean, and Central America. The business is divided into three segments. First and largest is Community Banking, which provides traditional banking and mortgage services in all 50 states through a combination of branches, ATMs, and online services. Wholesale Banking provides commercial banking, capital markets, leasing, and other financing services to larger corporations. Wealth, Brokerage, and Retirement provides financial advisory and investment management services to individuals.

As of the end of 2015, Wells Fargo had $1.78 trillion in assets, loans outstanding of $905 billion, and shareholder equity of $193 billion (this latter figure is up 53 percent from the end of 2010, a sign of health). Based on assets, it is the third-largest bank holding company in the United States. The company expanded its footprint and market share—which is close to 10 percent of all U.S. banking services—considerably with the 2009 acquisition of Wachovia. The bank maintains its uniquely strong "Main Street" orientation, focusing on consumer and small business customers and less on large corporations, investment banking, and other "Wall Street" endeavors. At present, it is the U.S. market-share leader in commercial real estate, middle-market commercial lending, mortgage origination and servicing, small business landing, auto loans, and retail deposits. It holds the number two position in debit card issuance, number three in total deposits and full-service retail brokerage, and number four in wealth management. The loan portfolio is split 50–50 between consumer and commercial customers.

The company is also an innovation leader, for instance, with experiments with a new 1,000-square-foot "minibank" with personalized service, interactive technologies, and large-screen ATMs, and in mobile banking which, it estimates, 15 million customers are using at present.

The bank's success is more based on fees and services than most. About 54 percent of income originates from interest margin (the difference between interest charged and interest cost); 46 percent originates from an assortment of fees. Of that 47 percent, the brokerage and financial advisory operations generate 35 percent, deposit service charges 13 percent, mortgage banking fees 17 percent, card fees 10 percent, banking fees 11 percent, and seven other small categories account for as much as 5 percent apiece.

Financial Highlights, Fiscal Year 2015

Wells Fargo continues to rebound from the Great Recession more successfully than most of its brethren. Loan losses and nonperforming assets continue to drop, and the so-called "Tier 1" ratio, a measure of equity to total assets, has improved from 8.3 percent in 2010 to 12.54 percent at the end of 2014, healthy by banking standards. For FY2015, the company also reported charge-offs for nonperforming assets of 0.36 percent, up slightly from 0.33 percent in 2014 but down from 1.36 percent in 2011; allowance for loan losses of 1.37 percent, down from 1.51 percent last year and 2.56 percent in 2011; and nonperforming assets down to 1.40 percent from 1.72 percent in 2014 and 3.37 percent in 2011. In line with these numbers, the loan loss reserve has dropped from $15.7 billion at the end of 2010 to $2.4 billion at the end of 2015. These figures all deliver a picture of vastly improved financial health and asset quality, and we like the fact that the company presents these figures clearly on their "Investment Profile" page (www.wellsfargo.com/invest_relations/investment_profile).

These figures, while indicating health, also brought improved performance. Strong loan growth in commercial and industrial segments and in credit cards was offset by a decline in interest margin; together these led to a 2 percent revenue gain for FY2015. Due mainly to increased interest expenses, net income was down slightly but an 80 million share decline in share count (1.5 percent) led to a 5-cent increase in per-share earnings. FY2016 looks to be considerably stronger with revenue gains in the 6–7 percent range and a net income rise forecast as much as 10 percent, largely based on market share gains, operational efficiencies, and more favorable trends in interest rates. Fully blessed so far by the Federal Reserve, the dividend should rise above $2.00 by the end of the decade if not before.

Reasons to Buy

Wells Fargo has cleaned house and strengthened its brand as the prime Main Street player in the consumer and commercial banking industry. We like its solid financial base and its growth in noninterest income (fees, etc.) that insulate it against possible interest rate hikes, and its reputation in the marketplace.

We like its relatively small footprint in the more volatile investment and international banking circles; results should prove steadier in a crisis than many of its brethren. Shareholders will be rewarded with ample return in the form of share price appreciation, dividends, and some share buybacks as time goes on, although buybacks may attenuate in an effort to retain strong capital ratios—in this industry, that's not a bad thing. And we also don't think it's a bad thing that Warren Buffett, through his Berkshire Hathaway business, recently upped his stake 2 percent to 479 million shares, or 19 percent of his stock portfolio—his largest position.

Reasons for Caution

Headline risk continues to abound in the banking industry. Wells Fargo is still deeply involved in mortgages, and any sign of trouble on the mortgage front will obviously hurt, although recent settlements of litigation related to mortgage-lending operations reduce this risk somewhat. Banking is a complex business—more complex than we like—and hence our minimal inclusion of financial firms on the *100 Best Stocks* list; only the best, as they say. The interest rate landscape continues to be a bit hard to predict and may cause some short-term profitability hiccups as "wholesale" interest rates rise faster than "retail," but in the long term, the company is well positioned to handle any rise in interest rates and may even benefit from it.

SECTOR: Financials ◻ **BETA COEFFICIENT: 0.90** ◻ **10-YEAR COMPOUND EARNINGS PER-SHARE GROWTH: 8.5%** ◻ **10-YEAR COMPOUND DIVIDENDS PER-SHARE GROWTH: 3.5%**

		2008	2009	2010	2011	2012	2013	2014	2015
Loans (bil)		843.8	758	734	750	783	811	850	905
Net income (mil)		2,655	12,275	11,632	15,025	17,999	20,889	21,821	21,604
Earnings per share		0.70	1.75	2.21	2.82	3.36	3.89	4.10	4.15
Dividends per share		1.30	0.49	0.20	0.48	0.88	1.15	1.35	1.48
Price:	high	44.7	31.5	34.3	34.3	36.6	45.6	55.9	58.8
	low	19.9	7.8	23.0	22.6	27.9	34.4	44.2	47.8

Website: www.wellsfargo.com

GROWTH AND INCOME

Welltower, Inc.

Ticker symbol: HCN (NYSE) ◻ **S&P rating: BBB** ◻ **Value Line financial strength rating: A++** ◻ **Current yield: 5.0%** ◻ **Dividend raises, past 10 years: 10**

Company Profile

What's in a name? The first bit of news about Welltower, Inc. is the name itself—which was changed from the rather descriptive-but-nondescript Health Care REIT in mid-2015. Same company, different name. The same company that comprised our first entry into the real estate investment trust space for our 2014 *100 Best* list, and as the entry is still quite "well" in our view, it remains on our list under its new name.

Welltower is a real estate investment trust investing primarily in senior living and medical care properties primarily in the U.S. but also in Canada and the U.K. The business—and we think it's a good business, not just a real estate portfolio—operates in three primary business segments. The first and largest is referred to as the Seniors Housing "triple-net" segment and is involved primarily in owning senior housing properties, including independent, continuing care, and assisted living facilities, and leasing them to qualified operators like Sunrise Senior Living and Genesis Healthcare in return for a steady income stream. This segment currently owns 705 properties in the U.S. in 42 states, but is concentrated in high-cost urban areas mostly on the coasts, and contributes about 30 percent of revenues. There are now also 60 facilities in the U.K. and 14 facilities in Canada.

The second and fastest-growing segment is the Seniors Housing Operating segment, which operates some of the facilities owned by the

REIT and others owned by third parties. It operates 233 properties in 35 states, 103 in Canada, and 52 in the U.K. and contributes about 58 percent of revenues. The third major segment is Outpatient Medical, which owns and sometimes operates 250 outpatient medical centers including skilled nursing facilities in 36 states, contributing about 12 percent to revenues. The company sold its last hospital and its life sciences facilities in 2015 and 2016. In total, Welltower owns and/or operates some 1,426 properties in three countries. Welltower employs a conscious and stated strategy of being in markets with high barriers to entry and with a more upscale, affluent retiree base—this is part of why we feel it is a good business, not just a real estate play. Markets such as Boston, New Jersey, Seattle, and major coastal California cities are territories for Welltower. The top five markets are New York, Philadelphia, Los Angeles, Boston, and greater London. The average revenue per occupied room in the seniors operating segment is $6,550 per month, some 52 percent higher than the national senior housing industry average. (For the triple-net segment, this figure is $1,331 per bed/unit per month.) In the markets in which HCN operates, the cost of the average single-family home runs 74 percent higher than the national average, and household incomes are 40 percent higher. Eighty-five percent of facilities are in the 31 most affluent U.S. metropolitan areas. Occupancy rates are 87.2 percent in the seniors housing triple-net segment, 91.0 percent in the seniors housing operating, and 95.1 percent in the medical facilities segments. The facilities are newer, more attractive, and desirable, as a trip through the company's website at www.welltower.com will show.

The REIT continues to grow, with new investments of $4.8 billion in 2015 mostly in the seniors housing segment to be operated by existing partners. As mentioned, certain non-core assets like life science and hospital facilities were sold. The strategy and focus are more sharply aligned with the idea of "differentiation" and providing an "infrastructure platform that emphasizes wellness and connectivity across the continuum of care"—or pleasant, well-appointed alternatives to the traditional facilities usually offered to both healthy and less healthy seniors.

REITs, obviously, play on the real estate market, and in the Welltower case, in the high-value-add REIT segment of healthcare. You're also investing in the aging population—which is expected to grow 40 percent by 2024 against a 9.1 percent growth in the population as a whole. In this case in particular, you're investing in the ability and willingness of the more affluent segments of the elderly population to spend for a pleasant retirement.

REITs are typically good income producers, as they are required by law to pay a substantial portion of their cash flow to investors. The accounting rules are different, and REIT investors should focus on Funds From Operations (FFO), which is analogous to operating income; net income figures have depreciation expenses deducted, which can vary in timing and not always be realistic. Funds From Operations (FFO) support the dividends paid to investors.

Financial Highlights, Fiscal Year 2015

Acquisitions, stronger pricing, and slightly better occupancy drove revenues up about 15 percent in FY2015. Per-share Funds From Operations (FFO) rose about 6 percent over FY2014 (3.1 percent on a same store net-operating-income basis), while the dividend was raised another 4 percent. Continued strength in pricing and occupancy suggests a 12–15 percent revenue and 5 percent FFO increase for FY2016 with similar to slightly higher FFO increases on moderating revenue gains in FY2017. As the REIT structure implies, those FFO increases should readily translate into similar dividend increases. The company continues to add a modest number of shares to fund acquisitions and to approach a goal of 60 percent equity as noted in the following.

Reasons to Buy

Welltower continues to be a solid, relatively risk-free, income-oriented way to play the steady growth and trends of the healthcare industry and the aging demographic. Rents—and rent growth—are better than average, and its income payout is stable and growing. Longer term, the company estimates that senior housing rent growth will exceed inflation by 1.7 percent, that the U.S. population over 75 years of age will grow some 86 percent over the next 20 years, and the 85+ population will double—all factors supporting a healthy growth story.

Some 88+ percent of revenues were estimated to be derived from private pay sources in 2016, up from 87 in 2015 and 83 percent in 2014. With the concentration on private-pay services, Welltower will avoid some of the exposure to Medicare utilization management initiatives and related cutbacks that many others in the sector are exposed to—and an improving economy will only help further. We like, and most in the industry agree, the expansion into the U.K., which positions them well for other fertile pastures overseas. The company also avoids exposure to debt and interest costs better than most REITs, with a target debt of 40 percent of total capital (they have currently managed this down to 47 percent).

Reasons for Caution

Because of their differences from ordinary corporations, it may be difficult to understand this investment, particularly the financial performance of REITs, especially a complex REIT such as this one, which has both traditional property investments and operating company investments. There are some rumors of competitive pressure and oversupply in the seniors real estate market, but we feel confident that Welltower is playing in the stronger, more exclusive niches. One could also question, going forward, whether retirees will be as well-heeled as they are today, with deterioration in retirement savings and increased costs. Finally, there is some sensitivity to rising interest rates, and while real estate prices have rebounded well since the Great Recession, any hiccup in any sector of real estate is likely to affect this issue.

SECTOR: **Healthcare** ❑ BETA COEFFICIENT: **0.43** ❑ 10-YEAR COMPOUND FFO PER-SHARE GROWTH: **3.5%** ❑ 10-YEAR COMPOUND DIVIDENDS PER-SHARE GROWTH: **3.5%**

	2008	2009	2010	2011	2012	2013	2014	2015
Revenues (mil)	551.2	569.0	680.5	1,421	1,822	2,880	3,344	3,858
Net income (mil)	150.3	161.6	84.4	155.9	294.8	93.3	505.0	883.8
Funds from operations per share	3.38	3.13	3.08	3.41	3.52	3.80	4.13	4.38
Real estate owned per share	55.9	49.3	58.4	72.5	66.9	74.9	69.5	75.8
Dividends per share	2.70	2.72	2.74	2.84	2.96	3.06	3.18	3.30
Price: high	54.0	46.7	52.1	55.2	62.8	80.1	78.2	84.9
low	30.1	25.9	38.4	41.0	52.4	52.4	52.9	58.2

Website: www.welltower.com

CONSERVATIVE GROWTH

Whirlpool Corporation

Ticker symbol: WHR (NYSE) ❑ S&P rating: BBB ❑ Value Line financial strength rating: A+ ❑ Current yield: 2.1% ❑ Dividend raises, past 10 years: 5

Company Profile

Whirlpool is the world's leading home appliance manufacturer in a $120 billion global industry. The company manufactures appliances under familiar and recognized brand names in all major home appliance categories including fabric care (laundry), cooking, refrigeration, dishwashers, water filtration, and garage organization. Familiar brand names include Whirlpool, Maytag, KitchenAid, Amana, Jenn-Air, Gladiator, and international names Bauknecht, Brastemp, Indesit, and Consul. The Whirlpool brand itself is the number-one global appliance brand and is number one across all four major world geographic regions. Seven brands within the branded house generate over $1 billion in annual sales. Based on FY2015 sales, the product breakdown is about 28 percent refrigerators and freezers, 29 percent fabric care, 18 percent home cooking appliances, and 25 percent "other." About 49 percent of Whirlpool's sales come from overseas. Although results have been mixed, the company has invested heavily in overseas markets especially with the recent acquisition of two moderately sized international firms: Europe's Indesit (another billion-dollar brand) and China's Hefei Sanyo. Latin America is a big emphasis too. The acquisition strategy keys on adjacent businesses, many to open or gain critical mass in international markets.

In an industry not traditionally known for innovation, Whirlpool has striven to be an innovation leader in its industry. This has manifested itself both in new products, product platforms, and contemporary styling within those platforms; and in manufacturing and supply-chain efficiencies, such as a global platform design for local manufacture of washing machine products, recalling similar achievements in the auto industry. Such gains are key in this competitive, price-sensitive industry. The company also has initiatives to build lifetime brand loyalty and product quality, improve water and energy efficiency and quietness of operation, and add more interesting and decorative colors to some of its products. More recently it has marketed specialized "smart" appliances; one example is the Whirlpool 6th Sense Live app, which allows owners to operate a washing machine remotely for convenience and to save energy.

Overall, the strategy is to expand the business through innovation, brand strength, and geographic coverage; then to expand margins through supply-chain and cost-structure efficiency.

Financial Highlights, Fiscal Year 2015

For several years the company has ridden the coattails of an improving economy, an improved replacement cycle for old units, improved demand for today's more efficient appliances, and operational improvements. Then it ran into a bit of a speed bump in 2015 in the form of currency and emerging market headwinds, particularly in Brazil and China. For that year, which got off to a good start, revenues were still up a healthy 5 percent; cost synergies led to a stronger 9 percent gain in net earnings. The dollar and emerging market effects will hurt FY2016 more than FY2015, with roughly flat revenues—however, brand strength, an improved sales mix, and cost savings from overseas manufacturing adjacent to local markets will all serve to improve margins and increase earnings in the 12–14 percent range with very strong cash flows. Forecasts call for revenues to advance once again in FY2017 in the 2–3 percent range with earnings rising once again, somewhere in the 8–12 percent range. Low double-digit dividend increases look likely after a 23 percent raise in 2015; moderate share buybacks also provide strong returns to shareholders.

Reasons to Buy

Long a dull, boring business, Whirlpool has made shopping for an appliance more interesting and has profited handsomely from its efforts. If you shop for an appliance today—take washers and dryers, for example—they work better, they're more energy efficient, they use less water, and are more technology enabled. In short, they're better products, and guess what: They're more expensive and more profitable for the manufacturers, too. Operational improvements, higher-product value add, and a gradual increase in premium brands have driven operating margins from the 6–8 percent range six years ago into the 10–12 percent range; these improvements look to be permanent, beyond the effects of a strong business cycle. We like the way the company wrings ever more profit out of a modestly growing or even flat sales base.

We like market leaders, particularly companies not content to sit on their laurels while others close in around them. Whirlpool used the Great Recession and ensuing recovery as a wake-up call and an opportunity to streamline its businesses and to put some real strategic thought into how to drive its brand assortment and international portfolio to achieve better results.

The company continues to innovate toward better products and internal processes. We like their "Purposeful Innovation" motto. Long term, we see more opportunities to develop "smart" appliances, which can work together with smartphones and other residential management applications to deliver better, more energy-efficient results. Too, the company is building critical mass in overseas markets. Cash flows and investor returns are solid and rising. More than most, the management team is a plus with a recognizable pragmatic and strategic approach to managing this business.

Reasons for Caution

By nature, the appliance business is highly competitive and cyclical. In addition, consumers with more disposable income have of late been opting for fancier, more expensive foreign brands, like Bosch and LG, a trend that could hurt if it continues. We believe that Whirlpool is countering this trend by adding elegance, advertising, and channel support for its top-tier brands and products—as well as a few "foreign" brands of its own. Commodity costs, labor issues, quality issues, and shifts in consumer preferences, while favorable now, are perpetual risks. Weakness in emerging markets has emerged as another. But overall we don't find much dirty laundry in this story.

SECTOR: **Consumer Durables** ◻ BETA COEFFICIENT: **1.70** ◻ 10-YEAR COMPOUND EARNINGS PER-SHARE GROWTH: **5.0%** ◻ 10-YEAR COMPOUND DIVIDENDS PER-SHARE GROWTH: **5.0%**

		2008	2009	2010	2011	2012	2013	2014	2015
Revenues (mil)		18,907	17,099	18,366	18,666	18,143	18,768	19,872	20,891
Net income (mil)		647	328	707	699	559	810	907	987
Earnings per share		5.50	4.34	9.10	8.95	7.05	10.03	11.39	12.38
Dividends per share		1.72	1.72	1.72	1.93	2.00	2.38	2.88	3.45
Cash flow per share		13.90	11.37	16.91	16.54	14.05	17.53	18.80	21.43
Price:	high	98.0	85.0	118.4	92.3	104.2	159.2	196.7	217.1
	low	30.2	19.2	71.0	45.2	47.7	101.7	124.4	140.5

Website: www.whirlpoolcorp.com

AGGRESSIVE GROWTH   NEW FOR 2017

WhiteWave Foods

Ticker symbol: WWAV (NYSE) ◻ S&P rating: BB ◻ Value Line financial strength rating: B++ ◻ Current yield: NA ◻ Dividend raises, past 10 years: NA

Company Profile

Here's one for the Millennials. But wait—not just the Millennials, but for the millions of their older (mostly) American brethren who for one reason or another have seen the light and reformed their eating habits to "eat more healthy." After years of including an assortment of traditional food processors like Smucker and General Mills on our lists—all of whom are dipping their toes into the healthy food market—we decided we wanted to cleanse ourselves of the bad stuff for at least one pure play in Food 2.0—and we think we've found it in WhiteWave Foods.

Spun off from the large commodity milk producer Dean Foods in 2012, WhiteWave Foods manufactures, markets, distributes, and sells branded plant-based foods and beverages, coffee creamers and beverages, organic premium dairy products, and organic produce. The company's five segments and products include:

- Americas Foods & Beverages (24 percent of FY2015 sales) includes plant-based foods and beverages, including Silk and So Delicious branded beverages such as soymilk, almond milk, coconut milk, and cashew milk, So Delicious Dairy Free plant-based yogurts, ice cream, and frozen products, and Vega plant-based products. Silk and So Delicious are number one in their respective markets; Vega is number two.
- Premium Dairy (20 percent) includes the rapidly growing Horizon Organic (milk, but extending into other dairy including a line of packaged cheeses and even macaroni and cheese) and Wallaby Organic (yogurts, also extending into adjacent products). Both of these also hold the number one position.
- Americas Fresh Foods (15 percent) includes organic salads, fruits, and vegetables such as packaged salad greens, fresh and frozen fruits, and vegetables marketed under the Earthbound Organic name (number one in market) and others.
- Coffee Creamers and Beverages (28 percent) includes the International Delight line of plant-based creamers and other dairy-related beverages (number two in market).
- Europe Foods & Beverages includes various plant-based foods and beverages, such as Alpro (number one position) and Provamel brand beverages, and plant-based alternatives to yogurt, culinary creams, desserts, and margarine. Overseas sales account for about 15 percent of the total.

Financial Highlights, Fiscal Year 2015

Overall, the combined Organic/Natural/Non-GMO food category grew 12 percent in FY2015 (versus 1 percent for foods in total). Not surprisingly, WhiteWave grew slightly ahead of this pace, with a 12.5 percent rise in revenues and a more substantial 20 percent rise in net profits as price increases and volume-driven operating leverage took hold. Continued market and brand strength will drive revenue increases in the 10 percent range through 2017 (we think this might be conservative) while scale and other operating improvements should raise margins and thus profits in the 15–20 percent range each year. For now, this rapidly expanding business pays no dividend and is not buying back shares as it adds new capacity and infrastructure to increase product and geographic coverage, and innovations to continue to expand its offerings and its geographic footprint into markets like Canada, Mexico, and China.

Reasons to Buy

What got us onto the WhiteWave wave originally was being sent to the store to buy—not just any milk, but *organic* milk. And there it was after a short venture into the refrigerated natural foods aisle—in a well-displayed and marked assortment of bright red half-gallon milk cartons—Horizon Organics. We checked the flavor and checked the price—over five bucks for a half-gallon. Being well outside of our own personal food ecosystem and well familiar with paying about a buck eighty for equivalent "regular" milk, we realized we were onto something quite new and lucrative. Eventually, this experience led to the inclusion of WhiteWave on the 2017 *100 Best* list.

We like the strategy. Get into the path of favorable consumer tailwinds such as health and wellness, convenience, "permissible indulgence," personalization, and environmental and social awareness—and ride these horses to the finish line ahead of the others vying for their share of this lucrative and strategic business. It has worked so far, and the company has combined a very healthful mix of product and packaging innovation and strong branding (and brand extension into adjacent foods) to separate it from the pack ever further. As the company likes to point out, organic foods are growing at three times the rate of conventional foods, and four times for plant-based categories—giving growth rates of 30–40 percent in many of its top lines. Research also indicates that 67 percent of the population prefers minimally processed foods, up from 24 percent in 2006.

We feel that such tailwinds aren't about to shift anytime soon, and they should make WhiteWave a winner for years to come. We like the fact that the company has achieved distribution in conventional grocery and staples channels, not just natural foods channels like Whole Foods and similar. We also think the company could be an attractive takeover candidate for a larger food processor looking to accelerate its presence in this lucrative niche.

Reasons for Caution

The natural foods category has been historically fickle; what is today's trend may be passé tomorrow. The whole category has gone through its ups, downs, and changes since the 1970s, but this time we think it's here to stay, and WhiteWave has established its presence and done its marketing homework to the point where we think it will be the trendsetter, not the trend follower.

As tastes change, so can the economy; a sour economy might knock a few of those five-dollar half-gallon milk cartons out of shopping carts. Too, the definition of "organic" and "minimally processed" can and has changed over time; this market tends to follow the latest research trends and not all of the research is in agreement. Competition in some subsegments is fierce and is likely to heat up as more "conventional" producers get on the bandwagon. Finally, the excitement about this category and WhiteWave's pure-play success in it has brought a stock pricing and behavior more like a new tech stock—this pick is definitely more exciting but also more risky (especially with no cash returns) than our traditional *100 Best* stock.

SECTOR: **Consumer Staples** ◻ BETA COEFFICIENT: **1.44** ◻ 10-YEAR COMPOUND EARNINGS PER-SHARE GROWTH: **NM** ◻ 10-YEAR COMPOUND DIVIDENDS PER-SHARE GROWTH: **NM**

	2008	2009	2010	2011	2012	2013	2014	2015
Revenues (mil)	—	—	—	—	2,289	2,542	3,436	3,866
Net income (mil)	—	—	—	—	111	129	178	213
Earnings per share	—	—	—	—	0.73	0.74	1.00	1.19
Dividends per share	—	—	—	—	—	—	—	—
Cash flow per share	—	—	—	—	1.07	1.21	1.65	1.89
Price: high	—	—	—	—	17.0	23.6	38.6	52.5
low	—	—	—	—	14.2	14.7	21.9	32.4

Website: www.whitewave.com

PERFORMANCE ANALYSIS: *100 BEST STOCKS TO BUY IN 2016*

ONE YEAR GAIN/LOSS, APRIL 1, 2015–APRIL 1, 2016,
EXCLUDING DIVIDENDS

Company	Symbol	Price 4/1/2015	Price 4/1/2016	% change	Dollar gain/loss, $1000 invested
3M Company	MMM	$164.95	$167.53	1.6%	$15.64
Aetna	AET	$99.15	$113.71	14.7%	$146.85
Allstate	ALL	$71.17	$68.23	-4.1%	$(41.31)
Apple	AAPL	$124.43	$109.99	-11.6%	$(116.05)
Aqua America	WTR	$26.35	$31.93	21.2%	$211.76
Archer Daniels Midland	ADM	$47.54	$36.47	-23.3%	$(232.86)
AT&T	T	$32.65	$39.05	19.6%	$196.02
Becton, Dickinson	BDX	$143.59	$153.49	6.9%	$68.95
Bemis	BMS	$46.31	$52.16	12.6%	$126.32
Campbell Soup	CPB	$46.55	$65.16	40.0%	$399.79
CarMax	KMX	$69.01	$51.75	-25.0%	$(250.11)
Chevron	CVX	$104.98	$94.26	-10.2%	$(102.11)
Clorox	CLX	$110.39	$127.38	15.4%	$153.91
CenterPoint Energy*	CNP	$19.87	$21.20	6.7%	$66.94
Cincinnati Financial*	CINF	$48.54	$65.96	35.9%	$358.88
Coca-Cola	KO	$40.55	$46.83	15.5%	$154.87
Colgate-Palmolive	CL	$69.34	$71.20	2.7%	$26.82
Comcast	CMCSA	$56.47	$61.87	9.6%	$95.63
ConocoPhillips	COP	$62.26	$39.78	-36.1%	$(361.07)
Corning	GLW	$22.68	$20.83	-8.2%	$(81.57)
Costco Wholesale	COST	$151.50	$158.25	4.5%	$44.55
CVS Health	CVS	$103.21	$104.82	1.6%	$15.60
Daktronics	DAKT	$10.81	$8.03	-25.7%	$(257.17)
Deere	DE	$87.69	$76.50	-12.8%	$(127.61)
DuPont	DD	$71.47	$63.91	-10.6%	$(105.78)
Eastman Chemical	EMN	$69.26	$73.66	6.4%	$63.53
Empire State Realty Trust*	ESRT	$17.65	$17.59	-0.3%	$(3.40)
Fair Isaac	FICO	$88.72	$108.80	22.6%	$226.33
FedEx	FDX	$165.45	$163.67	-1.1%	$(10.76)
Fresh Del Monte*	FDP	$36.47	$42.96	17.8%	$177.95

* = New for 2016

Company	Symbol	Price 4/1/2015	Price 4/1/2016	% change	Dollar gain/loss, $1000 invested
General Electric	GE	$24.81	$31.93	28.7%	$286.98
General Mills	GIS	$56.60	$64.96	14.8%	$147.70
Grainger, W.W.	GWW	$235.81	$234.38	-0.6%	$(6.06)
Harman International	HAR	$133.63	$86.75	-35.1%	$(350.82)
Health Care REIT	HCN	$77.36	$69.16	-10.6%	$(106.00)
Hillenbrand Industries*	HI	$28.58	$29.73	4.0%	$40.24
Honeywell	HON	$104.31	$113.23	8.6%	$85.51
IBM	IBM	$160.50	$152.20	-5.2%	$(51.71)
Illinois Tool Works	ITW	$97.14	$103.44	6.5%	$64.85
International Flavors & Fragrances*	IFF	$112.58	$116.38	3.4%	$33.75
Itron	ITRI	$36.51	$41.86	14.7%	$146.54
J.M. Smucker	SJM	$115.73	$132.52	14.5%	$145.08
Johnson & Johnson	JNJ	$100.60	$109.19	8.5%	$85.39
Johnson Controls	JCI	$50.44	$39.15	-22.4%	$(223.83)
Kimberly-Clark	KMB	$107.11	$136.20	27.2%	$271.59
Kroger	KR	$34.07	$38.32	12.5%	$124.74
Macy's	M	$64.91	$42.96	-33.8%	$(338.16)
McCormick	MKC	$77.11	$100.53	30.4%	$303.72
McKesson	MCK	$226.20	$157.41	-30.4%	$(304.11)
Medtronic	MDT	$77.99	$75.37	-3.4%	$(33.59)
Microchip Technology	MCHP	$48.90	$48.28	-1.3%	$(12.68)
Monsanto	MON	$112.54	$87.87	-21.9%	$(219.21)
Mosaic	MOS	$46.06	$26.84	-41.7%	$(417.28)
NextEra Energy	NEE	$104.05	$118.71	14.1%	$140.89
Nike	NKE	$48.92	$61.59	25.9%	$258.99
Norfolk Southern	NSC	$102.95	$82.97	-19.4%	$(194.07)
Novo Nordisk*	NVO	$55.29	$54.94	-0.6%	$(6.33)
Oracle	ORCL	$43.15	$41.16	-4.6%	$(46.12)
Otter Tail Corporation	OTTR	$32.17	$29.44	-8.5%	$(84.86)
Pall Corporation	PLL	$100.39	$127.20	26.7%	$267.06

* = New for 2016

Company	Symbol	Price 4/1/2015	Price 4/1/2016	% change	Dollar gain/loss, $1000 invested
Patterson	PDCO	$48.79	$46.35	-5.0%	$(50.01)
Paychex	PAYX	$49.62	$54.17	9.2%	$91.70
Perrigo	PRGO	$165.55	$126.73	-23.4%	$(234.49)
Praxair	PX	$120.74	$115.24	-4.6%	$(45.55)
Procter & Gamble	PG	$81.94	$83.53	1.9%	$19.40
Public Storage	PSA	$197.14	$275.52	39.8%	$397.59
Quest Diagnostics	DGX	$76.35	$72.57	-5.0%	$(49.51)
Ralph Lauren	RL	$131.50	$97.26	-26.0%	$(260.38)
ResMed	RMD	$71.78	$58.99	-17.8%	$(178.18)
Ross Stores	ROST	$48.97	$58.64	19.7%	$197.47
RPM International*	RPM	$46.67	$47.94	2.7%	$27.21
Schlumberger	SLB	$83.44	$72.17	-13.5%	$(135.07)
Schnitzer Steel	SCHN	$15.86	$18.94	19.4%	$194.20
Scotts Miracle-Gro	SMG	$67.17	$73.01	8.7%	$86.94
Seagate Technology	STX	$52.03	$33.69	-35.2%	$(352.49)
Southwest Airlines	LUV	$44.30	$44.56	0.6%	$5.87
St. Jude Medical	STJ	$65.40	$55.19	-15.6%	$(156.12)
Starbucks	SBUX	$48.97	$61.02	24.6%	$246.07
State Street Corp	STT	$73.53	$58.95	-19.8%	$(198.29)
Steelcase	SCS	$18.94	$14.93	-21.2%	$(211.72)
Stryker Corporation	SYK	$92.25	$108.52	17.6%	$176.37
Sysco	SYY	$37.73	$47.08	24.8%	$247.81
Target Corporation	TGT	$82.07	$82.76	0.8%	$8.41
Tiffany	TIF	$88.01	$73.77	-16.2%	$(161.80)
Time Warner	TWX	$84.44	$72.99	-13.6%	$(135.60)
Timken Company*	TKR	$38.08	$33.67	-11.6%	$(115.81)
Total S.A.	TOT	$50.01	$44.20	-11.6%	$(116.18)
Union Pacific	UNP	$108.31	$78.92	-27.1%	$(271.35)
UnitedHealth Group	UNH	$118.29	$129.82	9.7%	$97.47
United Parcel Service	UPS	$96.94	$104.95	8.3%	$82.63

* = New for 2016

Company	Symbol	Price 4/1/2015	Price 4/1/2016	% change	Dollar gain/loss, $1000 invested
United Technologies	UTX	$117.20	$99.97	-14.7%	$(147.01)
Valero	VLO	$63.62	$62.91	-1.1%	$(11.16)
Valmont	VMI	$122.88	$123.82	0.8%	$7.65
Verizon	VZ	$48.63	$54.01	11.1%	$110.63
Visa	V	$65.41	$77.59	18.6%	$186.21
Wal-Mart	WMT	$82.25	$69.06	-16.0%	$(160.36)
Waste Management	WM	$54.23	$59.17	9.1%	$91.09
WD-40 Company*	WDFC	$79.95	$110.69	38.4%	$384.49
Wells Fargo	WFC	$54.40	$48.45	-10.9%	$(109.38)
Whirlpool	WHR	$202.06	$183.31	-9.3%	$(92.79)

* = New for 2016

THE *100 BEST STOCKS* 2017, DIVIDEND AND YIELD, BY COMPANY

| Company | Symbol | 2015 | | 2016 INDICATED | | Dividend Raises, Past 10 Years |
		Dividend	Yield %	Dividend	Yield %	
3M Company	MMM	$4.10	2.6%	$4.44	2.6%	10
AbbVie*	ABBV	$2.02	3.7%	$2.28	3.6%	2
Aetna	AET	$1.00	1.2%	$1.00	0.9%	5
Allstate	ALL	$1.12	1.3%	$0.32	2.0%	6
Amazon*	AMZN					
Apple	AAPL	$1.94	2.2%	$2.28	2.7%	4
Aqua America	WTR	$0.71	2.6%	$0.71	2.2%	10
Archer Daniels Midland	ADM	$1.12	2.2%	$1.20	2.8%	9
AT&T	T	$1.88	5.3%	$1.92	4.9%	10
Becton, Dickinson	BDX	$2.40	2.4%	$2.64	1.6%	10
Bemis	BMS	$1.12	2.7%	$1.16	2.3%	10
C.H. Robinson*	CHRW	$1.57	2.4%	$1.72	2.3%	9
Campbell Soup	CPB	$1.25	2.8%	$1.25	2.0%	8
CarMax	KMX					
Carnival Corporation*	CCL	$1.10	2.3%	$1.40	2.9%	4
CenterPoint Energy	CNP	$0.99	3.9%	$1.03	4.6%	10
Chevron	CVX	$4.28	3.9%	$4.28	4.2%	10
Cincinnati Financial	CINF	$1.82	3.4%	$1.92	2.8%	10
Clorox Company	CLX	$3.00	3.4%	$3.20	2.5%	10
Coca-Cola	KO	$1.32	3.2%	$1.40	3.2%	10
Colgate-Palmolive	CL	$1.50	2.3%	$1.56	2.2%	10
Columbia Sportswear*	COLM	$0.52	0.9%	$0.68	1.3%	10
Comcast	CMCSA	$1.00	1.7%	$1.10	1.8%	7
ConocoPhillips	COP	$2.92	4.0%	$1.98	4.5%	9
Corning	GLW	$0.52	2.4%	$0.54	2.6%	5
Costco Wholesale	COST	$1.43	1.2%	$1.80	1.2%	10
CVS Health	CVS	$1.24	1.5%	$1.70	1.8%	10
Daktronics	DAKT	$0.40	3.1%	$0.40	5.0%	7

* = New for 2017

| Company | Symbol | 2015 | | 2016 INDICATED | | Dividend Raises, Past 10 Years |
		Dividend	Yield %	Dividend	Yield %	
Deere	DE	$2.22	2.2%	$2.40	3.0%	10
DuPont	DD	$1.48	2.7%	$1.52	2.3%	7
Eastman Chemical	EMN	$1.60	1.8%	$1.84	2.5%	6
Empire State Realty Trust	ESRT	$0.34	2.0%	$0.34	1.8%	1
Fair Isaac	FICO	$0.08	0.1%	$0.08	0.1%	1
FedEx	FDX	$0.80	0.6%	$1.00	0.6%	10
Fresh Del Monte	FDP	$0.50	1.4%	$0.50	1.0%	3
General Electric	GE	$0.88	3.4%	$0.92	3.4%	8
General Mills	GIS	$1.67	3.3%	$1.84	2.9%	10
Grainger, W.W.	GWW	$4.68	2.2%	$4.88	2.2%	10
Honeywell	HON	$2.08	2.3%	$2.38	2.1%	9
Illinois Tool Works	ITW	$1.98	2.1%	$2.20	2.1%	10
International Flavors & Fragrances	IFF	$1.98	2.0%	$2.24	1.7%	10
Itron	ITRI					
J.M. Smucker	SJM	$2.56	2.3%	$2.00	2.3%	10
Johnson & Johnson	JNJ	$2.92	3.0%	$2.68	2.1%	10
Kimberly-Clark	KMB	$3.52	3.5%	$3.68	2.9%	10
Kroger	KR	$0.38	1.4%	$0.42	1.2%	9
Macy's	M	$1.33	2.2%	$1.51	4.6%	8
McCormick	MKC	$1.60	2.1%	$1.72	1.8%	10
McKesson	MCK	$1.12	0.6%	$1.12	0.6%	7
Medtronic	MDT	$1.28	2.2%	$1.52	1.9%	10
Microchip Technology	MCHP	$1.44	3.0%	$1.44	3.0%	5
Monsanto	MON	$1.96	1.7%	$2.16	1.2%	10
Mosaic	MOS	$1.10	2.4%	$1.10	2.9%	4
NextEra Energy	NEE	$3.08	2.9%	$3.48	2.9%	10
Nike	NKE	$0.52	1.4%	$0.64	1.2%	10
Norfolk Southern	NSC	$2.36	2.4%	$2.36	2.4%	10

* = New for 2017

| Company | Symbol | 2015 | | 2016 INDICATED | | Dividend Raises, Past 10 Years |
		Dividend	Yield %	Dividend	Yield %	
Novo Nordisk	NVO	$0.90	1.9%	$0.96	1.7%	10
Oracle	ORCL	$0.51	1.3%	$0.60	1.5%	5
Ormat Technologies*	ORA	$0.24	0.7%	$0.50	1.2%	5
Otter Tail Corporation	OTTR	$1.23	4.1%	$1.25	4.2%	4
Patterson	PDCO	$0.88	2.0%	$0.96	2.0%	6
PayChex	PAYX	$1.52	3.4%	$1.68	3.1%	8
Perrigo	PRGO	$0.46	0.3%	$0.58	0.6%	10
Praxair	PX	$2.86	2.4%	$3.00	2.7%	10
Procter & Gamble	PG	$2.60	3.2%	$2.68	3.3%	10
Prologis*	PLD	$1.52	3.9%	$1.68	3.5%	4
Public Storage	PSA	$5.92	3.3%	$7.20	2.8%	8
Qualcomm	QCOM	$1.86	4.2%	$2.12	3.8%	10
Quest Diagnostics	DGX	$1.47	2.4%	$1.60	2.1%	6
ResMed	RMD	$1.18	1.5%	$1.20	2.1%	3
Ross	ROST	$0.49	1.2%	$0.54	1.0%	10
RPM International	RPM	$1.00	2.5%	$1.10	2.2%	10
Schlumberger	SLB	$2.00	2.0%	$2.00	2.6%	9
Schnitzer Steel	SCHN	$0.75	4.0%	$0.75	4.7%	3
Scotts Miracle-Gro	SMG	$1.85	3.1%	$1.88	2.7%	7
Southwest Airlines	LUV	$0.30	0.8%	$0.40	0.9%	4
St. Jude Medical	STJ	$1.16	1.7%	$1.24	1.6%	5
Starbucks	SBUX	$0.64	1.4%	$0.80	1.5%	6
State Street Corp	STT	$1.32	1.6%	$1.36	2.2%	8
Steelcase	SCS	$0.48	2.6%	$0.48	3.0%	6
Stryker Corporation	SYK	$1.38	1.7%	$1.52	1.4%	9
Sysco	SYY	$1.20	3.3%	$0.24	2.6%	10
Target Corporation	TGT	$2.15	2.8%	$2.24	3.3%	10
Time Warner	TWX	$1.40	1.8%	$1.61	2.1%	9

* = New for 2017

| Company | Symbol | 2015 | | 2016 INDICATED | | Dividend Raises, Past 10 Years |
		Dividend	Yield %	Dividend	Yield %	
Timken Company	TKR	$1.04	1.9%	$1.04	3.1%	8
Total S.A.	TOT	$2.80	4.4%	$2.73	5.6%	7
Union Pacific	UNP	$2.15	2.2%	$2.20	2.7%	10
United Parcel Service	UPS	$2.92	2.9%	$3.12	3.0%	10
United Technologies	UTX	$2.56	2.1%	$2.64	2.6%	10
UnitedHealth Group	UNH	$1.60	1.7%	$2.00	1.5%	6
Valero	VLO	$1.60	2.9%	$2.40	4.4%	9
Valmont	VMI	$1.50	0.9%	$1.50	1.1%	10
Verizon	VZ	$2.24	4.3%	$2.26	4.5%	9
Visa	V	$0.50	0.8%	$0.56	0.7%	7
Waste Management	WM	$1.54	2.8%	$1.64	2.7%	10
WD-40 Company	WDFC	$1.48	2.1%	$1.68	1.5%	7
Wells Fargo	WFC	$1.48	2.8%	$1.52	3.0%	8
Welltower	HCN	$3.30	5.3%	$3.44	5.0%	10
Whirlpool	WHR	$3.00	1.9%	$4.00	2.3%	5
WhiteWave Foods*	WWAV					

* = New for 2017

THE *100 BEST STOCKS* 2017, DIVIDEND AND YIELD, BY DESCENDING PROJECTED 2016 YIELD

| Company | Symbol | 2015 | | 2016 PROJECTED | | Dividend Raises, Past 10 Years |
		Dividend	Yield %	Dividend	Yield %	
Total S.A.	TOT	$2.80	4.4%	$2.73	5.6%	7
Daktronics	DAKT	$0.40	3.1%	$0.40	5.0%	7
Welltower	HCN	$3.30	5.3%	$3.44	5.0%	10
AT&T	T	$1.88	5.3%	$1.92	4.9%	10
Schnitzer Steel	SCHN	$0.75	4.0%	$0.75	4.7%	3
CenterPoint Energy	CNP	$0.99	3.9%	$1.03	4.6%	10
Macy's	M	$1.33	2.2%	$1.51	4.6%	8
ConocoPhillips	COP	$2.92	4.0%	$1.98	4.5%	9
Verizon	VZ	$2.24	4.3%	$2.26	4.5%	9
Valero	VLO	$1.60	2.9%	$2.40	4.4%	9
Chevron	CVX	$4.28	3.9%	$4.28	4.2%	10
Otter Tail Corporation	OTTR	$1.23	4.1%	$1.25	4.2%	4
Qualcomm*	QCOM	$1.86	4.2%	$2.12	3.8%	10
AbbVie*	ABBV	$2.02	3.7%	$2.28	3.6%	2
Prologis*	PLD	$1.52	3.9%	$1.68	3.5%	4
General Electric	GE	$0.88	3.4%	$0.92	3.4%	8
Procter & Gamble	PG	$2.60	3.2%	$2.68	3.3%	10
Target Corporation	TGT	$2.15	2.8%	$2.24	3.3%	10
Coca-Cola	KO	$1.32	3.2%	$1.40	3.2%	10
PayChex	PAYX	$1.52	3.4%	$1.68	3.1%	8
Timken Company	TKR	$1.04	1.9%	$1.04	3.1%	8
Deere	DE	$2.22	2.2%	$2.40	3.0%	10
Microchip Technology	MCHP	$1.44	3.0%	$1.44	3.0%	5
Steelcase	SCS	$0.48	2.6%	$0.48	3.0%	6
United Parcel Service	UPS	$2.92	2.9%	$3.12	3.0%	10
Wells Fargo	WFC	$1.48	2.8%	$1.52	3.0%	8
Carnival Corporation*	CCL	$1.10	2.3%	$1.40	2.9%	4
General Mills	GIS	$1.67	3.3%	$1.84	2.9%	10

* = New for 2017

Company	Symbol	2015		2016 PROJECTED		Dividend Raises, Past 10 Years
		Dividend	Yield %	Dividend	Yield %	
Kimberly-Clark	KMB	$3.52	3.5%	$3.68	2.9%	10
Mosaic	MOS	$1.10	2.4%	$1.10	2.9%	4
NextEra Energy	NEE	$3.08	2.9%	$3.48	2.9%	10
Archer Daniels Midland	ADM	$1.12	2.2%	$1.20	2.8%	9
Cincinnati Financial	CINF	$1.82	3.4%	$1.92	2.8%	10
Public Storage	PSA	$5.92	3.3%	$7.20	2.8%	8
Apple	AAPL	$1.94	2.2%	$2.28	2.7%	4
Praxair	PX	$2.86	2.4%	$3.00	2.7%	10
Scotts Miracle-Gro	SMG	$1.85	3.1%	$1.88	2.7%	7
Union Pacific	UNP	$2.15	2.2%	$2.20	2.7%	10
Waste Management	WM	$1.54	2.8%	$1.64	2.7%	10
3M Company	MMM	$4.10	2.6%	$4.44	2.6%	10
Corning	GLW	$0.52	2.4%	$0.54	2.6%	5
Schlumberger	SLB	$2.00	2.0%	$2.00	2.6%	9
Sysco	SYY	$1.20	3.3%	$0.24	2.6%	10
United Technologies	UTX	$2.56	2.1%	$2.64	2.6%	10
Clorox Company	CLX	$3.00	3.4%	$3.20	2.5%	10
Eastman Chemical	EMN	$1.60	1.8%	$1.84	2.5%	6
Norfolk Southern	NSC	$2.36	2.4%	$2.36	2.4%	10
Bemis	BMS	$1.12	2.7%	$1.16	2.3%	10
C.H. Robinson*	CHRW	$1.57	2.4%	$1.72	2.3%	9
DuPont	DD	$1.48	2.7%	$1.52	2.3%	7
J.M. Smucker	SJM	$2.56	2.3%	$2.00	2.3%	10
Whirlpool	WHR	$3.00	1.9%	$4.00	2.3%	5
Aqua America	WTR	$0.71	2.6%	$0.71	2.2%	10
Colgate-Palmolive	CL	$1.50	2.3%	$1.56	2.2%	10
Grainger, W.W.	GWW	$4.68	2.2%	$4.88	2.2%	10
RPM International	RPM	$1.00	2.5%	$1.10	2.2%	10

* = New for 2017

Company	Symbol	2015 Dividend	2015 Yield %	2016 PROJECTED Dividend	2016 PROJECTED Yield %	Dividend Raises, Past 10 Years
State Street Corp	STT	$1.32	1.6%	$1.36	2.2%	8
Honeywell	HON	$2.08	2.3%	$2.38	2.1%	9
Illinois Tool Works	ITW	$1.98	2.1%	$2.20	2.1%	10
Johnson & Johnson	JNJ	$2.92	3.0%	$2.68	2.1%	10
Quest Diagnostics	DGX	$1.47	2.4%	$1.60	2.1%	6
ResMed	RMD	$1.18	1.5%	$1.20	2.1%	3
Time Warner	TWX	$1.40	1.8%	$1.61	2.1%	9
Allstate	ALL	$1.12	1.3%	$0.32	2.0%	6
Campbell Soup	CPB	$1.25	2.8%	$1.25	2.0%	8
Patterson	PDCO	$0.88	2.0%	$0.96	2.0%	6
Medtronic	MDT	$1.28	2.2%	$1.52	1.9%	10
Comcast	CMCSA	$1.00	1.7%	$1.10	1.8%	7
CVS Health	CVS	$1.24	1.5%	$1.70	1.8%	10
Empire State Realty Trust	ESRT	$0.34	2.0%	$0.34	1.8%	1
McCormick	MKC	$1.60	2.1%	$1.72	1.8%	10
International Flavors & Fragrances	IFF	$1.98	2.0%	$2.24	1.7%	10
Novo Nordisk	NVO	$0.90	1.9%	$0.96	1.7%	10
Becton, Dickinson	BDX	$2.40	2.4%	$2.64	1.6%	10
St. Jude Medical	STJ	$1.16	1.7%	$1.24	1.6%	5
Oracle	ORCL	$0.51	1.3%	$0.60	1.5%	5
Starbucks	SBUX	$0.64	1.4%	$0.80	1.5%	6
UnitedHealth Group	UNH	$1.60	1.7%	$2.00	1.5%	6
WD-40 Company	WDFC	$1.48	2.1%	$1.68	1.5%	7
Stryker Corporation	SYK	$1.38	1.7%	$1.52	1.4%	9
Columbia Sportswear*	COLM	$0.52	0.9%	$0.68	1.3%	10
Costco Wholesale	COST	$1.43	1.2%	$1.80	1.2%	10
Kroger	KR	$0.38	1.4%	$0.42	1.2%	9
Monsanto	MON	$1.96	1.7%	$2.16	1.2%	10

* = New for 2017

Company	Symbol	2015		2016 PROJECTED		Dividend Raises, Past 10 Years
		Dividend	Yield %	Dividend	Yield %	
Nike	NKE	$0.52	1.4%	$0.64	1.2%	10
Ormat Technologies*	ORA	$0.24	0.7%	$0.50	1.2%	5
Valmont	VMI	$1.50	0.9%	$1.50	1.1%	10
Fresh Del	FDP	$0.50	1.4%	$0.50	1.0%	3
Ross	ROST	$0.49	1.2%	$0.54	1.0%	10
Aetna	AET	$1.00	1.2%	$1.00	0.9%	5
Southwest Airlines	LUV	$0.30	0.8%	$0.40	0.9%	4
Visa	V	$0.50	0.8%	$0.56	0.7%	7
FedEx	FDX	$0.80	0.6%	$1.00	0.6%	10
McKesson	MCK	$1.12	0.6%	$1.12	0.6%	7
Perrigo	PRGO	$0.46	0.3%	$0.58	0.6%	10
Fair Isaac	FICO	$0.08	0.1%	$0.08	0.1%	1
Amazon*	AMZN	—	—	—	—	
CarMax	KMX	—	—	—	—	
Itron	ITRI	—	—	—	—	
WhiteWave Foods*	WWAV	—	—	—	—	

* = New for 2017

Currently available from Value Line for individual investors

THE VALUE LINE INVESTMENT SURVEY®
The signature publication from Value Line is one of the most highly regarded comprehensive investment research resources. Published weekly, it tracks approximately 1,700 stocks in more than 90 industries and ranks stocks for Timeliness™ and Safety™.

THE VALUE LINE INVESTMENT SURVEY® — SMALL & MID-CAP
The Small & Mid-Cap Survey applies Value Line's data and analysis protocols to a universe of approximately 1,800 companies with market values from less than $1 billion up to $5 billion.

THE VALUE LINE INVESTMENT SURVEY® — SMART INVESTOR
This Internet version of the Value Line Investment Survey tracks approximately 1,700 stocks and offers sorting functions and custom alerts.

THE VALUE LINE INVESTMENT SURVEY® — SAVVY INVESTOR
The Internet counterpart of the preceding three Surveys, Savvy Investor includes every one of our 3,500 stock reports plus updates during Stock Exchange hours.

THE VALUE LINE® 600
Provides stock reports from The Value Line Investment Survey on 600 large, actively traded and widely held U.S. exchange-listed corporations, including many foreign firms, spanning over 90 industries.

VALUE LINE SELECT®
Once a month, subscribers receive a detailed report by Value Line senior analysts, recommending the one stock that has the best upside and risk/reward ratio.

VALUE LINE SELECT®: DIVIDEND INCOME & GROWTH
A monthly, in-depth report recommending one dividend-paying stock, providing extensive information about the company's finances, prospects, and projected earnings, along with follow-up on numerous alternate selections.

THE VALUE LINE SPECIAL SITUATIONS SERVICE®
The Value Line Special Situations Service is designed for those seeking investment ideas in the small-cap arena. It includes both aggressive and conservative selections every month.

A special 14-day trial of The Value Line Investment Survey — Smart Investor is available to individual investors with the code "100STOCKS" at www.valueline .com/100STOCKS.

485 Lexington Avenue, 9th FL, New York, NY 10017
www.valueline.com
1-800-VALUELINE